AMERICAN ERRAND

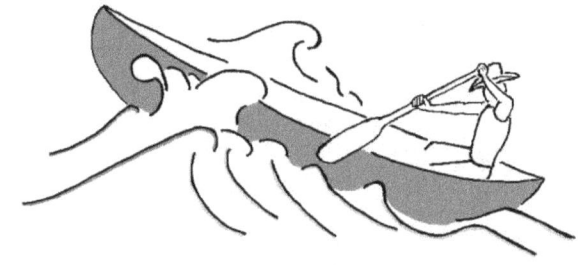

RIVERS OF THE NORTH
2nd Edition

James Sheldon

Copyright © James Sheldon
2016

All rights reserved

Library of Congress Registration Number
TXu 1-663-400

All rights reserved

ISBN 978-0-9827613-1-1

Sheldon Publishing
Winchester, KS
USA

For Father and Mother

Author's Note

There will always be room to grow, I know, I was not a mature Christian when I made the journey and wrote this book. But regardless of my newborn status, my heart was on fire for God and I firmly believed that as long as I kept putting one foot before the other in faith, He would bring good from my effort. I had been a bookworm before then, and my writing style herein reflects that stage of my life (spent in Victorian novels and Medieval Romances, perhaps the perfect background from which to tell of an adventure taken by a self-absorbed dreamer newly turned to God).

This book is a totally true account of my first 500 miles and a product of my entire 4,000 mile journey on the Lewis & Clark Trail. This is a journey from farm to farm, town to town, city to city, and vast wilderness, done solely by canoe and foot, with no cell phone, no back-up crew, and no doors to lock. In fairness to the people in this story, my literary portrait of them should be regarded as coming solely from my perspective (they just kept coming forward like angels out of the blue). Unless otherwise indicated, I use their real names (first names only). Location names are also given, which can help readers that wish to follow by way of Google Earth or other satellite imagery services.

Embellishment is used in this story only in a way that will be obvious to the reader, as in a reoccurring subplot woven in the form of humorous thoughts about a bumbling knight (me) and fearsome dragon (the river), which never takes the place of the story's action, but by way of thought process, serves to keep beauty and humor alive while struggling to survive the sometimes unforgiving force of nature, not to mention my ignorance (or just plain stupidity).

In both doing the trail and telling the tale, I have done my best to apply myself as God would have me do.

Thank you

PS: Today, I do mission work, traveling by horse and wagon from farm to farm and town to town, telling folks what I learned on the Lewis and Clark Trail. To see photos from the Lewis and Clark Trail, and my horse and wagon missions, please visit this book's website: www.americanerrand.com (go to the Author's Page for links to the wagon mission websites).

With heartfelt thanks, I wish to acknowledge my contents editor, and my map makers, three Christian volunteers who gave their time, effort, and expertise. Their professionalism, honesty, and generosity made this book possible. I also wish to acknowledge my literary editor, a highly regarded professional, and also a Christian, without whom this book could not be possible.

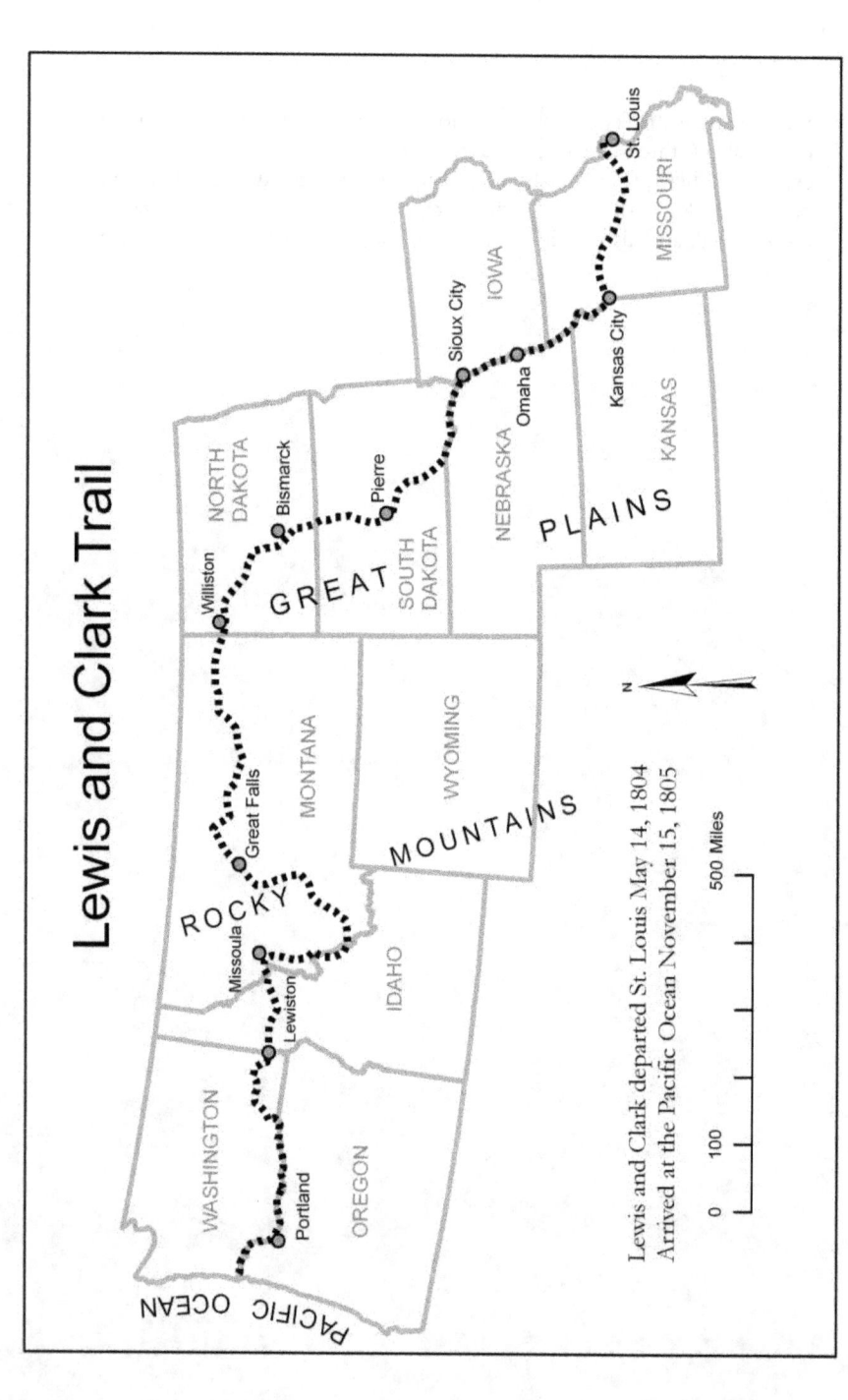

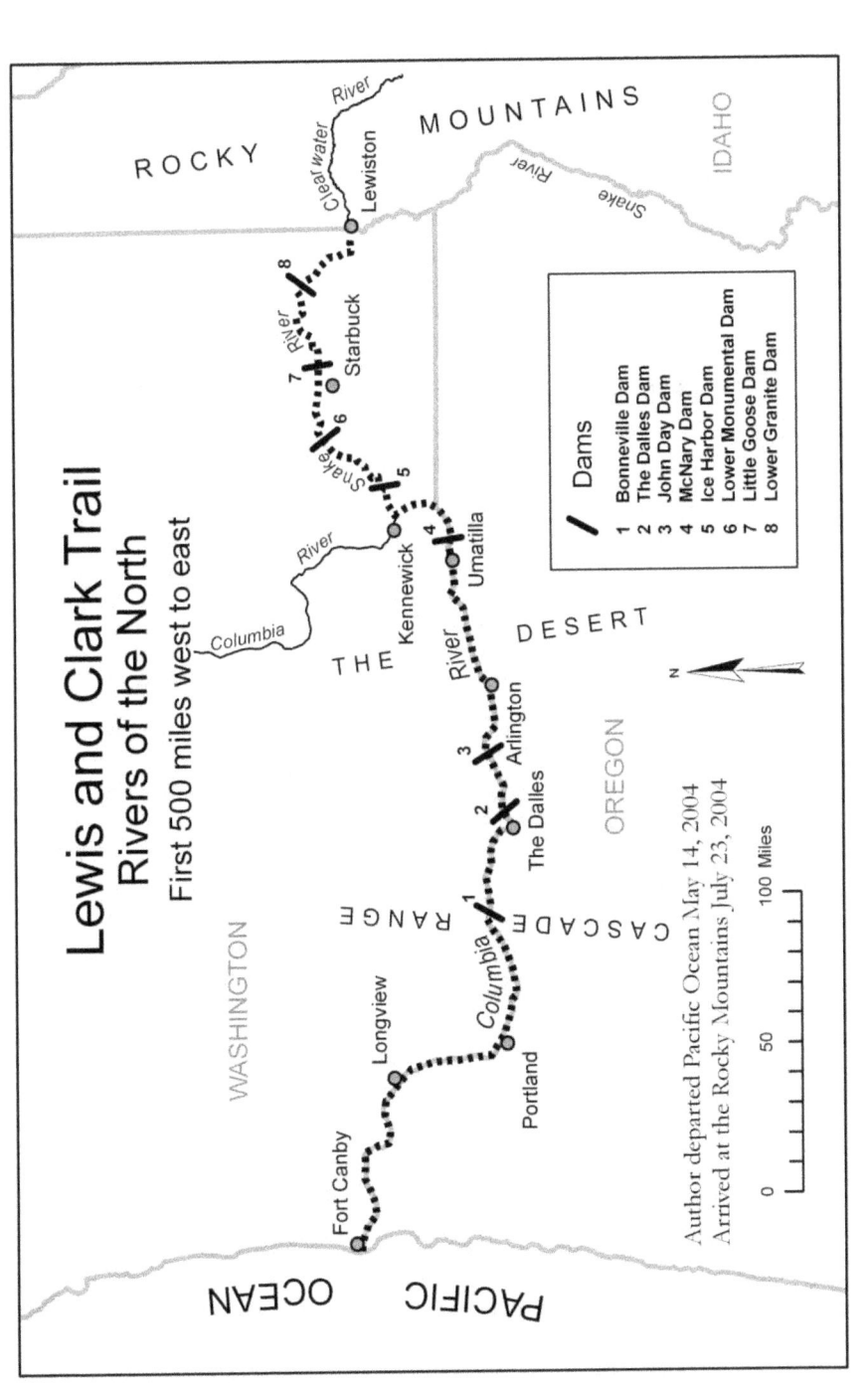

"TO THE STARS THROUGH DIFFICULTY"
Pioneer Motto of Kansas

RIVERS OF THE NORTH

Trail to Trail
Chapter I

"WE COULD MAKE THE JOURNEY. You know, like Lewis & Clark did. We could canoe the rivers and walk over the mountains."

James caught the light in his older brother's eyes. Frank, it seemed, had pulled the idea from thin air.

The family had gathered around Frank's dinner table just like every Sunday, and as usual they were enjoying a good deal of animated conversation. Frank, however, had hit upon something special. His idea opened a trail into the great wide-open and the two brothers were suddenly fixed on it like a pair of boys making far-flung camping plans.

Frank's wife Kathy was a level-headed woman and, seeing the two men heading into the great unknown, decided to intervene, "Frank, we would have to pull Megan out of college."

Frank's eyes filled with realization even as his jaw went slack. He turned to his wife and tried to backtrack but Kathy wasn't having it, "We would have to sell our house. You would lose your retirement. And..."

While Frank got a good reminding of life's realities, James sat immersed in his own situation. Certainly he would have liked to of had children but his ex-wife had felt differently, so he lived alone in a motor home at the end of a dead-end road. James wasn't without hope however. He had an old canoe and some camping gear tucked away. All that was needed was a good dusting off. He had some money in the bank, not a lot, but enough.

After an evening of family time, James took his leave with hugs and well wishes. He drove into the cool of night, beyond the city limits where the stars of November shone bright. On an empty gravel lane he followed the lay of the land, climbing the prairie-covered hills, descending wooded ravines. He went with thoughts on what his older brother had said, and such being the case, perhaps he felt something not so terribly removed from what

Captain Meriwether Lewis felt after President Jefferson laid out his plan for an expedition. Something like a spark to the heart. Not a thrill-seeking spark, but that spark that gives meaning to life.

James's home could be found at the end of Wild Horse Road in Jefferson County, Kansas. James didn't own the property but lived there by the grace of his friend and landlord Mark, a high-school teacher who lived with his wife and son in town. James wouldn't have moved there if he hadn't needed a cheap place to live. To his surprise, it turned out perfectly, secluded and beautiful, between rolling pasture and wooded ravine. And down in the crux of the ravine, immediately below James' motor home, a spring had carved a horse-shoe-shaped pool out of the rock. The spring pool was crystal clear, never ran dry, and rarely froze in winter.

On a rocky shelf above the spring, James had cleared undergrowth by hand to claim the excellent contour of the land which was shaded by a grove of walnut trees. And keeping with that flow, James had parked his old church bus behind his motor home so that both were parallel parked atop the rock shelf. Both motor home and church bus were of 70's vintage. The motor home was earth tone in color. The church bus was bright white with bold black Christian insignias and vivid stained-glass windows. In the summertime, both motor home and church bus appeared to sit in a grassy cove peppered with rocks and bordered by trumpeter vines in bloom. The walnut trees provided shade. A hand-buried line supplied electric power. A barn cat controlled rodents while her kittens played in the yard.

Monday as usual, Frank came to visit and also perhaps to check on James who was nine years his junior. And as usual, on seeing Frank coming up the trail, James's dog UB, though old and frail, barked and danced and wagged his tail.

"How's life at 'the compound?'" Frank asked with a wry smile, standing on a wooden pallet that served as a stoop.

"Good," James replied happily.

With Frank comfortably seated inside, James pulled down a large window shade on which he had mounted a map of the USA. "I've been thinking of what you said about the Lewis and Clark trail, and you know, I've come to realize, I'm in a good position to give this a shot."

Frank seemed worried. James might drown in the river, or fall from a cliff in the mountains. Moreover, Frank's fears were magnified by the lens through which he saw his little brother who for some years had been chasing after things that couldn't put a crumb of bread on the table. In fact, having gotten onto such a path, James had willingly given up a very successful business which he'd built from scratch. Fifteen years of hard work, apparently thrown away. James also sold his house and gave away most of his home furnishings. And things had only gotten "worse" from there. Most recently, James had made an ink pen from a falcon feather which, as far as he could tell, floated down from above. With the feather, James paid homage to his forefathers in verse by candle lantern. Only after showing his mystic feather to Frank had James learned it wasn't a falcon feather but a turkey feather.

Some months before finding the feather, James had found a long-forgotten pioneer graveyard with the help of a third-generation farmer. The old farmer had told James to walk past a giant cottonwood tree on the horizon and then continue until he found a wagon road hidden in tall prairie grass—,

"Find the road and follow it," the old farmer had said, purposefully neglecting to tell James what waited at its end. So James did as the farmer said and walked toward the cottonwood. Soon the farmer's place seemed a tiny island of trees in a sea of corn and soy beans behind. It sunk from sight as James went over the next rise. He skirted the edge of a pond that had filled with silt to become a cattail marsh with frogs singing in a chorus. From there the fields were taken over with hedge and hawthorn trees. James walked with a weave to avoid their prickly branches. On the other side of the wood, at the base of a long low rise, James came out in a virgin prairie, wide in girth, and featureless as the blue sky above. At once James noticed how the angle of the sun fell upon the native grass to betray the shadows of two parallel lines. There lay the wagon road. Its ruts were hidden even though they were deep in the earth. James followed their shadows with his eyes across the prairie, rising slowly to a hilltop where stood a small crown of trees. The trees, which must have been great in their day, had gone the way of those who lie below. Their bark had been stripped away, their storm-wrecked limbs bleached by sun and time. Below these wood skeletons, the graves lay concealed in a thicket. Only an ornate fence spear protruded here and there to tell of the Victorian age. Also, the top of a granite obelisk was just visible in the center of the plot. There the pioneers had laid their loved ones to rest. The last to be laid down was in 1895. And by all appearances, there hadn't been anyone to pay their respects in modern times even though the cemetery lay just ten miles outside a thriving city. But to be fair, local folk kept the place a secret for fear of thieves and vandals. The number of graves surprised James. And he should have seen it coming before he crawled into the thicket but, as he made his way from grave to grave, he realized that nearly all were children. So there James was on his hands and knees, getting closer to something he could not explain, thinking about how it must have been for those fathers and mothers who had to bury their young. And he realized, he did not understand the struggles of the past. He did not know the sum of his debt.

Some folks thought James crazy but in truth he was answering a call. He did not know what he was called to but only knew it to be right in his heart. And as for the Lewis and Clark trail, James saw it as an extension of the path he was already on, and he had already gone beyond the point of turning back.

Several days after James spoke with his brother Frank, their sister Patricia reached him through the modern magic of a telephone (and what would those pioneers have thought, had they known that a 150 years later, people at opposite ends of the Oregon Trail would be speaking clearly to one another through midair!)—,

"James," said Patricia, "you can do it. I know you can. And I want you to know that, at least on this side of the [continental] divide, I'll do everything I can to help you."

Throughout the winter James worked at meeting obligations unrelated to his dream except that they had to be done in lieu of beginning on it. Then in mid-March, James removed a tarp from atop his motor home to reveal a dusty canoe. He put the boat in a 9' x 26' over-the-road cargo-box he'd had trucked in to serve as a workshop. The cargo-box had a ceiling of clear fiberglass which let plenty of daylight in. James strung up plenty of lights so he could work day and night. Next he climbed to a luggage rack atop his church bus where a steel locker contained four large plastic tubs full of camping gear. James brought down his gear and took it into the cargo box where he laid it out alongside his canoe. He next went around behind his bus where a small wooden deck provided easy access through the back door. Above the door, a sign read, "FOLLOW

US, WE'RE FOLLOWING JESUS!"

James had made the inside of his church bus into a workshop. And a fine workshop it was, with workbenches and cabinets custom fit to the contour of the interior. The floor of the workshop was rubberized because it had originally been a school bus. Thus having everything he needed, James turned on the power and set about building the invention that had previously existed only in his mind, a lightweight portage system that integrated canoe, machine, and man.

Although James hoped to be ready in a month, he actually completed his preparations in seven weeks. His tasks included constructing a portaging machine, fixing up an old car that could be thrown away, getting his gear in order, figuring out an unrefrigerated diet, completing physical training, putting the compound into mothballs, arranging to have his rat-killing cat fed while he was away, and so on.

Based on logistical reasons to be later revealed, James decided to attempt the Lewis and Clark trail in reverse. In other words, he would go inbound on their outbound route (from west to east). Therefore James needed to find a way to get his one-man-expedition to the Pacific Ocean some 1,800 miles away. And that was how it came to pass that his friend and landlord Mark stood shaking his head while asking—,

"James, do you really think that this [junky old car] can make it over the mountains?"

The object of Mark's question was an automobile from the gas crunch days of the early 1980s, a real runt of a rust bucket with its interior gone to rags.

With a worried gleam, James looked up from the engine bay, "Yeah."

Mark could hardly keep from laughing.

"It'll make it," said James, wrenching on the grease-caked engine. "I'll make it, make it."

James had no choice but to make do, having neither budget nor time to afford better. In fact his plan was so short it ended at the beginning, beyond which he had no plan other than to put his boat in the water and paddle.

Mark went for a walk in the woods. Then upon returning, he approached James, "Hey James."

James turned to look.

"Does your brother know it's a good thing you're doing?"

"He'll come around," James replied, making out as if it were no big deal when in fact it was a big deal, and James had been going on faith that Frank would come around.

Next to visit came Joe and his daughter Ali who were curious to see the portaging machine James had built. Joe was a family hog farmer and close friend of James. Inside the cargo box, James's machine sat jigged up on saw horses so his demonstration was only a dry run, but that didn't dampen his enthusiasm. Harnessed into what he called his "walking machine," James showed Joe and Ali how it worked. He then explained how it folded to stow in his canoe when in the water.

At a local outfitter, James purchased six rubberized duffle bags. Also at the outfitter, James replaced old gear with new, purchasing a pair of heavy boots, a ground pad, and water filter.

For his nutritional needs, James consulted Patricia who besides being a registered nurse held a certification in wilderness rescue and survival. And because she understood James to have a budget, Patricia said, "There's a ton of food marketed for this sort of thing but when it comes down to it, it's still hard to beat rice and beans."

Finally, on a Sunday afternoon in late April, Frank paid a visit to the compound. Frank had been warming to James' plan for months despite real concerns for the welfare of his younger brother. James busted at the seams to show Frank everything. At dinner that evening, Frank displayed his original enthusiasm and then some, especially when he spoke of the "walking machine" and called his little brother a genius. Kathy's cooking tasted delicious as always. So all in all, James had as sustaining a dinner as ever there was. Then with hugs and well wishes, he drove home in ecstasy.

The first of May saw James ruled by a single thought, *"I must make my destination by May 15."* James believed May 15, 1804 to be the date Lewis and Clark set out on their epic voyage and, somewhat as a ritual necessary to keeping with their spirit—James meant to make that date. James had the date wrong, but time remained to get it right, as we will see.

James's knack for underestimating the time it would take him to do things measured second only to his desire to get them done. In fact James had so many things to do; he had no time for little things like testing his new water filter. Therefore he would have to wait until on the river. Then when he needed water, he would read the instructions.

Sunday dinner came round again too quickly and having caught adventure fever, Frank and Kathy had a list of ideas for James including an offer to equip him with a powerful satellite phone. Megan then chimed in, respectfully reminding her mother that phones required batteries and there wouldn't be many plug-INS along the river.

Kathy then asked, "James, does your walking machine have a brake? I mean, to get around those dams, you'll have to go up and down some fairly steep hills, won't you?"

While James looked on dumbly, he saw himself falling under the wheels of a machine that weighed over 300lbs when loaded. So he needed a brake, yet one more thing to fit into an already impossible schedule.

It took James a day and a half to build a brake (which shall be described later). Then, having packed his walking machine parts, gear, and food supplies into the aforementioned car, James couldn't find any place to put UB. The tiny hatchback had been packed so full, there wasn't a space left.

"However will I fit my dog in there?" James wondered.

UB wagged his tail while looking with hope to his master. UB couldn't foresee the discomfort that would soon be visited upon him but only sensed that dog-heaven lay just around the corner.

James's longtime friend Dale came to the compound with his dad Jim who was both farmer and trucker. Dale also farmed, and framed houses. Dale and Jim brought an over-the-road truck to haul away the empty cargo box in which James had built his walking machine and organized his gear.

By setting May 3rd as his departure date, James had allotted for the real possibility of an automotive breakdown; the idea being that in such an event, James could fix his car and have enough time remaining to reach the Pacific by May 15. But May 3rd had come and gone and James still had a whirlwind of loose ends to tie up. At last, with no time remaining, he simply told himself, "I have to go."

On the morning of Saturday May 8th 2004, James and UB drove to Frank's workplace in town. With full hearts, the two brothers embraced and bid one another farewell. "God speed," said Frank, "God speed."

James went west on I-70. At Salina, Kansas, he turned north on Highway 81. In Nebraska he took I-80 toward the Platt River where from as far back as Kansas, he had seen thunderheads rising. In fact he'd watched them rise all afternoon. So it came as no surprise when by 4:00pm or thereabouts, it wasn't sunshine that ruled the western horizon but a black wall cloud into which the highway disappeared. The storm flashed dimly, then died to blackness, only to dimly light up again like the pulse of a distant giant.

Rain drops began to dot James's windshield. Then as rain came in sheets, James felt glad about the new wiper blades he'd installed. James had also filled the washer reservoir and had done many other things to prepare but he couldn't control nature and when a big wind blast caught him off guard, he cried out, "Man alive!"

The Kansan counter-steered to correct the sail-like effect of the canoe atop the car. Dust from farm fields got blown up by wind, mixed with rain, and deposited on the windshield as mud. A mix of small debris flew horizontally right to left and James suspected a tornado. Driving at 20mph in near-zero visibility seemed too fast and yet James did so in hope of getting through the storm or finding an underpass where he might take shelter. Still hurrying more than he should, a road sign measuring 4ft x 4ft suddenly dropped before him.

James swerved and missed the sign with one part skill and two parts "luck." Then glancing back with a measure of pride, James didn't see that a second sign had fallen in his path.

A loud tinny noise erupted as car met sign. It could have been worse however and in fact the car ran over the sign rather handily.

James feared his car might blow over on its side because the canoe was functioning like a sail, indeed, a sail that measured so much larger than the car, the very sight of it made some folks burst into laughter.

Ever aware of his responsibility to other motorists, James kept within his lane but, all the same, his best intentions couldn't keep him from frustration, *"THIS IS ONE HECK OF A WAY TO START!"*

Like a runt in a litter, James arrived too late to every underpass. Meanwhile, hailstones kept hammering. Only after taking an exit ramp to a truck stop would James find shelter under the port of a drive-in diner which had been converted to a laundromat. The port quickly filled with like-minded motorists.

Soon the storm weakened so that only steady rain continued

along with flashes of lightening. James got back on the highway and proceeded. He would not record exact locations in his journal until he put into the Columbia River and therefore his exact location remains unknown except to say he was on I-80 somewhere near the Platte River when he saw one of the most awesome atmospheric spectacles of his life. Hundreds of travelers must have seen it. The storm had broken into a hundred smaller storms like mountain islands floating in a blue sky. And being nearly equal in size, the flat bases of the island storms formed a tiled pattern like a kitchen floor except on a cosmic scale. Meanwhile, from the western horizon aglow with gold, the sun extended its fingers to play upon the tiled pattern in every hue of silver. But the beauty of it came with a treacherous threat, for dancing between all the island storms was snake lightning. Snake lightning in amounts that had to be seen to be believed. And still that wasn't the half of it, for boldly set against the eastern horizon was a tremendous rainbow. James, who had lived in the storm-rich state of Kansas all his life, had never seen such a sky.

James understood there was a scientific explanation for what he saw up there in the atmosphere. Particles of light were bouncing off water molecules to make pretty colors. James knew all that but, just then, he wasn't thinking on such terms. He wasn't looking up at Heaven with his brain, but rather, with his heart. Such a thing could be compared to looking into a person's eyes and seeing the color blue while at the same time, seeing the soul behind the blue eyes. Of course James could not look into the eyes of God. But he could see that God was present, there amid everything, in the beauty of the rainbow, and in the terrible bolts of lightning. So it was that James marveled, and felt both uplifted and afraid.

Through the storm nebula James passed into night where growing tired, he entered a roadside rest area. Inside his car, James put his legs up on his gear and rested his head against the window. To make room for his gear, James had previously removed the passenger seat which helped his current situation a little. Still, it wasn't a thing that lent advantage to being a little tall. UB didn't take up much room and yet, he was packed in like a sardine, atop an ice chest in the back. UB was a terrier mix, mostly Boarder Terrier but taller and stockier with superb black and white markings. From his place atop the ice chest, UB could see out the windows but couldn't fall off the chest due to the gear around him. And because UB was thirteen years old, James had covered a life vest with a towel to make him a soft bed.

The Kansan slept hard and woke with birds singing.

From somewhere in Nebraska, man and dog proceeded to that place where I-80 began its assent out of the Plate River Valley. There James saw how the highway went up a series of grassy shelves rising to the western horizon. It would be his cars first test. There were motorcycles with bigger engines. In fact, such was the condition of the car engine; it died at every stop unless James kept the gas pedal depressed. All the more pleasant then to discover, the old car had climbed to 60mph. James made it return to 50 and tried his best to hold it there. Bigger hills awaited.

In Wyoming, James successfully made it over the first small mountain range and passed through the city of Laramie. He then proceeded on the high plain of the Great Basin Divide where due to a strong headwind, he could scarcely maintain the minimum speed limit of 40mph. Meanwhile, a solid stream of cars and trucks zoomed around him in the fast lane.

At least James wasn't blocking traffic. At least not until he entered a construction zone with only a single west-bound lane for as far as the eye could see—,

"This ain't good," James thought, glancing at the grill of a semi-truck in his mirror.

Interstate Highway 80 served as one of America's connecting arteries and James took no pride in blocking it, even on Sunday afternoon. He floored the gas pedal but the headwind robbed the engine of power. As a result, traffic backed up for miles. James obviously needed to get off the road but the shoulder lay torn up from construction work. Still he tried, only to find it too hazardous. Thus changing his mind, he tried to abort but a semi-truck encouraged him otherwise and, he was forced off the road.

So there sat the Kansan, looking like the fool of I-80, the goof who had blocked the vital artery of a nation, the misfit who got pushed aside, the nut who stuck out like a sore thumb, the butt of passing jokes, and target of scorn. Rightly or not, James could not help feeling a little downtrodden. After all, his cowboy hat was white, his face handsome, his shoulders broad, his legs long, and his arms muscular. His voice was strong, his eyes piercing. His thick dark hair was cropped short, his mustache peppered with gray. And what's more, he was proud of his heritage which sprang respectively from Puritan Priest and Crusader Knight. The Puritan had signed the Mayflower Compact. The Knight had received a fiefdom from the Pope. James got to take his place on the road once everyone else had passed. Shortly thereafter, James was forced off the road again. It happened in the exact same fashion as before. James did not give up though. He was determined to make his destination even while he took his responsibility to not block traffic seriously. Finally a semi-truck driver took pity and, James blessed that Good Samaritan for a full five miles.

Just across that imaginary line which separates time zones, James escaped the construction zone. The fact that the place to which he'd escaped seemed to fit his humiliation did not strike James as funny however. Indeed, it seemed James had arrived at the bleakest place in all of Wyoming. A lonely little filling station for people with cars like his, located just below the highway. Adjoining the station was an empty parking lot from which a single dirt road stretched to disappear on the high plain. That was the sum of it.

James pumped gas and went inside to pay where except for a South Asian clerk who waited on four young black men, the place was deserted.

At the counter, a wiry young black man grinned through gold teeth while twisting a simple question into something cryptic, "You like my smile? It's a nice smile, ain't it?"

The Asian answered with just enough humility and defiance to make a thinking man believe he had a scattergun behind the counter.

The group of blacks escalated, making sport of it. Meanwhile, James stood in line, silently steeling under the brim of his hat, *"Don't bring me into this... please."* And so it was, no one spoke a word to him.

From the restroom there came a black gentleman of about 35 years who corralled the youths and drove them away in what looked like a state-owned van.

Collecting himself, the Asian turned to James, "Is that all for you?"

"No Sir," James replied, "I'm needing to get out of this wind. Would it be alright if I were to hold up over there, on the edge of your parking lot?"

If the Asian's eyes betrayed him true, he must have been thinking, *"First that bunch, now this guy."*

In an attempt to soften himself, James removed his sun glasses, tipped his cowboy hat up, and briefly told what he was about. The Asian granted permission to day camp.

So it was on a chilly afternoon, the Kansan sat marooned on a high plateau with nothing to do but gaze on wind-twisted shrubs stretching like carpet to the horizon. He cracked his window, sank down in his seat, and tried to nap while the wind whistled in like a cry from across the plain. At last, after an unrecorded number of hours, the wind abated and he set off again.

The car ran well in the calm of evening, climbing grades at 60mph and descending at 70mph. So James felt relieved, especially in the construction zones. And wishing to avoid the wind of the high plain which would surely return on the following day, James drove until he believed himself beyond its reach. He then entered a roadside rest area where he spread himself over his gear and slept like a rock. The time was 2:00am. Whether or not James had crossed the Wyoming/Utah border cannot be known.

James woke to a beautiful morning, cool and crisp under blue skies of which he wrote in his journal: *"Making excellent time. Car runs great. Tired but satisfied, and determined."*

Driving on Interstate Highway 84, the Kansan pressed north through the state of Utah and into Idaho. He needed to make his deadline but, as his eyelids began to grow heavy, he feared falling asleep at the wheel. The solution he decided lay in a large cup of coffee, the idea being that he could catch up on rest later. So James stopped and drank a big cup, then drove directly into a dust storm where he had to pull over and wait it out. Of this he wrote: *"Wish I hadn't drunk that coffee."*

Pinned down in a rest area with other shelter-seeking motorists, James made a few journal entries in which he looked back over the past three days:

> "UB is hanging in there. He vomited three times on the first morning of our trip even before he got in the car. He wasn't eating, so I began sharing my roast beef with him and now he's spoiled to it. Living in the car is hard on him."

> "I have conversations at rest stops with other motorists but rarely do I mention my plans. Smalltalk mostly, between travelers who are happy to chase away the loneliness of the

road."

James's next entry addressed his current situation:

"Here I am writing in a dust storm when a large [heavy made] top portion of a rest area trash can flies sideways [and slams] into [the front left fender of] my car. It is like getting sandblasted out there! I don't even get out to see if there's a dent. It's kind of funny. Either that or I've gone crazy and am here laughing for nothing. What's it matter if it dented the car?"

In the next entry, James addresses his suspicion regarding the resistance he'd met with. And in fairness to James, he'd been on a long spiritual journey and felt like he'd finally gotten a green light from above only to have everything but the kitchen sink come at him. At least it seemed that way to James who felt tired but revved up on coffee while his car rocked and shook in a strange kind of twilight:

"The devil is throwing all he's got at me. Tornados, dust storms, highway signs, and trash can lids."

James didn't curse very often. That said, his path would soon place him in such need of God's mercy and grace, as to make curse words vanish from his vocabulary entirely. Presently, James made one final entry:

"...the wind grows violent. The car rocks and shakes. In amazement I see the windows are dulling from the sandblasting."

James felt relieved to discover his windows were not sandblasted but only appeared so due to the dust which clung to them. For 2½ hours he waited while the storm blew. Then the rain came and cleared the dust from the air whereupon a mountain range in the west caught James's attention. The Kansan realized he saw something important. The mountain range created a wind dynamic with its unique form. In fact the range acted like a dam holding back atmospheric pressure and, it just so happened that James's location lay directly where air pressure flowed in a torrent as if from a spillway below a dam. Realizing as much, James understood there to be an excellent probability for wind intensity to drop markedly several miles up the highway which ran parallel to the mountain range. Of course to prove his theory, James would have to drive there.

The wind broadsided James continuously for three miles. More than once it forced him to the shoulder where he second guessed himself. Nevertheless, he drove on with determination to match the wind, and the wind abated where he had guessed it would. He didn't know it but such was the force of the wind, it had broken his high quality luggage rack. Fortunately he would discover the problem in time to avoid disaster (especially in the event that the canoe fall off and hit a car behind, causing a crash).

Presently, James had the road to himself, at least until he looked in his side view mirror and saw a convoy of semi-trucks approaching. One truck after another passed in steady rain and each kicked up such a deluge that James could hardly see beyond his windshield. Equally dangerous, the convoy cut through a crosswind, creating a wind instability problem for him:

> "I had to take an exit ramp. I found a quaint little frontage road, a narrow blacktop with a sign that said road narrows ahead. That little road was made for my little rig. It was duck soup. In fact, I went driving alongside a small irrigation canal with ducks in it. I passed a small airfield with a crop duster parked out front, a bright yellow biplane with a huge radial engine. I crested a rise to see the interstate stretching into the distant Idaho landscape. And there beside it ran my little road. All this was set in fields lush with spring crops, or a single crop, I should say."

James was accustomed to seeing the crops of Kansas; wheat, corn, and soy beans. He had never seen a potato field. Ignorance is bliss, or so they say. James certainly felt delighted, for the road ahead shone like a fresh washed ribbon, rising and falling on the Idaho plain which besides being lush and green, appeared vast as a sea. And when it ended, it ended perfectly, at a truck stop where James could refuel and get back on the highway.

After refueling, James went into the restroom where he encountered something he'd never seen before. All he had to do was hold out his hand whereby some magic the paper towel dispenser sensed his presence and fed a towel directly into his hand. The Kansan went back out into the store and announced what he'd seen in the restroom. The clerk behind the counter replied, "Yes, isn't it just wonderful!"

James knew by the clerk's tone and smile, she truly meant what she said.

"Ma'am," he replied respectfully, "I have no wish to disagree with you, but I think a man should at least have enough strength to pull a paper towel out of a dispenser."

Back on the highway, James drove late into the night. Rain kept falling. The wipers beat back and forth. The wiper motor made ominous noises that foretold the end of its life. The headlights of oncoming cars glared in the windshield while at the same time, the fresh asphalt road surface soaked up light, making it difficult to see in a construction zone with two-way traffic.

At last, gaining a stretch of highway without construction or traffic, James had opportunity to reflect. He felt grateful for the culmination of events that had brought him to where he was even though he didn't know what he was supposed to do outside of attempting the trail by putting one foot before the other in faith. And being tired but passionate, he thanked the Lord with all his heart. But James was not a mature Christian. For even while he thanked the Lord, he promised he would not let the Lord down and, as if to assure the Lord that He had made the right decision, James claimed to be the right man for the job. His tired ramblings were suddenly blown away by a white sports car, its tires squalling on wet pavement directly beside him! The sports car spun around as if performing a trick that had it skidding backward directly in front of James! James cried out as the lights from the white car blinded him. Both cars went careening down the highway nose to nose! The momentum of the sports car carried it ahead and James could only watch with dread as it flew off the road.

Like greased lightening the sports car slid through wet grass. James's heart missed a beat as the mystery car missed a massive sign pillar by no more than 12 inches. Fortunate was its trajectory, for it remained on the good side of the fence where it crossed smooth turf like a skier on a lake until it came to rest.

So much fright! So much relief! Exactly what happened may never be known. James knew for certain he had been in his lane. He had very keen spacial ability and clearly remembered being in his lane. He suspected the driver of the sports car had not seen him until the last and, going too fast for conditions, swerved in an attempt to get around him only to lose control. James switched on his emergency blinkers and pulled over to get out. He hoped the occupant(s) of the car were okay even as he felt a measure of trepidation, like they might be crazies or something. No sooner had James gotten out however than the car pulled back onto the road and drove away, albeit at a reduced speed. Bewildered, James got back in his car. He did not try to understand what had happened beyond the simple analysis of a near disaster, but oddly, without consciousness of behavioral change; James would never again make such claims to God.

James could drive only a little further before he had to pull over for the night. He parked at the back of a gravel lot behind a truck stop where, overtaken with exhaustion, he felt ill. He could scarcely think or function at all. He tried to tend to UB's needs but UB had become despondent. Thus unable to help himself or his dog, James passed out in an area marked "TRUCKS ONLY."

While James lay snoring on his gear, UB lay losing his will to live. UB had always shown tremendous loyalty to James but he no longer had the physical ability to follow his master and the last few days had been terrible for him. Even before leaving Kansas, he seemed such a frail old dog; the cat stalked him whenever he went out to do his duties. But physical hardship wasn't the half of UB's anguish, for in all truth, his master had forgotten him.

At 3:00am, James woke to a bad situation. His loyal friend of thirteen years had thrown in the towel. Thus filled with dread and shame, James was transformed into a patient and caring being. He poured his heart into saving UB. First he apologized and asked UB to hang in there. UB responded to nothing. He harbored no will to get up, to go out, to eat, to live. James petted, pleaded, and promised that things would get better if only UB would hang in there a while longer.

UB came round slowly. James hand-fed him bits of moistened dog food with one hand while gently stroking him with the other.

Then they went for a walk and UB did his duties. By then dawn had broken. All that remained was to retake the road.

More rain, wind, and semi-trucks. James had had enough. He found an exit ramp and struck out on a two-lane black top which, running perpendicular to the highway, disappeared in the Idaho desert. For ten miles or so, James drove in the general direction of the Pacific Ocean before pausing at an intersection of rural blacktops where he pondered returning to the highway but decided to go north for awhile instead. So he went north, then west, then north. He was uncertain of where he was.

At last, James noticed a few cars traveling together and because it was seven in the morning, he guessed them to be country folks on their way to jobs in Boise, Idaho. So he followed them. More cars soon joined in so that three cars become four, five, six, and so on. On reaching the city of Boise, James saw long lines of traffic stalled on Interstate 84, and he knew he'd hit upon a fine bit of "luck." For had he not left the interstate, he would have been trapped in the traffic jam. Instead, he found himself at a perfect vantage point on the northwest edge of the city, right beside an entrance ramp to the interstate. So James retook Interstate 84 and proceeded with ease toward the state of Oregon.

In Oregon, James ascended the Blue Mountains where in steady rain he drove up and down grades until the breadth of the range had been crossed. Then, on the last blue mountain, James came before a sign that read: "View Point."

Following the sign, James drove up a short winding road that ended at a high precipice. He parked his car in an asphalt lot large enough to hold a hundred cars. The lot was empty. The time was four in the afternoon. James got out of his car and stood alone in such a place as to inspire appreciation for that craftsmanship that no hand of man is capable of producing. The rain had ended. Everything shone wet and clean. Gray clouds went unbroken to the horizon yet appeared so thin as to be melting away. Forest-covered mountains fell abruptly to treeless plain below. Treeless plain extended to the very curve of the earth itself where far, far away in a desert, James glimpsed a glimmer of sun on water. Fleeting though it be, James had gotten his first look at that from which this book takes its subtitle.

James's next order of business was to descend "Cabbage Hill," a grade of no small renown by which travelers dropped from mountain top to plain. Once safe at the bottom, James sped across the plain, his heart filled with anticipation, his eyes longing to gaze upon what he'd glimpsed from the mountain top. It waited in the vast desert somewhere ahead and James could have no other thought than that of finding it. The sun burst through the clouds, illuminating the way. And then, James was there. He parked on a gravel lane, got out of his car, and went quickly to the edge of a desert canyon where he marveled at the spectacle below.

While James stood gazing into the canyon, something brushed against his leg, and looking to see what it was, he could hardly believe his eyes. UB had somehow followed him across the rough and gotten up on the same small boulder where, wagging his tail, he looked up as if to say, *"I still got some fight left in me."*

And so it was, James and UB stood gazing on the Columbia River, which Lewis and Clark had called, "The Great River of The North."

At 5:00pm, James struck out west on Highway 14 along the north rim of the river gorge. And while he hadn't expected to find the Kansas River, neither had he expected to find what he found. The hydroelectric dams in the gorge were huge but they were not the problem. The problem was in the river itself. The problem lay in the inescapable relativity of being a man on the edge of a cliff in a gorge that measured two miles wide and a thousand feet deep with a tremendous river at its bottom. Down there, the river foamed and marched in white-capped ranks like scales on a dragon's back, a dreadful dragon, mystically formed from the forces of wind and water.

"Whoa," thought James, who having done no research, couldn't know he looked on [what was arguably] the deadliest river in America.

Having witnessed enough without seeing much at all, James held onto the hope that he might get around perilous stretches of river by using his walking machine alongside Highway 14 which ran the canyon's north rim. He thought differently after observing how the notorious highway was driven.

By nightfall James had been reduced to scouting service roads, ATV trails, and even animal paths in hope that he might later use them to portage difficult stretches of water. And as he scouted, he kept telling himself, *"There must be a way."*

Because UB had pooped out, his master carried him with steps that gauged the depths of his own tiredness—,

"Tonight," said the Kansan, coddling his little dog, "we're going to treat ourselves to an inn."

Under normal circumstances, James did his best to keep himself clean-cut. He did his best to show courtesy and respect to every person he met. And having no wish to bring dishonor upon his native Kansas, he would not speak boldly about his plan. Why he would behave differently upon entering the spacious and finely decorated lobby of an upscale hotel located beside the Columbia River in the city of The Dalles cannot be known. What can be known is he was dirty and unshaven, like a man who lived under a bridge. The clock on the lobby wall read 10:00pm. James stepped up to the check-in counter where a slight framed night clerk appeared to be made of sinew or as the saying goes, tough-as-nails. Probably, it was the night clerk's job to wear two hats, one hat for welcoming guests and another hat for dealing with the occasional riffraff that drifted in off the river.

"Good evening, Sir," said James, "I need a room for the night. Oh, and I have a small dog."

Naturally, the clerk was suspicious but kept to a standard of courtesy and professionalism which spoke well of him. Thus he went about the business of checking in James. Meanwhile, James took the liberty of telling the clerk that he'd come from Kansas to attempt the Lewis and Clark route.

The clerk's eyes flashed up to betray what any sane man would have thought but, being a professional, he immediately returned to the work at hand.

"I mean to try the route west-to-east," James added, "I'm on my way to the mouth of the river." Then signing the bill, "I'll stop here on my way upstream, so you'll see me again, but don't look for me to arrive by car, I'll be in a canoe."

It appeared that James had flushed the clerk's stern heart into the open at last. Still, the clerk maintained his post even as his eyes spoke volumes. And in fairness, who could blame the clerk for wondering about James? After all, the river was right there, awesome spectacle that it be, for all to see.

James bid the clerk goodnight and retired to his room where he and UB slept like the dead.

After a good night's sleep, man and dog awoke much refreshed and happy. Scouting resumed after breakfast, but so much difference lay between looking [at the Columbia River] and being [on it], James would understand little of what he saw. The day meanwhile passed like a fast-burning fuse until James realized he'd been scouting too long. Then fearing he might not make his intended destination before nightfall, he set out for that place where the Columbia River met the Pacific Ocean.

Two-hundred years before, in November of 1805, Captain Lewis, Captain Clark, and their brave band of men, together and forever known as the "Corp of Discovery," made their final push to the Pacific Ocean. It took them two weeks to make that last ten miles, fighting for every yard through a tremendous winter storm. By all accounts, the devil threw his entire arsenal at them, but to no avail. After coming through such a fight, and being so very far from home, how they must have hoped that upon reaching the ocean they would encounter a trading ship. They found only the endless gray of a Northwest winter, cold wind and rain, day after day. And probably, that was why they named the point at which they reached the ocean, "Cape Disappointment."

Compared to Lewis and Clark, James had it easy, indeed so easy that he modified the name of the cape to fit his liking, *"Cape [anything but] Disappointment [just so long as I make it there before nightfall]."*

James's desire to stand where Captain Lewis had looked out over the ocean could be measured by the eternity James believed to have passed on the short drive between Portland and Longview. And in fact daylight had begun to wane as James went west from Longview on Highway 4. Seventy-five miles lay between Longview and the Cape. James put the pedal to the metal and the grossly underpowered car hit a onetime record speed of 80mph on a long straight-away going downhill.

The road wound through lush coastal mountains like a racetrack with many hairpin turns. James recalled the words of a man he had known as a kid, an old Indy driver from the days of raw courage when the track was brick and cockpits were open, *"Keep both hands on the wheel, left hand at ten o'clock, right hand at two. Concentrate!"*

Only by bending all his will upon it would James make his destination before nightfall.

Alas, with only one hundred yards to finish, James found his way barred by a steel gate. And because night falls first in a forest, time seemed to have run out. It wasn't dark yet however, and seeing how the road became little more than a path after the gate, James guessed a fort lay hidden in the trees just beyond his field of vision.

No guard stood post at the gate. In fact there wasn't a soul in sight but only a sign warning dire consequences for anyone who attempted to pass without permission. It cannot be known how, for it was neither recorded nor remembered but somehow James spoke with a woman, probably by speaker phone. The woman told James that he was late, yet he might still pass but only under condition that he go on foot.

James walked fast up the path that went through the woods to the fort. The fort came into view almost immediately. A lit doorway stood out in the waning light, and James went up the stairs to the door which had been propped open. Only a screen separated James from the guards who were posted in a small room that looked out over the inland approach. The soldiers were of the United States Coast Guard, and even though none among them looked to be a day over thirty, the professionalism and courtesy they showed would make any citizen proud to be an American. For his part, James stood upright and remarkably calm for a man burning with intent.

"Sirs, my name is James. I have come from Kansas, and I would like to see the cape."

"We are sorry Sir, but the fort is closed for the night. However, if you return tomorrow morning, we will be happy to give you a tour of the fort."

Crestfallen but no less intense, James stared in through the screen at the guards.

"Sir, we really are sorry," said the second guard who had read James's expression, whereupon the first guard added, "We must stand our stations, Sir, or we would give you a tour. There just isn't anyone here to give you a tour tonight. But as I said, there will be someone here tomorrow."

James remained at the screen but certainly no one inside felt the slightest threat from him, for while his disappointment was obvious, so was his acceptance of the rules. Still remaining on the stair landing however, James spotted a path that went up a ridge behind the fort and he knew that there went the very footsteps of Captain Lewis.

James was just that close. The layout of the place was such that, the fort faced to the inland side of the cape while a small ridge behind the fort sheltered it from the Pacific Ocean. James guessed the point of honor to be at the top of the ridge, only fifty yards up through the trees. There was the very place where Captain Lewis had stood, exhausted but victorious with all the Pacific Ocean stretching out before him.

"Sirs," said James, turning back to the guards, "allow me to make certain that I understand. If I return tomorrow morning and ask permission, then I can go up there and look out over the ocean?" James concluded his speech with a gesture toward the path.

"Oh!" cried the guard in realization.

"Is that all you want?" asked the other.

"Yes," replied James.

"You can go up there now if you like."

"Thank you," said James, breaking into a broad smile. "Thank you very much!"

James had left UB tied at the bottom of the stairs, and while UB had only the brain of a dog, he did possess a gift for sensing what James felt. Therefore upon reaching the trees, man and dog simultaneously bolted for the top of the ridge. UB pooped out quickly. James went back to swoop him up, then kept on until at last cresting the ridge; he stood on a cliff panting hoarsely with all the ocean stretching out before him. The point of honor was marked by a bronze plaque immediately before James, and inscribed upon it was a poem by President John F. Kennedy.

James found himself so high above the earth that every ounce of his will could not restrain a tear of joy. And when in such a state, the last thing James needed was to read a poem. Nor did it help that the whole of the western sky backlit the poem with a deep swath of crimson over sparkling silver water. Meanwhile, a coastguard soldier kept watch over the ocean from a cliff top turret only twenty paces to James's left.

So James stood on a cliff over the ocean at sunset feeling like the most fortunate man on earth, for he had successfully gotten himself to the beginning. He would not begin however, not until 200 years to the day that Lewis and Clark began their journey. James felt it a ritual necessary in keeping with the spirit of Lewis and Clark.

"The spirit of Lewis and Clark, along with the spirit of the pilgrims who came before and the pioneers who came after were all excellent examples of men and women who possessed what it took to build the home of the brave and land of the free. I have no words to explain that part of God they possessed, except to know it burns strong in the hearts of men and women that follow God into unknown territory. Here for the sake of verse, I will call it, 'The Goodly Light.'"

"The Goodly Light,
in the Corp of Discovery,
made each man a shining knight,
who in history's most vaunted errand,
carried Liberty's torch
to the distant sea."

As James would find in that neck of the woods called the Northwest, the path of his ancestors was still guarded by a fearsome dragon of wind and water (the Columbia River). Just above the river, in a fishing village roughly three miles from the fort, James lodged for the night. The next morning he drove back to the cape but not to the fort. Instead, he drove to a small parking lot nested in the jungle-like flora that covered the cape. There James found a sign that directed him up a foot path where, as he understood it, he would find a place dedicated to the teaching of Lewis and Clark.

After a walk that wasn't very far, James arrived at a ridge top above the forest where he found a modern temple, owned and operated by the state. People were filing into the place and James assumed them to be vacationers.

Entering the facility, James found himself in a foyer which served as a junction between different sections. A library stood through an opening to his left, a gathering hall through a door to his right. Behind a reception desk, a third opening led into a maze of small rooms that were closed to the public.

James remained behind while the vacationers were taken into the gathering hall to be taught about Lewis and Clark. James then approached a woman of retirement age who sat behind the reception desk—,

"Good morning Ma'am," said the Kansan, removing his hat.

"My name is James. And I've come from Kansas."

"And how may I help you?" replied the kindly woman.

"Ma'am, I'm suffering from some confusion as to what date Lewis and Clark began their journey. I thought they had begun on May 15. However, I have come to suspect they may have begun on May 14. And that is why I have come here. I'm hoping you can tell me the exact date of their departure from St Louis."

"You have come to the right place," the woman knowingly replied. She then brought out a book, opened it on her desk, and began to scan the text. James watched and waited with anticipation. His confusion would soon be cleared away. He would have his answer.

"Sir," said the woman with uplifted eyes, "Lewis and Clark did not depart in May, they departed in November."

Although only momentarily, James's former state of confusion suddenly advanced to the threshold of calamity. Then slowly shaking his head with a grimace, "Ma'am, I am sorry, but I do not think that can be right."

"Oh yes it is," replied the kindly woman, somewhat forcefully pointing her finger to the open text, "It says so right here. They departed in November."

So sure was the woman, James wondered if his scant research had cost him a mistake of such proportion, as to call his sanity into question. Fortunately, he suffered only a brief moment. Then realizing it could not be, he replied, "Ma'am, I am certain that Lewis and Clark left St Louis on May 14th or 15th. Of that much I am certain, it must be one of those two dates."

"No," said the woman, assuredly shaking her head at James. "It says right here in the book, they left in November. See?"

While James would not bother to read the text, he paid the kind woman his upmost respect and courtesy, "Ma'am, I am sorry, but that cannot be. November is the onset of winter. Lewis and Clark would not have begun then, not with winter at their heels."

At last the good woman looked a little uncertain, and after a pause, "Sir, would you mind waiting for just a minute while I do a little more checking."

"Please do so, and thank you Ma'am. This is a matter of extreme importance."

The good woman then brought out more books, but having no

luck, she called for a second woman who came from the maze of small rooms. The two women then pressed the search together. They brought books and pamphlets from drawers and shelves. They riffled high and low. And as they searched, they made comments between themselves about how the information had to be there somewhere.

While the ladies searched diligently on James's behalf, James wondered if the exact date had been lost to history. Then as if to put him under a spell, a voice came in through a doorway and lit upon his ear soft as a butterfly from the wood. In fact the voice came from the gathering hall and belonged to a speaker who at that moment was teaching the vacationers about Lewis and Clark.

> "Unless my ears deceived me, the teacher did not carry an inspirational tone as in speaking with appreciation for those white knights in buckskins collectively known as the Corp of Discovery. Instead, he was being politically correct, taking great care not to offend his audience by repeatedly stating that they were only men. Perhaps he did not mean to throw cold water on my heart, or perhaps he feared the fire that burned there. Whatever the case, if that fire died, so would my appreciation and gratitude for those to whom I owe my existence. Indeed, if that fire died, there would be no more flesh and blood following in the footsteps of a people who by their uncommon willingness to put their necks on the line, built the home of the brave and the land of the free."

Getting rubbed the wrong way, James's brain reacted like a bloodhound that identifies a particular sent, *"I know that tone and use of words, but I never expected it here!"* Then, in a manner of speaking, his heart shouted at his brain, *"Brain, perform your duty as seneschal of my house. Sound the alarm! Send out the signals! Tell the legs to march! We go to defend the honor of Lewis and Clark!"*

"Master," replied James's brain to his heart, *"I do not forget my station but, if I might provide a line of reason, I think we've been taken by surprise here, and here we are, already with so much on our plate, we cannot afford to rush into anything rash."*

"Brain, do you not know anything? Our very forebearers, upon whose

sacrifices we stand, are being bush-wacked! What's to rush into?"

"*Master,*" pled the brain, "*please listen to me. The path of our forefathers awaits us. It is the Great River of the North, a dragon of wind and water which, as we only yesterday discovered, is the most terrible in all America. So let us keep our focus. For it is so much, I have no capacity for more!*"

Fortunately at that moment, the good woman who had been working so diligently on James's behalf spoke up, "Sir, I believe we've found what you're looking for."

Because of his rare distraction, James could not know from where the two women had brought the man of old. Perhaps they had led him in from the library but in any case, directly before James stood a gentleman of such age, he may have soldiered in the great war of which all had been told. The gentleman appeared somewhat shortened by his years, which was normal for those who are long lived. Numerous buttons covered his cap (and perhaps served as amulets to ward off the voice of the teacher). Presently, the gentleman wore a bright-eyed smile that told of what he knew. In fact he was presenting a text, pointing to an entry, holding the book so that James might see for himself. The old gentleman then read aloud from an entry put down 200 years before. And so it was that all doubts were laid to rest. The correct date was May 14, which meant James had no time to waste.

> "The anger and disappointment I felt was not for those kind volunteers who went all out in their effort to help me. Rather, I sensed the LEWIS AND CLARK INTERPRETATION CENTER was, in thin disguise, a political tool in the hands of those who regard praise for my forefathers and mothers as being politically incorrect."

Being a man of his time, James assumed the journey to be 2,000 miles when in fact it was 4,000. In other words, roads are straight and rivers are not. James would figured this out in due time, along with a good many other things. Presently the date was May 13 which meant he had scarce time left in which to prepare. And because only a few miles separated temple from fort, he made his next stop at the fort (Fort Canby).

The Kansan went up the stairs to the same door he'd visited the evening before. And because it was not after hours, the soldiers allowed James inside where they impressed him once again with their high standard of professionalism and courtesy. Having told his plan to the ranking officer, James added that he knew nothing about the tide except for stories of men being swept out to sea and, he had no wish to join them. Tidal current in the Columbia estuary ranked among the most powerful in the world, a fact James learned only after returning safely home. Presently, the ranking officer introduced James to a tide table by which James might know which time slots were safe for travel and which were not. The tide table was a computer printout and, while a mariner might know exactly how to read it, James had never seen anything like it. The entire page was filled with:

05/13/04 Thu 03:05AM LDT 2.4 L O9:08AM LDT 5.8 H 03:26PM LDT 0.8 L 10:09PM L 05/14/04 Fri 04:09AM LDT 1.6 L 10:17AM LDT 5.9 H 04:15PM LDT 1.0 L 10:50PM L 05/15/04 Sat 05:09AM LDT 0.8 L . . . .

    James would need to learn to read the table. And contingent on his location on the river, he would also need to adjust the table with addition or subtraction. And assuming that he could accurately determine his location on the river, he would also need a secondary table called a tide-differences table with which he would know how much to add or subtract from the main table. Tide tables were not available at the fort, but according to the ranking officer, James could pick one up locally.

    James said he understood the tide table although in truth he only knew that he would in time. He thanked the soldiers for their help and then departed through the woods with desperation coming on like a creeping case of the flu. He was not without hope but only without a clue, and being without a clue, it pleased God that his only recourse was to follow his nose to a hometown café located in the fishing village of Ilwaco where he'd taken lodging the night before.

    The café sat where the main street of the town dropped to the river below. The exact time cannot be known but it was midmorning. James sat alone by a window that faced the river while a handful of townsfolk conversed like extended family. Other than that, the place was empty except for a man who, like the Kansan, sat alone. Everyone there seemed to know the man even as he kept to himself. He was old and white-haired, tall and stout, clean cut, stern in countenance, and most definitely possessed of a strength which only a river like the Columbia could put into a man.

After James had stolen a few looks at the man, the man looked back at James as if to say, *"Don't push your luck boy."*

James looked the man square in the eye and addressed him as honestly as he knew how, "Sir, my name is James. I have come from Kansas to attempt the Lewis and Clark route. I mean to start tomorrow and canoe to St Louis, if I can." Then looking out the window to the river beyond, James added, "The way I feel about that river is probably about the same way a person strange to Kansas would feel about a tornado," and returning his eyes to the man, "Sir, I don't mind saying, my heart is in my throat this morning."

The man gave no indication of surprise whatsoever but sized James up like a sea captain of old. Then with a wave of his hand, he summoned James to his table where he went directly to the point, "Have you a map?"

"No Sir."

Never had a sharper stare fallen on James. Then pointing through the glass to the river below, the man said, "Son, that business out there, that's deadly!"

"Yes Sir, I'm hoping you can tell me what you know about it."

James was told to sit, whereupon he heard what he needed to know straight from the horse's mouth. The seaman wasted no time on storytelling but went directly to the heart of the matter. And as he told of the river, his eyes livened, his stern face gave way to a smile until, at last, he seemed transformed into a younger man. Then wishing to make certain James got the best river map possible, the seaman took James to the town's port. There the seaman introduced James to Shane, a clean-cut young man who worked at the marina. The old man of the sea, whose real name James never learned, obviously felt proud of Shane. He spoke of how Shane grew up on the river and had been the star of the high school sports team. So it came to pass that two river men, one old and one young, shared their knowledge with James. On their recommendation, James chose a river map. They pointed to the map. They pointed to the river itself. They identified and explained a variety of things for James, but such details needn't be told here because all shall be known soon enough. Something worth knowing however was how the old man of the sea scoffed at the notion of a tide table. He said a man only needed his eyes to read the tide, and proceeding to tell how, he gave a few priceless lessons in commonsense. For James's sake however, he did order Shane to open a newspaper and read the time of tide, high and low, for May 14. He then said he must go but would be in the café at eight in the morning. James thanked him for his kind help and said that he would see him there. Then thanking Shane for his help, James took his leave, intent on scouting as much as possible with what time he had left.

From Ilwaco, James followed Highway 101 along the shore of the Columbia River to the fishing village of Chinook where, still following his nose, he drove to a campground where fresh cut grass grew lush under shade trees of which there were too many to count. To James, the camps of river people, there along the winding gravel lane, did not appear much different from those back home in Kansas where people vacationed along the shores of reservoirs.

If given the choice, James would have entered the campground on a tall white steed so to speak, but his ride bore more resemblance to a mange-ridden donkey. It had some ugly patches of bare skin, its wheel houses were rusted, a hodgepodge of foam pads banded together with duct tape made for a driver's seat, and as already mentioned, it died at every stop. As for James himself, he never wore anything other than a pair of blue jeans, a sleeveless white tee shirt, and white cowboy hat. Beneath his shirt, a cross from a bygone realm hung on his heart, made of black ebony and banded in silver.

In the campground, James drove directly to the office which stood at the center of the camp. There the campground proprietors, who were husband and wife, came out to greet him.

Climbing from his car, James said, "Howdy Ma'am, Sir. My name is James, and I've come from Kansas to attempt the Lewis and Clark route."

Don and Jean hadn't an atom of ridicule between them and still it only made sense that their eyes shone with amazement while they smiled and were amused. Immediately thereafter, another man came who undoubtedly felt the same. His name was Wade and he was obviously friends with Don and Jean.

All came together for handshakes, after which James resumed his speech, "I mean to put in tomorrow and go west to east, from the Pacific to St Louis, or at least that's my hope. I've had my canoe for twelve years, but I've never canoed anything bigger than the Kansas

River. So I've come out here, and I've seen your river, and I can tell you, the Columbia has sloughs that are bigger than the Kansas. In fact that doesn't begin to cover it. So the long and short of it is, I'm outside of my experience and, I'm hoping you might be able to tell me what you know."

At once the three set to helping James. And of them he would enter in his journal: *"The kindness of this trio was more than anything I could have hoped for."*

Straight away James was asked if he had a map, which he fetched from his car. And seeing it, they all nodded with approval, saying, "You've got the best map there is."

Jean then asked, "James, do you have a ___ radio?" To which James replied, "Ma'am, what's a ___ radio?"

"If you get into trouble, you can call for help."

"I didn't know there was such a thing."

"Do you have a cell phone?"

"No."

No small looks of concern passed between the trio, whereupon it was put to James that he needed a radio. He was told he could get one at any marina for about ninety bucks. James promised he'd look into it but added that chances were he'd have to make do without.

Wade then excused himself, saying he'd be right back. When Wade returned which was immediately, he placed two flares in James's hand and said, "Take those with you."

James didn't know what the flares were. He stood dumb while pondering over them. They were exactly alike, being red and white in color and shaped like candle sticks.

Realizing as much, Wade said, "Those are flares."

"Oh I couldn't take your flares!" James declared, having no wish to take another man's chance for rescue.

"It's okay," said Wade, pushing the flares back, "I've got more."

Having thanked Wade for his kind act, James then explained what he'd learned from the Coast Guard regarding the availability of tide tables and, he asked if any among them knew where he might get a tide table.

Don then excused himself, saying he'd be right back. When Don returned which was immediately, he placed a booklet into James's hand. Contained in the pocket-sized booklet were both tide tables. Hence began lessons on how to read tide tables which wasn't so complicated after all. James learned quickly, and Don insisted that James keep the booklet.

Next the map was opened up and poured over. James learned many things important to his survival. A true giant, the Columbia River measured five miles wide for the first 25 miles of its length going inland from the ocean. Thereafter it gradually decreased to a mile in width and remained so for many hundreds of miles. The volume of water that flowed from its mouth surpassed all other North American rivers flowing into the Pacific Ocean. Its mouth had a nickname known to mariners worldwide: "The Graveyard." In the graveyard, wind and current whipped up swells known to reach 50 feet in height! Obviously the Kansan, who meant to begin from the very lip of the mouth, would not be able to navigate in outgoing tide. Thus his time on the water would be spent in six hour intervals, each being the duration of incoming tide. Moreover, he would not be able to hug the shorelines and thus enjoy the safety of land but instead would have to navigate open water because that was the only way to make progress from point to point in the estuary. James would be miles from land. The water would be dangerously cold and in point of fact, any man who found himself in the unfortunate position of falling in could expect to die of hypothermia within twenty minutes.

It is not known how long the three men spent pouring over map and tide charts, more than an hour. They focused on the estuary because it was the first section of river, about 35 miles in length. Another section of river waited after that. And while different, each section would prove an extreme challenge. But now we have gotten ahead of our story, so let us return to James who was putting one foot before the other in faith.

James told Don and Wade that if all went according to plan, he would see them tomorrow, the idea being to stop there and camp on his way upstream. Then expressing his gratitude for their kind help, James took his leave.

Once again using Highway 101, the Kansan drove to the town of Long Beach located on the shore of the Pacific Ocean. There in twilight he found an auto tow service located on a corner lot. The place appeared to be closed for the night but a garage door was cracked open so James slipped in and shouted into the dark, "Is anyone home?"

A large man in coveralls appeared from a dimly lit doorway in the back. James told the man what he was about and the two men were immediately on good standing. The long and short of their visit was to salvage James's car. James said he meant to abandon his car on the morrow, out on the cape where he would leave key and title under the seat. James had become fond of the tiny car, but it had served its purpose, so there was an end to it.

James returned to the inn at Ilwaco where he worked past midnight making final adjustments to his gear. He would enter in his journal: *"It has been a full and productive day."*

The Estuary
Chapter II

Day 1, Friday, May 14

According to his tide table, James could shove off at five in the morning or five in the afternoon. He chose the latter hour and went to the café for breakfast where he met the old man of the sea. In the café, James's pure hearted intent saw him at home among the local folk. After breakfast, James went to the marina and looked at special radios but didn't buy any. Instead he drove across the Astoria Bridge to the town of Warrenton where he bought a wetsuit. It was a fine wetsuit although James would never use it. Back on the Washington side of the river, the Kansan continued scouting until time came to drive to the cape.

Arriving at the entrance to the cape, James found an armed guard blocking his way. The guard told James that a celebration was taking place at the fort to commemorate the 200th anniversary of Lewis and Clark, that all parking places were taken, and that James would have to turn back. James, who hadn't known about the celebration, told of how he'd come all the way from Kansas to put into the river, in that place, on that day. The guard, although armed, large-framed, stern in countenance and stiffly starched, was not without heart. Thus bidding James to give her a moment, she stepped away to make a radio call. On her return, the guard smiled and said, "You have a green light."

"Thank you Ma'am! Thank you very much!"

Inside the tip of the cape, James moored his canoe to a small pier beside a quiet parking lot ringed by forest and packed with cars. He then hustled back and forth from car to craft loading gear. A sense of urgency gripped him, his tide window was ticking away and he feared getting swept out to sea. He cut his right thumb pretty good but couldn't afford to care. He kept to his task and bled on his gear. Meanwhile, across the pond-like waters of the sheltered cove stood Fort Canby, inside of which the celebration must have been taking place because there wasn't a soul in sight. In fact, the cape seemed hauntingly quiet.

James was manhandling a large pack when, from the corner of

his eye, he caught sight of a lady (or perhaps we should call her a maiden, seeing that she was not married, and appeared to be younger than he). She looked metropolitan, college educated, a lover of art. She was slender, with dark hair, fair skin, and attractive features. She seemed warm not cool, perhaps of Italian or Argentinean blood. She came walking his way, rounding the bend on the lane that hugged the cove. Then coming before him, she said, "So you're the guy from Kansas."

Baffled, James asked, "How did you know?"

"Word gets around," she replied with a smile.

The Kansan hid his thumb, for he didn't wish her to fret over him.

"May I take your picture?" she asked.

James agreed to the maiden's request even as he begged her to forgive his haste, as he could pause only a moment, lest he be swept out to sea.

The maiden, whose name was Madya, said she understood. She then pointed her lens wherein James appeared so at ease with himself, the peaceful water of the sheltered cove made a fitting backdrop. James held UB in one arm while resting the other on a large pack. He looked like a typical hardworking American. In other words, had his paddle been traded for a spatula, his image could have been superimposed onto any of countless backyard barbeque shots. He appeared only a little tired from putting in long hours and, he possessed a hint of that pasty potato quality that comes with middle age. And here comes a place to tell that same as his photo was taken by coincidence, so would another photo be taken 500 miles upstream. But nothing of that photo need be known now. What can be known now was that James hadn't touched a paddle in seven years and whether he showed it or not, he was nervous.

Madya took down James's address so that she might send him the photo. Then bidding him well, she left him to his task. James thanked Madya for her kindness, and he would find her photo upon returning to his native Kansas so far away. There the pen of a maiden would gracefully tell how she often looked out on the river and thought of him; of how he must not of known what it was he faced, yet regardless of whether he lasted one day, one week, or just to the next town, she thought his errand noble and would like to hear from him. The maiden would have long to wait but the Kansan would reply. Now let us return to where we were, quickly, as had James returned to loading his craft.

Soon all that remained for James was to park his car, put the key under the seat, find his scruffy little dog and get in the boat. James would not forget the act of untying the rope which held him to the pier anymore than he would forget the feeling.

James shoved off into the calm of the cove. He put his paddle into the water. He glided forward. Then again, with another stroke, it came back like riding a bicycle. James brought his craft round in a leftward sweep to exit the sheltered cove.

As he came out of the cove, the canoeist did not look back, not while facing that which demanded everything of him. He looked for something other than water on which to get his bearings but so distant were the nearest landmarks, he couldn't distinguish islands from shorelines. Thus toward which to go was difficult to know and, although his map and compass lie before him, there was before all else a leap of faith to take.

"Start slow," came Frank's voice. "Start slow," older brother had said again and again. It was his first and last advice to James, "Start slow."

James had thought to meet the dragon of wind and water head on. He had planned to paddle two miles out to a string of elongated islands beyond which lie the main river channel where incoming tide flowed full strength. By gaining the main river channel, James figured he'd be able to make the port of Chinook before nightfall. However, there were other routes by which he might go, and as he exited the sheltered cove to see the full immensity of what he'd got himself into, he reconsidered his options as circumstance demanded, quickly!

In the meantime, the river waited patiently, and being the great dragon that it was, sunlight sparkled like fire from its mouth. Thus it beckoned the knight come hither. But loyal little friend that UB was, himself having gazed on it over the gunwale, did then look to his master with woeful whine, and truly did he tremble!

"Start slow," James told himself, "Start slow." And he veered toward the much nearer port of Ilwaco. In doing so, James put off his frontal attack. Thus contenting himself wisely, he flanked the beast to take its measure. So it was that the canoeist paddled across the west end of Baker Bay just inside the mouth of the Columbia

River. The gentle bay allowed him to relax. And as he relaxed, the realization of what he'd done began to sink in. The date was May 14 and he was on the river! Filled with joy, James began to sing as he navigated. Although he rarely sang, he sang heartily to sooth the affect of waves which weren't big to local folk but rose and fell enough to keep the flatlander on his toes.

Fearsome fights lie ahead for James. Truly, he would be tested to the full measure, but not on that day. A few drops of blood, a crimson stain on his paddle would be the worst of it there. Therefore comes a place to tell how the canoeist paddled and steered his craft. James sat at the back of his canoe, not in the middle like some soloists do. UB sat or lie on his dog bed between James's feet. The remainder of the canoe was packed with gear and provisions from stem to stern. The stem, to be known henceforth as the bow, was the front end of the canoe. The stern was the back end. The gunwales were the rails atop both sides of the canoe from bow to stern. James's canoe measured large, being 17' 4" long. Combined weight of canoe, gear, food, man, and dog totaled just over 500lbs. James didn't paddle his craft like the kayakers who continuously switch back and forth between right and left sides. Rather, James paddled on one side, using long powerful strokes to move across the water. Only when he began to tire from paddling on one side would he switch to paddle on the other. When he switched, he brought his paddle across behind him, thus throwing water from paddle blade to river and not into boat. James steered by means of a rudder technique in which he twisted his paddle at the end of each paddle stroke. By combining paddling and ruddering (pace and bearing) into one smooth move, being his stoke, he had that which is critical to efficient movement, being rhythm.

Because James sat in the stern of his craft, he pushed his load before him and, by such means, immediately realized his craft to be a handful. And yet as he would soon learn, size and weight could be advantageous in rough water. On his brother's advice, James had made a cover tarp for his canoe. The cover tarp snapped to the gunwales and would prove indispensable (especially in rough water). The color scheme of his canoe was dark green on which the silver tarp fit tight as a drum with the gunwale like a ribbon of black trim between. Inside the canoe, a speckled beige interior had a pleasant appearance and felt smooth to the touch.

UB, who'd been whining continually, changed his tune and happily so, when into sight came the Port of IIwaco. James also felt relieved and, spurring a bit, continued until safe within the stone walled port.

Total distance traveled wouldn't add up to two miles and although pathetic, at least James was alive. Alive, and absolutely delighted. So much so, that the work of carrying loads of gear was pure joy. Up and down the jetty-like wall of the port he went, making many trips. He carried his canoe up last, then got out his toolbox and laid out the various pieces of his walking machine. First came some one-time assembly work and because the thing was of his own making, James performed each task handily. In fact James relaxed by working with his hands, and because plenty of daylight remained, he felt no need to rush. He'd been rushing for months to make that day and there it had turned out just as beautiful as could be imagined, with the wide mouth of the river opening to the sparkling ocean, and the forested slopes coming down to the little fishing village above. Plus there wasn't a soul around (although one might expect to find a crowd in such a place). So it was that James sat with tools in hand, assembling parts, fastening nuts and bolts while taking in sun and shine, feeling a sense of accomplishment and adventure that was truly sublime.

Once James had his walking machine assembled and loaded, he harnessed into the lightweight pulling frame, clipped UB's leash to his belt loop and set out for town. Immediately, James discovered the brake didn't function properly. The brake was the only part of the machine he hadn't tested, being that he'd built it at the last. So James stopped at the marina and borrowed an electric drill from Shane. Then having relocated the brake, James continued up the hill and into the town of IIwaco.

Straight away, people stopped and smiled. Many came forth. There was excitement. In fact, James hadn't gone a block when a group of teenagers, four or five in all, young men of fourteen or fifteen years came running to see what the Kansan was about.

"What is that?" asked one of the boys.

"It's my walking machine," James replied.

"Where'd you get it?"

"I built it."

The boys gathered round, marveling and asking questions. So

James explained how his amphibious machine worked: Whenever the canoe was in the water, the rectangular pulling frame folded back on its hinge to lay flat atop the front half of the boat. To move from water to land travel, James first assembled the components of a two-wheeled cart previously stored in the canoe. (James had ordered the cart from the back of a magazine, cut the cart apart and redesigned it in a configuration that fit his needs.) Next the assembled cart fastened to the bottom of the canoe by a system of stays and straps.

"Cool," said one of the boys upon hearing how the tires were made of the same stuff that bullet proof vests were made. James then explained the rectangular pulling frame and its components, all of which he had built. He showed the boys how the pulling frame attached to the canoe via a special cross member that spanned the gunwales at the bow. With pulling frame folded forward and cart in place underneath, the canoe became something of a rickshaw. But unlike a rickshaw, the pulling frame had a fore-and-aft hinge design which gave it a double action, thus the unit floated in rhythm with whomever was pulling it. So bumps in the road were not transferred to the puller but dissipated through the design of the machine. The puller harnessed into the pulling frame via a mountain rescue harness which James had modified. The harness was not restrictive but allowed good freedom of movement. The harness had no buckles or clips to unfasten, so if the occupant needed out of it in a hurry, he could jump out simply by throwing up the pulling frame which was made of lightweight steel tubing. The pulling frame surrounded the occupant and had a front crossbar with black rubber handgrips. By pulling in harness while pushing on the crossbar, a man could move a heavy load up a steep grade. A cylindrical pad on the rear crossbar served as a back pad for comfort and stability when going down a grade. Overall the machine had a clean and simple design. All welds were clean. All steel had been acid-scrubbed, primed, and painted silver. The harness was black, same as the backrest, handgrips, and wheels. The tarp snapped down tight to give the look of a silver lid atop what was not only a canoe but also the body of a cart. Streamlined from front to back, the walking machine measured 23 feet long and weighed 300 pounds when loaded. It had a simple color scheme: silver and black with a body of forest green. To park it, James only needed to step out of the harness, draw a budgie cord from the front, and hook it to a carabineer on the frame to lock the rig in a tripod-like position. For the record, James would not employ the silver tarp for land travel during the first seventy miles of overall travel.

"What's that?" asked one of the boys who had wandered round behind the rig.

"That's my brake," replied James with the proud smile of a craftsman. "Do you like it?"

All the boys agreed that they liked it. James then explained how prior to the brakes construction, he'd thought to make it from bicycle parts but due to time concerns, he'd made it from parts-on-hand instead. From white pine, James had made the body of the brake which had a V-shaped interior that fit to the front (or rear) of the canoe. The wooden brake body was painted white and sheathed entirely in bright 18-gauge aluminum. Lines of tiny screws appeared like rivets. A ¾-inch-thick hard-rubber pad was housed in the bottom of the brake body. A winged angel made of 18-gauge aluminum graced the front of the brake body like a battle ram from a medieval war ship. Its two-dimensional figurehead reflected the love of her maker even while betraying a cheesy crafts-show quality. Her arms were poised like an ancient Egyptian with palms turned up. Long flowing hair framed her face. A modest gown concealed her shapely form. A halo made clear she was of Christian design.

The one-piece brake made for quick storage inside the canoe when traveling by water. On land, the brake easily secured to the cart via four 2-inch-wide aluminum straps that extended up to the gunwales. When deployed the brake worked as follows: If while traveling down a steep grade the load could not be managed, James could stop the rig by pulling the bars of the pulling frame upward which would immediately drive the brake's rubber pad into the road surface. And that was why the brake was armored; its principle demanded it, lest it explode from the impact of a fully loaded cart bearing down on it.

"And that's how it works," James concluded, "except I didn't have time to test the brake. So when I set out walking from the port, I found that the heels of my boots caught on it, and I had to remount it back here on the stern."

"That's too bad," said one of the boys, his expression turning from enthusiasm to disappointment.

"Oh but it couldn't have worked out better," James assured the boy. "You see, when I walk down a grade, I'll be placing my boots further out in front of myself, like this. So my heels won't catch on the brake after all. So I can still have the brake up front when needed. At all other times, I'll keep it back here on the stern. And look here; see how the rubber brake pad protects the stern tip from getting worn through when the cart is parked? As a result of correcting my mistake, I've gained an entirely new feature. You see how well things can work out."

James briefly showed the boys how he'd made the slow-moving vehicle sign (a triangular reflector same as those used on the back of farm tractors). The sign had a one-piece design made from 18-gauge aluminum and included an extended mount that James hand-formed to fit tight over the stern. Thus the sign snapped on and off the stern quickly. And because the sign fastened to the top portion of the stern whereas the brake fastened to the lower, neither component got in the way of the other. Both sign and brake stored in the canoe for water travel.

The boys were inspired and, as they went away, James overheard one say, "Someday, I'm going to do something like that."

James smiled up to Heaven, then harnessed into his walking machine and continued into town with UB walking happily alongside.

Traveling a block further, man and dog put themselves up in an inn as evening fell. There James laid his head down and thought of all the uplifted spirits he'd seen, and of the kindness of so many people. So ended James's first day on the Lewis and Clark trail, it had been a good day.

Day 2, Saturday, May 15

James wore a wristwatch but timekeeping hadn't yet occurred to him (he would improve at such things). Suffice to say, he rose after a good night's sleep. He fed and took UB out. He shaved, packed, and loaded gear from room to machine. He then harnessed into his rig and set out on a beautiful spring morning. At the café James proudly parked his rig before plate glass windows where all could see. For breakfast he had eggs over easy on white toast with hash browns, sausage links, and orange juice and coffee. He found no lack of conversation there. In fact, word of his errand seemed to have gone before him, which surely explained the admiration of one very lovely maiden.

"Although I yearned for marriage and family, I could not return her ardent looks. I could not because my errand allowed no time for all that goes into courtship, marriage, and family. To credit the young woman, it is no bad thing that she be impressed by a man (any man) who pulls a 300 pound cart. After all, it's honest work. Honest work indeed, and if my ego has not laid me so low that I claim what is not mine to bestow, then in the maiden's eyes I understood, those who are young at heart can still believe in that which is pure and good."

From the café, James proceeded to the port where he unloaded and disassembled his walking machine, then loaded his canoe. The old man of the sea pointed to the river and gave final words of advice. James thought it surprising how quickly time had gotten away. And so it was, with a firm handshake, words of thanks and well wishes… he paddled out the port gate and into the wide open.

By James's estimate, Baker Bay was twenty-five-square miles of open water just inside the mouth of the Columbia River and he would have to cross it at its widest point if he wished to make port before the changing of the tide. It goes without saying; he paddled hard:

"I was not used to so much water. The bay was like a sea to me. I feared the tide. I didn't want to get sucked out to sea. It was just over five miles across the bay. I covered it in less than two hours. I knew no challenge there except for my own fear of the unknown and the waves on the water which were small to local folk but seemed large enough to me."

In time James would discover that entry to one port was pretty much the same as any. Landscapes would change over distance but the basic construction of the port would remain the same. Each port was protected by strong stone walls and usually attached to a small town. In making port, James would paddle through a single narrow opening in the port wall to gain the protected area within. And because sailboats were docked in every port, and because their masts rose above the protective walls, they could be seen like banners from afar. Therefore James would learn to look for them when out on the approach.

The old man of the sea had warned that, upon entering the Port of Chinook, the way to the boat landing wouldn't be obvious. By following his directions, James entered the port and paddled to the landing as if he'd been there before when in fact he had not.

Wishing not to obstruct the fishermen who brought their motorboats in and out of the water, James moored his canoe to a small wooden dock located in an out-of-the-way corner. He then made a dozen round trips carrying gear and provisions up a wooden ramp to a gravel parking lot above. Returning to the dock below, James worked to assemble the wheeled carriage for his cart. He used caution not to drop any tools or bolts between the planks and into the water. Then with wheeled carriage assembled, James pulled his canoe from the water and attached the carriage to the bottom of the canoe body (he did this work while yet on the wood planked dock). Meanwhile, a lone onlooker came to stand at the edge of the wooden ramp above. The onlooker, who was up in his years, spoke no words but watched from under the brim of his straw hat while leaning on a walking stick. He appeared highly interested and yet, standoffish. He was obviously a man and yet, not an inch taller or stouter than a boy of ten. James thought him an enigma but as to who was more enigmatic between them cannot be known. In any case, the Kansan addressed the onlooker in the same friendly no-nonsense manner with which he spoke to everyone—,

"Good morning, Sir. My name is James, and I've come from Kansas to attempt the Lewis and Clark route, west to east."

Vernon had come to the river for the 200th anniversary of the Lewis and Clark expedition. He didn't say so at the time but only continued to observe James. Meanwhile, so narrow a space did James have on either side of his walking machine, he just could get around it to work without falling off the dock and into the water. Moreover, he had to go back and forth and from side to side around his cart a number of times in order to center and secure its body atop its wheeled carriage. Such work was far from being second nature, so James was truly involved when for some reason Vernon abandoned his standoffishness and came down the plank to observe the assembly process up close. Up close, like maybe all Vernon ever wanted was to be a part of things. Whatever the case, a comic dance began in which the two men went shuffling like a pair of pigeons on a ledge, going one way, then back the other way, excusing one another and so forth until, begging forgiveness, James suggested it might be better for Vernon to watch from where he'd been.

Continuing, James unfolded the pulling frame and installed its harness. He then harnessed in and pulled his rig up the plank and onto the gravel above where he attached the brake and slow moving vehicle sign. Then with gear and supplies stowed in cart, James changed his tennis shoes for walking boots, clipped UB's leash onto his belt loop, harnessed into the pulling frame and stood ready to go.

Vernon asked if he might come along, and James thought that would be just fine. Then as they were heading out, a man in a big black SUV pulled into the parking lot and introduced himself as Dan, a friend of Wade's. Nothing more need be told of Dan at this time except that he drove away as James set out for town with Vernon walking alongside at a brisk pace. Vernon possessed a wealth of knowledge regarding the famous history of Lewis and Clark. James possessed only a basic schoolboy's understanding of the legendary expedition, and confessing as much, listened intently.

The pair of walkers soon arrived at an intersection where they had to bid one another farewell because James had made plans to stay at Don and Jean's campground whereas Vernon had his camper in another campground.

Having gone left at the intersection, the Kansan entered the town of Chinook where a good many folk came out to see him. Formal and friendly as ever, James took pleasure in their attention. In fact they strengthened him with their enthusiasm, and he would need all the strength he could get. They took pictures and asked if they might interview him for their newspaper. With some fast thinking, James made a policy he would keep to the end. He made known how much their interest meant to him even as he said he would give no interview without first making it to St Louis. But if he made it to St Louis, then he would re-drive the route just as soon as he could afford to, whereupon he would be happy to give interviews to those who had asked. Thus the people not only respected James's wish but remained happy.

On advice from the townsfolk, James chose a café for lunch and because the café had no window facing the street, James drew no attention from inside as he parked his rig outside. Thus he entered the café without fanfare and found it to be a hopping place. In fact it was so crowded, the waitress sat James at a table with a couple who weren't done eating! Moreover, the young couple appeared to be experiencing some lover's problems but to their good credit showed no resentment toward James. Nonetheless, James felt bad for intruding. Then as fortune would have it, a woman came in from outside and proceeded through the din to where the Kansan sat—,

"I just got the news," said the woman, having come to stand before James, "and Sir, I want you to know, I think what you're doing is wonderful."

Suddenly everyone wanted to know, and no sooner had James told them than they all wanted him to succeed, particularly the young couple who, knowing something of the river, gave directions to the best campsites. Others joined in. So they had good conversation and good food. And when the young couple departed, they appeared to have forgotten their troubles.

James paid his bill, complimented the chef, harnessed into his walking machine and resumed pulling toward Don and Jean's campground. Along the way, James came before an old gentleman who sat alone in the yard of an abandoned high school. The man appeared to be a retired sailor and James couldn't help noticing how he fit into his surroundings as though made for a painting in a frame. His hair had been bleached white by sun and time. The concrete bench on which he sat appeared bleached white by sun and time. The abandoned high school, which had bevels and ramparts like a castle, also appeared bleached white by sun and time. And finally, the seaman's look was as clean and solid as the old-fashioned concrete on which he sat.

"Where are you going in that thing?" asked the old seaman.

James stopped and replied, "Sir, I'm attempting the Lewis and Clark route, west to east."

"I'm proud of you."

"Thank you Sir," said James, and continuing, he told of how he'd stood beside the river some days before, watching it flow around the pylons beneath the Astoria Bridge. But even as James told of what he saw, he was in fact ignorant, for he was yet to witness the power of the tide.

"Son," said the old seaman, turning ominous, "don't go under that bridge at Astoria."

Perhaps it was nothing more than the way in which the moment unfolded, being surreal, like finding the ghost of a white knight sitting before his abandoned castle. Perhaps it had to do with the fact that James had yet to meet the dragon and therefore, he couldn't know what he faced. In any case, James would not forget the warning.

At the campground, James received a warm welcome from Don, Jean, Wade, and Dan, whom James had met briefly at the port. Don showed James to a good campsite, and Wade and Dan came along saying they wished to help James with his tent. Thus began the second comedy of the day. James had purchased his tent four years earlier when his old tent had torn, but he hadn't used the new tent or even had it out of its duffle. The new tent had a simple design, yet there stood three grown men reading instructions and scratching their heads. Finally, James decided he didn't need instructions. Thus bending a tent pole nearly to its snapping point, James managed to force it into an eyelet. In such a way, James installed two of the three tent poles.

Dan stood back to view the contorted tent, "That can't be right."

Soon, James discovered the correct eyelets, "Oh, here we go. I've got it now."

So the tent went up and James was right pleased with it. James then went with Wade and Dan to the camp of John and Jack who were cooking some crabs they'd caught that day.

After introductions, James was given a fresh-cooked crab. James had never tasted fresh crab. He attacked the thing, breaking and eating it with such passion that bits of meat and juice flew six feet in every direction. It was true, the men were laughing even as they sought to get clear of him.

Fortunate had James been for meeting men of such hospitality. In fact, James would find such fortune all along the way, like panning in a stream rich with gold. The only catch was, the gold was guarded by a dragon—as well it should be in the home of the brave.

Presently, the men with whom James shared company were all a bit older than he, most if not all being Nam vets. And James, who felt comfortable in their midst, thanked them for their kind hospitality. So the five men continued in laughter and good conversation, speaking on variety of subjects until James caught sight of a man striding the lane that passed beside the camp.

"Vernon?" asked James, somewhat surprised.

Vernon stopped, having realized it was James.

"How are you?" asked James.

"Oh, I'm fine," Vernon replied. "They told me that your camp was over there," he added, gesturing down the lane.

"Yea," James replied. "I've got a nice spot. It looks west over the bay."

James then turned to the others, "This is Vernon, I met him today at the port," and turning back to Vernon, "Vernon, this is Wade, Don, John, and Jack."

Vernon looked about as relaxed as a wet cat when suddenly John barked, "So what are you doing? Just walking around, or what?" John meant no harm with his big booming voice but Vernon looked like he might go up a tree. Instead, Vernon extended his hand to offer what may as well have been his free pass to anyplace in the Columbia River Basin—,

"I wanted to show James my Lewis and Clark postage stamps."

Wade was first to go forward, and James was on his heels. Everyone liked the stamps. James felt sure they were the best he'd ever seen. The men invited Vernon into camp and offered him fresh crab. James assured Vernon that it was good but Vernon declined and went away as quickly as he'd come.

Without missing a beat, the five men carried on as before, laughing and having a good time until alas, James drew dire—,

"I saw an old gentleman on my way here. He told me not to go under the bridge at Astoria and, I don't know, maybe it was only the way he said it but, I think I ought to take his advice."

"A kayaker drowned there a week ago," said one of the men, also turning dire.

"Was it a week ago?" asked another. "I thought it was two weeks ago."

"I can't remember, people drown up and down that river."

"Yeah, a lot of people."

"Stay clear of the pilings James," said Dan, referring to the flood fences that stood in the river. "That's what got the kayaker. Stay away from the pilings, and you'll be fine."

With evening on the approach, James thanked the men for all they had done. He then went with UB for a walk to the water's edge. By the time man and dog returned to their tent, night had nearly fallen. James crawled into the tent behind UB. UB had a nice little scrap of foam rubber for a bed with a towel atop it. James had a ground pad and lightweight sleeping bag. He slept like a rock.

Day 3, Sunday, May 16

Don and Jean would accept no camping fee. Instead, they said they liked what James was doing and wished him well. James thanked them for their hospitality and then proceeded to town where he parked his rig beside a large café. Rain had begun to fall so James set UB up under the cart before going in for breakfast. James ordered his usual and had pleasant conversation but because he sat in a wing of the café, there weren't many people near him. Therefore when the last couple left the wing, James remained alone, quietly finishing his breakfast.

"James."

James looked up from his meal, "Vernon, how are you?"

"I'm fine. May I join you?"

"Yes, of course."

Vernon took a seat and placed a piece of notepaper before James, "I made a list of resupply points between here and Portland."

James picked up the paper, "That's very kind of you Vernon. Thank you."

"You might want this also," Vernon added, opening a Lewis and Clark leaflet on the table before James.

"You've probably seen dozens of these tourist pamphlets," Vernon continued, "but this particular one is pretty good. See, it's a map specific to this area. It shows the original Lewis and Clark route with their campsites."

"Oh, well how about that," said James who hadn't seen a single pamphlet until then, although he would see dozens of them henceforth.

"James?"
"Yeah."
"Would it be alright if I walked with you?"
"Sure, if you don't mind the rain?"
"I don't mind."
"Alright then, let's get going."

James, Vernon, and UB set out walking toward the port. And as they went along the road, James remembered the old seaman's warning, *"Don't go under that bridge at Astoria."* Thus deciding he needed to test his walking machine anyway, James scratched his plan to put into the river at the Port of Chinook. Instead, he continued pulling his cart east along the shoulder of Highway 101 with the Astoria Bridge as his new objective (5 miles ahead). Past that, James would decide when he got there.

The rain came down steady, making the morning gray and chilly. UB meanwhile, who wasn't leashed, had fallen behind to become a picture of misery. Fortunately for him, his master stopped and made a bed inside the rig where he would be warm and dry.

Having toweled UB off, James placed him inside the cart under a blue tarp. James had previously piled his gear and provisions in the center of the cart to balance the load over the single axle. Presently, James readjusted the cargo load to compensate for UB because the principle of his walking machine demanded balance. UB however didn't understand the principle of the machine but only wanted to see outside. Therefore while James pulled the cart, UB poked his nose out one side, then the other. And while UB only weighed nineteen pounds, his movements compounded a much larger load balanced on a single axle. The result wasn't good. The hinged pulling system meant the cart and its puller floated semi-independent of one another in a design that depended not on a solid frame but instead on a nearly indiscernible see-saw rhythm that kept man and machine in harmony. Presently, as James was forced to counter UB's movements by exerting pressure up and down on the pull bars while walking, the harmony got lost and, the see-saw rhythm became exaggerated to the point of comedy. UB caused the body of the rig to teeter, and James made it totter. The rig became a teeter-totter.

"Excuse me Vernon," said James while rain water dripped from the eve of his parka hood. James then unharnessed, set his machine in its park position and went to peer under the tarp where UB peered back at him.

"You're messing me up."

UB hesitated.

"Lie down," James said in a fake growly voice.

UB hung his head and got back in bed.

James harnessed in and resumed walking along the shoulder. It was Sunday on Highway 101, arguably America's most famous tourist fare. Rain fell steady while a change of climate, diet, and drinking water took its toll on James. And once again, UB had gone on the move inside the machine. Therefore instead of walking easy, James struggled to control a 300 pound teeter-totter. And with UB hidden from sight, what passerby could possibly have known what was wrong when each time the machine went wacky, James turned his head and barked, "Lie down!"

As usual James spoke somewhat formally, "Vernon, you're going to have to forgive me this morning if I seem distracted. I've got a lot going on just now."

"That's alright," said Vernon, and he launched back into talking about the history of Lewis and Clark and what James could expect in the next 100 miles.

Vernon not only possessed passion for his American heritage but could maintain a strong stride in spite of his years. As a practical matter however, Vernon had to turn back. Therefore the two men shook hands and parted ways with well wishes. Then as it would be with so many men and women, James hoped to see Vernon again someday.

The rain ended and the day brightened. James pulled his rig along a wide gravel shoulder where people parked their cars to fish and enjoy the day—,

"Hey cowboy!" shouted a young woman, "where you going in that thing?"

"Just as far as I can, Ma'am!"

After walking a few miles further, James arrived at a place where the highway entered a tunnel. And because traffic flowed heavy and many motorists didn't have their lights on, James feared they may not see him in the dark tunnel. A yellow signal light sat on a post outside the tunnel entrance and James understood he could push the button on the post to start the caution light flashing (the theory being to warn motorist of his presence in the tunnel). James let UB out of the cart and asked, "What's your time in the 100 yard dash?"

It would have been an absurd question except James meant it. The Kansan knew he couldn't run through the tunnel with his dog in the cart. The thing would fly out of control. So there knelt James, petting UB and wondering what to do, when along came Dan in his big black SUV.

Dan pulled over and the tinted glass came down, "Need some help?"

"Yeah."

"What can I do?"

"Could you follow me with your emergency blinkers on?"

"You got it."

James could hardly believe his good fortune. He harnessed in and clipped UB's leash to his belt loop, "UB, we're going to have to run."

The old dog wagged his tail fiercely.

At the first break in traffic, James set out running as fast as he could. "Run UB! Run!"

By the time James had made it 1/3 of the way through the tunnel, traffic had stacked up behind Dan and, so hard were people laying on their horns, James may as well of been inside a trumpet! James made it out the other side and pulled over on the shoulder. Dan gave a thumbs-up and drove on. James had become winded and could have doubled over but instead, he stood tall and waved at each motorist while they exited the tunnel. James did so in a formal and courteous manner as if to say, "Howdy. My name is James and I've come from Kansas to attempt the Lewis and Clark route." And almost every motorist waved back.

James and UB continued winding along the river with narrowing shoulders and ever increasing amounts of traffic. Naturally fearing an accident even as he kept off the road, James said prayers in which he asked God to protect the motorist, himself, and UB. At one point with no shoulder to pull on, James pulled his rig in the ditch like a beast of burden.

Arriving at the Astoria Bridge and seeing how the river lie calm beneath it, James wondered why he struggled to pull his rig along the road (he would know soon enough). He didn't go on the bridge which would have taken him across the river but instead, he passed the bridge entrance and struck out on Highway 401 which continued east along the north shore of the Columbia River.

Rain fell in spits as James reached a rest stop just east of the Astoria Bridge. The rest stop consisted of a long flat patch of mown grass and small trees between Highway 401 and the Columbia River. A low central building served as information center while scattered throughout the park were picnic tables under small shebang-styled shelters. James parked his rig and took care of UB before lying down to rest on a bench under a shebang.

Soon there came a volunteer from the information center. Her name was Marjorie and she staffed the information center along with her husband, Jiggs.

"Are you okay?" asked Marjorie in a grandmotherly tone.

"Yes Ma'am, I'm fine," replied James who wouldn't admit to feeling ill.

Marjorie, who had lived long enough to know when a man was lying, took to mothering James. Then, after drinking the juice she brought, James fell asleep. Marjorie came periodically to check on James but did not disturb him while he napped.

Upon awakening, James noticed the tide had changed, and bringing out his field glasses, he got a bird's eye view of how the tide flowed to the sea. For all his fear of it, James had no idea just how powerful the tide truly was. And so it was, he understood the old seaman's warning, without which he may have lost his life.

Feeling better, James thanked Marjorie for her kindness and set out pulling east along Highway 401 until at last, having pulled all day, he found a primitive access road that dropped to a small rocky beach hidden in the trees between highway and river. No town lie there, nor were any people or structures in sight but only mountains, trees, river, and a primitive boat launch called the Knappton Ramp.

James had no wish to put into the river after pulling a 300 pound cart for ten miles. In fact he'd been keeping his eyes peeled for a place to camp only to lose count of the no-trespassing signs along the way. Nor could James proceed further by road because the road left the river there to climb the coastal mountains. So James had come to the end of the road, the end of the day, the end of his strength, and still he stood between a rock and a hard place. It seemed he had no choice but to take to the river.

Perhaps the dragon of wind and water had been waiting there all along, licking his big chops and rubbing his paws together. Perhaps he said, "I hope you enjoyed your 15 minutes of fame."

James looked through his field glasses across two miles of open water to a landmass called, Grays Point. The distant shoreline didn't appear all that hospitable and that wasn't all bad. By his map, James saw how there weren't any roads over there. Therefore it would be primitive and, providing the shoreline wasn't too rugged, there would be a place to camp. James wasted no time but set about the business of unloading gear and provisions from his rig. He then backed his emptied rig into the water and launched his boat. Next he went about the work of breaking down the wheeled carriage so it could be stowed in the canoe first because it wouldn't fit any other way. And while it was simple enough, the amphibious process of changing from land rig to water craft took time, even with experience.

At last, James only needed to change his walking boots for tennis shoes. In fact he was tying his tennis shoes while sitting on a rock beside his moored boat when as fortune would have it, Dan, who was returning from wherever he'd gone that day, saw James and turned off the highway to drive down the rugged little road that went between the trees to the primitive beach below.

"*What are you doing?*" Dan asked, getting out of his truck, grinning like James might be half crazy.

"I'm going over there," said James, pointing a shoe across the water.

"Why?" asked Dan.

"I need a place to camp."

"Don't do that."

"Why not?"

"Because it's late, and you're tired."

James finished tying his shoe and stood up, "There's no place to camp here."

"Yes there is."

"Where?"

"Across the road," said Dan, nodding inland. "Come, I'll show you."

While the two men walked toward the highway, Dan spoke about how a change in climate, water, and diet could affect a man. Dan said he'd seen men affected by it in Nam. He said he'd suffered from it over there himself, and he gave it a name, but James failed to remember it for his journal. It was something-syndrome. Dan said a man only needed rest to cure it. Having crossed the highway, Dan pointed to the remnant of an old logging road that blended in with the forest almost perfectly. In truth the road wasn't more than two muddy tire ruts filled with stagnated water and overgrown with stinging nettles. The air there buzzed with hungry mosquitoes and, there weren't half so many slugs in all of Kansas.

"I know it doesn't look like much," said Dan, "but I think there's a spot back there." He then waited while James went to check it out. And sure enough, not thirty yards beneath the forest canopy, on the edge of a mountain slope; James found a flat patch of dry ground just big enough to camp on.

"I found it," James shouted.

Right gratefully did James shake Dan's hand who then went on his way, for it had gotten late and James had precious little daylight left for making camp.

No more had Dan driven away than perhaps, the dragon pinned his ears back while squinting and grinning like one who'd been cheated out of ill-gotten gain. Perhaps in an ominous tone, the dragon said, "I'll see you later," whereupon he submerged beneath the waves.

So quickly did night approach, James had to run as he carried loads of gear back and forth across the road. From water's edge to camp he ran until only his canoe remained which he carried atop his shoulders. Then in near darkness, he stomped down nettles and erected his tent with a flashlight. The Kansan meant to break out lantern and stove to calm his fierce hunger but fiercer yet was his exhaustion. He literally could help himself no longer. He had found the end of his strength. He was sick with exhaustion, and he had yet to face the dragon.

No more had James crawled into his tent than a vehicle stopped on the road and aimed its headlights on his camp. With his last ounce of adrenalin, James exited his tent and went toward the glaring headlights in which he could see nothing except the silhouette of a man on the approach.

Continuing forward, James couldn't help remembering all the no trespassing signs he'd seen that day, not to mention Dan's words, *"Eh, nobody's going to care."*

At last, halfway between camp and road, James met the dark

figure—,

"I got to thinking you might be hungry," said Dan, holding out a grocery bag containing beef franks, oranges, apples, drinking water and doggy treats.

"Ah, Dan," said James with great relief. "Thank you, Dan. Thank you for all your kind help." Then in a tone at once direly frank and laughing with good fortune, James added, "You don't know how much I needed this."

Dan smiled and said, "When you cook those franks, give the broth to your dog. That's what I do anyway."

James said he would do so. Then parting with words of thanks and well wishes, Dan took his leave. James immediately thought to bring out his cook stove. He thought on it for all of five seconds, then devoured the franks raw along with everything else while UB wolfed the dog treats.

James couldn't know it but his need for strength would soon be such that the meal he nearly skipped may have been one too many, and the difference between living and dying.

Day 4, Monday, May 17

The Kansan woke in the dark wood to find he'd slept as if under a spell. His wristwatch read 8:00am and like a man late for work, he skipped breakfast to get underway. Still he had no small amount of work to do before he could shove off. Items had to be packed and because his six rubberized duffle bags opened at one end only, packing took time. Other items like his bedroll and plastic gear locker had to be waterproofed by various designs of his own making. Then he began the work of hauling loads, after which came a second round of packing to trim the canoe so it would sit level in the water. All said and done, there were many chores which needn't be told here but are better left to the progression of this story. All that need be known here is that, by working hard, James stood ready to shove off at 10:00am.

From the Knappton Ramp, James paddled past Gray's Point before continuing east into open water. To his left lay Gray's Bay. To his right lay Cathlamet Bay. In between the two bays, the river measured eight miles wide. So altogether the estuary was twelve miles wide! It was something to see, nothing but river and sky stretching out to meet on the horizon where a lone cloud puff floated like a beauty mark on the face of Heaven. And as for the air in that place, it was so fair, the sun could muster no more than a gentle caress. Meanwhile along the distant periphery, forested land points appeared here and there like mystic realms veiled in haze.

"It truly was like paddling into a storybook."

But where was the dragon? Perhaps in all of nature there existed no beast more deceiving, for so neatly had the fire king groomed his scales into waves, he appeared to be robed in a million armor plates floating like mirrors in the sun. He was magnificent. And while he napped, the knight paddled his heavily loaded craft in more water than a sane man might care to find himself. But it was a good day for learning, being that the waves were small to local folk. Our novice was kept on his toes in the knowledge that he mustn't spill, not in water like ice and more than two miles to the nearest shoreline.

At 1:30pm the tide would change and when it did James had to be off the river. Therefore having paddled seven miles due east, the canoeist had no choice but to land on Harrington Point which wasn't a bad thing. James found an excellent little beach on which to day camp. And although the stony beach was manmade, James wouldn't see another soul there for the duration of his stay. James washed his clothes in the river, then strung a line on which to hang his laundry. He shouted as he bathed in the icy water. Then because he could not drink the brine, James took a jug and went listening for a brook which he found tumbling down a mountain slope.

On his way back to camp, James found a "No Trespassing" sign and realized he was on private property. He then saw a freshly poured foundation set back in the trees. Nobody was there, but somebody had been building their dream cabin, and James had camped on their dream beach. James felt bad but couldn't do much about it until the tide changed. To James's credit, it would be the only time he knowingly trespassed in his 4,000 mile journey. Still, he was only a man. He was weak. So he cooked and ate his first hot meal in 36 hours. Then with a full stomach, he propped his head on his bedroll and lay soaking up the beauty of his surroundings.

The tide would not change until 7:15pm, a late hour for a novice to put into the river. So James pitched his tent and got a good night's sleep.

Day 5, Tuesday, May 18

At sunrise James cooked and ate breakfast. Then came time to do dishes; UB washed and James rinsed. Finally, James made some adjustments while loading his canoe to distribute weight more evenly based on his experience with waves encountered the day before. Then upon the changing of the tide (8:00am), man and dog shoved off.

Thanks to Don and Wade, James understood the morning of May 18th marked a time in which the tide flowed extra strong. It would be a time for caution, and, a time to take advantage of the powerful incoming tide. Whereas James had come only twenty miles over the previous three days, he hoped to make eleven miles that afternoon and thus reach the fishing village of Skamokowa. Plus the shoreline to Skamokowa would be a straight shot east which meant James looked forward to a day spent near land.

From Harrington Point, James paddled east along a shoreline which although rugged was land nonetheless; very comforting, and beautiful, directly beneath forested slopes that rose sharply to an elevation of 350 feet.

James hadn't gone far when he spotted a flood fence ahead and because James would encounter many such fences, this was a place to describe what a flood fence entailed. A flood fence is a giant picket fence, made of telephone poles, anchored in the river bottom with poles protruding above water level approximately six feet and spaced approximately 18 inches apart. A flood fence often begins at the shore and extends directly into the river. In length a flood fence could measure from one-eighth mile to one-half mile long. A flood fence works in principle like a snow fence but instead of preventing snow from drifting onto a road, a flood fence prevents silt from drifting into a shipping lane. Therefore to make a long story short, a very big fence stood ahead and our novice needed to get around it.

Don in particular had taken pains to explain the perils of a flood fence for James. A flood fence was a very deadly thing. To help understand why, let us imagine the force of a mighty river passing through a half-mile long picket of phone poles spaced too close together for a man to pass between. If a man didn't see a fence in time, or if he misjudged and came to close to a fence, the tide could easily pull him to the fence even as he fought to escape it. And once against the fence, there would be no chance for escape. His boat would be rolled over by the motion of water passing beneath on its way between the poles. He would be spilled out. He would find himself pressed against the fence by the full force of the river. He might be crushed even before he could drown. And that wasn't all, a hidden peril lay off the end of the fence. Don had called it "strange water," but whatever its name, there existed some kind of fluid dynamic which could draw a man back to the fence if he got too close while trying to go around its end. In other words, a man who cut it close around the end of a fence might discover his folly too late and be swallowed up, never to be seen again.

To position himself to clear the fence, James paddled 1/4 mile away from shore. In doing so, he entered the shipping lane. James had seen the shipping lane on his map, marked by a pair of neatly dotted lines running parallel to one another. Of course he'd been warned to watch out for ocean freighters but so far he hadn't seen any because until then the shipping lane had been on the other side of the river. Only there had the shipping lane crossed the river by angling between two elongated dredge islands to emerge directly behind James.

With his entire focus on the flood fence ahead, James stabbed and dug with his paddle to keep his craft true in the shipping lane where a confusion of current, tide, and wind whipped the river into something ugly. Ugly, as in a great swath of ever-shifting rapids and eddies. Thus with his hands full, James did not think to look behind him. He did not see the ocean freighter come out from between the dredge islands like a train from a tunnel!

> "I was in position to clear the end of the fence and, although intense, all was going well when a strange droning sound came over my shoulder, and turning to look, I cried out for God like a terror-stricken child."

Big as can be imagined, the ocean freighter's black bow turned up the river like a great iron plow, roaring as it came straight on.

James was good as dead. If he paddled for shore, he would be caught in the fence. If he raced to escape round the end of the fence, the ship would overtake him. And in that place, where even the fences were on a giant scale, he probably wouldn't make so much as a blip on a radar screen.

"Shock and despair, impossible to describe, except to say that, if only I'd had the luxury, I would have burst into tears."

Out of time, the Kansan made a dreadful decision. He must charge directly into the path of the oncoming ship. He must cross its path to get to the other side of it, to escape to the open waters of the river beyond. It was a horrible thing to have to do, but it was his only chance.

James cried out at the top of his lungs, "Please God, help me!" And stabbing his paddle into the river, he brought his canoe about with every ounce of his being.

"Please God, help me!" James cried out in terror, putting all he had into another paddle stroke, pushing forward to begin his charge.

"Please God, help me!" digging with his paddle, digging to save his life. Every stroke was to save his life. All the strength in his heart and soul, James poured it out. Digging with his paddle. Digging with arms and shoulders, back and chest. Glancing up with his eyes. Seeing the giant. Charging into its path. Charging in a fury. Shouting for the Almighty. Shouting for His help with every desperate stroke.

As his brain transferred all strength to his upper body, James's legs began to shake uncontrollably.

"Lord God, give me strength!" James cried, reaching the end of his own, feeling himself slipping, glancing up at the behemoth, shoveling with his paddle, digging for all his worth, digging as if to expend his life on each and every paddle stroke. James was in fact getting clear of the ship. He saw it was so. It looked as if he might make it. It appeared he was going to make it. Indeed, he had made it. Never had a man used himself up so rapidly. And still James knew that a whale of a boat would make a whale of a wake, so he kept on brutally, digging, pushing his exhausted body to put as much distance between himself and the ship as possible.

James soon reached a small island where, stopping just 50 yards off shore, he laid his paddle across the gunwales and rested his spent body upon it. Then with labored breaths, he lifted his eyes to heaven, "Oh Lord, thank You!"

Not a minute had passed when came a loud crashing noise and, looking in the direction of the noise, James saw the ship's wake roaring down the island's beach. A black wall it was, boiling with sand and debris, taller than any man, coming with such might as to tear James limb from limb. The sight of it was too much for James to bear. He cried out for God, cried out in disbelief, cried out in a hurt tone that wished to understand why he had been delivered only to be tossed back into the jaws of destruction.

Seeking escape, James stabbed his paddle into the river and took a leftward angle away from the oncoming wake. He raced to reach that part of the beach still ahead of the wake. He dug like an exhausted madman. He dug even though it was hopeless. Pure instinct drove him toward the island beach: *Get to land! Jump from the boat! Let the wake have the boat. Get to land! Save myself (and UB) from destruction!*

"Master!" cried James's brain, "We won't make it! Come about! Come about!"

Coming about without a second to spare, James brought his craft in line with the wake which, as fortune would have it, did not break and expend its energy. The wake didn't break because James hadn't quite made it into the shallows along the island. Therefore, and in contrast with what happened (with the ship) when James really had needed to do what he had: James had seen the wake rolling straight down the beach and, because he hadn't understood what he was seeing, he had gone into a panic like a rabbit who runs out in front of a car. Fortunately in James's case, the car passed before the rabbit could get himself under its wheels. Therefore the wake did not roll over James like a wall of destruction but rather, having caught him by the stern, it lifted him up high, then set him down before a succession of secondary wakes took him up and down like a carnival ride. James didn't count the wakes. They just kept coming, awesome big wakes, one after another. Up and down James went with all that power passing underneath.

When it was over, all the flatlander wanted was to stand on dry ground. He didn't land on the little island however, not after seeing how the wake had rolled down its beach. Instead he paddled around its eastern tip and landed on a small desert isle called Miller Island. At the same time that James landed his canoe, two men landed a motorboat but James did not speak to them because they were well beyond earshot. They had come to the island from another direction and immediately set out walking into its sandy interior. James guessed them to be marine biologists doing research on birds who nested on the island.

Like a minnow who escapes a largemouth bass, James wouldn't be going back to the shipping lane. In fact James had his map out, studying a broken network of shoreline across the river locally known as "the islands." The islands made up a flood plain three miles wide and extending 20 miles east along the southern border of the estuary. The islands were divided by channels, marshes, and sloughs. And because big ships couldn't go in there, it seemed a perfect place for a canoe except that Dan had warned of it. Dan had said that all those channels and sloughs running this way and that made it difficult for a man to keep his bearings. Presently, James thought that getting lost in a calm little slough didn't sound all that bad. First however there was the river to cross. So James ate a food bar, called UB back to the boat, and shoved off.

The battle between knight and dragon had only begun; the knight who sought an ancient path to a new frontier, and the dragon who guarded it. Neither was showing any love for the other. Straight away the wind began to rise and with it arose the waves. Then as waves began to white cap, James fought to keep from being tossed over (ever aware that if he spilt, he would be in frigid water). He had no choice but to go with white-capped waves running hard west to east even as he fought to angle his way south.

Next the waves began to roll as if upon a beach, but there was no land. It made for a strange sight, long white lines rolling on a dark plain of water. Before James could understand what he saw, he ran aground. James could hardly believe it, for there he sat in a canoe with miles of water all around, and he'd run aground. In fact, he'd gotten snagged on Snag Island. Nor had he a choice in the matter. The wind had blown him there.

At once the breakers turned his craft sideways and would have rolled him over except that his canoe had such a shallow draft, the waves had expended most of their energy by the time he ran aground. But the breakers were not completely spent, and as the first

one almost rolled him over, James shouted like a novice, "Hey!"
Then, when the second breaker soaked him, he shouted that much louder, "Hey!"
Perhaps the dragon was only having a little fun with the knight, kicking sand and water in his face.
The novice leapt from his craft which in turn made his craft more buoyant, so it floated in the ankle-deep water. He then unfolded his secret weapon and, without need of wheels or harness, pulled away from the bothersome breakers.

"If ever a place deserved to be called a nether realm, it was on that ankle-deep plain of water beneath a perfect mix of sun and clouds. For there the great wide-open took on a beautiful new dimension, and I couldn't help laughing while using my walking machine in the middle of a river. UB meanwhile, who'd been forced to hunker down for the sake of maintaining a low center of gravity, got to come out of steerage and enjoy the sunshine."

The Kansan hadn't pulled a hundred yards when pausing, he asked himself, *"What if I fall into a patch of quicksand?"*
He'd heard stories of quicksand on the Kansas River, stories of men being swallowed alive, more myth than reality. Then again, James had sunk to his knees in many a sandy shallow on the Kansas River. Presently, the sand beneath his feet felt firm. So he continued while keeping a firm hold on the frame of his machine, the idea being that he could pull himself out of trouble should the need arise.

After pulling for a half mile, James reached deep water. He then got back to business as did the waves which had only gotten larger. In fact James didn't know it but the fishermen had gotten off the river due to rising wind and waves (and their boats were much larger than his, not to mention having motors). So the canoeist had his hands full while, wave by wave, he drew nearer to the shelter of the islands.

Specifically, James hoped to gain a slough between Marsh Island and Brush Island. A mere half mile remained but it seemed a far greater distance for James who, having entered into a realm beyond the limits of his ability, fought on the edge of disaster from one foaming white crest to the next. Then as fortune would have it, he caught sight of several fishermen who had retreated to a sheltered shoreline and, he knew by their concerned postures, they would come out if he went into the river. They were many hundreds of yards away and would take a shellacking if they left the protection of shore and still, James believed they would come to his aid if need be. And that was a good thing to know because as James drew within one-hundred yards of safety, the dragon came on like a man who tries to stomp a cockroach before it can escape into a hole. It was a furious few final moments that saw the battered knight giving it back as best he could until at last, he made the opening and escaped into the network of islands.

The wind abated, the water calmed, and James found himself on a peaceful flood plain carpeted in green vegetation and thick with marsh birds. He first navigated the slough between Marsh Island and Brush Island, then the channel between Long Island and Horseshoe Island. Then paddling with steady intent, the canoeist entered the channel between Aldrich Point and Tronson Island.

So it was that James made his first crossing of the Columbia River in which he paddled eight miles, navigating on a diagonal from Harrington Point to Aldrich Point. And for the record it was six miles as the crow flew but James wasn't a crow and he wasn't a daredevil either. He was a man on a mission.

> "Although I did not know what I looked for, God had put the weight of what I looked for in my heart, and by such means, made me feel the gravity of it".

If James had to guess, he would have guessed himself to be in the world's largest marshland. Many of its channels were wide as rivers, big peaceful rivers. There were no roads or bridges or boats but only wide open solitude and, feeling a sense of infinity, James smiled up to Heaven while cloud puffs passed across the blue. James then continued for another 1½ miles without seeing a soul until he came upon a man cleaning a large fish at the end of a small wooden dock. Other than the man on the dock, James saw no other sign of civilization except for a cement boat ramp surrounded by gentle marsh grasses.

The man on the dock remained so focused on cleaning the fish, he didn't notice as the canoeist glided by in the swift tidal current.

James brought his craft around in a rightward sweep to land in the reeds alongside the ramp. Then stepping into the reeds, James said, "Good day to you Sir."

The man jolted, "You scared the heck out of me!" Then smiling in bewilderment, "Where'd you come from?"

"Sir, I come from Kansas. My name is James, and I'm attempting the Lewis and Clark route. I'm going west to east. I put in at the mouth of the river on May 14, and I hope to make Saint Louis in two years. Today I've come from across the river, from Harrington Point."

"*You've been out there?*" the man asked in disbelief, and not waiting for a reply, he added, "That's no place for a canoe! I just came in from there and I have a good-sized fishing boat and I got tossed around pretty good!"

James smiled like a man grateful to be alive, "Sir, it's just good to be out of the water."

In astonishment the man gazed on the Kansan who yet stood shin deep in the reeds. Then out of the blue, the man asked, "Would you like my wife to fix you a tuna sandwich?"

"Sir," James sincerely replied, "I don't know of anything I'd like better."

Having secured his boat, James placed UB on dry land and then went up on the dock. The man, who was very courteous, asked James's forgiveness, saying that he should first finish with the fish so it wouldn't spoil. James assured the man that he ought to continue. James had never seen a sturgeon before although he figured the man was cleaning one. Therefore he asked, "That's a sturgeon, isn't it?"

"Yes."

"How much does it weigh?"

"Sixty pounds," the fisherman replied. Then having finished cleaning the fish, Art rinsed his hands in a bucket whereupon the two men shook hands.

One hundred yards from the dock, Art's wife and daughter were busy preparing lunch in the shade of a tarp that had been strung to shelter their work table. The family of three had come from Portland to camp at the remote river access which, according to James's map, had no name.

Art introduced his family, "James, this is my wife Sherry and our daughter Monica."

James couldn't help being touched at heart, for there they were, the only souls in that place, willing to trust and share what they had with a stranger. Even so, James remained formal, not standoffish formal but outgoing, buck-upright, straight-laced, and friendly.

The sandwiches were made and the four went to the dock to sit and sup together. James complimented Sherry on her sandwiches which were delicious. Monica, who wasn't yet a woman but on the threshold and holding the promise of great beauty, went running back to camp only to return with a treat for UB. UB accepted the treat happily but when Monica tried to coddle him, UB made a loud bark at her. UB never bit or bared his teeth but he could bark as though his mouth were a cannon. Whenever he did, his entire body convulsed and his front paws came off the ground. James apologized to Monica, who was a sweet girl. He then warned UB for his bad behavior although he did so mildly in the knowledge that UB had had a rough day.

Having told of his experience earlier that morning with the ship and its wakes, James added that, surprising as it may sound, he'd heard that a tugboat traveling at speed could throw off a tremendous wake, much like that of a big ship, albeit a result of proximity and not size of vessel. Art confirmed it to be true and added that James should be careful. The conversation changed to more pleasant topics and James was invited to camp there for the night. James declined even as he thanked Art, Sherry, and Monica for their hospitality. He then took his leave, intent on making hay while the sun shined, or more accurately put, before the changing of the tide.

With two hours of favorable tide remaining, James had hardly been back on the water fifteen minutes when the marshland began to stir, and turning to look over his shoulder, he saw that the whole of the western horizon had turned dark and ominous.

Perhaps it was the dragon. Perhaps he had taken wing. Perhaps in his own language, he was saying, "I hope you enjoyed that sandwich because you're going to need it."

The knight paddled hard and kept watch over his shoulder. He needed a place to take out before the storm hit but the marshland had come up against the coastal mountains, so the shoreline had turned rugged. Further out from shore, the waters of the flood plain, so peaceful and inviting only a short time before had turned into a windswept swath of whitecaps. So the novice was nearing a dilemma, getting closer by the minute when he spotted what looked like a giant wooden barn overhanging the water on stilts.

Bleached and battered by rain and shine, its windows broken out, the great gray barn stood alone in the shadow of the storm like a lonely ghost who haunts a forgotten backwater. The barn was in fact an ancient cannery that had been condemned. Therefore James passed it by, having read the government postings that warned people away.

No sooner had James passed the cannery when he saw a tiny cluster of homes huddled between river and mountains. A remnant of the old cannery town, incredible as it seemed, still clung to life. Clung to life, like the haunt of some rough characters if James had to guess, looking at a ramshackle row of backyard docks, rising and falling, clanging and banging in the wind shadow of the cannery ruin. "Keep Out," read one posting. "No Trespassing," read the next.

James hesitated until the last moment, then came about and charged for the last dock because it was either that or the storm would carry him past like a leaf on the water.

Having tied off alongside a floating plank way, James went up a narrow walk that ended at the back door of a small one story house. UB meanwhile struggled to get from boat to dock even as the rough water denied him. Seeing as much, James returned to the boat—,

"Stay!" he hushed, "Or sure as heck, some big dog will come running out here and kill you!"

UB did as his master ordered.

Deciding against knocking on the back door, James chose instead to gain the front door by way of passing through the sideyard. The old house wanted not for character and still it cannot be described because nothing was recorded due to the fact that James operated in a state of high awareness and therefore remembered little of trifling details.

On the front porch, James knocked and waited but no one answered the door. He knocked again and still no one came. He then turned and walked into the street where to his immediate left, the road disappeared in dense forest. Directly across the road, a mountain brook tumbled down a steep slope but due to jungle-like foliage, James could only hear the water. There wasn't a soul to be seen and in fact the place seemed hauntingly deserted. Then carried on the wind came what sounded like a lawn mower, faint though it be.

According to his map, James had found the tiny community of Clifton, remotely located at the end of an unspecified road. James followed the road until having walked a block to the other end of town, he saw a man on a riding lawnmower.

"Sir!" James called.

The man shut off the mower and dismounted.

James cut to the chase, "Sir, I've docked my canoe down there behind the yellow house. I didn't want to trespass, but the water was rough and (James gestured to the storm front), back home in Kansas, when the sky gets to looking like that, it usually means there's going to be trouble. So I went to the yellow house to ask if I might have permission to access to the road, only, I don't think anyone's home."

"No," said the man, looking in the direction of the yellow house, "he's not home." The man then fell silent.

"Sir," James asked, "would it be alright for me to access the road, to get off the river?"

In order that the man might see for himself, both men went to the yellow house where, looking from street to river, they saw UB in the canoe, anxiously staring back at them while bobbing up and down in rough water. The man broke into a smile and said it would be okay. James thanked the man and immediately went to work carrying loads of gear from canoe to roadside. He brought his canoe up last, carrying it atop his shoulders. James then brought out his tool box and went to work assembling his walking machine. Meanwhile the man, who had gone back to attend his own business, returned with a curious look, and seeing him coming, James stood up and offered his hand, "My name's James."

"Keith," said the man, shaking hands.

While assembling his walking machine, James explained it for Keith. In turn, Keith told James the history of Clifton which had been a boomtown back in the days of the cannery. With the cannery had come the railroad, the river ferry, and a good many homes although most were long gone. James didn't ask what had gone wrong, for so disheartening had his own path become, he could only nod to the channel below where waves had risen to such an extent, as to make a frightful sight—,

"I thought it wouldn't be so rough here in the shelter of the islands," said James, unable to hide his disappointment.

"That's pretty much the standard for this time of day," Keith replied.

The Kansan could only shake his head in dismay.

"It's really no place for a canoe," Keith added, sounding sane and certain, although with a hint of mercy, as if to let James off the hook, so he wouldn't have to feel ashamed for throwing in the towel.

Turning from river to road, James brought out his map and asked Keith where the nearest camping area could be found going east by land. Keith pointed to a small campground but like the saying goes, "From the Fire to the Frying Pan," there was a problem—,

"Can you pull your rig over those hills?" Keith asked, looking into the coastal mountains with concern.

"I've been wanting to find out," James replied with an honestly painful grin.

Exchanging words of thanks and well wishes, the two men shook hands, after which Keith departed.

"A storm was upon me. It was late in the day. I was hungry and worn out. A small mountain range stood before me. I had no chance of pulling ten miles to the campground before nightfall. But I figured I'd be okay, so long as I could find a place to camp along the way. That is, if I could find something other than no trespassing signs. First I needed to find water. The estuary was brine and my water filter didn't work on brine. Water tumbled down a slope just there but because I wasn't familiar with the area, I feared it might be somebody's dishwater. I decided to wait until up in the mountains where I hoped to find a brook beside which to camp."

Before getting started, James balanced his rig by making adjustments in the distribution of his gear. He then harnessed into his machine but hadn't taken a step when a man in a pickup truck came alongside. The man looked out his window with amazement. James smiled back, fast coming to understand that just about everyone liked his walking machine.

"What is that?" the man asked in a strong friendly tone.

"It's my walking machine," James proudly replied. He then told his name, where he was from, and what he was about.

"How much weight are you pulling?" asked the man.

"A little better than 300 pounds," James answered.

"And you're going to pull that over those hills?"

"I don't see as I have a choice," James replied.

"Ah heck James, you don't need to do that! You can camp right over there by my place. There's a nice spot, right beside the river. Come on down to the house. I've got to drive ahead and get these groceries to my wife, but you come on down. I'm right at the end of the road. You can't miss it, about two-hundred yards is all. I'll show you. There's a good place to camp. It's beside an old ferry landing. You can put into the river in the morning. The water will be calm then. James, you don't want to pull those hills. I know, those are steep!"

James felt right glad to be talked out of it. Bob drove ahead while James pulled his rig through some trees at the road's end before entering a small clearing where he once again saw Bob. James never asked and therefore Bob's profession cannot be known but, although not a large man, Bob had the hearty nature and duds of a logger just come home from work.

"I'll show you the campsite," said Bob, walking down his driveway. The two men then proceeded another hundred yards or more on a small gravel lane until they reached an abandoned ferry landing.

"Will that work for you, James?"

"It sure will," James replied, greatly relieved to have a place to rest. "Thank you, Bob. Thank you for your hospitality."

"Ah heck James, it ain't nothin'." Then nodding toward home, Bob said, "I have to go. I'm taking my wife to dinner in town. Are you all set here, James? Do you need any food or water?"

"I could use some water," James replied, "If you have an outdoor spigot where I could get a gallon, I'd greatly appreciate it."

"That'll be fine James," and Bob told James where to find the spigot. Then with words of thanks and well wishes, the two men shook hands and Bob departed.

James had previously seen the ferry landing from the water where it had appeared as a dilapidated wooden skeleton with government postings warning people away. Seeing it from land was different however. It still had postings out at the end of its rock jetty where the wood pier began, but the jetty itself stood solid as could be. Atop the jetty, a tiny lane provided an excellent view of Clifton Channel. James chose to camp in the natural windbreak of a blackberry thicket located beside the entrance to the rock jetty. And although the wind yet blew, it appeared the storm would blow over. Therefore James took his gallon jug and went to get water before pitching his tent.

While walking to Bob's house, James met Bob who walked in the opposite direction with a gallon of water in hand—,

"Here's some water for you James," and Bob offered the gallon jug.

James refused it, seeing it to be store-bought and therefore expensive. "Bob, I don't mind drinking tap water."

"My house is on well water James, it might make you sick."

"I can run it through my filter," said James.

"If you want some cooking water, that's fine. But take this gallon of drinking water, will ya?"

"I feel bad about taking your good water."

"Ah heck, it ain't nothin'. Here, we have plenty of it."

James took the water and thanked Bob. The two men then went to the house so James could get some cooking water from the wellhead. While there, Bob introduced James to his lovely wife, after which the couple departed for a nearby town.

Due in no small part to exhaustion, names would sometimes slip from James's grasp, particularly at the end of the day. The dragon was to blame. But the dragon wasn't all bad. For although only a brut of wind and water, he had a role to play in God's plan, being that of honing our knight errant like a blade while simultaneously bringing him into near helpless states of exhaustion and placing him at the mercy of strangers.

Deeply grateful for the hospitality he'd been shown, James made camp and got a good night's sleep.

Day 6, Wednesday, May 19

James had just finished eating breakfast when along came a man holding a miniature antenna as though he were looking to find a TV signal.

"Howdy," said James.

"Hello," replied the man.

The two men shook hands and exchanged names. Jeff was a state biologist looking for tagged fish with his portable antenna. He was young, outgoing, and generous with his knowledge of the river. James was happy to explain his walking machine which sat parked beside his tent. So the two men had a pleasant conversation before parting with well wishes. James didn't know it but he would see Jeff again.

UB washed and James rinsed dishes. James packed his ground pad, sleeping bag, tent, cooking gear, and other items before loading them into his walking machine. He then pulled the lane that ran atop the rock pier to where the wooden pier began, a distance of approximately fifty yards. James then unloaded all his gear and got out his tool box. He disassembled his walking machine. Next he carried loads of gear down a steep riprap bank overgrown with weeds. He brought his canoe down last, balancing the one-hundred-pound craft atop his shoulders while carefully searching with boots in weeds to get a firm footing from one piece of riprap to the next. Then came the business of loading a canoe in swift tidal current along a broken shoreline. James would become conditioned to his environment but as things stood, he hadn't yet put his paddle in the water and he felt plumb worn out.

Because James had chosen the fishing village of Cathlamet as his objective, he would have to cross the river again. Cathlamet lay only five miles away however and therefore James anticipated an easier trip than the fifteen miles he traveled on the previous day. Plus it brightened James's outlook to think that a big juicy steak waited only five miles upriver.

Although not recorded in James's journal, the sky appeared gray and overcast, no storm threatened, and the temperature was mild. James crossed Clifton Channel straight away and because he crossed on a diagonal, he paddled one mile through waves which, while not large, were big enough to make him feel thankful for reaching Tenasillahe Island.

Paddling parallel to the island shore, the canoeist reached the east end of the island where he entered a calm and sandy little slough which reminded him of the Kansas River. James liked the little slough and, he wished the entire journey could be so easy. Coming out the far end of the nameless slough, James entered the channel that contained the shipping lane. Needless to say, James stopped to look and listen carefully in both directions for big ships. And sure enough, a grain barge came down river.

Understanding he mustn't allow the wakes to catch him in the shallows, James moved into deeper water even as he stayed far away from the barge itself. Then while waiting for the wakes to come, the canoeist waved at the barge, although from hundreds of yards he couldn't know if anyone saw him. James then paddled to gain momentum and control before meeting the initial wake bow first. Up and over the wake James went, after which followed a succession of secondary wakes like moguls on a dirt bike track. James went over the wakes without event, then paddled like the dickens to cross a mile of open water before another ship came.

Reaching land was sweet relief. The land he reached was called Hunting Island but it was in fact the north shore of the river although technically an island because of a small slough which divided it from the mainland. James turned east and paddled alongside the island shore which was a cut-bank, meaning the river had cut into it, eroding it to expose a long continuous slice of rich dark earth like a cake that had been cut, which in this case contained many roots due to a dense forest of deciduous trees. The trees spread their canopy over the calm reflective water, and traveling under their eve, James saw how a carpet of fallen trees lay shimming below with barren branches reaching up through the flux. So it was with trees above and trees below that the canoeist passed where few boats could go. And as would often be the case, he marveled as he went. He passed beneath an American Bald Eagle which kept watch from its perch not twenty feet above. Both man and bird turned their heads and shoulders slowly to keep eye contact with the other until at last, they were looking back at one another. Further on, James saw a fisherman in a small rowboat. The two men said hello in passing. The canoeist then continued along a gradual leftward bend until that which he sought came into view. Less than a mile ahead, on a hill above the river, the hamlet of Cathlamet sat as though made for a postcard.

"Boy howdy UB," James said with delight, "it's going to be steak tonight!" Then spurring a bit, he continued until safe within the stone walled port.

At the Port of Cathlamet, James worked to transform his water craft to land rig. His amphibious contraption stirred up curiosity as always and by such means James met Chuck, a sturdy-made trucker on a fishing trip with a few buddies. Chuck had his camper parked atop the main wall of the port where a wide strip of grass served as a camping area overlooking the river. James told Chuck of his intent to test his walking machine on the hill that went up to town, and also, James was concerned for his gear, as in not wanting to leave it just anywhere.

"James," said Chuck, "that hill's a bit steep, so if need be, you're welcome to park your rig next to my camper."

"Thanks Chuck," James replied. "If I can't get up the hill, I'll do that." James then departed to give the hill a try.

> "Geometrically, the angle of the hill made it easy for me to maintain balance between myself and my machine while going up the grade. And because the harness held me semi-suspended within the frame, I could really lean into it. The machine did nothing to get the load up the hill but rather, it made the most of my strength, so that I could get the load up the hill."

The walking machine passed its test with flying colors. So James was happy (and winded), having reached the top of the hill. Directly before him stood the town's bed and breakfast, a splendid old house with flower lined steps rising to a large front porch overlooking the main street of the town. Up the steps went the Kansan with visions of a hot shower and clean linen. Then having rung the buzzer, he let himself in where he met Audy, the lady who owned the place.

"Howdy Ma'am, my name is James and I come from—"

"I need you to get your dog out of here!" Audy interrupted, at once urgent yet courteous. "My husband is acutely allergic to dogs!"

"Oh gosh, Ma'am, I'm terribly sorry," said James. "Come UB. Come boy!"

James led UB outside and clipped his leash to the walking machine. He then returned to the bed and breakfast, "I'm very sorry about that, Ma'am."

James explained his business to Audy who thoughtfully suggested they ask her next door neighbor Rudy if James could park his rig behind his house for the night (and UB could sleep inside it). So they went to ask, and Rudy was happy to help. James then pulled his rig between the two houses and parked (and locked) it at the back of Rudy's driveway. James next carried his gear up to his room which took many trips. By then evening had fallen, and because James could not afford to miss dinner, he skipped showering and shaving so that he might have dinner before the café down the street closed.

Outside the café, James tied UB to a post before going inside.

"Ma'am," James said to the waitress, "I know I smell bad and I apologize for it. I've been on the river for a few days. I would have cleaned up first but, food comes first." Then as James followed the good-humored waitress into a busy dining room, he added, "You may want to seat me accordingly."

Chuck happened to be dining there with friends and, on seeing James, he happily asked, "James, how the heck are you?"

Having forgotten Chuck's name, James should have said, "Sir, I apologize, I have forgotten your name. Would you please give it to me again so that I may remember it?"

"It doesn't reflect well on a man's character to forget another man's name, but should he then try to cover up his embarrassment by trying to be clever or cute about it, he only adds insult to his own injury. Unfortunately, that is exactly what I did."

James had no more than sat at his table when for whatever reason, UB started howling so loudly, James felt obliged to get up and formally apologize to a group of ladies seated beside the window. James then returned to his table where, with UB still howling, he ordered a king-sized platter of seafood instead of steak. He then cleaned his plate except for two deep fried things which were slimy and green on the inside. Guessing them to be clams, James slipped them in his pocket for UB.

After dinner, James took UB for a walk before bedding him down inside the walking machine where he petted him to sleep. James then snapped the tarp shut and went to his room where a hot shower never felt better.

James sunk into bed and slept like a rock until midnight when UB began howling with such determination, it had to be heard to be believed.

James got his flashlight, went downstairs, let himself out the front door, ran down the sidewalk, raced up Rudy's driveway, unsnapped the tarp and said, "Shush!!!"

UB cringed even while wagging his tail.

James delivered the riot act in hushed tones, "You've gotten to ride and enjoy scenery while I've pushed and pulled this load. Now darn it, it's your turn to 'toe the line!' "

UB seemed to understand if not the situation at least the strain in his master's voice and what it could mean if he failed to obey.

Hoping that UB would obey, James returned to bed where he fell fast asleep. Then, at 1:00am, he woke to hear UB howling like no tomorrow.

James did what he must. First, he lifted UB out of the machine, "You darn dog!" Second, James spread out his bedroll. Third, he took UB's bed from the machine and laid it beside his own. And finally, James laid himself down to sleep on Rudy's driveway.

UB did a victory dance around his master.

"Lie down you darn dog!"

Flat on his back, James gazed up though trees to Heaven above, *"Lord,"* he thought in frustration, *"Here I am paying seventy bucks to sleep on some man's driveway."*

No more had the Kansan finished his thought when, carried on the silence of night, there came the sound of a man suffering a horrible coughing attack (which was not Audy's husband who suffered allergic reactions to dogs). On hearing the coughing attack, James realized his own good fortune.

> "I was healthy and getting healthier with every step I took. My soul had been set free and I had been put on a path that I could not have dreamed of, all because I had put my life in God's hands."

Feeling deeply grateful, James began to laugh at his present situation. Then reaching over to stroke UB, he said, "It's okay boy, I don't think that bed and breakfasts were meant to be a part of this trip."

Shortly thereafter, James jolted awake in the realization that he lay on a stranger's driveway after all. So he retrieved his slow moving vehicle sign and propped it at his feet. Thus satisfied, James slept like a rock.

Day 7, Thursday, May 20

At approximately 7:00am, James awoke to find himself lying directly before a full-sized pickup truck that hadn't been there when he'd gone to sleep. As a first order of business, James knocked at Rudy's door to express his gratitude, apologize for UB's howls, and explain why he'd slept on the man's driveway. From the start the two men got along well. Rudy said the truck belonged to his girlfriend who presently fixed bacon and eggs inside. Rudy then invited James in for breakfast but no more had James begun in when Audy showed up in motherly fashion—,

"There you are!" said Audy. "I've been looking all over for you. Breakfast is ready. Hurry! The other guests are waiting."

"Yes Ma'am."

"Please, call me Audy."

"Yes Ma'am. I mean, Audy."

James did as Audy ordered. He brushed his teeth and went to the dining room where he met Doug and Terry, a married couple from Oregon.

"Did my dog wake you?" James worriedly inquired.

"No," replied both Doug and Terry, glancing at one another to confirm that neither had been awakened.

"I take it he was barking?" asked Doug.

"Howling," James replied, and he went on to tell of the night before.

"If I may ask," said Doug, "what prompts a man to do something like this [the Lewis and Clark trail]?"

James told of Sunday at Frank's dinner table and how he'd been in a good position to give it a try. In doing so, James told the mechanics of how but not the reason why. He didn't know why, he only knew that God knew why.

The conversation continued and, while not a prerequisite for good human chemistry, it didn't hurt that all three were Christian. Closeness soon formed and they might have spoken all day had checkout time not come. But checkout time did come and James vacated his room with just five minutes to spare.

On his way to port, James was happy to discover his walking machine worked as well going downhill as uphill. At port, James pitched his tent on a strip of green grass atop the wall of the port with a fine view of the river. He then seated himself at a picnic table where, under a heavy blanket of clouds, he spent the afternoon working on his journal. Then it got chilly, so he moved into his tent and continued working.

About dinner time, James heard a car on the lane beside his camp. A voice then called, "James, are you there?"

James went directly from his tent, "I was just thinking about ya'll," he said, smiling at Doug and Terry with delight. "I was feeling a little sad because I only knew your first names, so I had no way of getting in touch with you."

"We wondered if we might treat you to dinner?" Doug asked.

"Thank you," James replied, "I'd like that very much."

Doug, his wife Terry, and James went to town and enjoyed good food and good conversation. James told of his previous uncertainty regarding the date on which Lewis and Clark departed Saint Louis. Therefore he mentioned his stop at the Lewis and Clark Interpretation Center at Cape Disappointment, to which Doug echoed—,

"The Lewis and Clark Reinterpretation Center."

James picked up on Doug's title-modification at once and, the two men shared a knowing smile. Nothing more was said about it perhaps because they were in good spirits and didn't want to spoil their dinner lamenting the "politically correct" culture to which Lewis and Clark had fallen victim.

Doug and Terry returned James to his camp and, like so many men and women he met along the way, James hoped to see them again someday.

Back at camp, James shook hands with Rudy who'd been waiting for him there. Rudy then introduced James to a kayaker who wasted no time making known his extensive experience in the field of river travel. Then, and in no uncertain terms, the kayaker proceeded to tell the canoeist how he could save himself a lot of trouble by giving up his canoe paddle for a kayak paddle. Thus began a battle of wills between canoeist and kayaker until the kayaker gave up and said he respected the canoeist if for no other reason than because he was so stubborn. Rudy and his friend then departed with well wishes.

James next went to say hello to Chuck who camped nearby. James told the story of sleeping in Rudy's driveway and both men got a good laugh out of it. James then returned to his camp where he hit the sack and slept well.

Day 8, Friday, May 21

James understood that if he were to succeed in his errand, he must capture it on the page. It couldn't be put off. It couldn't be done later. Human memory wasn't that good. Therefore James spent the day writing and it was a good day for it, being gray and overcast. At 5:00pm he took a break and called home to speak with family and friends. Afterward, he went to the grocery store with UB. Back at camp, James cooked and ate a steak and salad. After eating, he sat at a picnic table beside the river, writing until darkness fell.

Man and dog slept well.

Day 9, Saturday, May 22

James awoke to find the port socked in by cold wind and rain. He walked to town for a big breakfast. Then on his way back to camp, he stopped to ask the advice of an elderly gentleman who lived in an old motor home parked there at the port—,

"I'd intended to shove off at noon with the changing of the tide," said the Kansan, "but with this wind and rain, I'm not so sure."

"I'd wait till tomorrow!" said the old timer, and seeing his certainty, James took his advice.

Fortunately, James and UB had an excellent tent and therefore remained comfy despite the nasty weather. James made use of his time by working on his journal.

During an afternoon lull, a man named Scott came walking his dog, and, having struck up a conversation, the two men set out with their dogs for the grocer where James needed to buy cheese. Along the way, James and Scott chanced upon a third man named Chris. Thus began a three-way conversation on the main street in which

Scott and Chris appeared to be on different sides of a political fence with regard to whether or not a man ought to shoot a coyote. James had a mind to let the coyotes live so long as they weren't looking to kill chickens, etc.

No sooner had James returned to his camp when Chris showed up and asked him to church in the morning. James thanked Chris, accepted his offer, and agreed that Chris would pick him up at 9:30am Sunday morning. James then returned to work on his journal and caught it up at 5:00pm.

No more had James finished his journal than the weather took a turn for the better and, he met another man who was walking his dog. Ken looked to be a man of the sea with his sturdy frame, white hair, sailors cap, and positive air. Ken lived in a sailboat docked there at port, and having introduced himself, he pointed out his craft which wasn't so different from James's home back in Kansas. UB and Ken's dog went on patrol while their masters sat on a bench atop the wall of the port and had a good conversation.

Next a woman who knew Ken came, and she also took a seat on the bench. Younger than James, single, twice pretty, and petite with a figure of flawless proportion (not to mention locks to prove a brunette could rival Rapunzal), Kathleen was a fisheries biologist by trade who had come for a weekend retreat to the sailboat her father had left her. Tired but relaxed from putting in long hours, Kathleen was easy to speak with. So the three sat talking at length until Kathleen asked James to dinner and, he readily accepted.

James and Kathleen drove to town, got a booth by a window in the café and got along with ease, speaking until well after dark. Afterward, they returned to the port, said good night, and shook hands.

> "What Kathleen felt as she returned to her boat cannot be known but I returned to my tent with a natural measure of reluctance."

James had no more than gotten in his tent and closed his eyes when along came a man playing a guitar and harmonica like some kind of Christian Bob Dylan. James could sleep through almost anything, so it hardly mattered that the man sat down to play on a bench not thirty feet from his tent. However, James felt fairly certain that the evangelist wanted him to come out. So he went out to listen and after the first song, the two men shook hands. Don, who had been out evangelizing all day, told a story of his youth. Apparently, Don and his father and mother and brothers had set out to ferry sixty head of cattle to an island for grazing. They transported the cattle on a motorized barge but engine problems developed halfway to the island and, matters went from bad to worse. Too many cows got to one side of the barge which then tipped, spilling the entire herd into the river. Don and his family also went into the river but by the grace of God were able to climb back onto the barge. Unfortunately, only three head of cattle swam to shore. The rest of the cattle, which were prone to follow one another, swam round and round in a big circle out in the middle of the river until all drown.

James rubbed his tired eyes and looked out into the night. He could almost hear the cattle mooing in the dark.

Don, who was himself something of a holy flood, had told the story so vividly as to make one wonder if, as the cattle went under the waves one by one, the last one realized its mistake, for only then, when it had none left to follow could it finally look around, and being too weak to swim any further, the last thing it saw was the shore.

Don then said a very sincere prayer for James, after which he departed.

James could not sleep. But in all fairness, his sleeplessness was as much a result of repressing sleep as anything. He drifted off at roughly 3:00am.

Day 10, Sunday, May 23

James sat on a picnic bench under gray skies waiting for Chris. Chris and Don where roommates, which was something James had learned from Don just before Don departed on the night before, even though until that point neither was aware that the other knew Chris. Chris came at 9:30am, whereupon James thanked him for his kind offer and told him he would not be going to church with him. James then returned a booklet that Don had given him the night before. The booklet showed pictures of Heaven, of children petting lions and whatnot. It was the kind of thing that skeptics scoffed at but not James.

"I have not seen Heaven but I've seen reflections of Heaven on earth. God paints wonders before me, and in the mist of His paintings, people come from the blue to help me along my way. Beyond this, I have no vision of Heaven. But if I did, it would be one of paddling my canoe beyond the veil of death, where the water goes calm as glass, reflecting blue sky, only to realize the reflection was no longer a reflection, and no sooner would I realize it, then I would land at His feet, there on the shore of His Kingdom."

Presently on earth, James gave Chris a note in which he thanked the people of Chris's church even as he respectfully declined while figuratively saying that a man might go with Jesus across the sky in a X-15 rocket or, in a canoe, and it wasn't James's place to judge which was better but rather to know which fit him better. Thus commending one another to God, James and Chris parted on good terms.

James next walked to town and had breakfast. On his return to camp he got out his map and showed it to Ken who had come along the lane. The map showed the river to be three miles wide, consisting of two large channels on either side of a massive island called Puget Island, which was itself home to many sloughs and marshes.

"See here," said James, pointing to his map, "First I'll cross the north channel, then I'll enter Puget Island via this slough, then I take this slough, then this slough, and finally this slough which comes out [on the other side of the island] in the south channel."

"You can't do that!" exclaimed Ken.

"Why not?" James asked.

"Because," said Ken, pointing to the last slough on the map, "you can't get through there."

"But I have a canoe," said James.

"It doesn't matter," replied Ken, shaking his head, "You can't get through there. Look, all you have to do is follow the north shore of the island to its [east] end, then you can cross to the south channel."

James was apt to listen to Ken because Ken was a white-haired man who looked to have the river in him, not to mention he lived in a boat. All of that changed however when Ken made a sympathetic reference to the kayaker who had tried to get James to change his style.

James looked sideways at Ken.

"Now just hear me out," said Ken, and he went on to pitch the case for the kayak paddle. Ken then said he had a kayak paddle in his boat and welcomed James to try it out. Ken suggested that James paddle around inside the port. James had yet to take his walking machine apart however and therefore couldn't test the paddle at that time. Instead, he asked Ken to go and get the paddle so he might look at it, which Ken did. The paddle was silver and black and came apart for storage. Deciding it worth a try, James got out his wallet and bought the paddle for thirty-five dollars. It was a mistake but only because the paddle did not suit James. As for Ken, he had been genuine in his belief that the paddle could help James. Therefore, Ken cannot be faulted.

Ken pocketed the cash and said, "I met a man who did what you're doing. It was some years back. He started in St Louis so I met him when he was about to finish. Man you should have seen this guy, he was tough, tough as steel!"

"It'll make me or break me," said James.

"Ah, you'll make it," Ken assured.

The Kansan sat gazing at his new paddle while the questions in his mind went ahead to vanish into the unknown. He didn't see Kathleen step before him.

"Hi, James."

"Kathleen," said James," standing and removing his hat.

Kathleen told of a spring festival taking place nearby. Then finishing her speech, she asked, "I was wondering if you'd like to come along."

Feeling torn, James earnestly replied, "I'm sorry Kathleen. Truly, I would like to. But the tide will be changing at two, and when it does, I have to go."

To no avail the maiden reminded the Kansan that the river would still be there on the morrow. She then went away and James set about the business of breaking camp.

While James transformed land rig to water craft, the wind began to rise. Perhaps the wind rose on account of the dragon. Perhaps the dragon had sat up to scratch like a beast who feels the stir of a flea.

The knight kept an eye on the river while making ready to shove off. Conditions were deteriorating but James knew he only needed to get across to the big island where he could then continue in a network of sheltered sloughs.

At 2:00pm, James shoved off and, as he paddled out the port gate, a fisherman coming in shouted a warning, "IT'S GETTING ROUGH OUT THERE!"

Seeing a squall coming upriver, and hoping time yet remained to get across, James quickly put his kayak paddle away and got out his trusted canoe paddle. He could just as easily have retreated to the safety of port but, there was always reason to retreat from the Columbia River. In the meantime, St Louis wasn't getting any closer.

Giving thanks for his path, James promised his best and dug with all his might. He charged into the channel. He charged because in that place a mile was no small distance to cover. He charged to keep his command over the ugly water, lest it gain control and overtake him in the confusion. And what confusion there was, the likes of which James had not seen. Forces of wind, current, and tide collided to buckle the river like dough under fist blows. James fought hard to keep his craft upright and true. He maintained his course even while pushed in every direction. He got knocked around but not overtaken. He shrank from no wave but attacked all comers, driving his paddle into each, thrusting to overtake as he must, so as not to be overtaken.

Halfway across, James took comfort in the knowledge that the port watchtower always stood manned and therefore someone probably watched and would send help if necessary. James hadn't informed the men in the tower of his departure, but being as there wasn't another boat on the water, James's chances for being seen were good.

Up the river came the ever-darkening cloud, turning the water before it. James paddled like mad and, without a second to spare, made it across the river and into the opening of a narrow and deep-set slough. The squall then struck, bending and whipping every tree and bush with such force, James could only imagine how ugly it must have been out on the open river.

The squall turned out to be a wind storm and not a rain storm. Rain came but only in spits. The wind came hard but not terribly hard in the sheltered slough, and because it came at his back, James made excellent time.

The protected slough presented a good opportunity to bring out the kayak paddle, which James found to require a certain grace and finesse that he did not possess. Thus stowing the kayak paddle away, James chose to ignore Ken's advice regarding the route he'd seen on the map, the very route that Ken had strongly warned against.

To paddle through Puget Island as a means of reaching the south channel, James first paddled three miles east through Bernie Slough. He then continued east in an unnamed slough for another 1½ miles. The worst of the storm passed as he turned south into a third unnamed slough which led to the vast interior of the island where fields of reeds stood tall as Kansas corn, and woods made of low-grade trees grew thick as weeds. It was a place as green as any land, yet through which no man could pass without a boat. In fact James had arrived at a nether realm between water and earth.

Without pause, the unwitting novice paddled into the natural maze.

His dog began to whine.

"Don't worry, boy," said James, patting UB, "You're old dad knows what he's doing. All we need to do is watch the tidal flow and follow the compass."

Then arriving at a junction, "See the current? That means we turn left here."

And paddling deeper into a network of natural hallways running through reed beds, "See the current? We'll turn right here."

A little further yet, and checking his compass, "See how well this is working UB? We'll turn left here."

Then with only a little confusion, "Gosh, I'm not sure where we went wrong. That's alright, we can backtrack."

And backtracking, "Ah! You see? We missed our turn, that's all."

An hour later and hopelessly lost, James passed though an opening in the reeds, whereupon glancing about in disbelief, he thought, *"How could this be possible? How could I be back at the beginning [of the maze]?"*

Although James felt dismayed to find himself back where he'd begun, on the bright side, he knew where he was. Not only that but his mistake presented an opportunity for him to return to the north channel by way of a marshy cove 100 yards away. Such a thing was possible because the first two sloughs had run parallel to the north shore of the island, so James had never been far from the north channel while he made eastward progress through the island. Only the third slough had run to the interior where it appeared (by the map) to connect to a forth slough which then connected to the south channel on the far side of the island. The only problem was that the map did not indicate a maze. Still, James thought the maze to be a safer route than the north channel because the north channel would lead to an encounter with a series of flood fences off the end of the island, and taking wind and current into account, the flood fences might force him into a place called Cape Horn, and he had been warned about Cape Horn.

To boil things down, James wasn't attempting a complicated route for nothing. Rather, he had weighed the dangers of the different routes and had chosen the one he believed to be safest. If he could make it through the maze and find the forth slough, then he might gain the south channel where the flood fences would not be a problem. He would still have to pass the fences, but off their south ends where he would not risk the perils of Cape Horn. Thus believing he knew where he'd gone wrong, James turned his craft around and paddled back into the maze.

As the crow flew, the maze measured only a quarter-mile wide, which was no small thing for a man in a canoe.

With uncertainty second only to determination, James made it through the maze and, after a total of 1½ hours searching, found the "fabled" forth slough through which no man could pass.

"This is it," James told UB who remained skeptical as they entered a shadowy wood where nothing stirred, save for the shrill cries of unseen creatures, as though to welcome the newcomers into a folktale.

> "No tree distinguished itself in that place, no lily flower blossomed, no bright songbird flew, no refreshing breeze blew. Indeed of it, sunshine scarcely knew."

The canoeist ducked to pass beneath a fallen tree trunk, then another and another while spidery limbs reached out from either shore like countless fingers coming to covet the newcomers. The limbs were dead as dead could be and yet, the deeper James went into the wood, the more they crowded him. The tidal current slowed and then stopped altogether. The scum thickened. The air became heavy with the scent of rot and, rounding a bend, the slough ended in an inescapable tangle.

Perhaps our unfortunate novice had blundered into the lair of an ill-favored spirit who lay in wait for a host. Then again, maybe it was only the feeling of being lost in a grim wood on an island in the middle of a river that made him give over to frustration and bark like a wild beast. Whatever it was, something stronger already burned in James's heart. Thus like a fortress repels a besieger, the evil that gripped him was quickly cast off.

James apologized to God for having shouted a four-letter word repeatedly. Also, James knew he'd found the exact spot where Ken had placed his finger on the map and said, "You can't get through there!"

Backing up, James came about and felt glad to get out of there despite his disappointment. He had no intention of giving up on finding a passage through the island however and therefore, he put his hope on a slough he'd passed in the wood about an eighth-mile back. There he had spoken with a fisherman on an old wooden dock at the end of a path which snaked into the wood on a tongue of land. James had asked the man about the forth slough but the man only said he was strange to those parts. Presently arriving at the fork where the man had been but no longer was, James set out paddling west even though he needed to go south or east. The new slough, which had no name, did contain a tidal flow and therefore held some promise.

As the tidal flow grew, so grew James's hope until having paddled roughly one mile, the muddy slough became a rocky stream with an opening in the forest 100 yards ahead.

"We did it UB," James said as they broke out into a small cove ringed with pine trees.

In the south channel, James paddled due east along the shore of Puget Island for two miles. Then from the east end of the island, he proceeded up the middle of the Columbia River. The storm had passed so conditions weren't bad, especially in the wind shadow of Puget Island. And that was good because James paddled directly between a series of flood fences and the shipping lane. James hadn't put himself in a situation like the one at Harrington Point. Rather, he had put himself in a dangerous place but, as a choice between the north or south end of the fences, the south was the safer of the two. So it was with flood fences on his left and the shipping lane on his right that James paddled in hope of reaching a point one mile ahead where he planned to turn away from the fences and cross the shipping lane in order to gain the safety of a slough which lay between Wallace Island and the south shore of the river.

Arriving at the point at which he hoped to cross the lane, James stopped to look and listen in both directions and sure enough a ship was coming. So he waited until the ship had passed, then paddled toward its wake to gain momentum with which to meet the wake bow first and, by such means, go up and over it in controlled fashion. After the first wake, he paddled through a succession of large secondary wakes, ever aware that he mustn't let them tip him over in the icy water. Then a second ship came along, and a third. All three ships were cargo carriers heading for the ocean and threw off wakes relative to their size. James rode out their wakes in the aforesaid fashion, all the while hoping for an opportunity to cross.

At last, when the lane cleared in both directions, James paddled hard to get across. To James it seemed highly intense, digging for all his worth, paddling his boat just as fast as he could. However, when taken on scale, James was like a box turtle trying to cross a highway and, unfortunately, he had only gotten a third of the way to safety when he spotted a tugboat approaching at a clip.

The canoeist bore down on his paddle to arrest his forward motion but it was too late to keep his distance from the tug. They were in close proximity and therefore, based on tales he'd heard, James could only hope against hope that the tug captain would behave uncharacteristically and throttle back a bit.

Having made eye contact and perhaps reducing his speed a bit, the captain looked away and continued past while James told himself that surely someone aboard the tug would keep watch behind to see how he faired. Then came the tug's wake, which resembled nothing James had seen. It had a multi-angled face like that of a liquid diamond flowing beneath a knifelike crown.

The only advantage the Kansan had was that he had no idea of what was about to hit him. So he dug hard and charged the wake because although only a novice, he understood he must overtake it. Either that or it would overtake him.

"Hang on UB!"

The canoe was pitched up on its stern where for one graceful moment in time, it stood like the vein of a sundial atop the wake. Then as the bow fell, James anticipated going into the secondary wake like a torpedo dropped from a dive bomber. The five-hundred pound load came down with a tremendous wallop and splash. Thanks however to a good and sturdy-made craft, the big canoe recovered just in time to climb the secondary wake which, while large, was not of the dangerous diamond design.

James gave thanks to God, then paddled like the dickens in hope of getting across the shipping lane and into the safety of Wallace Slough.

After paddling east one mile into the ¼-mile-wide Wallace Slough, James landed on a sandy beach in a sheltered lagoon located at the western end of Wallace Island. It was a primitive place, having no road or other development. It lay only seven miles as the crow flew upriver from Cathlamet, but it had been over ten miles as the canoeist knew (excluding the maze). James hustled to make camp and cook dinner. His diet shall be described but not yet. All was done as dusk faded to darkness. James then laid himself down in deep exhaustion but could not surrender the fight. Fortunately, he wasn't long awake.

The River Proper
Chapter III

Day 11, Monday, May 24

After a good long sleep, James sat eating his breakfast when along came some kind of official government boat. The cruiser could come no closer than one hundred yards because the tide had gone out and left a large mud flat where once had been a lagoon. So the cruiser came as close as possible, whereupon a man stepped out on deck and began shouting and waving his arms.

"Hey..." shouted the man on the boat.

James feared himself to be in some trouble. Perhaps he had camped in a bird sanctuary?

"Hey, James!" shouted the man, "Are you alright?"

Recognizing the cruiser from a description given to him some days before, and putting two and two together, James suspected the man to be a fisheries biologist he'd met at Clifton. Therefore he shouted, "Jeff, is that you?"

"Yeah."

James felt relieved, and working his way along a dry stretch of shore, he managed to get within forty yards of the boat.

Jeff continued, "We saw your tent, so we thought we'd stop and see how you were getting along."

"Thanks," James shouted, "I'm good. I'm waiting for the tide to change, then I'll be off again."

The two men continued their conversation for several minutes. Then with words of thanks and well wishes, the research cruiser motored away.

James had slept late in the knowledge that the tide would not change until 3:00pm. He hadn't anticipated a mud flat where there had been a lagoon however, and because the mud was too deep to cross, he had to portage a few hundred yards to gain a firm shoreline.

Upon shoving off, James realized that the incoming tide no longer overcame the outward flow of the river. In other words, the current flowed against James and would remain against him henceforth. It had been expected, but it had occurred sooner than James had anticipated. Thus began James's first experience ever canoeing against current.

The canoeist paddled east through Wallace Slough for three miles, then continued for another three miles along the Oregon shore in waters far removed from the dangers of the shipping lane.

Safe conditions could not last in a realm that changed with every mile, and so it came to pass that the great river funneled into a bottleneck measuring only one half-mile wide by one mile long.

In the bottleneck, James paddled extra hard in hope of getting through before a big ship came. Unfortunately, he was only halfway to safety when along came a supergiant. The massive ship came dieseling for the ocean and, due to the closed in nature of the bottleneck, James could put no safe distance between himself and the ship. Having no other choice, our novice took to the field and prepared for battle so to speak. The supergiant sent forth its wakes—great walls of water charged in ranks—and no sooner had James seen them coming than he came about and paddled like heck in the opposite direction.

Perhaps the dragon, who'd been laying in wait for the knight, let out a roar, "This time I have you!"

Almost anyplace else and James would have been wrecked if not drowned but, almost incredibly, like a rare gem set in a cliffy shoreline, there lie a tiny patch of beach that made for a natural boat ramp.

No sooner had James made the beach than he leapt into action like a man in a fire drill. First he saved UB. Next he ran back and forth, hurling bags of gear to safety. Then time ran out even as his boat wasn't yet unloaded. So James grabbed the pulling frame and, with a yank, threw it up and down around himself, whereupon pulling mightily, he drug his boat away literally an instant before the first wake struck with bone-breaking force.

James watched as a succession of wakes pummeled the shore. Then to his amazement a phenomena occurred. The giant ship had gone and yet, it had displaced so much water in the bottleneck that a reverberation dynamic began in which wakes crashed off shores and then raced back toward opposite shores only to crash into rebounding wakes. In the resulting chaos, the bottleneck became like an arena filled with wakes like phantom bulls made from the invisible forces of nature, charging in every direction, colliding in violent impacts, disintegrating in sprays of water, only to form up again.

Perhaps it was only the dragon, thrashing and shouting, "I'll kill you! So help me, I'll kill you!"

Meanwhile from the safety of shore, the knight laughed because it looked like a giant bathtub.

> "I know it sounds like I was crazy but I was not. I was after something. I knew it only in my heart, knew it like rock solid knew it, knew it was God, knew it was right, never identified it until after I reached St Louis."

Determined to make the most of his six-hour tide window, the canoeist continued east through the bottleneck before entering the safety of Bradbury Slough. In the 3/8-mile-wide slough, James paddled along the south shore of Crims Island for three miles until he reached its eastern tip where he passed behind a flood fence to gain the opposite side of the island. Then paddling west along the island shore for a few hundred yards, James landed his canoe on a stretch of sandy beach.

The Kansan had paddled against current for six hours straight with only a brief pause in the bottleneck. He had made better than ten miles progress. The time was 9:00pm.

The island beach measured thirty feet wide and made for a long gentle strip of sand between water and bluff. It would have been good for camping except it had no sufficient elevation to counter the danger posed by a series of flood fences that adjoined it. In other words, if the river were to rise overnight, anyone camped on the beach might be swept into the flood fences. Therefore James turned his attention to the bluff behind the beach. The bluff consisted of hard-packed sand and measured forty feet high. It stood nearly vertical but due to a peppering of grass clumps that grew on its face, James managed to carry loads of gear up it somewhat like climbing a ladder to a roof. He did so slowly, being at the end of his strength, the end of the day, and because he did not wish to slip and fall.

James brought his canoe up last, and as long as it rested on his shoulders, he could think of nothing but reaching the top so that he might get out from under its weight! But to take his canoe straight up the bluff would have been impossible, so James went on an angled traverse, searching out notch-like tusks of grass on which to secure a foothold. It was painfully slow business going from one foothold to the next, what with each move being a one-legged leg-press under a one-hundred-pound canoe, balanced not on level ground but on the side of a bluff.

"Master," asked James's brain, "why are we carrying the canoe up a bluff?"

"We're going to the top," replied the heart, beating hard.

"Master," implored the brain, "you need only allow me the honor and privilege that is my duty and I am certain to find a solution that will suffice with only half the effort."

"You needn't propose any such solution," the heart replied. "You need only remember your first duty and coordinate the arms and legs."

At the top, James stowed his gear back into his canoe and snapped the tarp down tight. By the light of a crescent moon, he pitched his tent. He didn't cook because nighttime had come and he felt deeply exhausted. So he lay in his tent with eyes closed, eating handfuls of dog food (something he would do only a few times during his journey).

Man and dog slept well.

Day 12, Tuesday, May 25

Emerging from his tent at approx 8:00am, James was awestruck, for there he stood on an island carpeted with wild flowers under a morning sky that shone pure as crystal. Songbirds did sing, and all around, mountain slopes were of the richest green. Sweet were the fragrances that floated on the breeze. Soaring eagles plucked up fish with grace and ease. And as for the river, it seemed a dream, so peaceful did it sparkle in brilliant sunshine. But that wasn't the half of it. For way up high, concealed until that moment from his eye, a nether realm appeared to float like a continent in the sky. It was the volcano, Mount Saint Helens. And while at first it appeared inconceivable for anything so large to be hidden from sight, in truth it was no mystery. The clouds had kept her concealed for days, only to unveil her at the perfect place and time. The Kansan stood in perfect wonder and delight. For not only had the volcano queen come out, she had come out in full regalia. Her pure white train covered the whole of the eastern skyline, her colossal snow crown

glimmered in the sun, and by some mystery, which made her base invisible—she appeared to float.
After breakfast, James worked on his journal.

"I suppose that somewhere along this stretch of river, someone will say this place isn't anything more than an old dredge island. But the way I see it while canoeing after my forefathers, this is paradise on earth. And to prove it, here I sit recording it exactly as it is."

Except for his canoe which remained atop the bluff, James made ten round trips carrying gear to the beach below. And while he went up and down the bluff with many a huff and puff, he couldn't help but notice the carcass of a cow, all dried up in a heap, and looking rather rough. Because a small herd of cattle grazed on the main segment of Crimes Island just to the south, James assumed that the unfortunate cow had crossed from the main island to the smaller island during low tide whereby it climbed up the gentle south slop before crossing to the north side where it fell down the bluff and died of its injuries. At least James assumed as much while trying to figure out how to get his canoe down the bluff. He didn't think himself in danger, but he certainly didn't want to fall if he could help it. Thus getting an idea, he carried the pulling frame back up the bluff and bolted it to the canoe. Then holding on to the cross bar, he eased the craft over the side and lowered it down step by step, digging his heals into the sandy soil as he went until he had made it safely to the bottom. In doing so, James once again used his walking machine to get out of a situation for which it wasn't constructed. Feeling pleased, James made his supper on the beach. He then loaded his craft and shoved off with the changing of the tide.

The time was 4:00pm and like the day before, the incoming tide no longer overcame the river but only slowed its flow. Hence with every mile James traveled upstream, the current grew stronger against him.

The canoeist paddled along the Oregon shore for one mile before entering an area where the river narrowed to a width of three-quarter mile. The current increased significantly in the bottleneck but James evaded the worst of it by hugging the shore where irregular cliffs hindered the flow. The canoeist still had to fight to make progress however, especially while going around those parts of cliffs that protruded into the river. And the bigger the outcrop, the stronger the current that flowed around its base. This was because each outcrop acted like a partial dam, blocking current only to have it rush around its end. In addition, each outcrop blocked wind pressure on its downstream side. Therefore, opposing currents of wind and water built up pressure on either side of an outcrop before rushing around to meet off its end. The opposing forces of wind and water made friction which distorted the river's surface into micro-rapids better known as washboards. Each washboard measured twenty to sixty feet in length with individual ripples measuring from four to eight inches in height.

So the new challenge for our novice was to push his 500 pound load through each washboard. He dug for all his worth, putting himself into it with back, shoulders, and arms. He used long heavy strokes and, it was all he could do to keep the force of the river from turning him back. He paddled through one set of washboards, then another and another. And each time he succeeded, he gained a small victory which added to his confidence.

The ¾-mile-wide channel continued straight east for two miles with no island barrier to stand between canoeist and cargo carriers. Twice, modest-sized freighters came along, dieseling for the ocean, and James paddled out to meet their wakes before returning to the business at hand. Now and again, cliffs created blind spots and James feared going around one only to see a supergiant. Such was his fear while paddling below a particularly rugged set of cliffs that appeared a terrible place to get caught by a giant. Terrible indeed, and the biggest ship he'd ever seen did in fact enter the bottleneck at that moment. At first James saw only the giant's gray bow as it entered the upstream end, then more of it appeared, and more of it, and more of it!

Grabbing his field glasses, James saw a series of super wakes rushing forth like white-capped walls of death. He paddled like mad to get away. His only hope lay in gaining the protection of a slough located directly ahead but, time ran out.

In desperation, James convinced himself that he could find a way to secure his boat among the slabs at the base of the cliff where he might ride out the wakes by bracing among the rocks. Thus he paddled toward the cliff. Fortunately, he saw his folly and came about to charge the oncoming wakes (which had expended themselves to a good degree even as they remained very large).

James made it over the first wake, and the second wake, and the third. Then came a loud report as the first wake crashed the cliff directly behind. The sound of it brought James's head around whereby he saw the second wake crash the cliff, and he knew he would have died had he sought refuge there, or at the very least suffered grave injury.

In knowing he had made the right decision, James took comfort and that was good because oncoming wakes were as numerous as rows of corn in a field. And looking out among their approaching ranks, James spotted a diamond surface flashing beneath a knifelike crown—,

"Diamond Wave!" he shouted, warning himself as much as UB, knowing what they were in for, not knowing if they would survive it.

Up the diamond wave went the big canoe, semi-airborne amid the spray. And when it had come down with a wallop and splash, and all the wakes had passed, James gave thanks!

Continuing into the shelter of an unnamed slough opposite the shipping lane from Walker Island, James had no more than reached its safety when the wind rose and the sky darkened. Perhaps the dragon was to blame, but in truth, the dragon was only of wind and water and not a flesh and blood beast who could be frustrated by a man in a canoe. Still, James had once again escaped only to have a storm come upon him. It seemed hard to believe, and in fact James shook his head in disbelief.

Through cold blowing rain, James fought the current and took heart simply because he could make progress against it. Slow but steady, he made his way up the river. *"Hard work,"* he would write in his journal, *"Very hard work."*

The storm passed as James emerged from the unnamed slough to find himself opposite the Port of Longview, which as he could see, was not for canoes. There the ocean freighters gathered round mountains of golden grain like farm fish at feeders. Mountainous piles of grain were themselves dwarfed by an oil refinery located immediately behind. The oil ran through a vast maze of pipes below a forest of smokestacks steaming white.

The port may have been a small fish among industrial ports but it wasn't small to the Kansan. James marveled from his canoe, lifting his eyes to the highest tower where blazed a flaming crown of fire. Meanwhile, a droning sound seemed to come from deep in the earth, as if a great diesel engine were turning the globe. James expected to see men working there amid the steel and smoke but there wasn't a man to be seen. In fact the place appeared to have been automated so that men were no longer needed.

"Once-upon-a-time, the seaport would have rung with shouts from dock and deck, come from men who hoisted loads with block and tackle, muscle and sweat, there beneath the mast and sail, and the eye of the captain upon the rail."

Presently, James saw a realm of machines without a man to be seen. Not one man. In vein he searched with his eyes, but it seemed the machines had swallowed up the men. James felt a warning sense in his heart which lasted but a moment and passed without thought. He then turned his eyes from the port and returned to the business at hand. The time was 8:30pm.

Opposite the port, the south shore consisted of a large beach from which two flood fences protruded. Local fishermen sat on the beach in lawn chairs with fishing poles propped on sticks. Behind the beach in some woods, their cars and trucks, numbering a dozen or so, sat parked on a primitive network of dirt and gravel lanes. Swimming wasn't allowed on the beach (it would have been suicide due to the flood fences that adjoined it). Between the beach on the south shore, and the port on the north shore, the river was a fast-flowing bottleneck measuring 3/4 mile wide. The day had entered its final hour of light. James had been fighting the river for five hours without rest, and, it pained him to see the flood fences standing in his path.

Doing as he must, the tired paddler moved several hundred yards out into the powerful current of the bottleneck. He had almost made it around the first flood fence when, getting caught in the "strange water" which Don had warned of, he found himself being pulled backward toward the end of the fence and quite possibly, the end of his life.

The fishermen rose from their seats while James fought savagely to escape a liquid conveyer belt of rapid waves that bounced him up and down like a rock on its way to a crusher. Then, somehow, almost incredibly, James managed to get to the outside just a bit whereby he checked his backward motion and began to pull away.

Escaping by the slimmest of margins, James shook his head with a painful grimace while looking at the men along the shore as if to say, *"Boy howdy, I ought to have been more careful!"*

James's embarrassment wasn't the result of taking a risk but the result of getting tired and making a mistake. Presently in no position to harp over mistakes, James remained focused on the business at hand. He hoped to reach the Port of Rainier that day and in fact he could see the lights of the tiny port on the Oregon shore just three miles ahead. Daylight had all but run out however and so extreme was his exhaustion, he had no strength left with which to get around the second flood fence just 1/4 mile ahead. Therefore he came about and paddled for shore.

Landing 1/8 mile upstream of the fishermen, James had only just dragged his craft onto the beach when two young men came in his direction.

"Do you have a cell phone?" asked a doughy teenager with a glum expression.

"No," replied James, and seeing a small car stuck in the sand he asked, "Are you stuck?"

"Yes."

"I've been stuck before," James said as though it were no big deal. "You can dig yourself out, but [on this beach] there might be broken glass, so don't use your bare hands. Use a piece of drift board for a shovel, or a hubcap. Then gather up rocks and sticks and put them under your wheels."

"I wish we had a shovel," replied the teenager.

"You don't need a shovel," James assured in a positive tone. "It's only sand."

"You really don't have a cell phone?"

James had neither cell phone nor shovel, but as fortune would have it, a 4x4 pickup came exactly then and stopped directly beside him. It was a fine looking truck of 1960s vintage, light blue and set up on large wheels. From inside the truck a good-looking couple in their late 20s or early 30s gazed out on James with concern. The man spoke first in a tone at once cautioning and caring, "Man, you can't just go out on that river and, I mean," and pausing before spitting out what he meant to say, "that river kills people!"

James dropped his eyes, "Yeah, I cut it too close out there," he admitted before looking up to tell that he'd come from Kansas to attempt the Lewis and Clark route.

The woman spoke next, and softly as women do, expressing her concern for James's welfare. The man then gave James an excellent bit of information which would allow him to reach the Port of Rainier early the next morning, weather permitting. The conversation then ended with words of thanks and well wishes whereupon the teenagers came forward to ask the man if he would pull them out of the sand. The man, who hadn't been aware of their presence until that moment, looked on them with disdain for which he couldn't be blamed. Nevertheless, he did pull them out.

James pitched his tent on the edge of the wood with his craft and gear secured alongside. By that time the beach lay abandoned under a pitch-dark sky. No rain fell, nor had any fallen for the past hour and a half. James and UB went out on the sand to sit beside a large drift log. The soft sand felt good, plus the smooth surface of the log made a fine backrest. James pealed an orange and gazed across the river. The big port was a sight to see. Thousands of light bulbs made it look like a galaxy unto its own. And taking it in, James said to his dog, "I've been looking forward to this orange all day."

Man and dog slept well.

Day 13, Wednesday, May 26

Acting on information given by the man in the blue truck, James had set his wristwatch alarm for 5:30am in order to catch the incoming tide before it ended at 8:40am. By such means James hoped to reach the Port of Rainier that morning instead of waiting until late in the day to shove off. Of course it all depended on the weather and at 5:30am, rain pelted his tent. So James hesitated for fifteen minutes while petting UB and hoping the rain would let up, although it did not.

In moderate rainfall, James skipped breakfast and worked fast, doing his best to keep his gear dry and, except for his tent fly which he put away wet, he did a good job. Next James carried his boat and gear to the water where, glancing at his wristwatch with surprise, he saw 1¼ hours had already slipped away. He shoved off and paddled out to clear the aforementioned flood fence. He could have shoved off in front of the fence, but due to strong current, he thought it safer to begin behind it. Needless to say, he kept well away from its end.

No more had James cleared the fence than the full force of the river came against him. And that wasn't the half of it, for the wind, which (unbeknown to him) had been his ally against the current for the past two days, presently came against him. And with both current and wind against him, he had to fight with all his might just to make a few yards. It seemed impossible, and with thousands of miles to go, he couldn't help wondering if he'd bitten off more than he could chew—,

"Of course I have," he said, laughing out loud. Then turning grim, he continued into a driving rain.

The novice had paddled only a few hundred yards when the rain turned extreme and, himself not yet being seasoned to the extremes he would face, he made for shore and took refuge in a shebang-like shelter made from a hodgepodge of various materials. The shebang stood behind a housing subdivision which meant James could use his walking machine if need be (a good thing to know in an otherwise miserable situation). Fortunately, the rain moderated after fifteen minutes, whereupon James unfolded his pulling frame and set out towing his craft through the shallows along the shore. By such means he gained another hundred yards before a change in the shoreline forced him back into the river where powerful current, wind, and cold rain came against him.

To gauge his progress, James looked to shore and saw how one paddle stroke with all his might put into it earned him one yard of progress. And so he fought, gaining one yard at a time.

Never had three miles seemed so great a distance. Twice, big ships sloshed water into James's canoe, adding weight to his load. Rain also came in where the tarp was not deployed in the area around and behind James. UB had gotten soaking wet even though he lie under the eve of the tarp. In fact UB appeared to be a case for concern, but James couldn't do anything for him until they reached port. The river simply would not allow it. Still, it wasn't easy for James to see his old friend shivering and groaning in the hull of their boat.

"I'm sorry boy. Sorry for getting us into this," James said worriedly.

Next James paddled under the famous Lewis and Clark Bridge which spanned the Columbia River between the city of Longview and the town of Rainier. Of the bridge James would make the following journal entry: *"The bridge, as seen from a canoe, was so large it made me dizzy."*

Two miles out of three yet remained, and a sobering fight to the finish it would be. James made the Port of Rainier at 8:40am, exactly at the end of his tide window.

"UB, we've made it."

The Port of Rainier wasn't made of stone but of a patchwork of floating docks surrounding a boat ramp. Above the ramp lie a tiny park with pavilion and bathroom. Having the park to himself, James used the pavilion as a staging area for his gear which he arranged into a fort for UB. James then spread out his tent fly to dry on a picnic table under the pavilion. Wind and rain continued but, under the pavilion, the wind acted as a drying agent. Next James returned to his empty boat and swamped it intentionally. He got in the water with it, all the way, to clean it. It didn't matter that James got wet, he had already gotten as wet as a man could get. Soon the canoe which had been full of grimy black sand, shone like new. James next turned to working on his gear which he did under the pavilion. He cleaned everything. It took three hours. Finally, James changed into clean cloths and, as he would enter in his journal, *"It felt good to leave the dirt and grime behind."*

Because there wasn't any place to camp at the port, James set out for town in his walking machine, but he hadn't gone twenty paces when a man who looked to be in his mid-sixties came with a walking cane in one hand and a brown bag in the other—,

"I've been watching you," said the man, and with a smile he handed over a bag containing apples, cookies, and orange juice.

"Sir," said the Kansan, altogether heartfelt and somber from his fight with the river. "Thank you, Sir. Thank you for your kind act."

"That's quite a rig you have there," said Jim.

James thanked Jim and then asked if there were any places to camp around. Jim replied that there were no official places but named several places where James might camp with permission from the sheriff. Jim felt certain that arrangements could be made.

James explained his walking machine to Jim as the two men went walking into town. They moved slowly for Jim's sake, as he obviously suffered some physical disability.

James asked, "Is there a café in town?"

"Are you hungry?" replied Jim.

"Yes Sir, very."

"Why not come with me to the shelter," Jim said. "I'm on my way there now. We can both get a free meal."

Thrown by what Jim had said, James was at a loss for words.

Seeing as much, Jim added, "Don't worry, the food is good there."

"I don't think that would be right," James said, realizing that Jim was homeless or something similar. "I'm able to pay," James added, "So I should pay. Fair is fair."

"Well alright," said Jim, and he gave directions to the café up the road.

James thanked Jim and then asked, "Would you like to come to the café with me?"

"Ah, no thanks," Jim replied.

"Are you sure? It's on me."

"No, but thanks anyway," and gesturing in the other direction, Jim added, "I should be going."

The two men shook hands and parted with words of thanks and well wishes. James would regret not learning more about Jim even as he continued to believe he did the right thing.

In the café, James ate while UB sat outside howling at the top of his lungs. Breakfast was eggs over easy atop white toast with hash browns, sausage links, orange juice, and coffee.

From the café, man and dog got a room at the inn across the street. In doing so, James made a mistake with regard to finding the spirit of Lewis and Clark. "The goodly light" as he would sometimes call it, did not come on with the flip of a switch in a hotel room. Jim had told how to find campsites in urban terrain, and James, who knew what it was to aim high and succeed, was still quite a lot more spoiled than he knew. In time, the necessary correction would be forced on him but that is very far ahead of where we are now, so let us return to James and UB in their room at the inn, in the town of Rainier.

From observing his dog, James would make the following

journal entry:

"UB, who used to make a little ritual of eating his dog food one piece at a time on the floor several feet from his bowl, doesn't do that anymore. Now, when I put his food down, he eats like it's the last meal he will ever get."

James also had changed after being on the river just 13 days. There had been milk and honey in the kindness of the people and in the beauty of nature. And there had been the dragon of wind and water from which the knight received ample cuts and scrapes (none of which he attended to in the slightest). So there was James, standing before a mirror, and in that mirror he saw a man he could not recognize. It wasn't because the skin had darkened, nor was it because the muscles had grown more defined. It was the look in the eyes. James didn't know whose eyes he saw. It truly astounded him, and even frightened him. He went away from the mirror and sat down. He had goose bumps. He got up and took another look at the man in the mirror. He didn't know what to think. He felt tired so he lay down on the floor and slept with UB at his side. Then waking some hours later, he returned to the mirror and felt relieved to see himself looking back, although he could still see something of the other fellow. Of this no more can be told until after James had returned from his dinner.

James showered, shaved, and went for Mexican food across the street: fajitas with steak, chicken, and shrimp. And because James sat outside on an empty patio overlooking the river, UB was allowed to beg at table. Rain fell lightly while man and dog remained dry under a large umbrella. UB pressed his case with hopeful eyes, and James fed him shrimp tails.

After dinner James retired to his room where he lay awake for fifteen minutes before unrolling his ground pad to sleep on the floor. There wasn't anything wrong with the bed but rather, James liked his ground pad.

James slept from 8:00pm to 3:30am. Then awake, he sensed the presence of the man in the mirror. The man in the mirror was there in the room, and because James's mind was rested, he saw who it was even in the dark. Maybe James didn't see as clearly as herein defined but he sensed well enough. The man in the mirror was a jungle mechanic who could do whatever it took to get the job done. Born from James's will to survive, the jungle mechanic had gotten out of his cage, so to speak, because outside of a Kansas tornado, the Columbia River with its wind and water dwarfed any dragon that might fly out of the sky.

So it was that the Kansan lay in darkness, wishing not to see the man in the mirror, sensing that to have him out, to run freely about, would lead to evil because the only law a jungle mechanic knew was the law of the jungle. Then for some unexplainable reason, a water pipe in the wall behind the mirror went "tap, tap, tap" as though a certain somebody in the mirror wanted out.

Of course James knew it was only a water pipe in the wall behind the mirror—a strange coincidence, there in the dark. James was only tired. He had bitten off more than he could chew. His nerves were a little worn, perhaps more then he knew.

"Tap, tap, tap."

James told himself it was only water coming up from below and not some entity sensing opportunity by which though trickery it might play upon his fear to gain a sympathetic ear. At least James heard no voice, saw no image, smelled no smell, but only the tapping, growing impatient.

"Rap! Rap! Rap!"

The state of the Kansan, being akin to a frightened animal by that point, frozen in fear, with senses bare and unhindered, could perhaps only be described in verse, as an inaudible whisper, from the ether:

> *In the darkness, I am here,*
> *come to prey upon your fear.*
> *Lest you wish to draw me near,*
> *call upon the one in the mirror.*
> *For he alone knows what to do.*
> *He alone can bring you through.*

"Lord Jesus, protect me! Lord Jesus, protect me! Lord Jesus, protect me!" James repeated even though he needed to ask only once. The pipe fell silent immediately and made no more noise for the duration of James's stay. Only in hindsight (long after he wrote the above verse) would James understand that his "fear" had been of death (in the river), and because he had wanted to live, his temptation had been to put his faith in his own strength (the jungle mechanic). As for the jungle mechanic, he was locked up, back in his cage so to speak, but only for now, and so, we haven't seen the last of him.

If ever so briefly, James broke down, "Oh Lord," he said in a grateful tone, wiping a tear from his check, and there under Heaven, fell fast asleep.

Day 14, Thursday, May 27

After breakfast at the café, James returned to his room where he poured over his map in hope of finding a way forward. Likewise, he knew he must reduce the weight of his load. Nonessential items like his camera would have to go. But first his journal had to be caught up while his memory remained fresh. So he sat down to write beside his window where, looking out on torrential rainfall, he felt grateful for the roof over his head.

Breaking for lunch, James went to a Mexican restaurant across the street and asked for a waiter he'd met the evening before, a tall, handsome, charismatic young Hispanic. On the evening before, James had declared the food the best Mexican he'd ever had. In response, the waiter had claimed responsibility for the food. James had then asked the young waiter if he had cooked the food. The waiter replied that he had not. Naturally, James looked at the waiter a little sideways. The waiter then claimed to have taught the cook everything that his grandmother had taught him. Wisely or not, James took the waiter at his word and thus thought him full of promise. The waiter then glanced over his shoulder and, seeing no sign of his boss, kept talking. Soon the two men were discussing the waiter's hopes for opening his own restaurant. And truly, the young waiter could hardly have picked a better person to speak with on such matters because James had lived the small business dream. Therefore with his entrepreneurial spirit kindled, James told of a university town located thirteen miles from his home. James said the town was a showcase of ethnic restaurants and had a whole lot of money floating around. In such a place, and with all the waiter had going for him, he should make it if he were dedicated and had good business sense. Moreover, James said he would assist the waiter with connections if he could, and in fact James knew men in that town who enjoyed having first-class food close at hand.

Presently, when James asked for the waiter, another Hispanic man who appeared to be the manager of the restaurant met James in the foyer. The manager began a conversation with James on the topic of pretty women. All was kept in good taste even as two men smiled and laughed. James didn't know it but the manager was tactfully questioning him in an attempt to learn his "sexual preference" for a reason that shall now be revealed.

While the two men were yet speaking, the aforementioned waiter showed up only to get chased from the foyer by the manager who browbeat him with frustrated if not carefully chosen words. James meanwhile heard and saw and therefore realized that his goodwill had been taken advantage of or at the very least confused for something he'd never been.

The manager returned to the foyer, picked up a menu, and while gesturing for James to follow, made a conciliatory comment about how men such as themselves liked pretty ladies. The manager then assigned two pretty Latino maidens to wait on James

After dinner, James returned to his room and caught up his journal. He then brought out his gear for a thorough reorganization in which he sacrificed many things including his wetsuit and camera to reduce the weight of his load so that he might make progress against the powerful current. Finally, by the time he'd finished, it was bedtime.

James slept well.

Day 15, Friday, May 28

Like most small towns, Rainier couldn't have been better for the man on foot, what with the café, inn, grocer, hardware store and post office all within a one-block radius. Therefore after breakfast at the café, James found everything he needed. At the post office he found boxes and tape with which to ship home his unneeded gear. He found outdoor health-food bars in a store that sold unwanted goods from the shelves of other stores. As indicated on their packaging, the food bars contained protein, fat, sugars, and the like.

The food bars were near their expiration dates but that didn't bother James. Back in his room, James packaged gear to be sent home and thus reduced his load by fifty pounds according to the scales at the post office. James didn't ship the kayak paddle home, having already dispensed with it in a place where only a river lover could find it (be they canoeist or kayaker). While going about his chores, James received help from friendly local folk and, while so engaged, took the opportunity to interview them with regard to the route ahead. In such a way, James gathered information that would help him develop a plan for the morrow. He did his laundry and then returned to his room where he got everything ready for morning.

By the time he'd finished getting ready, it was time for bed, but before hitting the hay, in his journal he would say: *"It was a good and productive day."*

James slept well.

Day 16, Saturday, May 29

After breakfast at the café, James returned to the inn where he unsnapped his tarp only to find an astonishing amount of rainwater in his cart. Whereas some rainwater had gotten in at Cathlamet and had to be bailed, there at Rainier James counted twenty gallons as he bailed them out. Fortunately, James's gear was not in the canoe but in his room, so no harm had come from the leaky tarp. The novice had made his tarp to snap down against the top of the gunwales when he should have made it snap to the outsides of the body just below the gunwales. Fabricating a new tarp wasn't an option, so James would have to live with what he had.

On the bright side, having lightened his load the day before meant less gear to pack which enabled James to maintain a low cargo profile even as he kept the load balanced over the single axle. A low cargo profile meant James could deploy his tarp for overland travel and the tarp still shed a lot of rain despite the aforesaid design flaw. Moreover, the tarp kept big waves from swamping the canoe. So the tarp would remain indispensable.

At 10:00am, James and UB set out on the eastbound bicycle lane of Highway 30 which ran between river and mountains. James looked forward to testing his walking machine as well as getting a break from the river. On the day before, he had asked the local folk about any hills he might encounter because his map didn't show whether the highway lay flat on a flood plain or rose and fell in mountain foothills. The local folk had assured James that the road lay almost flat. But as he would discover, almost flat didn't mean the same thing between mountain folk and plains folk. The gentle grades required effort but were by no means backbreaking. At least they weren't backbreaking so long as James kept his back straight.

"The walking machine forced me to keep my back straight. If I didn't keep my back straight, the machine punished me. Likewise on relatively level surfaces, the machine forced me to walk upright. UB didn't ride in the machine but walked alongside. I maintained my natural state of locomotion largely independent of the machine even while extending said state to the machine. This walking rhythm, or man/machine integration worked so well, I couldn't have been more pleased with it. Thus I proceeded in complete confidence."

"These are perfect pulling conditions," James told UB as light rain fell from an overcast sky. Cool was the air. Wide, clean, and smooth was the bicycle lane. Friendly were the motorists who passed on the two-lane blacktop. Out of sight, out of mind was the river, concealed behind a wall of vegetation.

Perhaps the dragon made a part in the trees like a peep-hole through which he spied the knight with a giant catlike eye. Perhaps he shouted, "Hey, sir knight, the fight's over here!"

As for our novice, he felt no cowardice or shame but to the contrary was enjoying great satisfaction and exhilaration, making good time under his own power, pulling his rig through a land more lush than any he'd known. And besides that, there would be ample opportunity to fight the so-called dragon. So it was on that day, James found joy in the simplest of things, like watching his little friend prance ahead with his tail straight out. UB was growing young so fast; James couldn't have believed it had he not seen it with his own eyes.

Passing motorists gave thumbs-up, waved, honked, or simply smiled in amazement. A few people stopped to ask questions. One man asked if he could take photos of James's walking machine. James felt apprehensive in the knowledge that not all men walked upright through the world. The man seemed honest but some men, if given the chance, would steal James's design. Therefore James wrestled with himself momentarily (a conference took place between his heart and brain). Then, James made a policy with/and private to himself in which the importance of his errand overruled any worry he might have about theft of invention. Bob then took pictures of James's rig after which the two men had a brief but good conversation. Bob, who'd been a reporter, asked if he might write a freelance story on James. James thanked Bob for his interest even as he told of his policy regarding interviews (being that he would do none before reaching St Louis). Bob gave his phone number and James gave his word to call (which he did). Then with well wishes, Bob departed.

As James understood it, eighteen miles lay between the towns of Rainier and Saint Helens with no eateries between. And because James had already grown weary of freeze-dried camp food, he didn't plan to stop and cook but planned to get by on beef-jerky, apples, and food bars. James had a stash of rice and beans which he ate from occasionally but he considered it as backup food. James would soon design his own diet based on a natural craving for red meat but presently, all he knew was hunger. Therefore when he came to a clearing in the forest and saw an old red tavern of low-roofed design sitting in a gravel depression with a couple of pickup trucks parked out front, it hardly mattered that it looked to be the haunt of every fist fighter in the county, just so long as there was a chance of getting an honest-to-goodness hamburger.

In the smoky tavern, James's brain adjusted his eyes to the dark. A clock on the wall read 1:30pm. A jukebox played in the corner. A group of good old boys stood round a pool table with their girlfriends talking nearby. James took a seat and waited at the bar with hope of getting some real food.

"The bartender was nowhere to be seen and that jar of pickled eggs looked about as appetizing as the modern camp food I'd been eating."

Soon a man hollered around a corner from which appeared a woman who asked, "What can I get you?"

"Ma'am," replied the Kansan, "do you make hamburgers here?"

"We sure do."

James smiled, "Then Ma'am, I'd like the biggest you got, with everything on it."

"What are you drinking?" asked the bartenderess.

"Just water Ma'am, thank you."

After the bartenderess disappeared into the back, James struck up a conversation with the man who had alerted her to his presence, and the two men spoke at length. The man told of his youth spent on the river with his father. And while the man told his story, the bartenderess brought James one of the best hamburgers he'd ever had. So James enjoyed good food and good conversation. Then with words of thanks, well wishes, and a firm handshake, James harnessed into his rig and set out pulling toward the town of Saint Helens.

The road flattened, the miles passed, and James did all he could to keep UB going—,

"Keep walking, UB. You can do it. Do it for your daddy. That's a good boy! Do it for your old daddy!"

For the love of his master, UB pushed himself until he could go no further. Then with words of praise, James laid UB on a bed inside the machine. The little dog had walked seventeen miles. And yet, UB was soon on the move inside the machine. James, who himself suffered the effects of pulling their cart, tried in vain to talk UB into cooperating. Lucky for them, James would soon fix the teeter-totter problem to the complete satisfaction of both.

At approximately 6:30pm, James stopped at a mini-market on the approach to Saint Helens where he purchased a bottle of orange juice and then sat to rest on a bench with people gathering around. Some folks stopped because they had seen James pulling along the highway. Others stopped to use the market, then saw his walking machine and wanted to know about it.

"I saw you earlier today," said one.

"Where are you headed?" asked another.

"How does this thing work?"

And yet another, "Why are you doing this?"

With no small appreciation, James courteously answered all questions. In reply to the "why" question however, James only put his fist to his chest and said, "That, is in here."

"I did not assume to know the design of what I sought. In a matter of speaking, a grail is a grail and still it might be short or tall, fat or thin, blue or green, wood or ceramic. I did not know. Nor did I engage in discussions regarding what it might be when after all the dragon who guarded it was on the field and no amount of discourse would get me around him."

However much James inspired the folks at the quick market, they inspired him. And as they departed, others came to keep the Kansan company, none of which was wasted on a man far from home. He still had difficulty recalling names for his journal but that was something he would improve on over time.

James hadn't been there long when a car pulled up and out of it came two women, one brunette and one redhead. The redhead came forward not with prideful mien, but with a body and face that had undoubtedly earned her much approval throughout her adult life. And being of an age younger than James yet old enough to be comfortable, she simply asked if she might have a seat on the bench beside him. The Kansan bid the fair maiden sit and they spoke at length in wholesome fashion.

"It was surprisingly easy," said James, concluding a speech on the principle of his walking machine for her.

"I'm sure!" the maiden positively agreed, "I saw you on my way to Rainier. You were moving right along. Then I saw you here and, I had to stop."

UB meanwhile, who also received no small attention, wagged his tail like an old dog with a new lease on life.

Next a man named Mike came and said he enjoyed taking his wife and kids out in his boat but he had neither seen nor heard of anything like what James did. Mike was enthusiastic and the two men spoke at length. Then concluding their conversation, Mike took out a twenty dollar bill and offered it, saying, "Get yourself a good meal."

"Thank you, but I have money," James replied, refusing the bill. Only then did James see how he had pained the man. Thus in a reversal James accepted, said a sincere thank you, and promised to get a steak dinner.

At last when none remained, the clerk who worked in the mini-market came out. And James had been hoping she would.

James had never given special consideration to women who lifted weights but the slender west-coast girl had him distracted. Shannon looked to be about twenty-one, measuring 5'8" or 5'10" with long straight blond hair. James measured 6 foot and a little better with boots on. So James and Shannon sat and talked, wanted to talk, talked about anything. And while they did, James thought, *"How can I ask Shannon to dinner? I have no car. I don't know where the eateries are. I don't even know where I will lay my head tonight. Well, I'll just tell her. Then, if she wishes it as I do, we'll find a way."*

James opened his mouth to speak but, at that very moment, the manager of the market exclaimed, "Shannon!"

The chide jolted the maiden to her feet.

"We have customers!" added the manager, herself on her way into the store at a double step.

"I've helped you into some trouble," James said ruefully, also standing.

Shannon hesitated for a split second then ran away to her duty, which made her all the more attractive.

James harnessed into his machine. Meanwhile in the course of hurrying out to assist a customer at a gas pump, Shannon returned just as James pulled away. And if for nothing else, both were glad for a chance to bid the other farewell.

"That was meant to be," James told UB, believing the manager's intervention to have been no coincidence, instinctually knowing that if he were to reach the gate of St Louis, he must maintain total commitment.

The next mile proved the longest of the day. First UB wore out even as James tried to encourage him on—,

"Keep walking UB. You can do it. Come on boy. Dig down and find it. Do it for your old daddy."

UB tried but could go further, so James put him in the machine along with a few kind words. James then continued with precious strength left with which to counter the teeter-totter effect.

At approximately 8:00pm, James reached Saint Helens where, on the edge of town, he flagged a man down—,

"Sir, if I may ask, is there a campground at the port?"

"No, there's no campground at the port," replied the man.

"Is there any place to camp in town?" James then asked.

"No," replied the man, and knitting his brows in thought he

added, "I am certain of it. I know this town well, and there is no place to camp."

"Is there an inn?"

"Oh yes. Straight up the road."

James pulled to the inn, stowed his gear in a room, and proceeded directly to a nearby eatery. UB howled while James inhaled a big plate of fried chicken and then laughed at himself for doing so. James felt very pleased regardless of his exhaustion, for he had pulled his rig twenty miles. And while he had no way of knowing it, he would never again know such perfect pulling conditions.

Man and dog slept well.

Day 17, Sunday, May 30

Having come to a place only a day away from entering a major metropolitan area, James had major reservations. After all, from every big city came news of crime. And traveling by canoe as it were, natural forces could force James ashore at any moment. If blown ashore in gangland, James might find himself in a no-win situation. He had a pistol but it was for protection from bears in the wild, not from humans in the cities. And such being the case, he kept it unloaded and buried deep in his gear.

"With regard to the upcoming city, I had already met several upstanding men and women who lived there, and therefore I would not want my decision to go around the city to be taken as anything but a safety precaution made necessary by the fact that, without the protection of walls, doors, or locks, it seemed the best option for a man who knew not where he would find himself at the end of each day."

To get around the City of Portland, James would have to cross the river in a place where even the best conditions promised danger. Specifically, James planned to cross at a place where the Columbia River, Lewis River, Lake River, and part of the Willamette River came together in a 4-way confluence beside the town of Saint Helens. Once across the confluence, James planned to enter Lake

River. On Lake River, James could parallel the Columbia River for ten miles before entering Vancouver Lake on the outskirts of Portland. Once across Vancouver Lake, James planned to assemble his walking machine and portage across the northernmost tier of the metropolis. And because the Columbia River made a ninety degree turn there in the city, James could skirt the city on a straight line back to the river. In effect, he would be cutting a corner on an elbow. That was his plan.

To begin, James checked out of the inn. Then coming out of the lobby, he found three maids standing in a row beside his walking machine.

"Good morning," said the Kansan to the maids, each of whom appeared to be in her twenties.

After a brief conversation, one of the girls asked, "What's your dog's name?"

"UB," James replied.

"UB," echoed the maid, "how's that spelled?"

"The letters UB are his initials," said James who had not given UB his name but his initials. James regarded the initials as UB's only name. Presently however, James was distracted by thoughts of the river crossing and therefore concluded by telling that UB's initials stood for "Under Bite."

> "UB's protruding jaw not only causes his lower fangs to jut but leaves his lower front teeth exposed which creates the appearance of a smile. Additionally, when UB was a pup, my one-hundred-pound-hound bit his head, so UB's eyes are not the same and in fact his entire face is out of kilter. Remarkably, his abnormalities fit together in such a fortunate way, as to make an adorable little dog."

Presently none the worse for wear, UB smiled up at the maids while wagging his tail. Meanwhile, a pall fell over the maids, like a spell of sadness in which their lips were sealed and their eyes were downcast.

Only then did James see his blunder. One of the maids had a pronounced overbite.

Knowing not what to do, James suddenly went down on his knees before the injured girl. Then while petting UB softly, James spoke from his heart—,

"UB, you're such a trooper, I wouldn't have any but you," and James lifted his eyes to the girl.

She appeared to understand and, if there was more James could do, he knew not what. So he harnessed into his machine and bid the maids farewell. They in turn wished him luck.

Due to the day before, neither man nor dog could walk worth a darn. Fortunately, the port was only a mile from the inn. James didn't stop for breakfast along the way because he had a tide window to catch.

At the port, James converted land rig to water craft and paid the port fee as always. He then set out on a route suggested by two men he'd met the day before at the mini-market. The two men had warned of extreme danger in James's original plan for crossing the confluence. Presently taking their advice, James paddled 1/4 mile straight out to an island where a string of cabin cruisers were moored. Upon reaching the unnamed island, James did as he must and angled between a pair of wooden piers. As he did so, a lady on one of the piers let out a gasp for fear James would be swept under the pier.

"Howdy Ma'am!" said the Kansan in a strong friendly tone, as though to assure her that he knew exactly what he was doing.

Due to heavy inland rains, Bonneville Dam had opened its floodgates sixty miles upstream which made the river channel flow with what local folk called a "ripping current." On the bright side, the high water had flooded the island beach, which in turn enabled James to cut behind a flood fence by paddling on what would otherwise have been dry land. So the flood water saved James the time and effort of portaging around the fence.

Beyond the fence, the canoeist gained the opposite shore of the island and landed on what remained of its flooded beach. He then used his field glasses to study the confluence where, seeing the danger of which the men at the mini-market had warned, he felt all the more thankful for their advice. The route they prescribed was the least dangerous, which is not to say it wasn't dangerous, for in fact it was extremely dangerous.

With no ships in sight, the canoeist attacked the river like a man possessed, pitting his every atom against ripping sets of rapids and vortexes for a distance of 3/4 mile in a crossing that would never be forgotten. Then, having reached the safety of the north shore, he gave thanks to God.

"I didn't understand it at the time but the wind broadsided my canoe like a sail as I crossed and kept me from being swept away."

Continuing east, James hugged the Washington shore, ducking under the lines of fishermen for a distance of one mile until he reached Austin Point where he entered the vast but calm mouth of Lewis River. In the mouth of Lewis River, James aimed for the mouth of Lake River which according to his map and compass lay straight ahead although he couldn't establish visual contact, so vast were his surroundings.

Having paddled directly to the mouth of Lake River, James found safe haven in Lake River which was, in reality, a peaceful slough. In Lake River, James continued east for an unrecorded number of hours, canoeing through what appeared to be a tall-grass prairie. By such means, and quite unexpectedly, James entered a floating village. Not a group of houseboats but real houses, fifteen or twenty in all, each full of character, with porch steps descending to streets of water. It was like nothing the Kansan had ever seen. Open garage doors revealed motorboats within. And seeing how ducks filled the roll of chickens, he laughed with delight. Then passing a couple sitting on their front porch, James told what he was about. In turn, they came to the rail and wished him well.

Just beyond the floating village, James passed beneath a bridge made entirely of wood. From there the little river ambled through a flatland wilderness of tall grass and cottonwood stands with foothills in the background. The water became so calm, as to mirror the blue sky above, with a white cloud puff floating here and there. And watching the bow tip glide in a reflection of Heaven, the Kansan fell under a spell of enchantment so complete, he may as well have been wearing buckskins.

James struck camp at 8:00pm, having traveled a total distance of fifteen miles. It wasn't an ideal campsite, being a sliver of ground where the river came up against a railroad track. James felt grateful to have it anyway. He feared going any further, lest he end up in the suburbs of Portland. Presently a railroad truck with flashing lights slowed down for a look at James. The truck continued and James hoped a decision had been made to let him stay.

That evening, trains shook the ground as they thundered past not twenty yards away. Between trains, a giant colony of herons made a tremendous racket from a rookery in a stand of cottonwoods directly across the river. James always thought herons to be timid birds but apparently when in large groups they become like baboons. Backlit by a deep orange sunset, countless bird heads bobbed up and down screaming, "Ka, ka, ka, ka, ka!" Then another thundering train. Then more, "Ka, ka, ka, ka, ka!" It's a wonder James slept at all but in fact he slept well.

Day 18, Monday, May 31

Although James had never knowingly eaten tofu, it had seemed a smart way to go when planning his journey because it could be kept fresh without refrigeration. To make breakfast for example, James only needed to take a tofu briquette from a vacuum-sealed pouch, break up the slimy and colorless briquette in a skillet, sprinkle in the tiny packet of egg-flavored powder and presto; imitation scrambled eggs!

Forcing yet another spoonful of imitation scrambled eggs into his mouth, James swallowed with a sour expression. Such problems had a way of demanding resolution.

The canoeist shoved off and soon reached Vancouver Lake on the outskirts of Portland. Vancouver Lake measured roughly three miles across in every direction and James sought a public boat ramp on its opposite shore but, once again, he couldn't distinguish land marks at distance even with field glasses. Thus he went by compass heading and, in spite of worry, found the boat ramp without difficulty.

At the ramp, James assembled his walking machine and set out on a gravel lane which turned into a narrow blacktop extending straight through grassy lowland flats to the city yet two miles distant. The day meanwhile had turned sublime but James took little notice, himself being consumed with the business at hand.

Despite prior scouting, James hadn't understood that a flood plain lay between lake and city and therefore, being unsuitable for development, there would be no suburbs through which he might find safe passage. Likewise, he had taken a basic grid of lines on his river map literally and not as a representation of a vast network of city streets.

Confused and surprised, James entered the city by way of a Hispanic barrio. Roughly six blocks into the barrio, James stopped on a street corner where he stood looking at his river map and shaking his head. He needed to ask directions and in fact a group of Latinos had already noticed the Kansan who, with his little dog and cart, had gotten lost on their turf.

"I can't believe this!" James thought, fearing that he might be heading into the very situation he'd been trying to avoid.

The Kansan parked his rig and began walking toward the Latinos who were playing basket ball on a court. UB remained behind with instructions to bark if anyone came visiting.

> "I felt uncertain as to whether or not I should ask directions and, by such means, betray the fact that I was lost. After all, it only took one gang connected man to go and tell others that opportunity had come knocking."

Fortunately for James, he was not in a ghetto but a barrio. And himself knowing the difference, he figured he'd be alright even while he remained concerned in the knowledge that he knew nothing about his location and therefore might be on the threshold of a ghetto. Later, upon relating this experience to a fellow Christian, James would be asked if he thought God knew the difference between ghetto, barrio, or suburb.

> "It is a question to be grateful for, and I know I'm in no position to judge. But while God may love all his children equally, and see their sins whether hidden from the world or not, I am certain He knows the difference between a barrio and a ghetto with relation to my situation, walking with my feet on the ground."

Presently, James hadn't taken ten steps toward the Latinos when he spotted what was perhaps the only Caucasian in the neighborhood, a white woman in an old pickup truck of Japanese design.

Thus he came about on a dime, "Ma'am!" and holding up his map like a flag, he angled to catch her at an intersection where she had stopped.

While the woman looked on with uncertainty, James did his best to reassure her with a friendly expression even as he came on with long swift strides. Only after arriving did James see the man in the driver's seat, and just as suddenly, the air filled with tension while men of different worlds sized one another up.

> "I had no wish to betray the weakness of my position to a man who might hate me."

With only a second to gauge the man, and sensing suspicion but not ill intent, James broke the silence, "Ma'am, Sir, thank you for waiting. If I may ask, is there an inn at the intersection of Hwy 501 and I-5?"

Having received directions to the inn, James expressed his gratitude and then moved on quickly so as not to appear lost any longer. But as it turned out, he hadn't gone a hundred feet when he heard a booming stereo thumping bass beats, and turning to look, he saw a "ghetto cruiser" crawling in his blind spot. It was sleek and shiny, crouched down low on wild wheels with dark tinted glass that kept him from seeing inside.

"This is exactly what I'd hoped to avoid," James thought, *"the gang bangers have sniffed me out."*

The modified SUV crept up alongside James, whereupon he turned his head to the impenetrable glass. He neither smiled nor waved. And for the record, his pistol lie buried at the bottom of a big duffle bag which was itself under a tarp that was snapped down tight. So his gun was well beyond reach, and unloaded.

At once the electric window came down and James could not help but smile, for there sat four honey-colored maidens clad in jewels.

> "The maiden closest to me had an awesome smile, with eyes as big, dark, and glossy as pools of joy on the wild side. As to whether she was a gangster or not, I could not care in that moment, such was my relief on seeing her expression, which appeared to be of pure happiness."

"Sir," cried the maiden, "now I know I've seen it all!"

Delighted by her enthusiasm, James smiled back while telling his business. Then, as they drove away, the peril-tongued maiden hung her head out the window and, looking back with sincere expression, gave James a "thumbs up."

James felt joyful in the possibility that he could inspire just about anyone, although he remained cautious.

Next the ethnic man and white woman returned to give James a new set of directions because the original set contained an inaccuracy which would have thrown him off. Needless to say, James felt grateful, for they had taken the trouble when they could have left him to it.

While they were still motoring alongside, the ethnic man said, "Hey Cowboy."

"Yes Sir."

"You all come back now, ya hear!" And shooting a grin at James, the ethnic man sped away.

James laughed even as he shook his head at the ethnic man's bad hillbilly impersonation. He then pulled hard to beat the onset of night because, happy though he be, he feared the streets might not be so friendly after dark.

James went left, then right, then left, then right, and so on. Eventually, he entered a district of outdoor cafés where preppie looking people sipped fancy coffee drinks. From there it was a cake walk, so to speak.

As soon as James had secured his gear and walking machine at the inn, he went to a steakhouse across the parking lot. The time was 6:00pm and, over a period of two days, James had eaten one helping of tofu eggs, a few food bars, a little beef jerky, two bananas, an apple, and an orange (all of which equaled approximately one meal).

"Sir," James told the head waiter, "I've had one meal in two days." James spoke no other words but only thanked the waiter for showing him to a table.

At once a waitress came and offered a menu which James courteously refused, "Ma'am, I know want I want."

"And what would that be?" asked the waitress.

"The biggest steak you got, with a baked potato and salad please."

"How would you like that?" asked the waitress.

"Rare."

"Yes Sir," and with a smile the waitress departed.

The staff rushed James's order ahead of all others and the sirloin was nothing less than excellent. With each bite, James felt his strength returning, and that was good because he was close, very close, to blacking out.

Back in his room, James had a good phone conversation with his brother Frank. Then as always when at an inn, James unrolled his ground pad and slept on the floor. It cannot be explained why he didn't sleep as well as usual.

Day 19, Tuesday, June 1

James went across the street for breakfast before returning to the inn where he purchased a map of the city. He felt surprised to see how big the metropolitan area really was, not to mention how much of it remained in his path. Fortunately the desk clerk knew the city well and helped the Kansan plot a safe course out. James thanked the clerk before returning to his room where he worked on his journal until lunch.

At the steakhouse, James ate the largest steak they had. He then returned to the inn where he met the manager, Eric. Eric had heard about James from the desk clerk and, being enthusiastic, offered his congratulations along with a ride to the grocery store. James thanked Eric but declined with regard to the ride because the grocery store was on his way out of town. James then returned to working on his journal but soon became hungry and went back to the steakhouse for another round of lunch. Back in his room, the Kansan worked on his journal for the remainder of the afternoon. He then returned to the steakhouse for a T-bone and seafood. Then returning to the inn, he worked on his journal while doing laundry. When he finished his journal, he worked on his gear until bedtime. Then after sleeping a few hours, James woke feeling out of sorts perhaps due to loneliness, fear of dying, and other weaknesses which for the most part are overcome when, having received the Holy Spirit, a man goes up in spontaneous spiritual combustion.

Remembering that God was in charge, James fell into a deep

sleep.

Day 20, Wednesday, June 2

After eating bacon and eggs at the diner across the street, James returned to the inn and loaded his walking machine. He then went into the lobby to check out where to his good fortune, Eric put together a care package from items there at the inn including fresh apples, oranges, bananas, and cookies. Eric came outside to take pictures but, as it turned out, his camera was out of film. The two men had a good conversation and then parted with a handshake.

James pulled east under Interstate 5 on Mill Plane Boulevard. He liked the bicycle lane but because the boulevard climbed a hill which would probably lead to more hills, he changed his plan in hope of staying on the flat streets of the valley floor near the river. He understood, thanks to the clerk at the inn, the neighborhoods would be safe. And thanks to Eric's care package, it didn't matter that the change of route would cost him a trip to the grocer because he had enough food to see him through to the next town. So he turned off Mill Plane Boulevard and proceeded by way of Gillis Street to Evergreen Boulevard.

Due to a complexity on his map, James suffered some confusion and as a result had to double back because Evergreen Boulevard ended at Highway 14 with no way through. In backtracking, he picked up Columbia Way, then continued east on Riverside before turning north on State Street which climbed steeply but only for half a block. James's error cost him two miles, after which he continued east on Evergreen Highway just the other side of Lewis and Clark Highway. Evergreen Highway, which was in reality a residential road, would continue out of town according to James's map.

No more had James gotten onto Evergreen Highway than along came a young man on a bicycle who'd gotten lost while in route to a job interview. James brought out his map and did his best to assist the young man whose name was also James. Shortly thereafter, two men in an SUV came to drive alongside while asking questions.

As always, James said he'd come from Kansas to attempt the Lewis and Clark route, west to east.

"So you're on a mission of self-discovery," stated the driver of the SUV.

"No," James replied, "I'm putting one foot before the other with faith that good will come of it."

"So you're looking to see if the grass is greener on the other side of the hill," said the passenger.

"No," said James, "it's exactly as I just told you." And looking perplexed, he asked, "Are ya'll from the press?"

"No," replied the men, laughing. Then wishing James well, they drove away. Only in hindsight would James wonder if the men had been speaking in code.

Next James met a man who'd come out to his mailbox. The two men had a brief but good conversation before James continued east, happy in the knowledge that his errand made just about everyone happy.

Seven miles from the inn and still within the city, Evergreen Highway had no curbs or sidewalks but traversed a valley slope with grassy ditches and country style mail-boxes belonging to modest homes amid trees that hid the river below. So the neighborhood had a rural touch that gave it a comfy feel, like a seasoned baseball mitt. There were no eateries and that was okay, James had no time to stop if he wanted to be out of the city by nightfall. He ate as he went, munching beef jerky, food bars, and fruit.

The sun burned unseasonably hot, man and dog drank lots of water, and James envied UB for his canine privilege of being able to "go" wherever he pleased. There wasn't much else to envy UB for, what with his little dog body being so close to the heated blacktop. It wore him out, so James put him in the cart and continued pulling along the old highway which the city had long since gobbled up.

Worse than coping with the teeter-totter effect, the heat wore James down until, having no other choice, he took UB from the cart and said, "You're going to have to walk boy, if only for a little while."

The tired dog employed one delaying tactic after another until his master got down on his level and addressed him with confidence, "UB, I know you can do this."

Being the good dog he was, UB got out front and led the way. So it was that man and dog proceeded in dire straits while motoring suburbanites, who may have been animal rights activists, gave James the evil eye.

At 4:30pm, UB veered into the grass and dropped on his stomach where he panted like a sphinx. James immediately parked his rig and put UB underneath to shade him from the sun. James then poured water over UB while petting and praising him for his considerable effort.

With UB taken care of, James sat numbly on the stern of his rig which, when parked, rested on the ground and made for a good seat. And in the natural progression of things, it was probably the act of sitting on his cart that provided the impetus for the idea that solved the teeter-totter problem—,

"If I were to adjust my gear in order to establish a level platform under the tarp and put UB's bed on top of it, then UB could sit atop the cart where he could see what was going on without having to move around."

Having made the necessary adjustments, James picked UB up and asked, "Will you stay put if you can see what's going on?"

James then placed UB on his bed, not in the machine but atop the cart.

James harnessed in and began pulling while UB rode. At first James kept close tabs by continually glancing over his shoulder. UB panted in hot sunshine but nonetheless enjoyed the scenery from his elevated position. UB no longer needed to move around within the cart to see out. Instead, UB stayed put like a sphinx, lacking only an umbrella (and perhaps a squirrel trained to flag its tail like a slave with a feather fan). So it was, the teeter-totter problem was solved!

On the outskirt of the city, James parked his rig in front of Fisher Cemetery and laid himself down under a tree to rest. With fourteen miles behind him, James rested only briefly before retaking the road. He had to reach the town of Camas. He knew so because people along the way had told him there were no campsites before Camas.

After pulling between river and countryside for three miles, James entered the small town of Camas by way of a quiet and well-kept residential neighborhood. Then, just one block inside the city limit and unable to go a step further, he sat on the stern of his rig with his elbows on his knees and his head hung low.

"Sir," called a voice, "Sir!"

James lifted his head as if from a slumber to see an elderly lady walking down a driveway. Her house sat back from the road and therefore having some distance to cover, the lady spoke in elevated tones but James couldn't understand what she said.

The lady saved her breath until, having advanced within earshot, she asked, "Are you alright?"

"Yes Ma'am. I'm only a little tired." Then gesturing to a no parking sign directly before him, James added, "I apologize for parking here."

"Oh don't worry about that!" and looking upon James with concern, "May I get you a glass of water?"

"I have water Ma'am, but thank you for your kind offer."

James apologized for not standing in the presence of a lady. He probably needn't have said more but feeling self-conscious about his lax behavior, he confessed, "I fear I've come to the end of my strength."

The lady assured James he ought to remain seated. The two then spoke for several minutes, whereupon promising a speedy return, the kindly widow went up the drive only to return with a bag containing an assortment of cheese crackers, bottled water, and candy.

Touched by her hospitality, James thanked Kathy kindly. The two then continued their prior conversation until, coming to the subject of marriage, James let it be known that he was, "divorced and not proud of it." He never said more than that to anyone with regard to his divorce, not because he had been a bad husband but to the contrary.

Being a lady, Kathy didn't pry but instead asked if she might give advice. James gave his permission and Kathy continued in classic grandmotherly fashion—,

"You're going to meet a lot of young ladies on your journey, and they're going to want to get hooked up with you, but don't you go getting hooked up before you've reached St Louis or you won't finish this thing!"

James laughed and agreed wholeheartedly. Still, he hoped to marry after completing his errand.

James thanked Kathy for her kindness and retook the road with seventeen miles behind and further than he knew to go. The time was 6:35pm.

James's next stop came at a mini-mart made from an old general store where he purchased a bottle of orange juice. There James met Roselle, a lady of about seventy, tall, slender, gray, and energetic. Kathy had called Roselle on the phone, and Roselle had come with pen and pad to get an interview for the local Lewis and Clark Historic Society. Coincidentally, three other women came round the Kansan who had already harnessed into his walking machine.

Bonnie was a lady of extraordinary beauty and good disposition to match. Two other women were in a car at the gas pump, parked just there beside James, Roselle, and Bonnie. James told the four ladies about his attempt at the Lewis and Clark route, going from west to east. Bonnie then took out a twenty dollar bill and offered it to James.

"That's very kind of you," said James, at once somber and heartfelt even as he declined.

"It's not because I think you're needy," said Bonnie, still holding out the twenty. "It's because I think you're doing a good thing, and I want to help."

James accepted and thanked Bonnie for her kind gift. The ladies then departed except for Roselle who remained with pen and pad at the ready. James begged Roselle's forgiveness, owning to his need for making camp before darkness fell and telling of his policy regarding all interviews.

Having learned James's plan to camp at the port, Roselle informed James that camping wasn't allowed there. She then made some inquires for James in hope that a tiny inn still existed in downtown Camas. Then, because the inn no longer existed, she gave instructions to an inn located three miles ahead in the small town of Washougal. James thanked Roselle kindly in the knowledge that she had saved him from wasting precious strength.

On his way to the inn, James stopped to eat at a burger joint and was happily surprised because UB didn't howl but contentedly watched through the glass from his place atop the cart. After eating, James proceeded east on Highway 14B, a four-lane blacktop. Traffic flowed heavily, there were no shoulders, and because James's rig measured 23-feet long and 3-feet wide, he felt uncertain about taking it on the sidewalk. So he remained on the road, praying that God protect the motorist, himself, and UB. No sooner had James finished his prayer when a police officer came alongside in his cruiser and courteously but professionally told James to get on the sidewalk because the highway was too dangerous. James happily obliged.

After pulling a total distance of 22 miles, James reached the inn. He unloaded his gear, secured his rig, and walked across the way for dinner. After dinner, James returned to his room and hit the sack. The time was 11:00pm.

Man and dog slept well.

Day 21, Thursday, June 3

After breakfast James decided to lie over for a day in order to reorganize his diet which had become a matter of pressing importance. He also hoped to catch up his journal and do laundry if possible. How he first met a lovely young lady named Sarah that morning wasn't recorded in his journal. However, it can be known that James had gone outside to check on his rig when first he saw the slender blond, dressed in soft shorts, getting something from the trunk of her car. Sarah had taken a room at the inn after a serious falling out with her husband. Sarah's parents lived far away but, mother was en route. Sarah would tell James as much but, just then, James only saw a beautiful blue-eyed girl of about 21 with no ring on her finger.

James and Sarah hadn't been speaking long when Roselle arrived with a plate of freshly baked oatmeal cookies. James thanked Roselle sincerely for her kind gift, then introduced the two women each of whom conducted herself in a manner that spoke to good breeding; the one young and beautiful, the other gray and wise. Sarah moved off a respectable distance to lean against a wooden pole where she lit a cigarette before turning her head to gaze at James.

James struggled momentarily, right or wrong, loneliness or lust, or both, he got a lid on it, and having mastered himself, he gave his full attention to the lady who had come for one reason and one reason alone, to help him survive the river.

"I photocopied a map of the port for you," said Roselle.

Taking map in hand, James saw how the layout of the port presented an unexpected problem. Roselle, it would seem, had once again saved him from difficulty. In fact, Roselle had been speaking with local fishermen and had obviously grasped that which lay just out of sight in a world where man had conquered nature even if only temporarily (she had sensed the dragon's presence).

"Roselle exercised such grace and tact even as she

voiced her concern for my welfare, it is a shame she wasn't captured on tape so that the old way might be preserved, that young ladies might know how to endear themselves to their men."

After Roselle departed, Sarah remained to speak with James for an hour. By then morning had nearly passed and James had much work to do. But there was Sarah, suffering some distress the source of which yet remained a mystery, not to mention she possessed every feature of physical beauty. How the two ended up sharing a high stair from which they sat overlooking the street cannot be known except to say that no sin passed between them. James didn't know what saddened Sarah, nor did he pry, but, after talking for another hour, Sarah confided (and it is suffice to say, she had cause to be blue). James assured Sarah that bad times would pass, adding only that one got to a better place one step at a time.

James and Sarah continued on various subjects until altogether they visited for a total of four hours. James then departed and walked a mile to the port where, due to inland rains, he saw high water and dangerous current—highly dangerous current.

From the port, James proceeded another mile to the post office where he mailed some photos home. He then continued to the grocery store and purchased a roast, bacon, eggs, bread, and the like. He also purchased a small Styrofoam cooler for which he had a special purpose. Then with arms fully loaded, he walked a mile back to the inn. In his room, he stored his food in the refrigerator. He then went for dinner across the way.

Returning to his room at 6:00pm, the Kansan felt dead tired as he laid out his gear and supplies for the purpose of reorganizing to accommodate a new diet. To begin, the small Styrofoam cooler fit perfectly inside his large plastic cooler, taking up only one third of the interior space. So James had a cooler within a cooler, in which to store meat and the like. In the remaining two thirds of the main cooler, James stored his bacon, eggs, fruit, and vegetables. He planned to cut the roast up into steaks. The tofu and egg-flavored powder would be left behind. As for the remaining dry food which had previously been stored in the cooler, James put it in one of his large duffles with other non-perishable provisions. By working hard, he completed his reorganization at 10:00pm. The added weight equaled that shed in Rainier but James didn't mind, he needed and looked forward to having real food. He caught his journal up at 11:30pm, then hit the sack and slept well.

Day 22, Friday, June 4

Just thinking about the swollen river put James's heart in his throat. In fact he seriously considered skipping it for the option of pulling the road. Throughout breakfast he thought about it. And even as he resolved to get back on the water, fear gripped him. He hoped to see Sarah again although he figured he shouldn't. He thought about stopping and knocking every time he carried a load of gear past her door. He imagined her in there, like sleeping beauty. Then, as he came to her door with the last armload, low and behold, her door opened.

Sporting soft shorts and t-shirt, Sarah leaned against the doorframe with a cereal bowl in one hand and a spoon in the other, her eyes fixed on his, "Hi James."

"Howdy," said James with all the deadpan surprise of a rabbit that gets hung in a snare. Indeed his errand hung in the balance, for there stood the damsel in distress, so very sweet and beautiful with all that sadness looking out from big blue eyes.

Sarah put a milky spoonful of cereal in her mouth and James got an idea, "Would you like some tofu with egg-flavored powder?" he asked, and continuing in complete earnest, "I was going to throw it away but, girls like tofu, don't you?"

"Yeah," said Sarah, smiling somewhat confusedly.

"I'll go and get it," said James. Then returning directly, he explained how to make tofu scrambled eggs. It was high-quality food after all, and Sarah seemed happy to have it.

The two stood in close proximity.

"Sarah," said James.

"Yeah."

"Take care."

"I will."

James could hardly say, "Goodbye." He pulled away in his walking machine and would later pray for Sarah's welfare and happiness.

No rain fell on that mild morning but as to whether the sun shone or not cannot be known due to James's focus on the business ahead. He made only one stop on his way to port, to get ice at a quick market where he took only a moment to speak with a man in a pickup truck who showed great enthusiasm. James then proceeded to the port where he began his land-to-water drill. First he unloaded his gear on a knoll above the docks, then took his empty rig down the hill, launched his canoe, and moored it to a dock. He then took the wheeled carriage back up the hill to disassemble it.

While James disassembled the carriage, a woman on a Harley motored into the park of the port, dismounted, and came walking toward him—,

"I've never seen a man pulling a canoe on wheels before," said she.

James slipped his wrench into his back pocket and took Sandy's hand, "Pleased to meet you."

Pretty and well made, Sandy appeared to be a young tomboy in leather and denim, "I saw you go past my workplace a few blocks back, and I told my co-worker I had to find out what you're about."

James told Sandy his business, then asked, "Do you like your Harley?"

"Oh yea," said Sandy, smiling broadly. "I just got it. I'd been wanting one for a long time."

Sandy pitched in and helped James carry loads of gear down the hill. They spoke while they worked, and when they had finished, the biker maiden asked the Kansan to be safe. He promised he would and they parted with a handshake.

Even at 120 miles from the coast, the ocean tide still affected the river. And because James was running late, the tide was going out but it no longer mattered because James had made up his mind, he wasn't going to wait for the tide to change. He felt ready. His gut told him it had to happen then. He wouldn't do himself any good by holding his nerve for hours before such a spectacle, swollen with rain and ripping with current.

Perhaps the dragon, having risen to his full measure, waited just outside the port gate. UB whined as if to tell his master, *"I don't want to go out there anymore."*

James charged out the gate. He charged to keep the ripping current from tossing him over and carrying him away. Then turning his craft to meet the river head on, he dug to overcome it. He had the wind at his back. His upper body was well rested. Yet try as he may, he could make no headway. He paddled desperately hard only to remain in place like a madman on a treadmill. At such a rate, he would soon be swept away. He could yet retreat, what with the port gate right beside him. Instead, he turned and charged into the middle of the river on a gamble that better water lay along the opposite shore. James had zero knowledge of what lay there, but he knew what must be done to get there—he had to fight through a mile-wide swath of ripping rapids and vortexes.

To his great relief, James found calmer water along the Oregon shore. Still, the going required all the endurance he could muster. Fortunately, he had gained more than he knew from three weeks of hard labor and human kindness. And James had also passed something of a crash course in the language of water. So he better understood what to aim for, and what to avoid. Therefore as his journal would say, he made his way on a sunny day.

Around a small point James fought to gain an easier patch of water where two fishermen sat anchored in their motorboat. At first the fishermen looked on as though the Kansan might be a few cards shy of a full deck, but they warmed up when James asked if they were having any luck. James didn't stop paddling because he couldn't afford to give up ground. So he bid them well as he paddled past and continued, yard by yard, into a series of islands along the south shore on a gradual bend in the river.

"I can do this," James told himself, laboring under a hot sun, making slow but steady progress.

Immediately after emerging from the islands, James lifted his eyes to Mt Hood. And while he couldn't have foreseen such a thing happening twice, once again he'd seen neither hide-nor-hair of a volcano until it filled the sky before him. Mount Hood stood like a white-robed king, a plum of steam, like a feather atop his shining helm. And below him, the Cascade Mountains stood like his soldiers, clad in evergreens, their snow helms aglow in sunbeams, their rock faces creased with rugged shadows.

His heart filled with wonder, James paddled toward the new realm but that wasn't the half of it, for no more had he rounded the last portion of the bend than the opening of the Columbia River Gorge came into view, and nothing could have prepared him for the view from his canoe.

Even at ten miles distance, the perfect U-shaped opening of the gorge seemed to stand directly ahead, shrouded in blue mountain haze, like a mystic gate on an unimaginable scale, rising up to the crystal sky.

"Oh, my!" said the Kansan, his drawl at once low, slow, and solemn, "Oh, my!"

As his errand demanded, James returned his attention to the business at hand where, according to his map, he should have made visual contact with a flood fence. The only problem was, he could see no sign of a fence. James didn't think the river so high as to cover the fence but rather wondered if he had not traveled far enough and therefore the fence was out of sight somewhere ahead. Or perhaps the fence had been removed by the Army Corp of Engineers who maintained the river. In fact the fence lay all but invisible beneath a thin sheen of flood water just 200 yards ahead. And because the strong but smooth-flowing backwater appeared to crawl with countless swirls and squiggles, it created a kind of natural camouflage that masked those disturbances which might otherwise betray the fence.

"At that moment, there came the only wakes I can recall on that day. The wakes came from a barge dieseling a half mile out. The wakes swept the entire field before me and, the fence was exposed in the troughs between the crests. In fact, the flowing series of crests and troughs made the fence appear to swim like a spiny sea monster."

The wakes subsided, the fence vanished, and the canoeist approached with caution until having drawn within yards, he saw the fence just an inch beneath the surface, shimmering like a ghost in the flux.

James knew better than to try and paddle around the fence. The current flowed impossibly strong out there. Nor could he paddle between fence and shore due to the lay of the land. With time and effort he could portage around the fence. However, if he could find an individual fence pole that lie an inch or two lower than the rest, he might be able to charge directly over the fence. James understood the danger. If the stern of his canoe caught atop the fence, the current would turn his craft sideways and roll him over. In such a scenario, anything that submerged to a depth of more than a few inches on the upstream side of the fence would be crushed.

"I didn't have a death wish. I wasn't out for a thrill. I didn't feel any need to prove myself. It wasn't about me. It was about something special in the hearts and minds of the pioneers who arrived at the shore of the Columbia River one-hundred and fifty years before, having already come thousands of miles through mountain ranges, deserts, and plains. The Columbia River made up the final leg of the Oregon Trail. Trail weary men, women, and children, they loaded their wagons and dreams on wooden rafts, then set out to run two-hundred miles of the most dangerous water anywhere on earth. It was an incredibly perilous thing to do, but then, it took such faith and courage to build the home of the brave and land of the free."

As mentioned, James used verse to relate that divine quality he called, "The Goodly Light."

"The Goodly Light,
had little families in wagon trains,
conquering mountains and windswept plains."

Due to limited resources, James knew he must make the journey in two years, and with 3,850 miles yet to cover, he could not afford to take the safest, longest, most time-consuming route every time he encountered danger.

The canoeist cased the fence by paralleling it, searching for a weak spot. Then, having spied a low piling, he turned away, arced round in a wide circle and came back toward the fence at the equivalent of a trot. Reestablishing visual contact with the low piling, James charged on a beeline so as not to miss his mark. Then, as he cleared the piling, the stern of his craft scraped on it. He came that close, but that was what it took. A half-mile later, he repeated the process, charging over a second flood fence. James next landed on a rocky but favorable shore and ate a cold lunch beneath Interstate 84 which had come to parallel the river with only a veil of green vegetation separating the two.

After lunch, James made slow but steady progress, gaining ground yard by yard for three miles. Then arriving before the mouth of what looked like a small slough, James entered it in the assumption that it rejoined the river further upstream. By entering the slough, James hoped to get a break from the powerful current. Soon however, James began to wonder if it wasn't a slough he had entered, but a primitive road. The flooded road gradually narrowed to become a flooded footpath in a willow thicket. Questioning the wisdom of continuing, James used his paddle like a pole to push his canoe along. Thus he proceeded squeezing through the thicket for another two-hundred yards until the path broke out to rejoin the river.

"We're not taking any more uncharted sloughs," James told UB.

No more had man and dog exited the thicket than they saw an island, half of which looked like a patch of Sahara desert with flowing sand dunes beneath a cliff that rose to the other half of the island, being a miniature forest of evergreens. It was a jewel of an island, set directly before the opening of the gorge.

Having landed on the island beach, the first thing to catch our sinner's attention was a sunbathing woman. Wearing nothing but a black g-string, she lay like a model atop the deck of a motorboat which had been beached on the sandy shore. No more had James approached her however than he realized she wasn't a woman.

Filled with disgust, James walked past without a word. Then spotting an older gentleman in a lawn chair, James continued toward the man but due to his angle of approach, James couldn't see until the last that the man was completely unclothed. Abruptly changing direction, James hadn't gone far when he saw a third man strolling willy-nilly across the sand, and he also was naked. More telling yet was the complete absence of women.

Going on a long shot that the other side of the island might be more to his liking, James walked to a sandy ridge and looked down the other side where he saw a father, mother, and several children playing on a beach beside their motorboat. All appeared normal there and, looking further up the beach on that same side of the island, a group of teens were having a beach party.

"I see what's going on here," James told UB, taking measure from the ridge top. "One side of the island is for 'straight' folks and, the other side is not."

Man and dog returned to their canoe with intentions of paddling to the other side and making camp but, no more had they shoved off than a man called out, "Wait!"

The Kansan turned his head, his eyes burning as if to say, *"Don't even think it!"*

"Over there," the man said with a scolding air, and he pointed across the water to a shoreline where a group of teenagers appeared to be in the process of deciding whether or not they should attempt to swim out to the island. Normally there would have been a land bridge connecting island with shore at low tide according to the map. Currently however, there was flood water.

At once James arrested his forward progress and waited to see what the teens would do. Knowing he couldn't hold his position for long in the current between island and shore, James remained along the island shore, saving his strength for an all-out charge should any of the teens get into trouble. Among the teens, four decided to attempt the 100-yard-wide swath of flood water. And while cause for concern, it wasn't an altogether uncommon thing for kids to do. The teens used the breast stroke, and the current taxed them, but the three boys and one girl made it across.

Next the younger teens that remained behind began to cross. "Turn back!" shouted one of the original four teens, standing breathless on the island shore, "Turn back! The current is too strong!"

Across the channel, the five or six youths obviously could not hear. Therefore in confusion they continued, whereupon the original four began shouting in unison at the top of their lungs, "Go back! The current is too strong!"

James felt relieved to see the younger kids turn around. They couldn't have made it. Meanwhile, the old man in the lawn chair may have put a towel in his lap so as not expose himself to the youths, but his actions cannot be known. What can be known was that the teens had to walk through all that on their way to the "straight" side of the island.

"The island was located right beside a busy interstate and adjoining a popular public park just outside a thriving city. A great many people had to know about it. I'm not gay but if I was, I would be telling my friends in Portland, 'Hey fellows, let's be the first to get out to that island and tell our guys to stop it! Let's get them to put aside their personal inner-entanglements long enough to see that what they're doing is bad for children, bad for us, bad for our Nation, bad for everyone.' "

    James felt relieved to find that the straight side of the island commanded a better view. In fact it was awesome, facing both the open river and the opening of the gorge just a mile upstream. James selected an excellent campsite on a flat patch of sand beside a bush that acted as a windbreak. His wristwatch read 6:30pm.
    After establishing his camp, James sat on his cooler trying to fix his water filter. He hadn't bothered to read the directions because the thing looked self-explanatory. The only problem was that it had broken almost immediately.
    "This confounded thing," James said, struggling with it. Then getting out the directions, he read how the user must be patient because if the handle were pumped too hard, the ceramic filter inside could rupture and become good for nothing—,
    "Darn."
    James yet had filter in hand when along came a man wearing a huge backpack, heavy hiking boots, and nothing more! The Kansan set his jaw and stared as though to say, *"Get the hell back over to your side of the island!"*
    The man did not enter James's camp but walked off without a word, although clearly in a huff. James then resumed work on his water filter but try as he may, he couldn't fix it. The wind then came up strong and, James saw a storm on the approach.
    Using his spare paddle for a shovel, James had only begun a rain trench when a powerful gust ripped up all the tent stakes and, in a move worthy of note, James caught his tent in midair. From then on every task became a challenge that had James finishing his preparations in near darkness. Then between lashing tent walls, he could only hope he'd tied everything down well enough. His wristwatch read 10:15pm.
    James slept well.

Day 23, Saturday, June 5

James woke to find the island deserted. Not only were there no people, even their footprints had been erased. Meanwhile, the sky hung just overhead like a heavy black quilt. The wind blew, and all had become wet and bone chilly.

The Kansan cooked and ate his breakfast while huddled against a bush beside his camp. Rain water dripped from cowboy hat to plate where, along with salt and pepper, there wasn't any shortage of wet sand. James's journal reads as follows:

> "I had bacon and eggs, with toast, orange juice, and coffee. Real food! The weather was horrible. The food was delicious! UB begged and got the bacon grease."

After breakfast, James worked on his journal in his tent. He hoped for traveling conditions to improve but when he caught up his journal at 2:15pm, the wind still bore cold rain by the bucket load. So James lay in a positive state of mind, thinking about all the kind people he'd met, and ten minutes scarcely passed before his tent walls glowed with sunshine.

James went outside, wiped water off his cooler, and sat for a lunch of tuna, summer sausage, a green bell pepper, an orange, two slices of bread, and a food bar. UB begged and got tidbits. The rain then returned and sent man and dog back into their tent.

"Our home just keeps getting smaller," James said to UB, petting and joking. "First we lived in a big house, then we lived in a small house, then in a motor home, and now, here we are in a tent."

With his journal caught up and his gear in order, James laid back and looked back on the day prior. At times he'd paddled for all his worth, fighting for every yard. At other times he'd paddled in easier water, whistling "Turkey in the Straw." He made up songs like "Paddlin' Fool." And of course, he could not forget seeing the opening of the gorge for the first time.

Presently wishing to see the opening again, James unzipped his tent and looked out through falling rain to see what looked like a great dark tunnel into which the river vanished. Lying back, James felt a might sick to his stomach and wondered if he'd accidentally used too many chlorine drops that morning because his drinking water tasted like a swimming pool. At last, he smiled and thought it funny that he had time to worry about such things. He noticed he'd worn the skin off his thumb while paddling the day before. He got out a dental mirror and looked inside his mouth where one of his molars had become infected. The infection had begun back home while making preparations for his journey. He had ignored it while racing toward his May 14 deadline. Since then, the infection had grown worse.

At 7:20pm the rain stopped, and going out, James had just gotten dinner started when it began to rain again so he tucked under the eve of the bush as best he could. Moderate rain made the slopes look misty while heavy rain could be seen coming along behind like a curtain. James didn't feel bad about the rain however because dinner called for two cups of water and, having no water filter, he'd been collecting rainwater from a tarp. James finished cooking as the heavy rain arrived. Then in the cozy shelter of his tent, he ate kung-po chicken and fell fast asleep.

While the knight slept, perhaps the dragon crept up on the beach (like in that cartoon where the coyote tries to catch the roadrunner) while sporting a pair of night vision goggles. Or perhaps he simply rose up out of the river like the giant he was and, filling his lungs to capacity, blew cold rain like fire from his mouth. Whatever the case, the knight awoke to a storm so fierce, his tent seemed on the verge of blowing apart. James prayed for protection while using his entire body to shore his tent from the inside, pressing hands and feet into the corners. And while not recorded, there must have been some relenting after which he fell back to sleep.

The Gorge
Chapter IV

Day 24, Sunday, June 6

James thought it great to be eating real food as he huddled under the eve of the bush with drops of rainwater falling from hat to plate. He had eggs on toast with bacon and orange juice. Directly after breakfast, the rain abated and James leapt into action. No more had he gotten his tent dried off and put away than the rain returned. James had yet to develop a consistent habit of timekeeping but probably, he shoved off at 8:00am.

In light rainfall, the canoeist paddled toward the mouth of the gorge a mile ahead. His journal tells of cloud puffs hanging about mountain slopes as though stuck in the trees like cotton balls, slowly dissolving under a black quilt that hid the mountain tops.

James entered the gorge, his journal reads as follows:

"I was so small. My heart swelled with the majesty of it all."

And:

"The rain increased, then came down like cats and dogs. I kept paddling, I had no choice [at that point]."

Rain came in soaking downpours with moderate rain between. One soaking downpour after another until, for the only time in James's journey, his waterproof parka became inundated. James added a fleece which helped to keep him dry. UB wasn't so fortunate, shivering and groaning in the hull. James worried for UB and still he had to keep paddling, moving one yard at a time up the vast river while swift current, cold wind, and downright violent downpours kept coming.

Eventually feeling he could take no more, James looked skyward and, wanting it to stop, he shouted, "GOD!" Immediately and very abruptly, a large wave broke over the stern and hit James square on the seat of his pants.

After a few minutes (and in the knowledge that until that point in his journey waves had crashed over his craft from every angle except the stern) James tried to make a mends, "Can't have life without rain." And the rain continued.

Upon finding a gentle riff of rocky shoreline, the Kansan stopped to tackle the problem of keeping his dog dry. He elevated UB's bed inside the boat, put a dry towel atop the dog bed, and put a sweater on UB. James also ate a quick lunch of summer sausage, apple, bread, a green bell pepper, and an energy bar. Then he was off again.

After paddling a total of 4.5 miles, James arrived at a group of three fishing boats anchored helter-skelter beside the shipping lane which no longer bore ocean freighters but river barges. And in fact a barge could be seen two miles upstream, coming toward the canoeist and fishermen who waited it out at the downstream end of Horsetail Flats between Multnomah Falls and Skamania Island. The fishermen looked ready for the North Sea in their heavy rubberized rain suits. James only waved in the poor conditions and they waved back. Then for sound reasons, the canoeist suddenly charged into the shipping lane, into the path of the barge coming on from two miles away.

"HEY!" yelled one of the fishermen in a tone that said, *"Don't do that!"*

But James had to cross the river there, and there wasn't any point in waiting on the barge. He fought through the ripping lane on an angle and then continued into the wide waters of Horsetail Flats. He beat the barge by a mile, but then, he had only done what he must. He crossed Horsetail Flats on a two-mile angle and felt no small relief in gaining the far shore.

In addition to learning the language of water, James had learned to use the wind. For example, in the aforementioned river crossing, James had purposefully ruddered and angled to maximize the effect of the wind that came upriver to glance off the side of his canoe like a sail. Time and time again, the canoeist would employ the wind as tiebreaker between himself and the current.

James continued paddling east along the north shore in what would be the wettest day of his journey. And certainly, it must have been a big Pacific weather front that had come against the mountains to pour into the gorge the way it had. For it came into the gorge like the spillway of a dam, the result being an almost black river of water-laden clouds flowing above. Indeed, James could see both rivers; the river above and the river below, with the walls of the gorge forming a tunnel between. And while one wouldn't have thought it an ideal day for sightseeing, the waterfalls were beautiful, pouring down from high cliffs.

At approximately 4:00pm, James went scouting for a campsite on a primitive beach. The only problem was that every inch of level ground stood under an inch of water. UB meanwhile, having done his dog duty, remained in his bed under the eve of the tarp with orders to stay put. James scouted further but found no patch of ground drier then a soaking wet sponge. Then turning back toward his boat, he saw UB having the time of his life, rolling on the beach which, as mentioned lie under an inch of water.

"No!" James shouted, upset in the knowledge that UB would be soaking wet then become cold, miserable, a possibly hypothermic.

"UB! Stop!"

Seeing his master coming full trot, the little terrier bolted for the boat.

"Stay!" James yelled, fearing the soaking wet creature would retreat to his bed which would then become wet, thus making it impossible to maintain his warmth.

> "There had been a time at the onset of our journey when UB couldn't get into the boat. Back then, he would try and then whine while looking to me for a lift over the gunwale."

Presently, UB cleared the gunwale like a gazelle. And sure enough, he got in his bed which became nearly as wet as himself. Being a matter of survival, James reached in and got UB by the nap of his neck. Then drawing him out, James brought UB up like a bear cub, "This is serious business out here alright, so you obey me!"

James dried UB off as best he could, then dug out UB's spare sweater. UB meanwhile shivered as though he were hypothermic, or scared, or both. James took the wet cotton blanket away from the dog bed in the knowledge that the bed itself consisted of dense nylon fibers which could not hold water. Additionally, UB's spare sweater consisted of high-tech material courtesy of an expensive outdoor shirt Frank had recently given to James. The shirt was drab blue and skin tight with a zipper in front like something a kayaker would wear. Frank didn't know it but James had cut the shirt up into a dog sweater (lucky for UB). With UB taken care of, James shoved off and continued east.

Another violent downpour came, then another, and another until James thought it so wet he could have tossed a fish in the air and it would have swam into the sky like a bird.

Alas it began to hail, but James could only laugh because by then he had already made eight miles in tough conditions and, as a result, he paddled on the cusp of reaching Bonneville Dam, his first major milestone. Therefore as hailstones bounced like popcorn from the tarp, and even though James had no visual contact with the dam several miles ahead, he knew in his heart, he'd already won the day.

Soon the hail tapered off, the wind died, and the water surface laid down flat. Then in a dead calm, the rain returned like James could not believe. Truly he marveled even as he bailed water from his boat. Never in all his life had James seen rain so heavy. But that wasn't the half of it, for even as the rain boiled the water, the gorge was suddenly illuminated as though an angel had thrown a switch to let in the sunbeams, and everywhere the sunbeams struck the boiling surface, a fiery veil sprung up to dance upon the river, shimmering red, yellow, blue, and green. It lasted but a minute, an awe-inspiring minute, until the sunbeams vanished and the rain moderated.

James next arrived at an eddy which only a force like the Columbia River could produce. The powerful eddy lay along the north shore directly after a narrow through which the river passed. James guessed the eddy to measure 175 X 300 yards in diameter. It spun in a clockwise rotation which made the river flow backward along the north shore. Thus seeking to capitalize on an obvious windfall, the canoeist paddled hard to maximize speed—,

"Boy howdy UB," said James as the shoreline flew past, "We may as well have a motor on the back of this thing!"

The eddy took the canoeist to the cusp of the narrow which consisted of a single land point to get around. The current turned against him there and, he just did get through. He then paddled one mile further to Beacon Rock State Park. The approximate time was 6:30pm. James had made ten miles as the crow flies.

Although not visible from Beacon Rock State Park, Bonneville Dam stood directly around the bend and James regarded it as a major milestone. And having gained it, even while he couldn't yet see it, he felt a profound sense of satisfaction.

> "There wasn't any time to celebrate but that was alright, the feeling of accomplishment was deeply gratifying and greatly rewarding."

James began the amphibious process. First he cleaned his gear, rinsing sand and dirt from his large plastic gear locker, ice chest, six rubberized duffle bags and one elongated duffle that held his sleeping pad. He also cleaned the various pieces of his walking machine. He carried his gear to a picnic bench on a grassy shore above the dock. He cleaned his canoe, then brought out his tools and began the business of assembling his walking machine. Meanwhile, a good many fishermen came and went—,

"I saw you on the river today," said a fisherman of about thirty years who looked like he may have been an All-American in high school. "Where are you going?"

James stood from his work, "Sir, to answer your question, I hope to reach St Louis. My name is James and I come from Kansas to attempt the Lewis and Clark route west to east. I began at the Pacific Ocean on May 14, and today I'm feeling good because I've made the first dam.

"Would you like a beer?" asked the fisherman.

"No thank you Sir," James replied. "I've got much to do yet."

"Well, would you like a soda pop?" the fisherman then asked.

"No thank you Sir, but I appreciate your kind offer."

Suddenly the fisherman flicked something like a John Elway pass across the water which, had James not caught, may have stuck to his chest.

"At least take that," said the fisherman, smiling.

"Thank you," James confusedly replied, not knowing what he held. In fact he held a bag of beef jerky which he ate while he worked. Meanwhile the fisherman moored his craft on the other side of the floating plank way where he also worked to get his gear in order.

"Sir, if I may ask?" the Kansan began. "Today I saw the river flash over like a rainbow, and I don't mean kind of, I mean it was glowing." Then pausing briefly, "Did you see it?"

"Yes, I saw it."

"I've never seen anything like that," said James, "Was that a rare event?"

"It happens now and then," replied the fisherman, his smile a mixture of amusement and admiration.

In a small green park above the dock, James got just enough of a break in the rain to pitch his tent. And when wet and exhausted in raw wind and rain, a perfectly timed pause in the weather wasn't taken for granted. UB meanwhile came out of his makeshift shelter to look on as if getting the tent up were a matter of life and death. Indeed, the little fellow shivered like a leaf, for he had truly suffered on that day.

Good thing UB had two beds, one for the canoe and one for the tent. So when James had thoroughly toweled UB off, he put him on a clean dry bed and covered him with a special blankie (made from the body of the aforementioned shirt). UB curled up on his bed and fell fast asleep. Perhaps he dreamt of endless meadows filled with rabbits and sunshine. Or perhaps he dreamt of the pretty miniature Collie who had lived across the street, back in the day, before his master had heard the voice (in his heart) that made him leave "normal" life behind.

While UB slept inside, James sat outside eating his dinner in the rain. He ate a large package of salmon, several slices of bread, a food bar, an orange-flavored vitamin drink, and an apple. By then four hours had passed since he landed, and in those four hours he had worked solid; taking care of UB, cleaning his gear, hauling loads of gear, assembling his walking machine, and striking camp.

Next came the task of drying his coat. James would have built a lean-to and dried his water-logged jacket over a fire if only he'd been traveling with Lewis and Clark in 1804. In 2004, he went to the public bathroom and dried his parka courtesy of a wall-mounted electric hand dryer. At least the lightweight coat dried quickly. James hit the sack at 11:00pm. Then with the sound of cold rain pelting his tent, being warm and dry never felt so good.

James slept like a rock.

Day 25, Monday, June 7

"PARK RANGER!" said a voice, piercing through tent walls with draconian authority.

James startled from sleep, "Oh!"

"YOU ARE ILLEGALLY CAMPED!"

James unzipped his tent and peered out through blurry eyes to see a green ranger uniform standing tall in gray morning light. Not only that, the robust woman who filled the uniform looked all business.

"Ma'am, I thought this was the campground."

"The campground's over there," the officer replied, pointing forty yards yonder.

James apologized and then explained what he was about. The good officer did not fine James but gave him time to move. The officer then departed. The time was 8:00am and the sky looked like rain. James skipped breakfast and broke camp in double-time. And because he had only cleaned the heavy dirt from his gear on the night before, plenty wet sand remained, so he cleaned his gear while stowing it away. The weather held and James stood ready to go by 10:00am. His first order of business was to find a fisherman who could tell him how to regain the river above the dam. Thus learning he would have to pull his rig ten miles around the dam with some hills along the way; James figured he'd better eat breakfast before setting out. He had no time for cooking, so he ate raw eggs and was surprised by the energy boost.

James never took any performance-enhancing drugs. Rather, he received what he needed from above.

> "In a manner of speaking, God had reached down and given me a vial of His own Spirit. Anyone who has faith can receive it. So it isn't given lightly. For while God may not require a man to make the ultimate sacrifice, certainly He expects him to appreciate those who have. For example, the pilgrims received God's Spirit, and they boarded the Mayflower, and within a year, half were dead and the other half had suffered terribly. But the pilgrims were not fools, they understood their dream to be an impossible one and still they went forward, and such is the power of faith, that

nearly 400 years later, their dream still lives."

James wrote the following verse regarding that unexplainable threshold where Reason ends and Faith begins, where men and women willingly put their lives on the line, and go forward with the "Goodly Light" in their hearts.

> "As pilgrims put to sea,
> and old world sank from sight,
> their minds besieged with fright,
> the goodly light sustained
> man and woman alike, who
> through trial of faith,
> became the wind in the
> sails of a new world."

James set off with his walking machine, and as he went he felt happy because one way or another, he was getting the job done. Within a short distance man and dog wound through the State Park, passed a clean little rural trailer court, and reached Highway 14.

Before beginning upon the highway, James observed a problem: There were no shoulders on which he might pull his rig but only a guardrail going round a mountain curve. Beyond the curve there was a wide shoulder but to get there James would have to pull on the highway itself. In addition to that, the guardrail would hide his slow-moving-vehicle sign from any motorist coming up behind (not to mention logging trucks). On the positive side, James could see a considerable distance looking west down the eastbound lane, and because the mountain curve had a concave radius as opposed to a convex radius, James knew he would be able to maintain good visual contact with the road behind. Therefore when the lane had emptied, he set out pulling as fast as he could, all the while keeping an eye out over his shoulder. He prayed as he went, asking the Lord to protect the motorists, himself, and UB.

As it turned out, no eastbound traffic came until James had gotten safely around the curve. From that point on, Highway 14 had a good shoulder except for a few places, but even then, nothing as bad as that first curve.

Upon reaching the tiny town of North Bonneville, James

stopped at a quick-market where he purchased a hoagie sandwich appropriately called the "Eighteen Wheeler." He also ate chips and drank a cranberry juice. James then set out pulling past Bonneville dam, the first dam to be built on the Columbia River.

No sooner had James passed Bonneville Dam than he looked down expecting to see an elongated lake. To his surprise there was no placid lake but only the same old river ripping with current.

With his hopes dashed, the Kansan shook his head in disbelief. He had done some scouting from his car on his way to the ocean but, as previously mentioned, it didn't do him much good. Fortunately, the river would widen a few miles upstream and the current would lessen as a result. As for the weather, James made the following entry:

> "The day was cool and overcast with some very light rain, perfect for pulling the road."

Up and down hills and around bends went the Kansan and his dog until having pulled ten miles, they arrived at the community of Stevenson which sat tucked alongside the river at the bottom of the gorge.

James had scarcely taken twenty steps inside the city limit when he met Tom and Cheryl, and Tim and Holly with their young son Morgan. Both were married couples who owned local businesses.

James told what he was about as always.

Tom then said, "You're the first man to make the dam."

"What?" James asked.

"No man has ever made it this far," Tom replied. "There was one fellow who nearly made it to the dam but, he drowned just shy of it."

"I can't believe that," James said courteously, intending no disrespect.

"I've lived here my entire life," Tom said, taking no offence even as he spoke with certainty. He then echoed what he'd said before, "You're the first man to make it to the dam."

James must have looked a little dumb as he confusedly shook his head. Meanwhile inside his brain, the newly gained information must have been racing toward the glory department for processing when, something like a trap door opened and, the information fell out of his memory.

Tom gave James his business card and said, "Call me if you need help with anything."

Holly then told James that, if he liked, he could come by her restaurant for a free meal. The Kansan thanked the good lady for her hospitality and promised to do so. He then asked if any camp-grounds were nearby and, learning there were none, he asked where he might find an inexpensive inn.

James entered the inn at the other end of town only to learn they didn't accept dogs. However, the clerk knew of another inn and, proceeding there, James met Angus the inn keeper. Angus showed James to a luxury cabin overlooking the river with green lawns and gardens. James decided the luxury cabin would be his reward for making the dam but only with regard to the dam as a milestone because in all truth James couldn't recall what Tom had told him. James would hear Tom's words repeated in days ahead, and he would always have the same reaction which was to totally forget what he'd been told. So he made no record of it in his journal even as he recorded his meetings with those who had given him the info. Only on the verge of paddling into St Louis would James recall the information. And he would be the first to tell, he gave himself a big advantage with his walking machine.

UB was so delighted with the luxury cabin, he probably thought the journey over and by some miracle they'd been returned to their former life. He wolfed his dog food and fell straight to sleep. James unloaded his gear and secured his rig, then walked a block to town for a steak, baked potato, and salad. He didn't go to Holly's because at that time Holly's restaurant served breakfast and lunch only. After dinner James retired to his cabin where he slept well.

Day 26, Tuesday, June 8

At Holly's restaurant, it wasn't easy for James to decide which he enjoyed more, eating good food or seeing a young entrepreneur work toward a dream. In addition to serving food, Holly had recently purchased two large ovens with which to bake bread for the area. Himself having been there, James would always have a soft spot in his heart for small business owners like Holly.

Returning to his cabin, James went about the business of checking and cleaning his gear. UB checked and cleaned his paws. James next went to work on his journal in which he wrote, *"There is so much to record."*

At lunchtime James went to town, ordered a hamburger at the eatery, and then went across the street to the tourist information center where he hoped to get a new map because his old map had ended at Bonneville Dam. The ladies at the visitor's center had no river maps. However, they did fix James up with two county road maps which included the river. James thanked the good ladies for their considerable effort and then returned to the eatery where he ate his hamburger while working on his journal. Back at the inn, James received help from Angus who made phone calls in hope of locating a river map. Angus's efforts were note worthy but in the end James would have to make do without. For the record, James's old river map had a phone number printed on it with which to order a new map covering the next section of river, but because the phone number was all but hidden, neither James nor Angus found it. Angus next showed James his sea kayak, and although a die-hard canoeist, James thought the sea kayak an awesome craft.

Shortly after viewing the sea kayak, James called home via a wall-mounted payphone just outside the inn's laundry mat. The laundry mat was housed in the main cabin along with the lobby and inn keeper's quarters, so it faced the parking lot and, if James lived to be a hundred, he would not forget what happened there. A car pulled up with the sun in its windshield, and out of it stepped a maiden of such rare beauty and form, she may as well have come from the pages of a storybook.

"Hello," said she, smiling at James.

"Hello," James echoed, intoxicated on the very sight of her, helpless even to take his eyes from her.

In the next instant, the maiden had gone on to the business of renting a cabin.

"Are you there?" asked a voice from the telephone. "James? Are you there?"

> "I couldn't help that such a woman had walked passed any more than I could stop being a man. A lonely man, with hope, dreams, and yes, lust. God knew it, and so did the

devil."

James's journal becomes a bit confused at this point but only in regard to the steps that brought him to the garden where he and the maiden would properly meet. As best the scene can be re-constructed: James returned to his room where, although love struck, he would not scheme to meet her even though he wanted to meet her very badly. After all, he had to stay focused on reaching St Louis, so he took his tent fly outside to shake it out, or dry it out, or something. While outside, James went to check on his laundry and because the shirt he wore wasn't completely clean, he took it off on an impulse and threw it in with the rest of the wash. James then set out for his cabin but, being without a shirt, he donned his tent fly like a golden robe (which he closed at the chest because after all, he wasn't living in the 70s).

Just outside the inn's laundry mat, the walk path split in two with the shorter path leading directly to James's cabin. The long path also led to his cabin but only after first winding around all the other cabins. With only a brief pause, James chose the long path in hope of a chance encounter with a woman whose name he did not know.

So the love struck Kansan in the golden robe went upon the garden path hoping with every step for something that seemed impossible when, as fortune would have it, the maiden stepped out on her porch at the exact moment he came round the corner.

Down the steps came Amy, smiling like sunshine.

Inside James's chest, his heart issued a final command for his brain, "Watch the shop."

"But master," the brain called after the heart in an injured tone, "I'm your high seneschal."

"Indeed you are," the heart replied as he flew away, "and like a good servant, you shall remain at your post."

So it was, James and Amy met in the garden outside her door. Amy had come from southern California and, low and behold, she had a little dog who at that very moment could be seen looking out from the screen door of her cabin. So James and Amy immediately had something to share besides their interest in one another (being their love of dogs). In fact James and Amy hit it off so good, both were soon sitting Indian-style on the garden path with scarcely any distance between, talking as though each were more than a little happy for meeting the other. The knight didn't tell the maiden about his fights with the dragon but rather, about the people who had helped him along the way. He told her they were like angels, and she understood his meaning without need of explanation. Meanwhile, so sweetly and completely electrifying was she, he would find himself at a loss for describing her.

"Happiness filled Amy's gaze and, when added to her awesome physical nature, made her a true icon of beauty. She must have grown up well protected which kept her innocent and wholesome even while, under the surface, tenacity flowed in her pioneer blood. In fact Amy looked to be the All American Girl. She may have been twenty-four but whatever her age, so radiant did she appear, as to be in the prime of life. And last but not least, if clothes betrayed the woman, then the woman was a classic good girl."

James had all but forgotten what trail he was on when, out of the blue, a second woman appeared from the cabin. The second woman (who looked to be Amy's mother) crossed the porch to stand at the rail where she gave James a stern stare.

Amy stood up at once and said, "James, this is my friend Jill."

"Pleased to meet you Jill" said James, also standing, yet to recognize that the two girls on vacation were, almost beyond doubt, mother and daughter (physical resemblance currently being masked by their radically different states; one happy, and the other unhappy).

"It's time for us to be going," said Jill to Amy.

Amy turned to James, "Jill and I were about to go to dinner, would you care to join us?" Then turning her eyes to Jill, Amy looked for approval.

Thawed by Amy's hope, Jill turned to James and said, "You're welcome to join us."

James accepted and then begged their pardon so that he might go to his room for his wallet and whatnot.

Like a good boy scout, James had an extra t-shirt in his emergency duffle which he emptied on the bed along with dry socks and pants, space blanket, matches, food bars, water purification pills, first-aid supplies, etc. James put the t-shirt on and went to join the ladies at a restaurant one-half block away.

At the seafood restaurant, the ladies ate lightly while James loaded up, eating his baked potato skin and all so that not one atom remained on his plate.

"Is your dog alright?" Amy asked.

"He's fine," James replied.

"He sure can howl," said Amy.

"That's why I put him over there," and James turned to look out the window where UB sat tied to a pole across the street and well away from everything except a set of railroad tracks. No one in the restaurant could hear UB but there in the window pane, something of a silent movie played out: UB threw his head back over and over, howling like a lone wolf while Amy's little dog looked out from a car window.

Having cut her food into small pieces, Amy ate two or three bites before asking the waitress for a carry-out box.

"What's the matter hon'?" asked the waitress. "Is it not to your liking?"

"Oh, no," Amy replied. "It's very good." Then with innocent glee, she pointed to her plate with her fork and added, "This is for my dog."

At that moment, James's brain crept up behind his heart with a rag soaked in formaldehyde, so to speak, and put the heart to sleep. It happened even as James remained unaware of it. Then in the wake of the coup, erroneous charges were drawn up against the heart for chasing after an impossible ideal. More serious however were charges for endangerment of mission.

James turned his eyes to Jill, "Jill, if I may ask, have you ever been married?"

Jill replied that she had been married for twenty-four years and had just been divorced. The stay-at-home-homemaker had two adult daughters. And if James understood correctly, Jill's husband had left her for a young woman.

"I have the greatest respect for you," said James.

"So do I," said Amy, turning to Jill with the tone and look of a loving daughter.

"Thank you," said Jill, momentarily shedding her dire expression, glancing between them both.

James appeared to be a little older than Amy when in fact he was probably a little older than Jill. It is true, he had grown that young!

But that was not the half of what made him attractive to the ladies, nor would he ever know or even stop to think about it, at least not until he had completed his errand. Then he saw it, but only after its shine had faded to become like a bed of embers in a hearth that had once blazed.

Presently, James drew an unspoken response from both women when he said, "I hope to get married when my journey is over, although I know not to whom."

Jill and Amy exchanged glances and then became more serious but only in a good way, hence the conversation continued. Then as they were quitting the restaurant, the ladies decided that James should have their e-mail address. And because Amy was "a bit transient just then," as Jill put it, Jill would give her e-mail with which James could reach Amy. James could pick up the e-mail address back at the inn. He needed only to stop by their cabin. So James and UB walked the half-block to the inn. Meanwhile, Jill and Amy drove but not because they were lazy. Rather, they had obviously taken their car as a place to keep Amy's dog because dogs were not allowed to stay in the cabins alone. James would have done the same for UB if he could.

At the inn, James knocked and Amy let him in. James closed the door, then remained standing a step inside. He had entered from the side of the cabin facing the street. Therefore he had entered into the bedroom at the back of the cabin. The fragrance of women filled his nostrils while lamplight fell soft upon a bed to his left. Amy sat looking up at him, just there on a plush footstool beside a matching chair. Across the bed, Jill leaned over a night stand, writing on a scrap of white paper.

"There," Jill said, putting down her pen, rising to look across the bed at James.

What happened next came without warning. The lamp on the night stand illuminated Jill, betraying her own very considerable beauty. For three long seconds she held his gaze, whereupon his heart awoke to the voice of his brain, telling him that perhaps it was she whom he should love. And unless his eyes deceived him, she had the same thought, and just as unexpectedly. A second wave of realization then swept over Jill. Her entire countenance changed. She looked as though she'd caught herself on the verge of doing something awful. And pushing the scrap of paper to James, her eyes went directly to Amy—,

"For Amy," was all Jill said, just two impassioned words to betray a mother's love.

Amy sat looking back and forth between Jill and James. Her mouth had come open, her eyes gone wide with confusion. And certainly James felt confused, for his heart had become servant to his brain!

"That's my e-mail address," Jill added, "but you can reach Amy with it."

James bid the ladies well and departed.

Back in his room, James needed sleep something fierce, but he had much to do. So he worked on his gear until midnight and then slept heavily.

Day 27, Wednesday, June 9

Deep in a dream, James heard a faint tap at the door beside his bed. He came around slowly, then got up and put his clothes on. The time was 8:00am. He felt Amy had been at his door. He went on the garden path, around the corner where first they'd met.

If ever James made a sad sigh, he certainly did upon finding that Amy had gone. Their little garden, just yesterday so full of spring, seemed to have suffered a frost overnight. So it was, the Kansan turned back toward his cabin. He wasn't so aware of what went on inside him but certainly the coup had been crushed in the night, the heart had been restored to its throne, the rebel brain shackled in a dungeon.

"It's not like a little wisdom is going to hurt us," the brain shouted, albeit his voice seemed somewhere far away, buried in the bowels of a castle.

"Wisdom?" mocked the heart, "From you, the very one who has cost me my happiness?"

"Master," pled the brain, "it's not my fault. After all, it was you who fell asleep. Do you remember? You dropped off during dinner, upon learning how Amy meant to give her food away to her dog."

"Yes," the heart ruefully replied, "I recall it now. And I can only imagine going before my Maker with such a sin as hers to confess." The heart then cried out, "IF ONLY MY OWN SINS WERE SO SMALL!"

The Kansan had all but gone back into his cabin when from the corner of his eye, he caught sight of a paper towel hanging like a scarf from the front of his walking machine.

Amy's note read sweet. She wished James well on his journey and said they would be cheering him on from California. She asked him to please send a photo of himself and "Yubi." She closed with a little something about angels, whereupon signing her name, she reiterated her e-mail address.

"Master," said the brain, "even I must admit, Amy isn't just any beauty. She is the very icon of an ideal and there's nothing wrong with that. Moreover, her character was genuine even if she might perhaps have told a little fib in an attempt to impress you. As for her wholesome nature, well, she might just be the last of a long-lost vintage, the Southern California Girl. You, on the other hand, are an aging knight from Kansas, 'on an errand for God and country.'"

"Very nicely stated my long-winded servant," said the heart. "Now come to the point!"

"Master, I'm going to speak to you in secret now, by way of our subconscious link, so you won't hear me, but you'll know what I say: *Master, other than paying Amy the common courtesy of a reply, you must forget about her.*"

A rumble something like thunder rolled down into the dungeon with such force, it shook the foundation.

"For the sake of our errand you must!" insisted the brain, entirely unswayed. "Master, if only we lived in the pages of a storybook, how sweet this could be. Amy would be your lady in waiting. With her scarf flying, you would ride into the lair of the dragon. Then having slain the beast, you and Amy would live happily ever after. But Master, this is no storybook. There can be no distraction here. Your courage and my concentration, every last atom of our shared being we must dedicate to this one task. We'll either make the gate of St Louis or go home in a box. This is true, is it not?"

From the silence came a solemn reply, "This is not about what I want."

"For God and country," echoed the brain.

Not to make light of James's effort or his errand, but only to keep things in perspective, this is a place to remember that James seldom had ten miles to travel between convenience stores. And not to make so much of it as to become like Don Quixote penning verses for his Dulcinea, but at the end of it all, the memory of Amy still warmed James's heart, and that was saying something.

"Amy was the kind of girl men dream of. As to why God made our paths to cross with chemistry that mixed so easily; perhaps He was giving me an opportunity to change course and take a different path of equal merit, before the point of no return."

James had been trying to call his sister Patricia since arriving in Stevenson. He hoped to see her for the first time in two years. Originally they'd planned to meet at the Pacific Ocean but had to postpone their meeting for a variety of reasons. Most recently, James had called Patricia from the town of Washougal and worked out a new plan: Since James could only approximate where he would be when Patricia got her next work break, it was decided that upon said break, Patricia would set out driving in the general direction of where James was, and, at the same time, James would look for a phone from which he would call her cell phone so that a meeting place could be pinpointed—,

"Pat, gosh I finally got through," James said happily, "I've been trying and trying. Where are you?"

"I just got home," replied Patricia.

"You're at home?"

"Yea, I'm sorry," Patricia replied, "I picked up [my daughter] Jenny and we were excited about seeing you but the weather got really bad in the mountains and my cell phone wasn't working so, without it, we didn't know how to find you. We considered driving up and down the river to see if we might spot you paddling but, in the end we decided it would be best to turn back and try again under better conditions."

Although disappointed, James was happy to speak with Patricia. James didn't have to explain to Patricia why he couldn't stop and wait for her. She understood he had to canoe up the Columbia River, up the Snake River, up the Clearwater River, and then hike 500 miles over the Rocky Mountains before the snows began.

After his conversation with Patricia, James returned to his room where he spread his newly acquired maps out on the floor. Then while studying said maps, James paused to bring out Amy's note. He would have answered her note that day if only he'd had her regular mailing address. James hadn't asked Amy for her regular address because doing so wouldn't have been proper. Unfortunately, James hadn't told Amy that e-mail for him was like something from another planet.

James caught up his journal at 1:25pm and then went to town for a hamburger. Afterward, he copied his journal at the visitors center where Amy (a different Amy) and Jamie helped him. James next went to the Post Office where a man recognized him and said, "You're the man who's canoeing the river."

A brief but good conversation followed after which the man wished James well and departed. James then proceeded to the mail counter where the clerk said, "Excuse me, but I couldn't help overhearing that you're from Kansas."

"Yes Ma'am, I am."

"I'm from Kansas also," said Sharon. "I was in 'The Topeka Tornado.'"

"Oh—," James groaned painfully, shaking his head, knowing what a Kansan knew about tornados.

Another brief but good conversation followed. James then got out his wallet to pay postage, but Sharon pushed the money back with a smile and said, "This is on me."

"Oh Ma'am," said James, shaking his head as if to say he didn't deserve the kindness that she and so many others had bestowed on him. He did not argue however but thanked her kindly. And truly, he was grateful.

Back in his cabin, James poured over maps then made a trip to the hardware store where he purchased a length of rope. From there he went to the grocery store. From the grocer, James went with two heavy food sacks under each arm. Back in his cabin, James went about his final preparations, organizing and packing. In the kitchen, he cooked a steak and made a salad for dinner. He felt drained like he might be coming down with the flu, so he prayed and confessed to running around with only a sleeveless t-shirt in the cool damp. He apologized for letting his new youth go to his head. He promised not to do it again, adding only, "But please, God, give me the strength to keep going."

Feeling better, James kept working. By 8:45pm, he had only two duffle bags left to pack. He had already packaged his perishable food so that it might easily be transferred from refrigerator to cooler in the morning. He finished the last task at 9:30pm, then went out on the deck and got into a hot tub where he soaked for a half-hour.

James slept heavily.

Day 28, Thursday, June 10

At 7:15am, James looked out his cabin window to see rain, wind, and large white-capped swells marching upriver in ranks. James had seen the swells in the gorge on his drive to the ocean but, he had yet to canoe in them because they only existed in the dammed part of the gorge. The reason that the swells only existed in the dammed part of the gorge were as follows: First and as already mentioned, the gorge acted like a spillway into which Pacific wind funneled with tremendous force. Second, the advent of the dams greatly increased the river's volume and consequently the river's ability to absorb and cycle out the wind energy. Third, the water had current that acted to compact the friction dynamic. The end result was that the gorge, a relatively small area in comparison to the ocean, became an impressive wave-making machine.

James went to town for breakfast and wished Holly well with her business. At the post office, James stopped in to wish Sharon well. Then returning to his cabin, the Kansan looked out on the river and because it looked deadly, he worked on his journal while keeping an eye out for better conditions. By 11:00am the rain and wind still blew but there had been some moderation. Therefore James decided to go. He didn't load his rig but pulled it empty to the water's edge to avoid cutting ruts in the wet lawn. Then with land rig transformed to water craft, he carried loads of gear from cabin to canoe. The waves made loading difficult but James stood ready to shove off by 1:00pm.

With high wind at his back, the canoeist paddled along the shoreline where waves were large but navigable in compare to out in the river where swells marched like man killers.

As the town of Stevenson fell away, a white pickup truck came and parked above the steep shoreline. A man hopped out directly and shouted, "You must be the man who's attempting the Lewis and Clark route?"

"Yes Sir."
"What's your name?"
"James Sheldon," shouted the Kansan.
"Good luck."
"Thank you, Sir."
There ended the occasional friendly riffs of shoreline that bordered the river in the gorge below the dam, to be replaced by cliffs rising directly from deep water, punctuated not by beaches but jagged outcrops of rock.

Five miles ahead of James, at the base of Wind Mountain, the river made a slight jog to the right before disappearing into the deepest part of the gorge. The radius of the jog began deceptively early however, just three miles ahead, and as a result, dangerous swells that presently marched a safe distance out in the river would come to crash against the north shore. And there was our novice, navigating the north shore.

"I had hardly gone any distance at all along the cliffs when I noticed the waves were getting bigger. Soon they were pushing me this way and that, demanding every atom of my attention."

The outcrops grew more frequent while, in the waters off their bases, boulders began to appear and disappear in the rising and falling flux. The waves, which had only gotten bigger, washed over the boulders and hit the cliffs with mounting force.

"With the wind pushing me in, and the cliffs hemming me in, I could no more have turned back if I had been on the event-horizon of a black-hole. In fact it took all my strength and skill just to keep my craft going straight ahead, and the worst of it lay ahead."

While James fought to keep his craft true, a large ship made to look like a paddle-wheeler came up the river roughly 1/8 mile to his right. The tourist vessel steamed with sightseers gathered at its railings on both top and bottom decks. Perhaps like James, the ship's captain had been waiting for better weather when, seeing improved conditions, he had embarked only to see conditions deteriorate.

Whatever the case, the ship turned around and steamed back toward the safety of port. Only later would James learn from local folk that everyone had gotten off the river except him.

Blowing along like a leaf on the water, James could at least be happy that no rain fell. Thus he went making the best of it, knowing not what waited even as he made excellent progress toward it.

"The wind came at an angle against the side of my boat and with every paddle stroke I ruddered to maximize its effect. I was really moving but, I felt I was on the edge of disaster."

Having no other route of escape, James knew he must reach Wind River Bay a few miles ahead in the shadow of Wind Mountain. Presently however, James arrived where the river began its jog. And having come to that point ever so steadily rising to a crescendo, perhaps the dragon of wind and water stood ready to orchestrate his grand finale. The knight couldn't have imagined anything worse but, something of a nightmare was set to begin.

"It began with a roaring sound. I thought it a train, running on a track that paralleled the river on a shelf 30 feet up the cliff. Glancing up, I saw no train but only small trees along the tracks, whipping like hurricane footage on television. Then the swells came crashing against the cliff, one after another, each more massive than any ships wake. And each time I managed to keep from being tossed over by a swell, I found myself atop its foaming white crest, bound for the cliff!"

Like a man determined to keep his life, the canoeist shouted, stabbed, and shoveled even as wind and waves carried him deeper into peril.

"Atop each foaming crest, the wind seemed bent on turning my canoe like a weather vane. But if I allowed the wind to turn me, the next swell would broadside and flip me over. I didn't want to get flipped over but if I brought my craft in line with the swell to avoid being flipped over, I would be carried into the cliff!"

From one foaming white crown to the next, the Kansan fought to keep his life. And as he did, he roared, "Hah! Hah!"

The wind roared back, the swells walloped the cliffs, and sprays flew in the air. The battle rose to a fevered pitch and, in the thick of it, James cried out like a child, "Please God, help me!"

> "The swells came against the cliff at an angle of forty-five degrees while I varied my own angle according to whatever the changing flux allowed between crests and troughs. In such a way I fought for every opportunity to keep myself off the cliff that stood roughly forty feet away. I ruddered hard with every paddle stroke and every stroke was desperate. I shifted my weight like a cat to counterbalance even as I stabbed and dug for stability. My dog hunkered in the hull and, although terrified, did his part to maintain a low center of gravity. Oddly, I cannot recall having my bow pointed away from the cliff although I must have kept an average angle of forty-five degrees to the swells even while swinging between wider degree variances. By such seesawing, I fought to reach Wind River Bay. And while I fought, I continuously glanced over my shoulder to time the next swell, so that I might attack it as it came upon me, that I might counter its effect, to push off it, so as not to be rolled over under its foaming crown. I never had control but fought off calamity from one second to the next. And save for the mercy of God Almighty, how I survived cannot be known."

Because James's focus was on staying off the cliff rather than going upriver, progress passed unnoticed but, over the course of an hour, it can be told that James truly came to understand the old saying, "If my strength holds."

At last, riding a swell around a cliff point, the canoeist coasted into the calm water of Wind River Bay. The change was dramatic, from madness to sudden serenity. And finding himself thus, James shed no tear but raised his eyes to Heaven and spoke with tremendous emotion, "Oh Lord! Thank You!"

In the next instant, James noticed a man on the cliff directly above. The man sat partway down the sheltered cliff on a natural seat of rock. He had a fishing pole in hand. His eyes simply stared and, he appeared to be astonished.

Stiffening with embarrassment, James spoke to the man in a severe tone, "Sir, I've never known anything like the last hour of my life."

The man seemed at a loss, but perhaps James appeared lit like a torch. In any case, no other words were spoken. James returned to the business at hand and paddled a half-mile to the boat ramp at the back of the cove. The time was 3:00pm. James had made only five miles progress but such was his relief in making dry land, it didn't matter. Then seeing that the boat ramp and parking lot were deserted, he laughed and said, "I'm the only fool in the valley."

While it felt wonderful to be alive, James couldn't help worrying about how to proceed. He wondered how things had become so treacherous. Then looking at his map, James saw his mistake. He hadn't taken the jog into account. Plus he couldn't control the weather. Thus learning from his first experience above the dam, James made a new plan. He would pull his rig on Highway 14 around Wind Mountain, thereby avoiding the remaining mile of the terrible jog. In fact such a thing was impossible but, James had yet to find that out.

Having assembled and loaded his rig, James pulled a half mile to the tiny community of Home Valley where he sat on the front porch of a general store enjoying an excellent hamburger. If James remembered correctly, the store owners were from Norway. At least they looked like Viking stock, and spoke with accents. Astrid was petite, blond, and pretty. Rolf was tall and muscular. Together, they made a fine-looking couple. They also owned the inn and campground there, nestled beside the river at the bottom of the gorge.

After setting himself up in the campground, James met Clayton who had come on a fishing vacation with his wife and friends. James told Clayton his plan for pulling around Wind Mountain by way of the highway, and Clayton told James about Drano Lake, a place where James could put back into the river after pulling around Wind Mountain. Then, and because it fit the topic of their conversation, James explained his logic for going inbound on Lewis's and Clark's outbound trail. The reason being that the Columbia River had roads along it whereas the Missouri River did not and therefore, James had decided to go west to east because it would allow him to use his walking machine to get around areas of overpowering current. Plus the idea of traveling in the direction of home appealed to James. James did not tell Clayton that the idea of doing the trail in reverse had come from his sister. Patricia had come up with the idea back in the early stages when, in a moment of doubt, James had called and said no man could canoe up the channelized portion of the Missouri River.

By the time James and Clayton finished their conversation, night had fallen, so James hit the hay. He was unable to sleep however due to his abscessed tooth which he decided must be taken care of. He had hoped that his sister, who was a nurse, would take care of it for him but, as we already know, their meeting hadn't worked out. So James dug around in his shaving kit and found a sharp wooden toothpick. He then went to the campground restroom. Fortunately, the restroom had plenty of light and a good mirror, not to mention it was clean. Also, it was midnight so all was quiet. James leaned over the sink and looked in the mirror while pulling his gums back to reveal a large bulge just below one of his molars. Then with his free hand he put the point of the toothpick to the abscess and with a firm motion pushed the toothpick into it. At once the mirror was splattered with blood and puss. James lowered his head and spit a mouthful of blood into the sink, then another. He cleaned up the mess and returned to his tent where he felt much better. The pressure had been relieved. James slept well.

Day 29, Friday, June 11

James took a shower at 6:30am, then made bacon and eggs with toast, a green bell pepper, and a quart of orange vitamin drink. He then broke camp and set out pulling east along Highway 14. His wristwatch read 10:00am.

"Before beginning my journey, I never thought it would take three to four hours to get moving each day. Therefore I understand why other men might wonder, themselves having never moved 300 pounds of gear and provisions 4,000 miles under their own power, day by day, keeping everything in working order, taking no breaks except to journal, working at a pace that would have any man breaking a sweat."

On Highway 14, logging trucks roared past but the shoulder was adequate and, James's tooth felt much better.

The Kansan understood the shoulder to be good all the way to the boat ramp at Drano Lake. However, well-intentioned folks didn't always give the most accurate information when led with hopeful questions about things that weren't plainly visible before them. Indeed, and as the miles passed, the shoulder slowly narrowed until alas, it disappeared altogether on a blind curve with a guardrail.

James could go no further unless he was willing to pull his rig on the road around the blind curve. Not a concave curve like the one James had faced at Bonneville Dam, but a convex curve. In other words, it was a totally blind curve.

James stood in harness, the terrible curve ahead, the terrible shadow of Wind Mountain behind. Odds were he'd make it around the curve okay but if a mother with a van load of kids suddenly came around and swerved to miss him at the last instant only to go head-on into a logging truck... James couldn't risk such a thing, and still, he dreaded going back to the river at Wind Mountain. So he just stood there with a pained expression, gazing at the curve for the longest time.

No more had James turned his attention away from the curve than, incredible as it seemed, he realized he stood at the only point in the entire stretch of highway between Home Valley and Drano Lake where a man might gain access to the river without having to climb down a cliff.

"I looked under the pines to see how the land sloped gently down to the water's edge not more than 100 yards away. There wasn't even any underbrush to be gotten through. It was a piece of cake. Indeed, I could see a picnic table down there. I could hardly believe my good fortune. Only then did I notice the 'No Trespassing' sign."

James couldn't be sure of his exact location but he had already passed Wind Mountain and probably stood on the flank of Dog Mountain parallel to a place on the river called Thirteenmile Point.

"Master," said James's brain to his heart, "with regard to this business of not trespassing, if I might interject with a line of reason."

Wrongfully, James decided it would be alright to break the rules just once for the greater good of his errand. And because he stood in a remote area, and because traffic flowed light, he didn't think anybody would see. James formulated a plan. First he would carry and hide all his gear in tall grass across the railroad tracks. Then with everything across the tracks, he would carry his canoe beneath the pines to the water's edge. Lastly, he would carry his gear to his canoe. He would move with speed and stealth. Then, he would be on his way up the river.

James had already carried his large plastic gear tub and cooler across the railroad tracks and stashed them in tall grass when along came a man in a pickup truck of Japanese design. The man got out of his truck and James greeted him somewhat sheepishly.

At once the man noticed James's rig and asked, "What's that?"

"That's my walking machine," replied James.

"Do you pull this thing?" asked the man, having spied the harness.

James told how he had built his machine but, the more the two men spoke, the less James trusted the man. Perhaps James's current state made him suspicious but, to James, the man didn't appear like other folks who had shown interest. Instead, the man seemed to be out for himself, looking and thinking of how he might profit from James's invention.

Next the man walked into the ditch, selected a used railroad tie that was still in good condition, and put it in the back of his truck. James recorded nothing of it in his journal (and memory has honestly been lost) but probably, James helped the man on request. Such a thing can be surmised because James retained a clear memory of standing behind as the man shoved the tie into his truck. James's location lends credence to a scenario in which he had helped the man to carry the tie. What can be known is this: When the man had closed the door on his camper shell and turned to James (perhaps to say thank you), James looked back at him as if to ask, *"Wait a minute, have you permission to take that?"*

Somewhat uncomfortably, the man made an elusive remark

about taking nothing more than an old railroad tie but, he said nothing about having permission to take it from the railroad company to whom it belonged. He then got in his truck and drove away.

James stood in a state of confusion. In fact he had lost his way between right and wrong. James sat down on the back of his rig and thought about his errand. He remembered the prayer he said each morning, the end of which was, at its core, his Errand: *"And Lord, I promise to go forward with all my heart and soul, putting one foot before the other with good intent, knowing I need only do so with faith in You, and You will take care of the rest. In the name of Jesus Christ. Amen."*

James was unable to keep his promise because he was a sinner, bound to stumble and fall, and yet so often when he stumbled, there came an intervention that allowed him to catch himself before he fell.

The Kansan fetched his cooler and gear tub from the weeds. Then having loaded said items back into his rig, he turned back toward Home Valley. He didn't want to face those swells at Wind Mountain but, he knew of no other way.

Perhaps the dragon, who cared little for sentiment, shouted from the shore. Perhaps his voice was broken by wind and trees so that only parts of what he yelled reached the road, "... trying to weasel your way around me ... you should have known it'd come down to this."

If only James had asked permission to access the river there, chances were good he would have received it. But James couldn't ask permission. He had to go blindly forward like Lewis and Clark had. James couldn't face the unknown that Lewis and Clark faced but he had to go like they had, not knowing what lay ahead, gathering what knowledge he could, and above all else, trusting in God. By faith alone could James walk in that Light that guided those who built the home of the brave and land of the free.

Back in the shadow of Wind Mountain, fear wasn't all James felt. He felt frustrated after pulling his rig six miles for nothing. He felt ashamed of his retreat. He wasn't stomping around in frustration but, deep down, his fear affected his temper. He wasn't beating his chest with false pride but all the same, he made a point of telling Clayton and company how he'd lanced his gum when normally he wouldn't speak of such things. So it was, the shadow of Wind

Mountain was upon James.

James sat with Clayton and friends on the porch of the general store eating hamburgers. Rolf came along and told of a tiny beach in a nearby park where James could put into the river and, by such means, keep from backtracking one-half mile to the boat ramp. James left his rig at the store and went to scout the beach. He first crossed the highway in front of the store, then walked over a foot bridge, continued through a shady State Park, crossed a ball diamond and entered a stand of trees via a dirt path. At the end of the short path, James found a secluded little beach with a single picnic table on which he fell asleep.

The Kansan hadn't slept forty minutes when his dog alerted him to the presence of a man on the path. James told what he was about and then asked the man, "Sir, if I may ask, do you live around here?"

"Yes I do," Don replied.

"Well Sir," said James, gazing on the river with a healthy measure of respect, "I saw some waves downriver, including some ship wakes that were big but none like these waves up here."

"Yeah," Don replied, "they can get pretty big. There've been times when I stood on the shore watching a windsurfer, and the swells were so big that, when he [the windsurfer] went down in the trough, the top of his mast disappeared. Then up he came on the next crest."

James could only shake his head. He didn't know the height of the mast on windsurfing rigs but, he figured they were tall enough.

"You know," said Don, "You could pull your rig on the highway across the river. It's an interstate highway, so it has a wide shoulder."

"That's illegal, isn't it?"

"That's Oregon over there," Don replied, "They allow bicycles on their interstate highways. And there aren't any signs saying you can't use the shoulders. In fact, there used to be a man who pulled a canoe behind his bicycle."

"You don't say?" said James, perking up.

"Yeah, Don replied. "But, I don't see him anymore, so, I don't know what happened to him."

Having such an option comforted James. If worse came to worst, he could wait for calm water (if such a thing existed), then cross over to Oregon and pull his rig along the shoulder of I-84. James thanked Don for his time and then departed.

Back at Rolf and Astrid's, James sat on a bench and worked on his journal until dinner at 5:30pm. Then, to afford the earliest start possible, James got a room to avoid breaking camp in the morning. Also to get an early start, James left his gear in his rig which he parked in a place that Rolf provided (the only time James didn't sleep with his gear). Subsequently, when Rolf saw James carrying his bedroll into the room and therefore learned that James wouldn't be using the bed, Rolf gave James a discount on the room. James hit the sack at 6:30pm and slept well.

Day 30, Saturday, June 12

At 3:00am, James got up and set out for the river. A fair night breeze blew as he pulled his rig on the trail. In darkness he carried loads of gear to the little beach below, and as he went up and down the dirt path, all was quiet except for the leaves that rustled in the trees.

James was so afraid; all he could do was repeat, "Lord, I'm so afraid. Lord, I'm so afraid," over and over again. And for the record, James had read the Gospels and still he either missed or forgot the part where Jesus tells his followers not to chant. James never chanted anyway, so maybe that was why he had missed that part, because it hadn't applied to him. But there he was, terribly afraid, chanting, "Lord, I'm so afraid. Lord, I'm so afraid."

After staging his gear, James disassembled his rig and loaded his canoe on a riff of sand in the sheltered cove. He took out his field glasses and trained his eyes on the wide river. Out there, in that faint glow that enters the darkness to let a man know day is coming, James saw the saw-toothed silhouettes, marching rank after rank like an army advancing under cover of dark. James knew he had to go out there and meet them. He could not seek safety in paddling near shore without ending up on the flank of Wind Mountain where that same army of swells would have him on the rocks. Instead, he had to paddle out and join them, for only then could he turn and ride them around the jog and into the entrance of the deeper gorge a mile ahead, where the walls drew close together.

To James's credit, he stopped his fearful chanting and said a proper prayer. He did not ask God to see him through but prayed in faith that God would decide what was best. Then shoving off, he went in silence.

At 5:25am, James paddled out to meet the dawn. He didn't know what he would find but hoped the night had soothed the river. He found neither foaming nor breaking swell but only well-rounded giants, each twice that of any ships wake. Indeed so peacefully did the swells lift and lower James one after another, he may as well of rode on the sound waves of a wonderful but frightful lullaby. For even as the swells marched in peace, each packed the power of thunder. Altogether they scarcely looked like water but rather, they had an other-worldly gloss, like a sea of liquid mercury, aglow with the golden sheen of a rising star. Mere words could not describe it. It was something born from a perfect meeting of power and serenity, as close as James could imagine to being in the palm of God's own hand.

Fingers of sunlight extended through the opening of the deeper gorge ahead, chasing shadows from slopes. The sky unfurled to reveal a perfect mix of crystal blue and, cloud remnants, like soft silken banners afire with the glory of a new day.

Taking long powerful strokes, the Kansan cut an angle through marching ranks to make certain he got far enough out into the river. Only then did he turn and ride the silent giants around Wind Mountain and into the deeper gorge. The longest two days of his life had only begun.

Having put Wind Mountain and Collins Point behind, James could once again paddle along the shore where there weren't swells but large waves. The waves were manageable because they traveled in the exact direction as James. Still, it was no free ride. James had to put himself fully into each stroke, and always at the end of each stroke, he ruddered with a firm twist of his paddle. Thus he used power and control to keep his craft moving forward in a straight line so as not to get turned cockeyed because while wind and waves could be used to beat the current, they could just as easily send him out of control.

A grain barge came and James rode out its wakes. Next, and because his location can only be assumed due to the fact that he would have no river map until after getting home to Kansas, James had probably rounded Thirteenmile Point when, entering the windbreak of the point, he saw two fishermen anchored in a motorboat off what was almost certainly the same private area he had seen from the highway on the day before. James would see no other fishing boats on the river that day. He waved and shouted hello, adding that he'd come from Kansas to attempt the Lewis and Clark route west to east. He did not stop or even slow down but continued with the business at hand.

Several days before, a well intentioned kayaker told James of an eddy that ran along the north shore from the backside of Wind Mountain to the bridge at Hood River. Therefore our novice expected to find a six-foot-wide band of water flowing backward along seventeen miles of shoreline! Also some days before, a fisherman who'd heard tell of the eddy went so far as to question its existence. Our novice assured the fisherman that he had it on good word. But of course the eddy was folklore, born of an illusion created by wind that blew so hard it could make a man believe the river flowed backwards. Also playing a part in the illusion was the riprap buttress of a train track that came to run alongside the river. The buttress made for a very straight shoreline wall which went to the canoeist advantage because it created a six foot margin of semi-navigable water while simultaneously channeling high wind to blow directly from behind. Such ideal-for-speed conditions required a focus that left no opportunity for sightseeing. Consequently, James would remember almost nothing of the gorge walls that rose nearly a thousand feet on either side.

Instead, James's memory would be like tunnel vision; a picture encompassing only the immediate area surrounding the bow of his canoe, of large waves on one side and large angular shards of volcanic rock on the other. The canoeist did scrape a rock or two along the way, and more than a few waves broke over the starboard side.

But that was alright so long as he could make the cove called Drano Lake before midday when the dragon of wind and water rose to full strength. To reach Drano Lake, James needed to paddle all-out along eight miles of shoreline, after which he hoped to hit the sack early then shove off at first light on the following day (for another morning of paddling in semi-navigable conditions). And because he hoped to make Drano Lake by or before 1:00pm, it came as no small surprise when he arrived at 8:40am!

Drano Lake was in fact the mouth of the Little White Salmon

River which had been artificially closed off by a large riprap wall to create a recreational fishing area sheltered from swells. By passing through its gate, James entered into something like a calm lake, with fishing boats here and there.

Having found a campsite, the canoeist made and ate a large breakfast. He then decided not to make camp but first to paddle back to the gate for a look at the river and, if possible, attempt further progress upstream. The only catch was that, once he went out the gate, there could be no turning back. The wind would not allow it. His wristwatch read 11:00am. The calm of morning had nearly passed. And what with the shore alternating between cliffs and riprap, he knew not where he would find the next place to escape if things got rough. Nevertheless, he decided to retake the river and continue east along the north shore, as per the following entry:

> "The wind blew and there were no shortages of waves [along the shore] but not swells, so I made very good progress."

James hadn't expected to make it as far as Hood River Bridge but, by late afternoon, he arrived there to see the windsurfers for whose skill and daring the place had become famous. There must have been two dozen windsurfers out in the middle of the river, athletes from all over the world, even as far away as Australia. In fact they were the best windsurfers in the world, come together in a place they had crowned, "The Wind Capital of the World."

James watched as the windsurfers rode the swells with their multi-colored sails, colorful as a kaleidoscope, going up and down and around in a spectacle reminiscent of a death defying circus act.

The white-capped swells prohibited James from crossing the river. Otherwise, he may have camped at the town of Hood River, known to be the Mecca of windsurfing. Presently on his side of the river, James came upon a beautiful string of micro-coves, each the size of a home garage and containing a patch of sand just big enough for a single campsite.

"Master," said James's brain to his heart, "shouldn't we be stopping for the night, especially in light of the fact that we've spent nearly every ounce of our strength and until this point had no chance to escape the river and may not have another chance for who-knows how-long?"

James's gut then chimed in, and while his gut couldn't think to speak, the feeling it made has been translated here for the purpose of telling this story, "Master, what kind of a curse makes this beautiful string of coves sit abandoned on a sunny Saturday afternoon at the height of vacation season?"

"You both tell the truth," replied the heart. "Brain, you are my high seneschal, but in this matter, I am predisposed to rule in favor of the gut. Therefore, we continue."

"Master," said the brain, "I agree the gut makes a point, or perhaps I should say a feeling for things that may or may not be. My concern on the other hand is for a real and present danger. We've been making hay for fifteen hours. The muscles are nearly worn out and, my reaction time is getting slow."

In a wind where a split-second delay put a beach out of reach, James let his opportunities pass one by one until he had passed the last micro cove. Then passing underneath the Hood River Bridge, he looked back and wondered if he'd gone a bridge too far. His wristwatch read 6:00pm.

Due to James's scant knowledge regarding what lay ahead, and also because the vast scale of his surroundings made it impossible to discern what lay ahead, not to mention the wind and waves that forced him to keep his focus on the immediate business at hand, but alas, no more had James gone under the bridge than he blundered into a new danger, which will now be told.

The Port of Bingen, unlike other ports, wasn't built to provide protection from the wind but instead opened to the wind for the express purpose of keeping fresh-cut timber trapped within it. So it had no gate but stood with its mouth wide open like a giant horseshoe made from imposing walls of riprap, atop which stood large cranes, poised for plucking up logs.

"UB, I think we've entered some kind of commercial zone. Oh well, according to my map there's a town up ahead, so there's bound to be a place to take out for the night."

Only after paddling a quarter-mile into the manmade bay did our novice realize his error—,

"Ah shoot! Ah shoot!" James shouted, finding himself in with a bunch of floating timber.

James came about and fought hard to escape. He angled south to avoid crossing the windy mouth of the bay. Then gaining the south side of the bay, he paddled west alongside a field of floating logs, all rising and falling together in the flux.

Fortunately, conditions in the bay were nowhere near as extreme as the open river. Still, the nearer James drew to the mouth of the bay, the more the wind and waves came against him until it seemed he would not be able to escape.

To gauge his forward progress, James looked at a log floating alongside and, by such means, estimated that one paddle stroke into which he poured every ounce of his strength gained him six inches. Nor could James let up for an instant, lest the wind push him back into the bay and hem him in with the logs.

At last, James made the point that separated bay from river. The point being the butt end of a massive wall made from shards of basalt on which large waves crashed and sprayed. James paddled wide to clear the point before turning his craft, whereupon the wind caught hold like a sail, his speed increased dramatically and, he was free.

Of course James's speed had not increased as much as the windsurfers at Hood River when the wind jettisoned them over the wave tops like a kite. Then again, James had been going against the wind with tremendous effort only a moment before, so the difference was relative. James had paddled hard, the wind had caught the canoe as he banked, and away he had gone.

Unfortunately, he went directly into the path of an oncoming barge!

Perhaps the dragon only kept the knight alive for the sake of his own entertainment, like a cat with a mouse, tossing him this way and that. Whatever the case, James escaped the front corner of the barge by less than thirty-five feet. Then finding himself alongside a moving barge, James's singular purpose in life became that of escaping the backwash. And perhaps even the dragon's jaw dropped when once again the knight got away. For low and behold, just between barge and riprap wall, an old tugboat lay half-submerged, and with a little maneuvering (which may have momentarily put our novice into the realm of world-class canoeist), he got behind it. No more had he done so than a wall of water crashed against it.

James gave thanks even as he'd had enough. He was spent. He

wanted off the river. But all he could see was a giant wall of riprap that appeared to go on forever. In fact, only a mile ahead, a small gate waited hidden from sight.

Relieved to find the gate, James entered a manmade recreational bay only to discover that in order to gain the public park at its west end, he would have to paddle against wind and waves for a distance of 1/3 mile—no small feat at the end of an intense 15 hour day.

> "Both park and bay were well kept but oddly deserted except for an old fisherman who suffered engine problems. He had limped in from the bay and was presently moored at the dock where he tried and tried to restart his motorboat. Meanwhile, as the old fisherman wore his battery down, two junior Hispanic gang-bangers (who had seen him limping in) came to stand on the dock directly above him like a pair of fledgling vultures."

The Kansan moored his craft to the dock, ordered his dog to stay put, and went toward the junior gang-bangers who were no more than boys, the older appearing to be fourteen, the other a year younger. Even so, the older boy appeared seriously hardened, as in not hiding any ill intent by way of stance or expression. He flew his gang colors loud and proud, like he owned the place.

"Are you okay?" James asked, standing directly before the younger boy, speaking in a tone neither friendly nor unfriendly but very seriously and clearly implying the question, *"What are you up to here—good, or no good?"*

"I'm okay," the boy replied. And if James read him correctly, the young man didn't have his heart into being a bad guy.

"What about you?" James asked, turning to the older boy, "Are you okay?"

The young man gave James the evil eye, then turned to gaze across the bay while keeping James in his peripheral line of sight. James stepped round in front of him, squared off like a drill instructor and repeated his question, "I asked if you are okay."

"Yeah, I'm alright," said the boy, his tone implying that he'd decided it better to reply even if he didn't want to.

"Alright then," James said in a tone void of pleasure. And perhaps the young man sensed it, but in any case James didn't get any thrill from putting him on notice. Nor did James react to the young man based on the color of his skin, but rather, on what appeared to be an evil temptation brewing in his heart. James then turned to the old fisherman.

"Am I glad to see you," the old fisherman said under his breath, and casting an eye toward the boys, he lowered his voice a notch more, "I'm afraid to leave my boat even to go and get my truck and trailer from the park."

"Sir," James replied in a strong tone, "I'm as happy to see you as you are to see me." Then watching as the boys drifted over toward his canoe, James added, "I had hoped to camp here but, I don't believe I will. I need to fill my water jug, though. Sir, can you tell me, is there a spigot in the park?"

Meanwhile, a second fisherman in the boat had buried himself in its engine bay for the sake of fixing a mechanical problem. And while he did not look like easy prey, his focus was on the mechanical problem and not the human problem.

"Sir," said James to the old fisherman, "How about I keep watch here while you go and get your truck? Then, after we trailer your boat, I'll go fill my water jug while you keep watch over my boat."

"Sounds like a plan," said the fisherman, and he went to get his truck.

Once the fishermen had their boat on the trailer, the boys went away on bicycles. James wasn't entirely happy to see them go because for all he knew, they would return with seasoned reinforcements. The fishermen stood ready and willing to wait while James went to get his water but James assured them he'd be fine and they departed.

While at the water spigot, James read a sign that forbade camping in the park but it hardly mattered by then because he had no intention of staying. So James shoved off, paddled out the same gate by which he had entered the bay, and proceeded upriver.

James hadn't gone fifty yards when it dawned on him; he was no longer in the deeper gorge. But that wasn't the half of it, for in emerging from the deeper gorge, he had entered a vastly different realm. In fact the change came so abruptly, it astonished him. Gone were the lush forested slopes, snow-covered peaks, and dense marshlands—replaced by a rocky brown terrain like something on the cusp of a desert.

Paddling another 200 yards, James noticed a piece of trash lying amid the riprap. The trash caught his eye because until that point in his journey, he couldn't recall seeing any trash, not even one piece. Presently he saw more trash along the bank which quickly became more cluttered until alas, it lay strewn with trash from top to bottom. There were discarded fishing nets, torn up tarps, bald tires, rusted buckets, and loads of miscellaneous debris.

James paddled on and, as he went, the trash thinned until once again the shoreline became clean. Very soon however there came another area as trashed-out as the one before, and after that, another.

> "At the center of each trashed area, a shabby Indian fishing platform stood like a monument to what happens when a people, any people, and for whatever reason, lose their land and culture."

The canoeist had come twenty-one miles as the crow flew, fighting to keep his craft true in the waves. He needed rest in the worst possible way but could find no friendly shoreline. Like a pony express rider who becomes exhausted, he nodded off, then caught himself just before he fell out of the saddle. He looked for a place to take out, anyplace, but there were only cliffs and grades, wind and waves.

At last, James spotted a riff of sand under a patch of shrubs in a calm corner where riprap buttress met rock outcrop. Behind the shrubs, at the foot of the outcrop, a grassy shelf appeared just wide enough for James's tent. First however, he had to get his boat and gear through the shrubs which, being of a variety found in a desert marsh, had tough stocks that snaked this way and that to a height of six feet.

James grabbed hold of the pulling frame and, while facing his canoe, drove with his legs as he pulled and twisted to get through the patch of shrubs which measured twenty feet deep. After he had finally fought through, he took a blue tarp from under UB's bed, opened it on the grassy shelf, and fell atop it, exhausted.

As if dead, man and dog lay side by side under a sky darkening with storm clouds. Meanwhile as things turned out, the grassy shelf wasn't anywhere as flat as it had initially appeared to be. In fact, it was no good.

Fearful of waking in a dark rainstorm, James forced himself to get up and go scouting for a suitable campsite, but the outcrop had no level or semi-level ground on which to camp. So James climbed a cliff to the top of the outcrop where, using his field glasses, he spotted another outcrop upriver which appeared to have a small shelf at its base.

Hoping the prospective shelf would accommodate his tent, James returned to his boat, pulled it back through the vegetation, and continued toward the outcrop that he'd seen from the cliff top. The outcrop looked like a mini mesa with cliffs rising 100 feet to a flat top of roughly twenty acres. In perspective, the outcrop, although massive, sat at the bottom of a gorge that dwarfed it.

At the downstream end of the outcrop, the rocky shelf lay under a carpet of green grass growing in soil only a few inches deep, below which lie solid rock, extending to the water directly below. Small to modest sized trees, which may have been elms, also grew on the shelf and cast their shade upon it. And due to the broken nature of the shoreline in that area, the waters around the shelf were calm. It would have been a special place, as beautiful as its Maker intended it to be, except that it was littered with broken beer bottles, pop cans, paper cups, and whatnot.

The trash was a "red flag" that had not been visible through James's field glasses. (The shelf wasn't wide enough for his tent anyway). So James moored his canoe alongside the shelf and set out on a footpath that ran atop it. By such means, he followed the base of a cliff to a notch in the bottom of the gorge.

Trees grew in the notch and, proceeding through them for another thirty foot, James entered a meadow no more than forty feet in diameter. The meadow was partially enclosed by a rocky crescent with a pair of bluish-silver pines at the back. The floor of the meadow was like peat moss, perfectly soft and flat. It would have been paradise lost if not for the beer bottles, soft drink cups, and misc debris.

Hoping for something safer, James scaled a cliff to the top of the outcrop. Then traveling along the cliff top, he used his field glasses to search for a campsite upriver but could see none. Nor did the top of the outcrop hold any suitable campsite, being rocky, uneven, and covered with course desert grasses.

Out of strength and with no place to go, James carried loads of gear to the meadow. He used up the last of his reserves getting his canoe through some tight spots between trees in the cliffy notch, then made camp at the back of the meadow beside the twin pines.

Exhausted though he be, James knew he must eat before sleep in order to replenish his strength. His wristwatch read 9:00pm and, he'd all but lit his stove when two men suddenly stepped out from behind the pines without a word. With a sudden rush of adrenaline, the Kansan went straight at them and although he bore no weapon, they froze in fear.

Seeing the fishing poles in their hands, James stopped, smiled, and said, "You scared me."

The two men appeared to be in their late twenties. One was white with a few front teeth missing; the other was an Indian with an interesting hat. As for UB, he may have been asleep in the tent. A brief but polite conversation followed. The two anglers then set out for the river and James returned to making grub. He ate a large steak, two pieces of bread, and an orange. Then as James prepared to retire to his tent, the two fishermen returned. They had caught a few fish, and bid James well in passing.

Having struggled to stay awake for hours, James struggled to fall asleep. His exhaustion ran so deep, he felt seasick from the give of his bed mat which measured only two inches thick. He drifted off at 12:00am and would have slept well if only the sound of a tarp snap hadn't opened his eyes. The time was roughly 1:00am and, fearing an animal might be getting into his provisions, James unzipped his tent to look out where to his surprise he saw the silhouette of a man. The man, who had heard James unzip his tent, slipped away on all fours like a spider that vanishes into surrounding shadows.

James yanked his head back into his tent. He couldn't know how many men there were anymore than he could know how far they were willing to go in a location removed from the eyes and ears of civil society. Suddenly sharp as a tack, he took his six-shooter and immediately slipped outside, using his tent for cover by crawling along its base to its backside. Meanwhile inside the tent, UB remained sound asleep.

Peering out from behind his tent, the Kansan surveyed the dark scene before him and sensed by whatever mysterious means God affords a man that a second man lurked in the shadow of the pine nearest to his tent. From there it took only rudimentary logic to understand that the second man was a wing man. In other words, had James pursued the first man, or even gone from his tent to his canoe, he would have put his back to the wing man.

Unaware that James had flanked him, perhaps the wing man waited for James to emerge from his tent.

James didn't think but instinctually sensed the picture before him and by such means understood that men who give over to creeping about on all fours in the night are largely dictated by the opportunity before them and therefore may go however far the opportunity allows so long as the risk of harm to themselves is not too great.

James would not think of firing his pistol into the shadow of the pine, but he could fire it into a safe area where no one would be hurt. Thus rising slowly so as not to be detected, he discharged his pistol into the ground a short distance before his feet. In doing so, he took a risk by exposing his position, trading away said advantage in hope that the shock of the blast would destroy any perceived opportunity held by the criminals. And in fact, so loud was the report of his 44 Magnum in that mini amphitheater of nature, it would have rattled most any man who didn't see it coming.

Having recovered from the initial shock, the wing man slipped unseen around the pine where he crawled up the rocky crescent, dislodging many small stones along the way.

James took cover at the base of the rocks where, in the event of an attack, he hoped to see them coming whereas he remained concealed in shadow. It was his only advantage in that place. Outside that, he was trapped between cliffs and river.

UB came next, sniffing his master out, sheepishly wagging his tail while looking up as if to ask, *"I messed up, didn't I?"*

"You could have barked," James said even as he understood UB only felt insecure due to the report of the pistol which had undoubtedly jolted him from sleep. "It's alright boy," said the Kansan, reaching to pet his dog even as he kept an eye out.

While James kept watch, this is a place to look at a journal entry which, although made much later, speaks directly about this event:

> "I met two men at a picnic table in the Dakotas, one a west-coast youth counselor who was canoeing a section of the trail west to east, the other an east-coast lawyer who was bicycling the trail east to west. They were not Christians, but

good men, a bit disillusioned perhaps, but maybe that was only a prelude to finding something better. The youth councilor told a story of a canoeist who, while doing the trail, got attacked in the night and was beaten badly enough for reconstructive dental surgery. The canoeist had chased off a pair of Indian boys who were attempting to steal his gear. To his misfortune, the boys returned with reinforcements. After hearing this, I recounted my story as told above. The youth councilor and lawyer agreed that in such a situation as what happened to me, they would allow the thieves to take their gear on grounds that such belongings weren't so valuable as to be worth whatever result might come from a confrontation. I told them it wasn't about the value of any gear but rather, the value of a principle. In other words, it was about right and wrong, and standing up against wrong for right. And I know what Jesus said about giving my shirt to one that takes my coat. And I am deeply grateful that my savior Jesus is rightly concerned with my soul, and not my material belongings. I take His lessons seriously. And I believe He allowed Peter to carry a sword not to protect His coat or shirt, but rather for a very commonsense reason, being that of keeping highwaymen men from prematurely ending His mission.

 From what I have since learned, I guess I could be sent to prison for the action I took that night on the river. Still, I have to stand for my belief. My point being that, although America is a nation of laws and not men, America stands on flesh-and-blood sacrifice, and all the legality and psychology and technology in the world will not preserve America if men refuse to stand in their own flesh and blood."

 Presently, James returned to camp where along with his usual duds, he strapped his gun belt to his waist. His black leather gun belt was western-style with brass bullets in its loops. His pistol was a bear gun, a stainless-steel western-style 44 Magnum target revolver with a 7½-inch barrel. James had owned pistol and belt for 25 years but, over the past 12 years, his guns had sat drawing dust. In fact, when James had gone to dig out his bear gun for his errand, he found the bullets to be so covered with patina, they were stuck in the belt loops like rusted bolts.

James couldn't know whether the ill-intentioned men would return. He was cornered in an isolated place which afforded them ample opportunity to do wrong so long as they were willing to face an armed man.

> "There wasn't anything to do but fight off sleep, stay alert, and keep watch all night. My adrenalin soon wore off. Then dizzy with exhaustion, I prayed for strength and remained awake."

Day 31, Sunday, June 13

> "At dawn it began to rain and I felt grateful because, to my way of thinking, criminals probably retreat from the light of day, especially on rainy Sunday mornings. So I thought it safe to get a few hours sleep."

James slept fitfully until 8:00am when, feeling he shouldn't stay longer, he got up. The rain let up just enough for him to towel his tent dry and put it away. He hauled loads of gear on the path. Then coming back for his canoe, he found it to weigh a ton, so to speak. In fact he couldn't lift it, so he dragged it. He got just enough breaks in the rain to get everything packed away dry. Then with everything ready to go, he ate a cold breakfast on the shelf beside his craft, all the while ready to jump and shove off in the event of unwanted company. Thankfully, breakfast went peacefully.

Immediately after shoving off, James looked back and gave thanks to God for his deliverance even as he turned to face the river. The rain must have ended at that time although not recorded in his journal. The wind was immediately obvious however but that wasn't necessarily bad although, had circumstances been under his control, James would have chosen a calmer day to enter that particular part of the gorge.

> "In that part of the gorge there stood a series of towers made of volcanic rock, each protruding from the wall of the gorge into the river like a castle tower into a moat except on

a far larger scale. And due to the immense size of each tower, the already colossal battle between wind and water got magnified around the base of each tower to form a black rapid. Black, for two reasons, the first being color, resulting from a combination of deep water made all the darker by cloud cover, not to mention the dark tower that loomed over it. The second characteristic from which a black rapid got its name was its frightening aspect."

In order to get through a black rapid, the canoeist developed a technique in which he employed his ally the wind. First however, he removed his hat as the wind off the point of each tower demanded. James then approached the tower by paddling as usual along the gorge wall. He didn't paddle out into the river to swing wide around the tower because that would have put him in the white-capping swells. Rather, James followed the gorge wall right up and into the nearly perfect ninety-degree corner where gorge wall met tower wall. James could do such a thing because the water lay relatively calm in the corner. Why the water was relatively calm in the corner wasn't known but certainly some dynamic was at play. Thus the waves didn't crash into the corner but rather, the water rose and fell with the kinetic flux of the river. Further out however, directly off the point of each tower lay a black rapid where, as with smaller rock points James had encountered, water pressure backed up on the upstream side of the point while wind pressure backed up on the downstream side. The pressurized forces then came around the point and, due to surface friction created by wind moving in one direction and water moving in the other, the water surface got folded up around the point to make a rapid called a washboard. Most washboards were small, as already known from earlier encounters in this story. A washboard became a black rapid when high wind and current collided off a point big enough to be called a tower or monolith. Such a tower or monolith served to compact the friction dynamic between wind and water. In other words, if one were to picture the water surface as the pleats of an accordion, then the washboard surface around an average point could be seen as pleats spread out whereas off a monolith the pleats were pushed together. So a black rapid was brief but violent. The word "brief" being relative to the size of the monolith, meaning that a black rapid could be as long or longer in length than a regular washboard off a regular point.

Only later would James understand the white-capped swells out in the river to be an option. Presently however, the canoeist had not developed the skill to navigate the swells, nor could he portage by land around the towers, so he had no other choice but to face the black rapids, which brings us back to his technique.

Once in the relatively calm corner created by gorge wall and tower wall, James turned his canoe away from shore and paddled as hard as he could while hugging the base of the tower. So he charged as if he meant to go from the point of the tower out into the river. But he didn't charge out into the river. Rather, in the instant the front half of his canoe broke the plane beyond the tower's point, ramped up wind pressure struck the front half of the canoe somewhat like a side-impact in an intersection and, taking his cue from the abrupt impact of the wind, James ruddered hard, his canoe wrenched like a weather vane struck by a gust and, he lurched into the rapid. Then in a battle between wind and water, the canoeist paddled violently hard, shouting as rapid waves broke over the gunwales. Once through the zenith of the rapid, water pressure took dominance over wind pressure. Thus while still in the rapid, there came a reversal of fortune which had James paddling like a madman to keep from being sucked back into the worst of the rapid where a loss of forward momentum would cause his craft to turn and roll over. More than once, he narrowly escaped.

Upon gaining the upstream side of a tower, James found refuge in the calm [upstream] corner where tower wall met gorge wall. There he said a word of thanks, bailed water, put his hat back on, and proceeded toward the next tower.

"I made good time but that wasn't important to me on that day. I needed to find a safe place to rest."

Such were James's hopes after getting past a series of monoliths when he came before the largest of them all.

"Through eons of erosion, surrounding rocks had crumbled away to leave this great tower of basalt. Dull and dark, it stood as testament to forces deep in the earth, and also to the force of man who had blasted a railroad tunnel through it."

James marveled at the towers awesome size even while he approached it like a man who had gotten the hang of things. Then, at a point one-hundred feet shy of its massive base, James struck an invisible barrier that blew his hat off and pushed his canoe back and away. James retrieved his hat from the water and stowed it behind his seat. He then went forward with added momentum which he believed would carry him through the invisible barrier. Once again he hit the barrier and not only did it stop him, it shoved him back with great force.

Retreating a sufficient distance to get up a full head of steam, the vexed canoeist dug his paddle into the river for all his worth and charged to ram the invisible barrier. Alas, he seemed to penetrate it only to get caught in it. It swirled his canoe wildly even as he put all his strength against it. He came within a breath of being flipped over, then got rudely chased back down the shoreline from which he'd come.

Beaten but not defeated, James retreated to the next monolith downstream which wasn't very far away. There he took refuge in its upstream corner—,

"Master," called a voice that seemed to come from a dungeon, "Let me out of here."

"Never!" replied the heart.

"But master, how am I to do my duty?"

At last, the heart decided to let the brain out, and the brain, being allowed back to his post, dusted himself off—,

"Master, look carefully and you will see that the tower is of such magnitude, it spins a giant pillar of wind before it."

"I see nothing!" the heart swore in frustration.

"Study the water surface, for it betrays the wind pillar."

"Where? How? Wait! Yes! I see it now!"

Once again the canoeist approached the tower. But unlike times before, he stopped shy of its invisible barrier. Then following the water surface with his eyes, he saw how it betrayed a pillar of wind rotating like a tornado. Of course it hadn't the power of a tornado or it would have sucked him up along with part of the river. Nevertheless, it had nearly flipped his 500 pound canoe over. So he studied the wind pillar to see how he might get past it. And sure enough, he could see a wind seam 150 feet straight off the tower's point, a seam between the wind pillar that rotated off the tower and the straight-line wind of the gorge. The seam was visibly betrayed by water sucked from the surface and atomized into something like spindrift in a snow storm, whereby it revealed what appeared to be a tear in the fabric of nature itself. Indeed, there lay a gap through which the canoeist might squeeze. Fortunately, the wind pillar rotated in a counterclockwise direction which meant it didn't collide with the straight line winds of the gorge but rather, it spun like an idler pulley receiving energy from a belt. Even so, the seam looked to be a violent place. And yet, however ugly it was, James decided the foaming swells were worse. His only other option was a long and dangerous retreat.

The canoeist did as he must. He paddled toward the seam some fifty yards out from the point of the tower. Then in an all out charge, James hit the seam and fought to maintain control. Inside the seam, a chaotic dynamic sucked up water and atomized it into a fine spray. The spray whipped about to betray the directionless nature of the place and although not the worst of James's worries, it impaired his vision like snow in a blizzard. Meanwhile, waves broke over the gunwales from every angle except the stern. The chaos worked to James's advantage only in that it mounted no organized force against him. Still, James just did squeeze through with a lot of digging, stabbing, thrusting, and shouting of good clean words like, "Haw! Haw!"

Perhaps the dragon should be given credit here for helping the knight to "keep it clean" by reminding him again and again of his need of God's mercy and grace. Need indeed, and when the knight was near defeat, with his life in the balance, he quickly came round to that age old plea—,

"Lord, help me!"

Having made it through the seam, James paddled to the calm corner where tower wall met gorge wall. There he gave thanks and bailed water from his boat. Years later, James would question what exactly the phenomena had been. Certainly it had been a wind eddy. Most likely it had been as James guessed; a giant roller-pin eddy standing on end, or perhaps an oval. Smoke would have told the tale. In any case, the canoeist felt fortunate to have gotten past it.

Having made good time, James soon reached the mouth of the Klickitat River which flowed into the gorge from the north. James's roadmap didn't show the small town that stood atop the gorge on the northeast corner where the tributary entered. Nor could James see any sign of the town from his location below. Instead, his hope lay in finding a boat ramp or park in the mouth of the tributary. Unfortunately, he found only impossibly steep banks. Fortunately, he saw a teenage boy and girl who just happened to be standing about under the bridge where Highway 14 passed over the tributary. The youths told James about a place to take out just a half-mile further up the Columbia.

Knowing how ugly the Columbia had become, James asked the youths if there was any place to take out up the Klickitat (from which he might then access the town that they had just told him about). The teenage boy shook his head in thought and then replied that there wasn't any such place. So it was, James thanked the teenagers and turned back toward the river.

Out on the river, James faced a problem similar to that at Wind Mountain with one major exception. Instead of a mountain sitting on a jog in the gorge, there was a desert marsh. Therefore James could attempt to fight his way around the jog and, should the swells get the better of him, he would not be driven into cliffs but into a bed of reeds. So James tried to fight his way around the jog and sure enough, the swells overpowered him. He had no choice but to come in line with the swells which shoved his canoe into the reeds like a spear.

Passing though the reeds, James discovered a lagoon enclosed on three sides by steeply forbidding banks. The lagoon was the size of two football fields placed end-to-end and running parallel to the river along the jog. The curtain of reeds grew along the jog as mentioned and in fact, so completely did the swells dissipate in the heavy curtain of reeds, the lagoon behind lay completely quiet and serene.

Perhaps the dragon had captured the knight in something of a live trap. Perhaps the dragon then came to sit beside the curtain of reeds where, admiring his sharp claws, he spoke through the curtain, "If you give up now, I'll let you live."

As for the knight, he had already unfolded his secret weapon and was towing his boat through knee-deep water along the shore of the lagoon. Thus emerging from the reeds on the upstream point, he executed a skillful launch in difficult water and escaped around the corner.

Perhaps the dragon remained beside the curtain, "I'm going to count to ten."

Just around the jog, James found an old ferry landing, which judging by its enormous size, had been a WPA project along with the dams in the days of the New Deal. The ferry landing was neither pier nor dock. Rather, it was a manmade notch with sidewalls carved from sheer rock, straight up and down, forming a giant ramp all the way to the top of the gorge! Its only other feature was a stairway that went up its east wall. Other than that, it appeared to be as empty as it was big.

James left UB tied to the canoe on a gravel beach in the mouth of the notch and then went to climb the stairway in hope of finding something above. His wristwatch read 2:00pm. The temperature was warm and the sky may have been cloudy.

At the top, the Kansan found a small campground and proceeded directly into it without realizing it was for Indians only. By such means James quickly encountered three modern Indian braves whose expressions lacked nothing except war paint. Fortunately, the Indians kept their cool even while their feelings were obvious; James was not welcome. The Kansan showed no disrespect, weakness, need, or hope but simply remained buck upright. Thus hiding the fact that he'd spent his last atom of strength and was in dire straits for a place to rest, he asked if he might camp there.

"No," reiterated the leading Indian, "you cannot camp here."

James looked inland, "Is there a town?"

"Yes."

"Where?" asked James, seeing no sign of it.

"A quarter-mile up the road," replied the Indian impatiently.

"I don't see any road," said James

Holding himself in check as though James were committing some gross violation that grew more intolerable by the second, the lead Indian offered a quick but accurate set of directions, "Go to the top of the ramp. There the road turns to the right, then left. Follow it and you will find the town."

By then some Indian women and children had gathered to see what the fuss was about. It cannot be known what tribe they were.

Their camp appeared to be neat and clean, a collection of older campers and pickup trucks in semi arid grassland with a deciduous tree growing here and there. James thanked them for the info and then returned to descend the stair.

Back in the notch, James couldn't forget how the Indians had looked like they already had news of the night before only from a perspective in which the cowboy was the bad guy. James didn't assume to know who the ill-intentioned men had been. He only knew the hostility he had just seen in the faces above. Therefore, while gazing up the long ramp, he wondered what village of hostiles awaited him. He turned to the river only to see white-capped swells like rows of dragon's teeth. His exhaustion ran so deep, there wasn't a staircase of words that descended to it. He was without friend. Nobody knew where he was. He had no river map to show where he was. His roadmap didn't show a town above. He didn't know where he was.

No more had James begun to assemble his walking machine than a young Indian man descended the stairs, walked to the water's edge, pitched a bucket of salmon steaks into the river and then returned up the stairs without a word. James had been warned from the start of his journey by Don and Wade that red salmon meat contained a natural toxin lethal to dogs and therefore UB mustn't eat any red salmon along the shore or he would die. So it was not unnatural that James wondered if the Indians were up to something. After all, since entering the realm beyond the mountains, James hadn't met with much to feel good about. Instead, he had found gang colors, trashed out landscapes, men who crept like spiders in the night, and a not-so-friendly encounter with an Indian tribe. Such things could breed fear in a man's heart. And when a man needed to keep his guard up, fear was no bad thing.

While UB complained about being tied up, James trained his eyes to see if any Indians hid atop the cliffs. Then turning to the task at hand, he proceeded to assemble his walking machine with grim thoughts. He feared trouble had found him. He feared what waited at the top of the gorge. And while he hoped he wasn't walking into a fight, his heart and mind began to prepare for the possibility.

Such was James's state when a pair of human figures appeared at the top of the ramp and proceeded to approach on foot. They were too distant to distinguish but James could see they had three large dogs, the biggest distinctly shaped like a German sheppard, a very big German sheppard. Mentally, the Kansan began to prepare for a worst-case scenario in which he might have to shoot the dog. He did not dig his gun out but continued to peel his eyes in their direction, trying to ascertain the situation.

At last, when the two human figures came into view, a great wave of relief swept over James. For walking his way was a pair of Christian maidens cut from pioneer cloth. The first maiden, who was in fact a lady, wore the cross of Christ upon a bright white shirt, itself tucked into a crisp pair of military camouflage pants. She was a striking beauty on a tall frame with awesome form and golden hair to her waist. But as stunning as she was, her presence outweighed her nature, being that part of her that spoke loud and clear without saying a word to let people know she was a Christian and wasn't making any apologies for it. Meanwhile, her German shepherd stood beside her with the appearance of a show winner and, if James guessed correctly, would protect her to the death in the absence of her husband. The second maiden was of medium height, well made, simply dressed, and sweetly disposed with a pretty face framed by long brown hair. Her dogs were Labrador retrievers. All three dogs were leashed. UB, who was also leashed, barked and wagged his tail.

"Ladies," said the Kansan with a welcoming nod, "am I glad to see you."

Good conversation followed but, due to extreme exhaustion, James would not be able to recall the ladies' names for his journal. He warned them of the salmon, told of the Indians on the cliff above, and asked if there were any white folks in town.

The maidens smiled and assured James that there were many white folks in town.

"I ran into some trouble last night," said James. "Two men broke into my camp, but they didn't get away with anything."

With a measure of concern, the lady asked, "You are armed, aren't you?"

"Oh yes Ma'am," James assured her even though the question would have seemed odd only 48 hours before.

The two women bade James goodbye, and as they went away, the lady turned to say, "God bless you."

Next to arrive was a young white man cut in the mold of a sky-diving, cliff-jumping, northwestern country boy. Behind his dusty jeep he towed some kind of hybrid cross between a boat and a jet ski designed specifically for rough water travel. James learned the young man was in fact a kite skier. Also telling, James noticed how the young man's gear looked well worn. The two men spoke while working on their respective rigs. Then having lashed his gear down tight, the kite skier made a phone call to make sure his buddies were up for some fun. Then bidding James well, the young man set out in his craft, zipping and splashing through waves along the shore.

The fact that the young man had left his slightly ratty truck there in the notch did nothing to reassure James who regarded the act more as a risk taken by a young risk-taker than a sign of a secure locality. Whatever the case, the aging Kansan felt glad to get away from the semiarid gorge and its intense wind that drove sand horizontally to blast eyes, face, and ears. Up to the top of the ramp James slowly pulled his rig. He then turned right, climbed briefly, made a left turn and climbed a bit further to the edge of town where he saw a large flag flying high on a pole.

In bold white letters, the black flag read, "KILL THEM ALL AND LET GOD SORT IT OUT."

James shook his head and laughed at the flag (which was on private property).

> "It would have been easy to take a picture of that flag, puff it into news, and make a few dollars to boot. I could have done that without ever having to face the river."

While focused on the flag to his left, James failed to see the hotel to his right even though he'd been told he couldn't miss it. Indeed the grand old hotel was a sight to see and yet, with no electric sign, it stood quietly behind large trees that bordered the street and James may have missed it if not for what happened next—,

"Where you going with that?" asked a woman with a kindly curious air, stepping quickly from porch to street.

"I'm going here, Ma'am," James replied assuredly, seeing the old-fashioned hotel sign directly behind her.

Penny wore the cross of Christ and possessed such character as to have stepped straight from a covered wagon, minus the dust. Penny was pretty and petit, with blond hair, brown eyes, and a timeless country dress. Penny's husband Jim came along behind. Jim was a big man, not heavyset but tall, large-framed, and, without putting on airs, appeared to be of some refinement.

Jim and Penny owned the old luxury hotel, built in 1906. And except to say that the place had been restored and was something to see, no description need be given until later. Presently, James found comfort in finding Jim and Penny, tremendous comfort. Jim showed James to a storage area behind a tall wooden privacy fence where James locked his rig. Penny then showed James upstairs to his room.

Apologizing to Penny for his state, James added that eating must come before bathing and therefore, he requested not to be seated in the dining room. Understanding his concern for the comfort of her other guests, Penny showed the Kansan to an Old West barroom which wasn't only beautiful but happened to be empty. There she gave him a menu limited to special entrees complements of a chef who came from Seattle on weekends. Penny then confessed her surprise at James's selection. James only smiled and shrugged. He wasn't a total stranger to five-star cuisine. Penny would return many times to check on James but presently left him to enjoy his excellent dinner.

"Master?" asked the brain.

"Yes," replied the heart.

"Master, only an hour ago we were desperate for a safe place to rest. Now here we sit, safe and comfy in a beautiful time-capsule, listening to classical music, enjoying food at the level of art."

"Yes, it's truly something isn't it?"

"But master, doesn't this strike you as being just a little strange?"

"No," replied the heart. "It is what it is."

"But Master, haven't you noticed? Whenever we're up against a wall, a door opens. When we need to put our tent up in the rain, the rain stops. Every time we turn around, someone's handing us money, baking us cookies, or fixing us a tuna sandwich. Pretty girls keep coming out of the blue. And if all that's not a little hard to believe, here come the Indians out of left field along with a hotel like something from *'Gun Smoke.'* "

After a brief pause, the brain lowered his voice to a whisper, "Master, I'm sorry to tell you but we could be in serious trouble here because, by my calculations, this can't be real."

Wishing only to savor the moment, the heart ignored the brain. And in fact, it was real.

Upstairs, James got a shower and retired to his room where he and UB slept like the dead.

Day 32, Monday, June 14

The old hotel stood quietly behind a row of ancient black locust trees that rose from well-like openings of red brick in a wide shaded boarder between porch and street. Going into the hotel was like going back in time one-hundred years. Just off the lobby, a sitting room afforded a view of the gorge via a great bay window. A spacious turn-of-the-century dining room also looked out over the gorge, with tall windows that let in the south sun to illuminate tables covered in white linen. A wood and leather barroom was an authentic relic of the Old West, and stepping out a side door, a shady garden made for a quiet place to enjoy lunch.

Breakfast couldn't have been better and Penny kept bringing more poached eggs, bacon, English muffins, orange juice, fruit, and cakes. Other guests sat here and there, talking and relaxing in the sun lit room. James would allow himself little time there however, for friendly as the folks were, he had work to do. First he did laundry in town a block away. Penny had given him laundry soap. In fact Jim and Penny had offered to drive James twenty miles for groceries but James declined because he needed almost nothing except ice.

While at the laundromat, James worked on his journal before returning to the hotel garden where, surrounded by red roses in bloom, he ate a perfectly delicious sandwich for lunch. Penny came and the two enjoyed good conversation but when the Kansan told the lady about the trouble he'd had, he wished for his words back, having seen the pained look in her eyes. For there they were in a sunny garden where she might escape if only for awhile, and there he had gone and reminded her of the shadow that had fallen on her realm. Penny explained how the area had come on hard times. Penny said nothing of her own troubles but James could see that the hotel hadn't been spared.

Intending not to pry but only to help, James made a few marketing suggestions. Penny then acknowledged the hotel to be up for sale.

"It's in God's hands," she said as she went away with worried eyes.

After catching up his journal at 1:15pm, James walked to town where all that remained of a once thriving community was a tavern, laundromat, and a depressing little market with scarce stock on its shelves. Whether by fault of her own or not, the Asian who owned both the laundromat and market charged high prices, thereby adding insult to the injury which appeared to have befallen folks all around.

Back at the hotel, James iced his cooler, took an hour-long nap and then organized and packed gear including his tent which he had hung out to air. By then dinnertime had come, so James headed off for town but not without first stopping to say hello to Penny and her guests in the sitting room. Walt and his wife then invited James to dine out of town with them. James thanked them kindly even as he declined, choosing to walk to town instead where he hoped to get a hamburger at the tavern.

As it turned out, the tavern wasn't open, and being Monday night, there wouldn't be any food back at the hotel either. Therefore James went to the little market where he reluctantly purchased some fried chicken that looked to have been some while in the display case at the checkout counter.

"Thank you," said the Asian, taking the exorbitant amount from James's hand.

No more had James stepped outside than an Indian barked, "Is that your dog whose been making a racket?"

"UB's a good dog!" James barked back, deciding the Indian to be drunk because his speech was slurred and he had some alcohol which he'd bought from the Asian. The Indian made no reply and James sat on the sidewalk to eat with his back to the wall.

Oblivious to everything but his master, UB wagged his tail and whined with hopeful eyes until James gave him a tidbit—,

"Tastes like cardboard, don't it boy?"

James couldn't know what waited on the trail ahead but Lyle was only the first in a string of small towns that, for lack of a more definitive term, had fallen on hard times.

No more had James finished his dinner than he saw the Indian who'd thrown the salmon steaks into the river on the day before. The Indian had stepped out of the laundromat next door and because James had gotten some rest, he no longer held his former suspicion. James also noticed how the Indian did not appear to harbor the resentment of the others. Therefore James stood up and spoke loudly to cover the distance between them, "Excuse me Sir, but may I ask what tribe you are from?"

The young Indian smiled and then loudly spoke the name of his tribe which regrettably cannot be given here because James failed to remember it. James then began toward the man, "Is that a local tribe?"

"From Alaska," replied Earnest. "Where are you from?"

"Kansas," James replied, and he proceeded to tell about doing the Lewis and Clark trail. James then asked if it might be possible to meet with the chief of the local tribe.

Seeing how his request caught Earnest off guard, James removed his sunglasses so that Earnest might see his eyes and know he was entirely serious, "I'm just a man who came from the river in a canoe," said the Kansan, "but if you could arrange such a thing, I would consider it an honor."

"I'll see what I can do," replied Earnest. Then with a firm handshake, the two men parted.

Back at the hotel, James bid Penny farewell in the knowledge of an early start. Likewise, Penny wished James well and asked that he be careful. Walt also wished James well. James then turned toward the staircase but, looking into the bar where a man in black leather sat alone, James paused to go and speak with the man—,

"Excuse my curiosity Sir, but I was wondering, is that your Harley out front?"

The biker pivoted on his bar stool, acknowledged that the motorcycle was his and told a little about it.

"Sounds like a nice bike," James said in shock. Meanwhile the man carried on as if everything were perfectly normal behind thick layers of rouge, lipstick, and mascara. Then having concluded his speech about his motorcycle, the man (who happened to be an Indian) said he had rode in from the city (which city cannot be known) and was just waiting on a friend.

James noticed the man wore a wedding band but unless it was a prop, James couldn't know what it meant. Straight away, a second Harley rumbled up and in walked a fat white biker who the Indian introduced as his friend. The white biker man didn't wear any makeup.

James excused himself and went toward his room only to meet

Penny in a hallway—,

"Penny," James asked in a confused tone, "there are two men in the bar and, I was wondering, are they planning on spending the night here?"

Penny looked like a girl who'd stepped on a tack, yet being unable to extract it, carried on as best she could, "Yes, they are."

"In the same room?"

Even more uncomfortably than before, Penny tried to explain that the men wouldn't be anywhere near James's room, but she was making a hash of it and James hadn't thought that far ahead anyway so, he was confused as to what she was saying. Therefore he went straight to the point—,

"Are they—

"I don't know!" Penny cried painfully, cutting him off in mid-sentence. Then hurrying away, she looked back to say, "I don't want to know!"

Why James pried cannot be known. He had been raised in a place where prying was considered rude. Presently however, James had been taken off guard and therefore temporarily thrown for a loop. And while he would regret pressing Penny, he would also feel that she hadn't been as upset with him as she had been with the situation in the bar. After all, Penny had told James just a short time before (while bidding him farewell) that she and Jim would be leaving the hotel shortly and would not return until the following day. And considering that Jim and Penny lived in the hotel, James didn't know what to think, but perhaps he thought too much on occasion. He only knew that Jim and Penny were good folks. And for the record, they had a man to watch the shop while they were away. Outside of that, it can be told that James did not hate the men in the bar.

Rather than worry about the men below, James laid down to sleep like his life depended on it because in fact it did. James meant to cross the river in a few hours and while he hadn't crossed it even once without creating a lifelong memory, he hadn't crossed it at all since entering the waters above Bonneville Dam. Therefore, and only because James lay on the floor directly above the bar, would he happen to hear what transpired below—,

Jim and Penny had left the hotel. The bikers were laughing. The time was approx 8:45pm and James had all but fallen asleep when an old pickup truck rumbled up, followed by the squeak of its door. Next came the sound of the lobby door opening and closing, followed by the soft voice of a maiden asking for James. James perked but didn't get up because as mentioned, he had a date with the river, and also because the entire episode happened so fast, it ended in a matter of seconds, as will now be told.

In a voice at once high-pitched, uptight, and fast-paced, the man with woman's makeup spoke on the heels of the maiden's question, and so curtly did he address her, he sounded as if he didn't care what she wanted but only wanted her to get out of there. The maiden then tried to explain but the man cut her off before she could get three words out. And again, the man sounded like he didn't give a hoot what she wanted but only wanted her out of his territory.

Directly thereafter, the lobby door closed and the old truck motored away. It ended that fast and James was left in a confused state of wonder. He had heard the maiden's voice before. He had also heard the sound of the truck before. From there it didn't take him long to remember that the maiden had been with Earnest at the laundromat. The truck had belonged to them. The young Indians had taken to heart James's request to meet with the chief. After all, James had told them where to find him, and it was yet daylight.

> "Had I been in the bar, I would not have allowed the man to mistreat the maiden. Likewise, the man had no right to injure Jim and Penny's goodwill with his rude behavior toward a person who had entered their establishment. I didn't care about any disrespect that had been done to me but, with regard to the ill treatment of the maiden and Jim and Penny, I was no happy camper."

James could go below, or he could stay on point. His heart beat for justice and felt the man should be put in line. James's brain reminded him that due to extenuating circumstances involving woman's makeup on a man and what it entailed, being that the man enjoyed special protection under the law which meant that, if James were to set him straight, then James might find himself up against those who had harnessed the awesome weight and power of the state in the service of hate. The heart reminded the brain that James would not be without friends in such a situation. The brain acknowledged as much, then reminded James of his errand, which required him to keep first things first and proceed toward St Louis in faith.

James closed his eyes and slept well.

Day 33, Tuesday, June 15

James's wristwatch alarm went off at 3:00am whereupon he arose at once, packed his ground pad, sleeping bag, and then made ten trips carrying loads of gear downstairs through the empty bar and outside where he loaded his rig beside the garden gate. He then pulled his rig down into the dark notch.

James knew he had to cross the river first thing. He had to do so before the wind came up. He needed to gain the opposite shore in order to portage the next dam. Fortunately the river passed through a narrow there at the old ferry crossing, so instead of being a mile wide, the river was only a quarter-mile wide, and 80ft deep. At the bottom of the notch, James unloaded and disassembled his walking machine. His journal reads as follows:

"I loaded my boat on the gravel beach, half in and half out of the water. As I did so, I confessed my fear to God. I'd seen how the middle [of the river] got when the wind rose. Presently there were no swells or white-capped waves but, the wind had already begun to come up. At 5:35am I set out, paddling and praying.

"Reaching the far shore, I thanked God for a fairly easy crossing. I then proceeded upstream until I found a good site to land and make breakfast. The sun came up over the edge of the gorge while I ate and, the river sparkled under a blue sky."

With dishes cleaned and stored, James shoved off and paddled east along the Oregon shore.

"My wristwatch read 8:00am. The river had calmed from an hour before when it looked as though the day would be windy. I paddled under a hot sun. The cliffy gorge gave way to large foothills of light brown grass contrasted by an occasional dark brown outcrop, and a sparse peppering of pine trees."

The canoeist paddled into the semi-arid region for several hours before seeing two fishermen along the shore near an abandoned barge. James said hello to the fishermen who wished him well as he paddled by. He then arrived before a land form along the south shore that looked to be either an island or peninsula. Uncertain as to which it was, James chose to navigate its open-river side. In doing so, he ran up against powerful current. At the same time, a headwind rose against him. So even though Rocky Island measured only a mile in length, James had to earn it one yard at a time.

No sooner had the canoeist put the island behind when he landed on a small beach to catch his breath. From there he noticed a footpath leading over a small knoll. Exploring the footpath, he found a larger path that took him to a lake where he saw a beautiful maiden sitting alone at the water's edge.

"Miss, am I intruding?" asked the Kansan with hat in hand.

The maiden turned her eyes to the Kansan who, fresh from his fight with the river, stood soaked in sweat. And while it cannot be known if she found him pleasing to look upon, he couldn't help noticing how fair she looked in soft shorts, open blouse, and bikini top.

"I was wondering if you might help me with some directions," James asked, and telling what he was about, he concluded his speech, "The current and wind have come up against me, but if that path over there leads to town, then I might continue on land with my walking machine. Can you tell me Miss, does the path lead to town?"

"The path does lead to town," replied the maiden, "but the path is under construction just now. They're paving it, so I don't think you could use your machine on it. However, if you can continue a bit further by river, there's another place to access the path and from there the path is paved." The maiden then gave directions. Meanwhile her small daughter had come running to play with UB who behaved like a good dog. The lake was obviously some kind of public area. It had a safe feel and, being a weekday, only a few folks were scattered about. James lingered to speak with the single young mother who was perhaps as lonely as himself. His errand pressed him however and, he took his leave after a brief but pleasant conversation.

Back on the river, James continued past a tributary that came in from the south called Chenoweth River. He then took out somewhere near Kindt Point on a tiny beach no more than one foot wide and twenty feet long. The beach lay between rock cliffs rising to a height of about twelve feet. Directly behind the little beach, a gentle bank of mown grass continued up to a paved bicycle path that paralleled the river. The time was approximately 11:30am.

James had arrived at the tidy outskirts of the city of The Dalles which sat along the Oregon shore directly below the Dam of The Dalles. Straight away James saw a young mother with her two little children riding bikes on the paved path. Together they made a fine looking crew and James approached like a gentleman who did not want to frighten them. The young mother provided the Kansan with an excellent set of directions. Then with well wishes and words of thanks, she and her children departed.

James spread his blue tarp under a large shade tree where he made a bed for UB among the gear. He then returned to the water's edge where he went to work assembling his rig. As he worked, a woman came with a pair of chocolate brown Doberman pinchers that weren't leashed. The woman apologized for her rambunctious dogs which were as big as they were beyond her control. James, who was down on the ground with his tools, assured the woman that her dogs were no bother even as he gently shoved one out of his way. In response, the offended animal squatted and defecated directly beside James. The lady, who remained helpless on the path, apologized. James assured her it was no big thing (although it was big). He then moved his toolbox and parts, and continued in an unsinkable state of satisfaction for reaching the second dam.

No more had the dogs shifted their attention than they both bolted as if in a race to see who could be first to James's duffle bags which must have looked like a colorful pile of chew toys under the shade tree. Knowing that UB lay hidden among the bags, James leapt to his feet and dashed after the Dobermans with a holler, but he may as well have been a tortoise after a pair of hares. The lady called out for her dogs to stop but they paid her no mind. Then, as they plunged headlong into mischief, something unexpected happened. UB went off like a bomb in their faces! It had to be seen to be believed, UB's shining moment! Taken off guard, the big dogs were momentarily driven back. Of course, UB may have died in the next instant except that James came barreling in like a mother bear and, flying fully horizontal, knocked one Doberman into the other like a bowling pin except that instead of a ping there was a thud, whereupon both dogs went down.

Bewildered but fast to recover their feet, the Dobermans drew up side by side in a stance meant to drive James from his gear pile. The dogs were not vicious but willful, very willful, and they clearly understood it was no longer a game. Fortunately, James had been first to recover his feet. He beat them to the advance by a second and, in doing so, denied them the confidence they were yet to regain—,

"*You think you can take me?*" James asked, his heart beating hot, his fluid brain planning their demise. UB meanwhile did not so much as bark but remained behind James, leashed to one of the bags. James would not harm the dogs unless they attacked but, if they did, he had a folding knife on his side, and such was his physical state by that time in his errand, not to mention the seriousness that the river had bred into him, he was not even a little afraid. Additionally, James knew his gear was good. His brother Frank had given him the knife as a gift before departing on his errand. The folding knife was difficult to see even while in plain view, having a mat finish and clip that held it at the ready, just at the top of James's pant pocket. Frank, who was a professional chef of many years, had sharpened the knife himself and then, seeing a vision of James underwater and tangled in rope with only the knife to cut himself free, Frank had sharpened the knife again, the end result being a blade so sharp, a man could not touch it without drawing blood.

The Dobermans turned and ran away.

The Kansan then turned to his dog, "UB," he began with a mixture of pride and amazement for the <u>U</u>ncommon <u>B</u>ravery he'd seen. "So long as I live, I'll never forget that!"

James then restrained himself for fear of adding to any upset the lady must have felt with regard to the shame that had befallen her dogs.

"Good boy!" said James, praising UB quietly while the lady went away without a word.

UB wagged his tail happily.

After bringing his walking machine under the shade tree, James stopped to eat a pack of beef franks, one jar of artichoke hearts, one large hunk of bread, one green bell pepper, and one quart of cranberry vitamin drink. He then began loading his rig and as he did, a man came along sweeping the paved bicycle path with one of those hand-held blowing-machines which had replaced brooms in the modern age of science and technology.

James introduced himself and told what he was about. The man suggested that James go to a nearby Louis and Clark historical sight only a mile out of the way. James said he would like to but he could not because the visit would require an added expenditure of two miles which he could not afford. The man did not understand what James meant even as he showed interest in a history that both men shared. James therefore decided the moment merited a heartfelt appeal so that the man might understand. Thus breaking with his formal attitude, James humbly explained the physical challenge of getting himself and his gear up the river. James then spoke about the distance he must yet pull that day if he were to have a resting place for the night.

"Oh I know that!" the man quipped, stopping to light a cigarette before launching into why James really must visit the historical site while near it.

The river had a way of erasing a man's tolerance for foolishness. James looked the obese smoker over and, deciding him to be detached from flesh and blood reality, assured him that he would not be visiting the site.

Not to be outdone, the man rebutted by way of raising a final point in which he seemed to suggest that James might soon meet with some real hardship—,

"Well," said he in a thoughtful tone, "you'll be entering the desert now."

The two men parted cordially, although both were disappointed with the other.

"No man sees anymore than a piece of the world. God alone sees everything. And it is worth remembering, the man had only wanted me to see something in which we both shared a common bond."

With his cart loaded, James harnessed in and pulled toward town on River Road. The time was approx 1:30pm. The sun beat hot on the pavement and UB got the worst of it, so James set him atop the cart.

Having entered the city proper, James came alongside a green park with shade trees, swing sets, and swimming pool. There James noticed a maiden watching him. She wasn't more than sixteen but stood out on the green with a beauty that might someday rival Amy, and that was truly saying something. James made the mistake of taking a second look and as he did, the maiden let the large beach towel in which she was wrapped fall away, leaving only a bikini to cover her extraordinary bloom.

James quickly looked away, knowing himself to be a sinner and fearing God, which meant he had some discipline and he cared. So the maiden was not in danger from him, nor he from her. And in fact this episode would not merit inclusion herein, if not for what followed—,

Next to catch James's eye was a water fountain and that was something he could not do without. While he drank, a Hispanic boy came along, and, because the Kansan also had a water jug to fill, he yielded the fountain to the boy. The boy, who was only seven or eight, took a drink, wiped his mouth on his arm and asked, "Sir, what are you doing pulling that canoe?"

"I'm doing the Lewis and Clark route," replied James.

The boy gave no clear indication as to whether he understood or not.

"Do you know who Lewis and Clark are?" James asked. "Have you learned about them in school yet?"

The boy only nodded.

"You have?" asked James, lifting his eyebrows as if looking for the truth.

"Yes."

"Alight then. You see how I got my canoe over there on wheels?"

"Yes."

"That's my walking machine. I use it to get around the dams. That's what I'm doing right now; I'm going around the dam. And once I get around the dam, I'll put my canoe back in the water, and then I'll keep paddling up the river."

The little boy nodded and ran away.

James shook his head and laughed to himself, then used his water jug to cool UB off, pouring and petting to work water into the dog's fur. While so employed, James saw that the boy had returned.

"Sir, are you working for a magazine?"

"No," James replied, amused, "I'm doing this on my own but, I hope to write a book."

The little boy disappeared as quickly as he'd come and James thought no more about it except to laugh at the intelligence of the question.

James then filled his jug with drinking water and stored it in his cart. No more had he finished doing so than the little boy came back—,

"Sir, are you rich?"

"No," James replied, laughing out loud. "I'm not rich. I have enough money to complete the trail. Then I'll be broke."

"You'll be broke," echoed the boy, obviously understanding what broke meant, suddenly looking afraid. "What will you do?"

"I'll get a job," James replied with certainty.

The little boy nodded, then ran away through the park.

Having grown curious, James followed with his eyes as the mysterious little fellow ran across the green. The boy went under several shade trees until having covered a distance of about sixty yards, he arrived to stand at attention before the very flower James had seen. The young beauty queen was sitting on a swing, brushing her long blond hair.

"Well I'll be," James said to himself, having been unaware. And for the sake of the maiden it must be told, she had at least acted with an innocent kind of tact, either that or her beach towel actually had fallen off by accident. In any event, she had put it back on.

James returned to the business at hand, and as he harnessed into his walking machine, the young queen's ambassador returned with her final question—,

"Sir, why are you doing this?"

"I'm doing this," James replied, "so people will know it can be done." Then bidding the boy farewell, he departed.

Arriving at a grocery store, James parked his rig in the shade of a small tree on an island of grass at the edge of the parking lot. After purchasing groceries, he had brief but pleasant conversations with passing folks while restocking his cooler and duffle bags. He kept busy as he spoke because he had much restocking to do and he had to work fast to keep food from spoiling in the heat. He couldn't transfer food from grocery bags to cooler until he had removed their packaging and then repackaged them in something less space consuming like a plastic storage bag. For example, a large roast came wrapped on a foam plate that James removed and discarded. In such a way, he not only made room for food in his cooler but also made room to get every cube of ice possible in there. Likewise, when purchasing food storage bags, James discarded the box that the bags came in then put the bags into one of their own, so they would fit into his food storage duffle. That was how it worked.

From the grocery store, the Kansan continued pulling through the City of the Dalles until he happened upon the local Chamber of Commerce. He parked his rig and went inside where a kind lady gave him directions on the route through town. She also gave him a lapel pin (which he later mailed home to keep with other gifts he received along the way).

Next is an episode (from the margin of James's journal) that was originally omitted from this story—,

Feeling the call of nature, James parked his rig on the shoulder and went down an embankment to a patch of shrubs possibly located between the river and road. There James met Dean, a young drifter. Dean was peering over the tops of bushes in fear of the police because, as he put it, they wouldn't let him hang out down there. Dean looked haggard from his lifestyle. He was still youthful however, and wiry, and even happy-go-lucky albeit in a sad way. Dean was highly impressed when James told him about doing the Lewis and Clark trail. The young drifter apologized repeatedly because he thought James deserved a beer and, he didn't have a beer to offer.

James next arrived at the public port of the city where he hoped to find a water spigot because UB appeared ill-effected by the heat. While at the port, a kind lady assisted James with directions on how to get across town without taking the interstate (via a road that traversed a hillside above the rail yards). Also at the port, a marine biologist gave James directions on how to portage around the dam. Having thanked both lady and gentleman in turn, James set out for the inn beside the dam at the far end of town (a distance of three miles).

James's journal reads as follows:

> "The sun burned hot and the asphalt smelt as if it were cooking. UB suffered in the heat even as he rode atop the cart. I kept giving him water and looking back over my shoulder to make sure he was okay. A good-looking brunette [who from her window saw me passing] came out to meet me. I apologized for my rush and moved on."

At 7:00pm, James arrived at the inn beside the dam. He first set UB up in their room then went directly to the inn's restaurant where he spoke with a waitress—,

"I apologize for my current state Ma'am, but just now food has to be the first order of business."

The young waitress laughed and told James not to worry about it, after which she took care not to seat him near anyone. And here comes a place to tell, James didn't smell or look like a pigsty. Rather, he was only a little gamey. He ate the biggest steak they had, along with a baked potato and salad.

Back in the room, UB lay exhausted, his eyes bloodshot from the heat. The poor old dog had been heavily taxed, and James felt more than a little concern.

James took a shower, then went straight to bed where glancing at the clock, he felt surprised to see the time was already 10:00pm.

James's journal reads as follows:

> "It had been a long day. I had made good progress. Twelve miles by land and water against current, head-winds, and afternoon heat [much hotter than previously encountered]. I felt happy because I had made the second dam. I considered it another milestone."

James and UB slept like rocks.

Day 34, Wednesday, June 16

At 7:30am, James began on a short list of things to do before departing. He needed to make a simple shade canopy out of cardboard for UB while he pulled around the dam. First however, James ate breakfast while his laundry dried. Then in the parking lot, he made a minor repair to his rig. While so occupied, he noticed the sounds of heavy traffic on the interstate highway and because he didn't like the idea of pulling alongside such traffic, he decided to remain at the inn another night and portage early in the morning when traffic would be light. By such means, he would also save UB from the afternoon sun, not to mention saving himself from making a shade canopy. So it seemed a good decision all around. With his extra time, James spread out his gear and did some needed maintenance work. The work took two hours, after which James ate a large roast beef sandwich for lunch at the inn's restaurant.

While at the restaurant, James asked to speak with a cook he'd met briefly the night before. Steve, as fortune would have it, just happened to be ending his morning work shift, so he clocked-out and took a seat at James's table. The two men then spoke for two hours. They spoke about dogs and divorce. They spoke about coming home from war (Steve was a Nam vet). They spoke about lots of things but mostly they spoke about the river. Fittingly, they sat at a table beside a glass wall that afforded a bird's eye view of river and dam.

Having been born in the city of The Dalles, Steve had spent many a day on the river from boyhood with his father to present. With pen and paper, Steve drew a detailed map covering the next one-hundred miles of river. He wrote many notes on the map that explained many things important to getting upriver. And that was good because James's roadmap gave no indication as to whether a town might have a grocer or not. In fact some towns indicated on James's roadmap no longer existed. With Steve's map, James would know exactly where the grocery stores were (not the quick-markets, but real grocery stores, however small they be), and also the hardware stores, and the locations of clean water sources which would be of great importance in the desert ahead. James thanked Steve and felt grateful even as he couldn't yet fully appreciate the value of what he received.

More than once, Steve stopped to address a point that James seemed incapable of grasping—,

"You're the first man to make it up this river."

Not knowing how to reply, James looked out the window and shook his head.

"I've lived here my entire life," said Steve, pointing sharply through the glass, "You're the first man to make it up this river!"

Of course Steve had spoken about modern times, since the construction of the dams. The conversation continued with Steve telling how his father had taken him to see the construction of the dam back when he was a small boy (and in fact the great gray dam was something to see, standing just there, through the glass).

"Look there," said Steve, pointing out the window, "the river is 255 feet deep there."

"No way!"

"Yes, I'm serious!"

"You must mean above the dam," said James, deciding Steve had accidentally pointed in the wrong direction.

"No," said Steve affirmatively, "right there, just downstream of the dam, there's a hole, it's 255 feet deep."

James wouldn't get his hands on a river chart for two more years but when he did, he would see the underwater contour lines that showed the river to be 255 feet deep. It cannot be told herein if the hole was natural or where the men who built the dam quarried rock but in any case, it was the deepest point in the river that James knew of.

With words of thanks and well wishes, James and Steve parted with a firm handshake. And like so many other men and women James would meet along the way, he hoped to see Steve again someday.

Outside the inn's restaurant, James went to get UB who sat tied to a tree some distance away. Halfway there however, James noticed a Mexican man who was looking curiously at his walking machine—,

"Do you like that?" James asked, at once bold but courteous even as he felt mildly suspicious due to things he'd recently seen which shall be told in a moment but not just yet. The man got frightened and began to speak in broken English. As best James could tell, the man said he didn't want any trouble. James tried to assure the man he meant him no harm but the man hurried away. James watched as the man joined a group of five or six Mexicans standing on a corner. James had noticed the Mexicans there before but couldn't understand what he saw, he knew nothing about illegal immigration. James had also noticed a group of Mexican men sitting in an old car at the park he'd passed the day before. It had seemed odd at the time, but James hadn't given it anymore thought. James honestly didn't know what he saw.

Returning to UB, James found his little friend shivering and crying under a tree. James hadn't known it but the pine tree under which he'd left UB produced a lot of sap. Additionally, the ground beneath the tree was covered in a layer of decorative wood chips. Therefore, the more UB had tried to get the sticky wood chips off, the more they had stuck to him. UB had wood chips stuck all over him. So much so, he looked to have turned into a cartoon character. James laughed even as he apologized. Then using warm water and soap, James spent hours carefully removing chips and sap from UB's fur and paws.

James next went to the lobby to mail home a map that he no longer needed. While in the lobby, he saw the night clerk with whom he had spoke on his way to the mouth of the river a month before. It appeared the night clerk had just come on duty—,

"Excuse me Sir, do you remember me?"

The clerk looked oddly at James, as if he did remember but couldn't quite place it.

"I was here a month ago," said the Kansan. "I was on my way to the mouth of the river. I was on my way to attempt the Lewis and Clark route. I told you I would canoe up the river and stop here on my way upstream."

Astounded, the clerk stared at James.

"It's me Sir, I made it."

The clerk's face brightened like a lamp come on from a dimmer switch until he stood fully transformed, no longer the stern old watchdog, but as bright a picture of joy as James had ever seen.

Back in his room, James worked on his journal. Then having caught up his journal and called home, James went to bed at 9:30pm. He couldn't fall asleep however because his tooth had reinfected. As for the fix that he employed, it shall be described only this once for the sake of avoiding needless repetition. First however, it can be told that the Kansan had an excellent set of teeth except for a crack in a molar which came from a shenanigan of youth and, the damaged tooth was the current culprit. James lanced the abscess as before and got a good night's sleep. The problem wouldn't go away however and in fact became a chronic infection that needed to be drained every third day or sooner as needed. At such a rate, James soon used up his toothpicks of which he had only three or four. James would then fabricate a tool from a large fish hook which worked well. And omitting any further description, all that need be known here is that James developed a routine in which he drained fluid from the abscess every third day or sooner as needed. No further mention of this shall be made except to tell that the problem continued for a year but with regular draining, brushing, proper diet, fresh air, and exercise, it went away on its own without antibiotics or pain killers.

The Desert
Chapter V

Day 35, Thursday, June 17

At 4:15am, James rolled up his ground pad and because it had to be rolled up small to fit in its sheath, James used his knees to keep it pinched while rolling it tight, very tight. After sheathing the pad, James rolled it up in a black plastic construction bag. He then twisted the open end of the construction bag tightly to keep water out, whereupon he secured it by wrapping a mini-bungee around the twisted bag's end to seal it like a twist-tie on a bread bag. He put a second bungee three-quarter of the way down the roll to keep the plastic tight. All said and done, the task of putting away his ground pad required five steps and used five components. It was only the first in a series of morning chores and unless James wanted to sleep in a wet bed that night, it had to be done right. In fact, every task had to be done right if James wanted to reach St Louis. And while so occupied, James never forgot that St. Louis wasn't getting any closer. Therefore by the time James shoved off or harnessed into his machine, he had usually worked up a sweat. Few men witnessed him breaking camp but those who did inevitably said something like, "I had no idea this involved so much work." The truth of the matter was that, whether James stayed in a tent or an inn, he had to move his home each time he traveled and, if he aimed to succeed, he had to take the necessary steps to preserve his home along the way.

James had hoped to be on the road at 5:00am but he wasn't ready to go until 6:00am, and because the inn's restaurant opened at that time, James decided he may as well stay and have breakfast.

At 7:15am, James pulled his rig onto the shoulder of I-84 only to have UB refuse to go. James couldn't understand the problem. After all, man and dog had been walking along highways from the start but perhaps UB had had enough.

"There's no other way," said James, tugging at the leash while UB planted his paws.

"UB, come!"

UB refused.

"There's no other way around the dam."

UB complied but only by walking as far from the road as his leash would allow.

James sugar-coated his voice while pulling UB back to the shoulder, "See how much easier it is to walk over here?"

Ignoring James, UB returned to walk in the rough where he soon drifted to the opposite side of a reflector pole—,

"Snap!" went the leash as it broke on the pole.

James knelt down and, while shaking the end of the broken leash at UB, said, "This is just like you UB. You always have to take the most difficult path!"

In the next instant, James heard the cars zooming by on the highway directly behind and, he closed his eyes and began to laugh at himself. The Kansan fixed his dog's leash with a knot, and they proceeded east for two more miles before arriving to where the east and west bound lanes of the interstate separated.

James parked his rig on what looked to be an unofficial parking area beside the north shoulder of the eastbound lanes. The parking area consisted of a gravel surface the size of two parallel parking spaces. No cars were currently parked there and the area was trash free. James unharnessed and surveyed the terrain between him and the river. A footpath (if it could be called that) went down a large buttress of basalt boulders, crossed a set of railroad tracks, and continued under the westbound lanes of the interstate which were elevated on tall pilings. The path then descended a riffraff bank and passed through a veil of vegetation before ending on a rocky sliver of beach beside the river.

While looking down the path, James recalled what Steve had said, *"It won't be easy,* but I've seen what you have [being one heck of a good portaging system], and with what you have, you can make it."

Exactly as Steve had done, so also had the marine biologist from the port given the same set of directions with the same pained expression. According to both men, there wasn't another way around the dam without a motor vehicle.

Having unloaded and disassembled his walking machine, James left UB topside and started down the buttress with his ice chest. The pitch was steep and the chest hindered his line of vision but with caution, focus, and balance he placed his boots from boulder to boulder until he arrived at a barbwire fence that traversed the buttress. The fence was old and partially broken down where the path intersected it. James managed to straddle it with cooler in hand even as the crotch section of his blue jeans barely cleared the top wire. And for the record, the geometry of a man crossing a fence on an incline doesn't square until one takes into account the uneven surface and the broken state of the fence. James proceeded to the bottom of the buttress where, having completed the hardest leg of the path, he failed to take into account the way in which the railroad tracks came round from under the westbound lanes of the highway like a tunnel. Nor did James take into account the traffic noise from the highway above. Fortunately, the engineer saw James at the last and laid on his horn. Without a second to spare, James saved himself with a quick spin and mighty step. Just two moves between life and death. It was that close. In fact, had James taken time to drop his cooler, he wouldn't have lived. Afterward, while boxcars flew past, James figured he had given the engineer a bad scare, and he would liked to have made an apology. He then thought about how unfortunate it would have been, had his great river adventure come down to getting run over by a train.

Once the tracks cleared, James crossed and continued down a riprap bank that seemed a cakewalk after the buttress. Then proceeding downward through a narrow band of vegetation, he emerged on a rocky beach where he stowed his ice chest in the shade of a bush to protect it from the morning sun.

Climbing back to the highway proved enough to wind a man and that wasn't a bad thing. Without pause James carried loads while UB waited in the shade of the canoe until only dog and boat remained. James carried UB first, then returned to hoist his boat atop his shoulders.

Balancing his canoe, James began down the buttress but had only taken a few steps when, due to the angle of the pitch, the stern hit the rocks causing both man and boat to fall forward. James's journal reads as follows:

> "My boots came down hard on untested rocks which moved with low grinding sounds but somehow, by no grace of my own, I regained my footing and didn't fall down or drop the boat. Realizing my mistake, I proceeded with sidesteps while keeping my canoe parallel to the buttress. By

such means I reached the fence where, attempting to straddle it, my blue jeans hung on a barb. I stood holding my boat over my head, looking down at my pants which were caught on the fence. Fortunately, I only had to rest the tip of the canoe on a rock which presented no difficulty due to the geometry of my situation. I then carefully reached down with one hand and freed myself from the fence. At the bottom of the buttress, I set the canoe down as gently as my remaining strength allowed; I dropped it hard on the rocks. I then went to look around the corner to make sure no trains were coming. No train came but I saw a barge called the *Tide Water* on the river. I then went back and got my canoe, crossed the railroad tracks, went down the riprap bank and through the veil of bushes to the river. Then with gear loaded, UB and I shoved off."

Several days before, on approach to the city of The Dalles, the walls of the gorge had given way to brown hills. Presently, the walls of the gorge came back to hem the river again. And entering into it, James saw something remarkable:

"The river went smooth as glass and became a natural mirror, one mile wide, winding like a ribbon, reflecting the great cliffs rising up to the blue sky for as far as my eyes could see. The temperature was mild because the air had yet to be heated by the sun. To call it awesome wouldn't do it justice. It was beyond awesome, like seeing a reflection of Heaven and, I felt grateful to be there."

When the morning grew hot, James found a shady patch of beach on which he stopped for a snack before proceeding upriver with his bow silently carving ripples in the glassy surface.

James paddled even as he checked his map which lay open before him. In fact he had two maps back-to-back in a soft plastic case. On one side was a roadmap, on the other Steve's map. Thus seeing that an Indian village lay ahead, James lifted his eyes from map to river and spoke aloud. But before his words can be made known, it is important to understand that, in returning to the river, certain fears had returned to James.

"It wasn't that I consciously felt afraid while out on the water in broad daylight but my fear affected me all the same. To understand such fear, I think a man would need to leave his home, walk to the nearest troubled area, camp out in the bushes amid trash and broken beer bottles with shadowy figures lurking about. Then having survived, a man would need to return to the bushes and camp some more but not before learning that in that same area there lived a number of men from another culture who hated him. In such a scenario, a man might be surprised to discover that a stranger lived within himself."

Looking at his map and seeing that an Indian village lay ahead, James's jungle mechanic kicked open the door of his cage and it sounded like this, "I don't want to be camped anywhere near those trashy thieving Indians!"

No more had the words left James's lips than a gust of wind came so abruptly from the dead calm, it seemed a slap in the face. James was not injured by the hand of God but, in a very real manner of speaking, such was the power of the warning, James's jungle mechanic got knocked back though his cage door just as he was stepping out.

All around, the glassy waters rippled and the mirror image of Heaven vanished. Shocked, James shouted up to Heaven, "I didn't mean it!"

The headwind continued to build.

Fighting against rising waves, James pled to undo what had been done, "I know, I'm a sinner too!"

The wind would not abate and James felt crestfallen because what had been a rare day would henceforth be just another struggle.

"Praise God, I got His message, which was not to allow my fear to turn into hatred."

Accepting what he believed to be the helping hand of God which on that particular occasion came in the form of punishment, James continued against the wind. And as he went, he ad-libbed an old song by Bob Seger, "Against the wind, I'm still paddling against the wind…"

It was hard work, very hard. In fact it became a battle in which it was all James could do to make it to Celilo Park which lay directly beside Celilo Indian Village.

At approximately 2:00pm, James landed at Celilo Park via a clean strip of beach adjoining well-manicured lawns with picnic tables under shade trees. Straight away James realized the park to be a rest area for Interstate 84. It struck him as funny because he had pulled in with his canoe for a rest. He carried his cooler to a nearby picnic table in the shade of a tree where he ate cold cuts, French bread, and a green bell pepper with a quart of cranberry vitamin drink. Meanwhile, two tourists came from opposite directions to see what the canoeist was about. Jim was an American and Alois a Canadian. The three men had a good conversation, the main topic being Lewis and Clark. After Jim and Alois departed with well wishes, James took a nap in hope that the wind would calm down. He snoozed, talked to his dog, ate more cold cuts, and snoozed some more while waiting on the wind to abate.

At 6:30pm, James shoved off and resumed against the wind. And here comes a place to tell, there were no swells when the wind came from the east. The east wind could raise waves with white caps but not swells. Presently, the waves were not white capped.

One mile east of Celilo Park, James arrived at a large bend in the river where, due to an optical illusion, he mistook a tiny island in the middle of the river for a large island along the far shore. James discovered his error only after paddling to the tiny island in the middle of the river. At that point it only made sense to proceed to the large island where he hoped to find a place to camp. In such a way, James crossed more open water than he otherwise would have and because he crossed on a large bend, his path of travel amounted to a shortcut of one mile.

Reaching the far shore, James entered a narrow channel which ran like a moat between island and shore. By entering the narrow channel (1/5 mile wide, or 1/5th the size of the main river channel), James began the second leg of his shortcut. This was because the narrow channel was relatively straight whereas the main channel dipped south around the other side of the island in a big semicircular radius. So the canoeist hoped to shave another mile, making a total savings of two miles (no small potatoes when paddling against the wind).

Inside the narrow channel, our novice marveled at what he saw. To his left, the walls of the gorge rose 200 vertical feet from water to shelf before rising another 600 feet to the rim of the gorge. To his right, Miller Island appeared a swath of barren desert hills rising steeply to a high plateau one mile wide and three miles long. Atop the plateau, an ancient Indian burial ground overlooked the channel. The channel lie deathly quiet between sheer rock walls and forbidding hills. Enclosed and cloaked in shadow with water that measured to 80 feet deep, the channel appeared very nearly black.

The current suddenly sprung to life and James found himself fighting for every yard. He hoped to find a place to camp, preferably away from the Indian burial grounds located on the downstream half of the island but as progress became a battle of inches, so did the island shore grow less hospitable until it became straight up and down.

With tall cliffs rising from black water on either side to make for something that looked like an entrance to a shadow realm, not to mention the freak current, James couldn't help but wonder if spirits of the unfriendly variety had come against him. Then, and quite suddenly, a cove opened to his right.

> "At the back of the cove, half hidden in a corner, a natural passage just a few feet wide went up like a ramp between sheer rock wall and steep sand bank covered with tall shrubs of the stout kind found in a desert marsh. I went up the natural ramp, between cliff and shrubs, whereupon coming out twenty feet above, I was pleased to discover a sandy little shelf."

James carried loads and brought up his canoe, then pitched his tent on desert sand. His wristwatch read 9:00pm. The fact that his camp lay hidden (except from the rim of the gorge) pleased James because he feared the Indians wouldn't want a white man near their hallowed ground. To his credit, James could have camped on the downstream half of the island near the burial grounds but chose the more difficult route to the upstream half.

With just enough time to make dinner, James cooked and ate a thick steak along with a large chunk of French bread. For dessert, he savaged a grape fruit while swatting at a swarm of mosquitoes that had found him. He then fled into his tent to escape the tiny blood suckers.

Man and dog slept well.

Day 36, Friday, June 18

At 4:00am the west wind woke James, and although he wanted to sleep awhile longer, he feared the wind would raise the swells and trap him on the island. He didn't think it life-threatening to be trapped on a desert island for days with scarce protection from harsh elements, but he thought it might be very unpleasant. A man could get worn out. In fact the desert had already worn James out and he'd hardly entered it.

James lingered but not for long. A sudden gust lashed his tent like a whip and sent him into action. He broke camp, working quickly but thoroughly. Breakfast would have to wait for the safety of the mainland shore.

At approximately 6:00am, James and UB set out toward the upstream end of the channel and a place called "Hell's Gate Point" which James had not seen on his map prior to entering the channel on the day before.

"I shouldn't have lingered," James thought, paddling hard in rising wind, gobbling a food bar and banana for strength.

Out in the narrow channel, the waves grew into small swells and began to whitecap. Conditions were rapidly deteriorating and, as a result, the canoeist changed his plan. He had hoped to follow the island shore east to its upstream end before crossing the river to the Oregon shore where he could continue east. Instead, he immediately struck out for the much nearer Washington shore.

Perhaps the dragon perched on the cliff above. Perhaps he looked on intently while clasping his paws before his mouth like a chess player who hides a grin.

The canoeist angled his craft so as not to be turned over by swells which, although not large, were almost beyond his ability. Then as swells grew larger, so did the distance across the channel seem to grow longer.

Sheltered water lay along the cliffs, and having arrived there, James felt he'd made it to safety in a nick of time when in fact he'd only drawn closer to danger. Closer to danger because he assumed the location of Hell's Gate Point to be somewhere on the east end of the island when in fact it stood directly ahead on the Washington shore. He could not see how the channel made for as perfect a wind venturi as nature could produce. Perfect because the narrow channel was of such design as to vomit swells from its mouth like cannon balls against a towering wall of rock, and that wall was Hell's Gate Point!

Perhaps the dragon had already begun a victory dance in the end-zone, so to speak, when an angel threw a flag down from Heaven. Whatever the case, the wind died, the water fell calm, and our novice continued in a clueless state of wonder:

> "A great wall of rock [called Hell's Gate Point] rose up on such a scale as to be awe inspiring. I passed directly beneath it. And quiet, it was so quiet!"

James had scarcely paddled a mile more when Maryhill Bridge came into view approximately two miles upstream. Seeing it, James decided not to cross to the Oregon shore as originally planned but to remain along the north shore so that he might get ice at Maryhill State Park. James didn't take out at the park but instead chose a primitive beach directly before the park. From the beach, James walked to the road above and then followed it into park where he found no ice but filled his water jug.

Back at the beach, James enjoyed a truly sublime breakfast camp; shaded, secluded, looking out at river and gorge, rising up to blue sky with Mount Hood for a centerpiece. The volcano that had once stood before him, presently stood far behind.

The east wind came up and James felt sorry because it meant a hard day awaited him. There wasn't anything to do about it except to pack up his cook stove, call his dog to the boat and shove off.

After paddling under Maryhill Bridge, James continued east along the north shore and while he went, he focused on the technique of his stroke in order to get all he could from his effort against the wind.

> "Fighting that headwind was hard work. Every stroke required a tremendous effort, then another, and another,

and another, and always ruddering the strokes, keeping the canoe pointed upstream even as the wind constantly tried to turn it back. And all the while, the desert sun burned hot!"

As the grueling pace continued, James felt happy simply for being able to make progress, slow though it be. Then looking across the river, James was struck by the fact that he could see both towns of Biggs and Rufus. James wouldn't have thought it possible, at least not by looking at his map but with his naked eye, he could see both towns at either end of a massive cliff five miles long. Biggs lay at the foot of Maryhill Bridge and Rufus was upstream just a few miles shy of John Day Dam. The interstate highway connected the two towns like a straight piece of string along the base of the cliff with cars traveling like ants between. It amazed James probably because he saw things through the eyes of a craftsman. He marveled at how much he saw; the river, the tiny towns, the great cliff between, and the cars going back and forth. It seemed a mural on a wall.

"That can't be."

Then checking his map, James lifted his eyes to look across the river again, "Well I'll be."

While paddling below high cliffs that rose directly from the water, James discovered a crack that seemed custom made for his canoe. So he backed in and tied off for a nap. His life vest made for a pillow on the stern while the gunwales made good foot rests. Stretched out and sleeping peacefully, James floated in shade between sheer rock walls rising to a swath of blue high above while a breeze came through although how cannot be known. The water rose and fell to gently rock the canoe as if in a lullaby and, in all likelihood, there was no finer place to nap in the world.

After a deep sleep of thirty minutes (approx 2:00 - 2:30pm), the canoeist awoke and ate ham, bread, cheese, and an apple for desert. He then set out to cross the river.

To cross the river with wind, waves, and current working against him, James paddled all out for an extended period with his bow pointed upstream on a forty-five degree angle. By such means, he managed to gain the far shore at a point directly across from where he'd begun.

Along the Oregon shore, James fought against a rising headwind until further progress became impossible. He then unfolded his pulling frame and set out towing his craft through shallows along a sandy beach that stretched for as far as the eyes could see without a soul in sight. Any other place in the gorge and James would have been stymied by the mere fact that such beaches didn't exist. In fact, James had often considered himself fortunate just to find a place to take out.

Perhaps feeling thoroughly fed up with the knight and his impossible "luck," the dragon sank beneath the surface to pull his ears and shout words that ought not to be spoken. In any case, the knight not only enjoyed having the beach all to himself but also, it came with a superb view of John Day Dam just three miles ahead.

"Whereas Bonneville Dam had appeared like a first attempt at dam building and Dalles Dam had appeared like a midpoint evolution, John Day Dam stood as the crowning achievement. With classic simplicity, it spanned the gorge on an awesome scale."

Having pulled his boat for a mile, James arrived at a sand flat peppered with tall desert shrubs and also a few ancient motor homes. The motor homes were occupied by folks living on the cheap, without modern amenities, which James could hardly imagine, himself knowing firsthand how a motor home without air-conditioning could heat up like a tin can in the sun.

James angled his canoe on the beach to create a band of shade for UB to rest in while his master went scouting. And because the stern of the boat remained in the water, UB not only had shade but also could get in the water. Such things were critical in desert heat so punishing, it could create an emergency in a very short time.

With UB taken care of, James scouted and found a primitive road that connected the sand flat to a county blacktop. Beside the primitive road, James made a crude shade shelter by tying a tarp to some shrubs. The time was 4:00pm and, after hauling everything from water to shade shelter, James well and truly felt the effects of a day spent in desert heat.

The tarp projected a 4ft x 4ft shadow onto desert sand, just large enough for dog, cooler, and gear if packed in tight. James remained in the sun, assembling his walking machine, his eyes burning with loads of sweat as he tried not to burn his hands on the black gunwales. The sun meanwhile moved across the sky more rapidly than James expected, forcing him to move his dog and gear several times to keep them in the artificial shade. He also carried UB to the water several times to cool him off.

About the time James finished his work, a woman who lived on the beach (in one of the old motor homes) came and told him how she hoped to get out of there someday. Linda wasn't asking for money but was only explaining how misfortune had seen her to where she was.

Linda's friend Mark came next in an old van. Mark, Linda, and James had a brief but good conversation, whereupon Mark offered James a ride to town. James declined even as he thanked Mark for his kind offer, adding that he must walk and paddle every step and stroke of the way. Mark and Linda then bid James well and retreated to a manmade patch of shade beside Linda's motor home.

With UB atop the cart, James set out pulling with narrow wheels sinking deep in sand, forcing him to labor if only briefly like a beast of burden who struggles to pull a cart out of a mud hole. From that point on, James would retain only foggy glimpses of that day, and the following day, and the morning of the day after that. What can be known is that the primitive road joined a blacktop which went up a gradual grade for a distance of one mile.

"Painfully slow, I ascended the grade. Like a hazy snapshot of the ground before my feet, one particular patch of blacktop is all I remember. I made it to Rufus where I purchased a bag of ice at a quick-market, then forgot to take the ice with me. I proceeded to the inn. I lay on the floor of my room. My head was cooked. UB was charred. My body was alright, but my head!"

The heat had come before James like a wall and because he didn't know how to surmount it, he feared it. He forced himself to get up and walk to the restaurant which according to his journal was down the street although he retained zero memory of getting there. He could record things but his long-term memory was shot and that was rare with regard to spacial detail. By his journal we know he ate the largest steak the restaurant had with a baked potato and salad.

Back in his room, James took a shower and hit the sack. His

wristwatch read 9:00pm. He had moved himself, his dog, and their home a distance of twenty-five miles as the crow flew from the Dam of The Dalles to John Day Dam in two days against current, headwind, and desert sun. According to James's journal, he felt happy as he closed his eyes and fell into a deep sleep.

Man and dog slept well.

Day 37, Saturday, June 19

At 6:00am, James went to the restaurant down the street for breakfast, then spent the morning working on his journal in his room. James also did laundry and restocked food supplies. Due to mild heat exhaustion, James would retain zero memory of Rufus except for the interior of the restaurant which many local folks visited. By such means, James figured Rufus to be a nice town. While at the restaurant, James had fish and chips for lunch and a good conversation with his waitress Fran.

Fran was of retirement age and had lost her husband only a year before. James would remember that Fran missed her husband very much. She asked James if he'd considered going through the locks at the dam simply for the experience of it. James was struck by what Fran said because until then he had regarded the locks as being for commercial shipping only. In fact James would have felt guilty asking the dam authorities to open the locks for him. After all, he was just one man in a canoe. Then realizing that it would indeed be a great experience, James thanked Fran for her suggestion and decided that in the event he made the last dam, he would ask to go through the lock.

Back in his room, James worked hard and caught his journal up at 4:10pm. He then turned his attention to his gear. For dinner James went to the restaurant then returned to his room where he called home before continuing with preparation and packing of food and gear. By the time James had finished it was 8:30pm, so he hit the sack.

James didn't sleep well because he had eaten a large order of ribs with loads of sauce, nor had he left as much as a speck of grizzle on plate or bone. It wasn't the restaurant's fault. They had two choices of ribs, James would remember that; one being lean, the other fat and saucy. Normally, James would have chosen the lean ribs but in his exhaustion he'd ordered wrong and because he knew it to be his mistake, he said nothing but ate the ribs without complaint. Therefore, the fat and saucy ribs were in his stomach for a night of indigestion.

James slept well enough.

Day 38, Sunday, June 20

At 4:30am, James ate breakfast in his room including five raw eggs. He then loaded his gear and set out to portage around John Day Dam via the shoulder of I-84. His wristwatch read 6:00am and, while not yet hot, the day promised to be a cooker. With UB walking alongside, James pulled east for five miles to Le Page State Park where a good many people were enjoying a beautiful summer morning. At that point James recovered his long-term memory (which of course he couldn't know he had lost).

No sooner had James pulled his rig into the parking lot above the boat dock when someone asked what he was doing, to which James gave his usual reply.

Another man then spoke in a tone that rubbed James wrong, "That's one way of doing it."

"It gets the job done," James replied curtly while thinking, *'It's hot, I'm trying to pull this load, and I don't particularly care for your tone of superior intellect."*

"Well," said the man, "you're going the wrong way."

If James understood correctly, the man had spoken about two different types of direction and both were arguable. And yet, the man had taken a contrite tone. James prayed every morning to treat each person he met with courtesy and respect even as he stood firm in his beliefs. So James did his best to make amends regarding his promise to be courteous whereby he ended up having a brief but good conversation with the man and his wife who came along after. Then with well wishes, James proceeded to the dock where he transformed land rig to water craft. UB meanwhile waited on a neatly mown lawn in the shade of a nearby tree.

Having launched from Le Page State Park, James paddled across the mouth of the John Day River before continuing east along the south shore of the Columbia River. The river measured one mile wide and went straight down from shore to a depth of 100 feet. The canoeist encountered no current probably because the flood gates at John Day Dam were closed. There wasn't anything to stop the desert sun however except for a cowboy hat under which the Kansan continued with his usual determination. In fact, so hot did James become, he took off his life vest which, until then, he had worn religiously. James hadn't removed his life vest for any reason other than the heat but, all the same, he would never put it back on.

"When I took my life vest off, a feeling came over me and I realized I had moved that much closer to following in the footsteps of my forbearers."

It is worth remembering that James's journey was not recreational but "re-creation-al." And to his credit, the knight would be the first to tell children that if they ventured out into the river without their life vests, the dragon would get them.

Presently hoping to beat the heat, James took off his shirt so that he might soak it in the river and put it back on, the idea being that wet cotton would wick heat away from his body. No more had James gotten his shirt off however than cars on the interstate began honking. Taken by surprise, James laughed in the assumption that some brazen maiden had started it. Then on second thought, he hoped it had been a maiden. In any case, James put his shirt back on and at once felt how well the wet cotton helped to cool him in the breeze.

After traveling for an unspecified period of time, the highway lay out of sight and no traffic noise could be heard:

"The sun burned hot and no cloud stood in its way but a breeze came from the west and, it was a beautiful day. I paddled east for another hour or two until I realized there wasn't a soul on the river except UB and I. Then, the water went smooth as glass. Silently, steadily, I glided in a perfect reflection of gorge and sky. On the heels of thanks, a lone white bird appeared, holding an altitude of approximately fifty feet above the river, coming straight down the gorge, straight toward my boat. I found myself caught up in a feeling for which words are hard to find, like getting a glimpse of Heaven. The white gull gave me a glance as it passed over without a sound, then continued until it had vanished from sight."

On either side of the river, a barren swath of desert measured no more than one mile wide below walls rising sharply to a height of eight-hundred feet. Vastly desolate and burning hot it was. At once beautiful and a little frightening but only as long as one didn't venture too far from shore in either direction of land or water.

Coming to a forty-five degree bend in the river, James decided to follow a straight line course through the bend as though laid out by a ruler to mark the shortest route. Doing so would take James from south shore to north shore and then back to south shore. By such means the canoeist hoped to shave 3/4 mile off his present course. There was a drawback however, being that he would have to paddle on a six mile trajectory through open river. In other words, he'd be far from shore. The river was calm however so James set out, aiming his bow toward a bend on the far shore some three miles distant.

As James crossed the river, the land he aimed for slowly grew in visual definition until, after a whole lot of paddling it came as a relief to distinguish individual rocks and shrubs. At last, the canoeist had nearly made it across when a barge came around the bend unexpectedly. James altered his course to avoid the barge, rode out its wakes, then continued toward the point of the bend where he hoped to land and have a snack before setting out to complete the second half of his short cut.

No more had James landed on the point and pulled his boat onto a riff of sand when, looking through a natural hedge of shrubs that lined the shore, he saw a small park. James hadn't known a park was there but in fact there lay a small park. Not a green park but a brown desert park, very neat and clean, although oddly placed under a blanket of heat waves in the middle of a scorching wasteland where the only sign of life came from the shrill cry of a cicada. The Kansan didn't enter the park but only peered through the bushes while wondering if it was one of those places built especially for Indians.

James had already drank a considerable amount of his water supply in the 107 degree heat and therefore his eyes were quick to find a water spigot in the empty park. Quick indeed, and as he eyed the spigot, he could almost hear Steve's warning: *"Do not go in those places set aside for the Indians!"*

If the Indians caught a white man in their park, they would cut him up and use him for fish bait, or at least they would like to as James understood it and that wasn't good, but James didn't know if the park was Indian territory or not. After all, there were no signs to designate it as such. At least no signs faced the shrubs along the shore from which James spied.

Walking half-sneak, half-nonchalant, James made his way to the spigot. Then glancing about, he bent and filled his water jug before walking quickly back to the veil of bushes that grew along the shore.

Coming through the bushes, James received a greeting from the east wind, whereupon he shouted, "Oh! I don't believe this!"

There wasn't anything James could do except get in his canoe and face the headwind. Nor could he safely cross back over to the other side of the river to complete his shortcut. So he paddled along the north shore by which means he quickly came to a well-manicured but deserted boat ramp previously hidden from sight. There James read a large sign warning all white men to stay out of the park.

James continued east along railroad grades and rocky cliffs. At 6:00pm, he began looking for a campsite, paddling and scouting until he found one at 7:45pm. His journal tells of the site:

> "The ground wasn't perfectly level and the coarse desert grass held many mace-like thorns but all-in-all it was a good site. Moreover, it wasn't trashy and I considered that a good sign [especially in lieu of a path that came down from somewhere, plus a fire ring]."

Having made fifteen miles in difficult conditions, James made camp in a state of exhaustion. Fortunately, he had a large T-bone steak pre-cooked from the restaurant in Rufus. So he didn't have to cook. As mentioned, James would remember very little of his time in Rufus but at least he knew a young waitress had carefully wrapped the steak in layers of foil on the evening before and, her diligence wasn't wasted on him. Along with his steak, James enjoyed a hunk of bread, one green bell pepper, and an orange.

After dinner, James took a long swig from his water jug, then looked at his dog and said, "Boy howdy UB, this Indian water sure does taste good."

James hit the sack at 9:30pm and thought it good. He slept well, waking only intermittently due to noises outside his tent which were nothing more than twigs in the breeze and nocturnal animals.

Day 39, Monday, June 21

At 6:30am, James got up tired but kept after it, packing, cooking, cleaning, and carrying loads. He shoved off at 10:00am or thereabouts. His journal tells how he kept cool in the heat:

"It was very hot breaking camp but seemed cooler on the water. A breeze came from the west and I made good time. The sun beat down hot! Not a cloud in the sky. Twice I jumped [from canoe] in [to] the river to cool off. Other times I took my shirt off and dunked it in the river before putting it back on. I also dunked my head regularly, using caution not to upset the canoe. I also dipped UB regularly. We were in the desert, learning how to meet our newest challenge—the heat."

After a lull, the breeze returned except that it came from the east. James noted that it felt good but made him work hard. He crossed the calm river and proceeded east along the Oregon shore. He slouched under the intense heat and doing so made his back sore.

"I found a rare shade spot just big enough to get my boat halfway into (under the eve of a low shrubby tree that clung to rocks which rose steeply from the water). I [tied off there and] ate one half block of cheese and a large apple. I then proceeded east."

The sun intensified, the temperature climbed above 105, and the breeze died. Fortunately, the weary canoeist found another patch of shade which, like the first, measured just large enough to shade half his boat. There James tied off with the back half of his canoe in the shade. He then laid his head back on the stern, put his feet up on the gunwales and fell deep asleep. For forty minutes James snored heavily under his hat. Then he was off again, paddling toward the town of Arlington which he could see through his field glasses some five miles ahead.

The east wind came up strong and the canoeist struggled to make progress. The last two miles made for a hard fight against headwinds and white-capped waves.

At 3:00pm James entered the Port of Arlington where his first order of business was lunch amid watered lawns and shade trees. The port and its park were a small manmade peninsula adjacent to the town. Across the bay of the peninsula, children played on the sandy beach of a swimming lake in the town park. The community of Arlington enjoyed a good layout because the town had been moved when the dams were built, and therefore, it had been thought through in advance of its reconstruction.

After lunch James began the business of assembling his rig, and while he worked, he enjoyed brief but pleasant conversations with local folks who happened by. A pair of retired couples, one couple hosting another couple who were visiting the community, stopped to see what James was about.

"Ladies, Sirs, my name is James and. . ." the Kansan continued, telling who he was, where he came from, and what he was about.

One of the men, a large-framed fellow who appeared impressed by James's effort, used old-fashioned straight talk to express his regret about a lack of "intestinal fortitude" in modern times.

Even though he agreed with the man, James refrained from comment in fear of coming off as a braggart.

James pulled his rig into town and got a room at the inn. The time was 6:00pm. In his journal, the following words were underlined, "I was cooked from the sun."

James fell asleep but forced himself to get up, take a shower, and go across the way for fish and chips with salad. He then returned to his room where feeling good about his progress, he fell fast asleep. The time was 8:00pm. Man and dog slept well.

Day 40, Tuesday, June 22

At 6:40am, James went searching for a map because his county maps covered only that section of the gorge between Stevenson and

Arlington. James looked at road maps in two gas stations but found only statewide maps, so he didn't buy any. He then went to the hardware store and purchased a small propane stove to replace his white fuel stove because, as he told the store owner, his old stove made his eggs taste like stove fuel. As James departed the store, the store owner said, "Keep the sunny side up, at least that's what they say."

The store owner's play on words brought a parting smile to James's lips.

Back in his room, James prepared to ship his old stove home by draining out the fuel. He also boxed up his broken water filter. On his way to the post office, James stopped at the hardware store and gave his old stove fuel (2/3 gallon) to the clerk, the idea being that someone could use it. The lady clerk then gave James a clip with which he repaired UB's broken leash.

"I wish I would have gotten names but so easy and casual were the conversations, I'm not even sure that names were exchanged."

From the post office James returned to the inn where he did laundry and worked on his journal before going out for a hamburger at 1:30pm. He then walked to the grocery store where he purchased steaks, bread, green bell peppers, apples, bananas, and grape fruits.

While at the grocery store, James overheard two men speaking about the river. One of the men looked reminiscent of an old miner, neatly dressed in his best duds for a trip to town. And because the man looked like he might know the river, James introduced himself and asked about the availability of firewood along the shores as one proceeded into the desert. Lake said he knew the river well, then courteously brought James into his audience while resuming a story he'd been telling the other fellow.

Lake, as James understood it, had had a near run in with Mexican drug runners out in the desert. James secretly thought Lake's story about drug runners to be far-flung when in fact James hadn't yet entered the territory from which Lake had come. Lake said he chose Arlington as a place to resupply because he could leave his boat at the port and walk to the grocery store without worrying about thieves stealing his gear.

In hindsight, James made the following entry:

"The town of Arlington, like the bulwark of its port on which the waves broke, had resisted the changes occurring in the desert beyond."

Back in his room, James caught up his journal at 3:55pm:

"I know I have a big challenge before me - the heat. It is 107 degrees in the shade. I do fear it. I have been thinking about it all day and have formed a plan: Rise at 2:30am, be on the water by 4:30am and paddle until 2:00pm. Then find a place to hold up and sleep until 2:00am. Then repeat. Plus drink a lot of water and dipping in water. A man almost has to get out there and experience it firsthand to understand [what it's like]; the railroad buttresses make for walls of basalt boulders and the cliffs are worse, so a man is boxed in on the water with no place to escape the sun. Plus he must push a 500 pound load up the river, one stroke after another. It isn't easy [but it sure was worth it]."

James packed his gear. He cleaned his cooler so that the melted ice could be drunk. He then went to the gas station where he purchased three bags of ice. He next went for dinner at the drive-in restaurant where he ate a hamburger and had a brief but good conversation with Zeke the grade-school football coach. Also, the waitress here must be given honorable mention for her beauty. Indeed, it seemed every community had a beautiful young waitress and Arlington wasn't to be outdone. James always appreciated beauty, although at times it pained him.

Back in his room, James caught up his journal at 6:30pm. He then prepared for bed. He prayed to be patient with UB, whom he had shouted at the day before. The heat had an adverse affect on James in that way but at least he would be quick to get a handle on it.

James slept heavily.

Day 41, Wednesday, June 23

James got up at 2:30am and did his best to break up bags of ice without making noise. He loaded food from refrigerator to ice chest then loaded his rig and set out with UB for the port. Arriving at the port at 4:30am, James found the river in a wild state. Like battering rams, large swells crashed against the port gate.

In mornings past, James had seen the west wind rise only to die out. Therefore believing that the wind would subside, he transformed his land rig to water craft. He then ate an abbreviated breakfast and stood ready to shove off at 5:50am, but large swells still crashed the gate. So he left his boat and walked back toward town with the intention of getting a full-fledged breakfast, after which he hoped to find navigable conditions. On his way to town, James passed a man out for a morning stroll—,

"Three days," said the man as he passed by, walking at a brisk pace.

"Excuse me, Sir?" James asked.

"Three days," replied the man, looking back even as he kept speed walking, "when it blows like this, it blows for three days." The man continued on, having spoken without the slightest hint of malice but rather as though stating a law of nature.

While eating breakfast at the restaurant in town, James met a man named Steve who was bicycling the Lewis and Clark route east to west. James and Steve had a good conversation while facing one another from tables alongside windows that looked out over the town park. They mostly spoke about the heat and how to deal with it. Then the same man who'd been out walking came and told James again that the wind would blow for three days. The man, who had a pleasant attitude, only wanted James to know what to expect and James appreciated that.

Returning to the port, James found the situation unchanged. Large swells with foaming white crowns crashed against the port gate, making for an impossible situation. So James went to sit atop a berm that overlooked the gate. James didn't sit in the wind but on a bench behind a wind wall where he waited with hope for the wind to die. While he waited, a man named Larry came along with his dog in a classic automobile, and the two men spoke for better than an hour on a variety of subjects including dogs, automobiles, and the weather in the gorge. Larry then wished James well and departed. James's wristwatch read 8:45am. Time to accept the obvious; the wind wasn't going to let up.

While carrying loads from boat to grassy flat above, James laughed while realizing that the Lord had answered his prayer from the night before. For there the wind had dashed his plan, causing him to do a whole lot of work for nothing, and yet, he didn't feel a single atom of frustration. Thus looking skyward, James said a word of thanks. Then while assembling his walking machine, two retired ladies came along on their morning walk. Formal but friendly as ever, James thoroughly enjoyed showing them his walking machine. Next came a couple with a girl who appeared to be their granddaughter and James enjoyed explaining his walking machine for them. They wished James well and went on their way.

It never entered James's mind to wait three days on the wind. Rather, he planned to strike out east using his walking machine on the shoulder of Interstate 84 early the next morning. The Kansan figured there must be someplace to access the river even if it was only a primitive access like the one he'd used at the Dam of The Dalles.

While pulling his rig back to the inn, James met a man named Neil who told about a place to access the river. The two men then parted with words of thanks, well wishes, and a handshake.

Back at the inn, James met Suzie the maid with whom he had a pleasant conversation. James asked Suzie if she knew the weather forecast. Replying that she did, Suzie relayed the forecast which was a hot one. James thanked Suzie and retired to his room where he slept for an hour.

Discovering that four eggs had broken in his ice chest (having been packed in like sardines), James went to the grocer. He went for lunch and then returned to his room where he caught up his journal at 3:05pm. He went to the hardware store and bought a blue tarp and some twine with which to make a shade shelter if need be. While at the hardware store, he had a brief but good conversation with a lady clerk who happened to be single and attractive.

After taking the tarp to his room, James went to the drive-in restaurant where he ordered two foot-long hot dogs with everything on them. While in the restaurant, James met a man named Jim and the two men had a good conversation, but as to what topics they spoke on, no record was kept. More than likely, they spoke about the river. James then returned to his room where he caught up his journal and hit the hay. His wristwatch read 7:30pm.

James slept well.

Day 42, Thursday, June 24

UB woke James at 2:00am. The little fellow needed to go outside. After taking UB out, James fell back to sleep. Then at 3:30am, James packed his gear and ate breakfast including five raw eggs. He departed the inn at 5:00am.

From Arlington, James pulled his rig up a long slow grade that climbed the side of the gorge before leveling off on a wide shelf one-hundred feet above the river. And because such distinctions aren't difficult to overlook, here comes a place to tell how the grade probably wouldn't have seemed like much to a motorist but only to a man pulling a moderately heavy cart. At the top of the grade, James found a sparse landscape of brown desert hills, coarse vegetation, and rock outcrops. Both road and shoulder were made of jet-black asphalt, and seeing as much, James pulled hard and fast to beat the desert sun that was sure to come.

"UB was just able to keep up. I kept an eye on him to make sure he was alright."

"You can do it," James told UB in an encouraging tone. "Do it for your old daddy."

Sensing the urgency, UB pushed himself hard and that was good because the less weight James had to pull, the faster they could go. And the more ground they could cover, the less chance they would find themselves on that jet-black surface at midday.

With a punishing pace, man and dog covered five miles in what seemed no time at all. Hence they came to a small gravel pull-off before a road sign that read "Heppner Jct ½ Mile." There stood a single tree which, although small, gave excellent shade. James took a break to eat a banana and a slice of bread with peanut butter. He then resumed pulling. He passed Heppner Junction and continued to a bridge over Willow Creek Canyon which, since the building of John

Day Dam and the subsequent rise in water level, had flooded to become something of a calm inlet. There was no public access to the canyon but a path just over a guardrail led to the water a short distance below. It wouldn't have been very difficult for James to put in there except for one problem; he couldn't see to the mouth of the inlet and therefore couldn't know what kind of water waited where calm canyon met windy gorge. Nor could James gain a visual vantage point by land. So he decided to pass it by. Before moving on however, he took the opportunity to carry UB down the steep path and gently toss him in the water. Then with his dog greatly refreshed, the Kansan continued toward the next exit another five miles ahead. James's wristwatch read 10:00am.

James and UB made good time. And although hot, a minuscule cloud puff hovered almost continually between the two travelers and the sun. So they went mostly in shade even while the sun beat down all around. James thanked the good Lord many times for that tiny cloud. And after reaching St Louis, he made the following entry:

"Instead of calling that little cloud a miracle (which it surely was), I would rather think it one of those things that happens when a man walks in faith."

Having pulled hard for ten miles, James couldn't go a step further even though his exit was in sight only 1/8 mile ahead. His strength had gone, his feet were mostly in pain, and still he felt overjoyed to see the exit because it meant he had beat the midday heat. UB meanwhile appeared so dire, as to be worthy of a medal.

Proceeding to the off ramp, man and dog descended to a remote gravel road that passed underneath the interstate highway. The road ran in a small desert ravine called Three Mile Canyon. There James met a pair of county workers who happened by in a pickup truck. The two county workers had no knowledge of the road going in the direction of the gorge. (The road was only two tire tracks with course desert grass growing between.) The county workers had only exited the highway for a pit stop. Thus wishing James well, they vanished up the ramp.

Looking down the road, the first thing James saw was a black swastika painted on a white bridge pillar like a marker to a trailhead. From there the road disappeared into a narrow gap between small cliffs where broken beer bottles and other telltale signs lay scattered about like the scrambled letters of an animal language.

James wondered if the swastika was the work of some dumb kid or if it was a warning marker by which White Supremacist told upstart Mexican Gangs to keep out, like a no trespassing sign that said, "DO NOT COME DOWN THIS ROAD!"

"Seeing the swastika, and having already been the beneficiary of so much kindness from my people, not only on the Lewis and Clark trail but, as the son of a widow, I could not help thinking of how, with the power of modern media, that swastika could be plucked up like a rotten apple floating in an ocean of goodness, plucked up and held up to falsely portray an ocean of people as being rotten through and through, like the Nazis did the Jews."

With instructions to bark if anyone came, UB remained beside the cart in the shade of the underpass. James scouted the primitive road in the direction of the gorge, whereupon going through a narrow gap between small cliffs, he found himself standing in the mouth of the tiny canyon that opened to the gorge like a high balcony in an opera house.

James stood before what would have been a beautiful vista and in fact a sign read PLEASE KEEP OREGON [AMERICA] BEAUTIFUL, but the sign stood absolutely riddled with bullet holes and trash covered the ground in such fantastic amounts as to be like carpet. James would not hold the man who had given him directions to the place in low regard however, for the man had shown nothing but goodwill, suggesting Willow Creek as the put-in point and Three Mile Canyon only as a last resort.

"My boat wasn't on a hitch behind a truck, so I couldn't just turn and drive away. Nor did I have doors to close and lock, or walls to sleep behind. Therefore in troubled areas, I had no choice but to walk in a nether realm between the primitive and the civilized, between the signs of the former and the rules of the latter. Such a mix could test a man, like navigating a river."

Going by the facts, being that bullet holes meant gunplay, destruction of state property meant anger, empty alcohol containers meant drinking, possible intoxication, and irrational behavior; James decided to strap his six shooter on. And here comes a place to tell, James never concealed his pistol. Either he wore it out where all could see, or he kept it unloaded and out of reach. The way James saw it, wearing his pistol wasn't so much about fear as it was a way of hanging a sign to let people know he wasn't going to take their crap.

Armed and harnessed, the Kansan pulled his rig to the vista where he began a long descent on the primitive road. He traversed on a downward angle, following little more than a path to the river ten stories below. Halfway down, the road deteriorated into a slide area peppered with loose rocks the size of footballs. James carried loads of gear across the slide area and then pulled his empty rig across before reloading it. Meanwhile, the face of the slope burned like an oven.

Only by using every atom of his strength and caution did James reach the bottom without losing control of his cart. He shed his gun belt on an empty beach at the water's edge, then walked into the sheltered water and fell over. The cool water felt good but James didn't tarry because trash lay scattered about and he regarded it as a bad sign. In fact James decided against unloading his cart but instead launched his canoe directly off its wheeled carriage. Nor did he take time to disassemble the wheeled carriage but only laid it atop his canoe and paddled away. The carriage made for a high center of gravity and that wasn't good for stability. But due to a long narrow island that made for something like a barrier reef (one mile long and approx 300 yards off shore), the chop was small in comparison to the open river.

Like an ocean oasis, the nameless island was a beautiful picture of white beaches and rich green vegetation. At its widest point, it concealed a rocky lagoon where a large colony of seagulls nested.

Having scouted the island, James returned to his boat and paddled around its east end. Then turning against the wind, he towed his canoe through shallows going west along the island's north shore until he arrived at a spot he'd marked with a stick while scouting.

". . . a section of beach measuring just wide enough to accommodate my tent, shaded by a wall of treelike shrubs that ran the length of the beach. The wind came across the water with its cooling effect while the convex curve of the shoreline kept it from blowing too strong. There wasn't a speck of trash anywhere. Plus the beach lay totally removed from where I had come, so there wasn't any trash to be seen at all but rather, the beach looked out over a mile wide swath of open river set before the awesome backdrop of a desert canyon. And still that wasn't the half of it, for the polished gravel that composed the beach on that side of the island possessed such a quality that, when wetted by waves that repeatedly ran up and receded, shone like semi precious stones."

James recorded it as his best campsite to date, dubbing it, "The Isle of Fantastic Rocks."

James set up his new cook stove which performed perfectly. Lunch was a large steak, bread, and a green bell pepper. The time was 12:30pm.

"I had made excellent progress. I was right on schedule. I figured I could pitch my tent, break down the cart, get the boat properly loaded and ready to go, then get to sleep early for a good start [at dawn]. Those were my thoughts while I sat eating and taking in the scenery."

After lunch, James went to collect a couple of small rocks he'd spied while eating. In doing so, he spied more rocks that looked too special to pass up. Thus he ambled about in the shallows, gathering rocks before his campsite—,

"Even the ugliest of these rocks would be special back home," James thought.

James decided to send the rocks he had collected to Frank and Kathy because they had a little water garden in their back yard and the beauty of the rocks came to life when wet. The rocks would add to James's payload until he could mail them but, so excellent were they, he decided it worthwhile. He figured on boxing and shipping them from the next town.

One rock had the quality of an ancient vase, being eggshell black with non-uniform pink squares surrounded by thin borders of pastel green. And the pastel green borders also connected the pink squares via a network of green pastel lines that ran like cracks throughout the eggshell black body. And the rock was uniform, being very smoothly polished with the same design all round. Also, it did not look as if its colors had been painted on but rather, different materials had been pressed together and then polished. Thus the pink and green parts were as insets in the black. It was a very special rock. Another rock, also the size of a small soap bar, had a grayish-green body with translucent white squares surrounded by thin black borders. In that rock, no black lines connected the white squares but flecks of black lay like stars throughout the gray green body. The Kansan had never seen such rocks. Another rock was translucent red in the size and shape of a strawberry with translucent white squares. Another rock was a mix of green and yellow in a pattern like woven wheat. Another rock was of the purest white, and another the purest black. Another was purple with darker purple bands like tree rings.

James gathered 29 rocks in all. As it turned out, Frank and Kathy did not put the rocks in their water garden but in a tray in their living room. Then when James got home and asked to borrow the rocks so that he might write of them in detail, Frank and Kathy reluctantly handed the rocks over while joking that James meant to keep them even though he promised to return them on the following Sunday (which he did).

While collecting rocks, James had a vision of a barge with a steam shovel scooping up his island paradise for sale to homes throughout suburbia, and he wondered if perhaps he shouldn't tell about it. Meanwhile, it just so happened that his position in the shallows gave him a more complete angle of sight over the mile-long beach, and as he picked up and admired the last rock, he realized he wasn't alone. Just two-hundred yards down the beach stood some kind of Robinson Crusoe, a man so dark and leathery, as to have spent a lifetime in wind and sun; his only covering, a tattered pair of cutoff blue jeans, and a beard like a bird's nest that had been pasted on his face.

Before the man caught sight of him, James managed to step back behind the wall of vegetation that bordered the beach. James then exited his camp through the wall of vegetation and by such means gained a low berm that ran like a backbone to the far end of the island. The vegetation concealed James as he went quickly on a faint trail atop the berm. Then at a point halfway to the man, James came to where the berm ran between river and lagoon. From there James continued with extra stealth, knowing he mustn't scare up the gulls in the lagoon and thus alert the man to his presence. A second curtain of vegetation between berm and lagoon helped to conceal James from the gulls. UB's location cannot be known except that he wasn't with his master and probably remained asleep at camp. Only on drawing near would James see that the man had dogs of his own but because James was upwind, none detected him. Also, the wind in the bushes helped to mask both noise and movement. James wasn't armed and intended the man no harm but only sought to get a better look before deciding whether or not to reveal himself.

From his hiding place in the bushes on the berm above the man, James got a good close look. It appeared the man had just landed. His ancient flat-bottom boat was made of heavy aluminum, with faded camouflage paint and a pair of outboard motors like un-restored antiques. Probably, the man had cut his motors and landed using a set of oars which were still wet. His three dogs had yet to come ashore. Behind his boat he towed a second boat that apparently served as a supply barge. Both boats were identical except the second had no engines. Also telling was the condition of the man's gear which looked to have been decades in wind and swells. As for the man, he wasn't big but entirely made of muscle and sinew tightly wrapped in a thick leathery hide from which a pair of eyes seemed like windows to the wild itself.

"I think I'll pass on striking up any conversations today," James thought, ever so slowly moving his foot to take a step back even as he kept an eye on the fellow. But as he shifted his weight, a stone dislodged and rolled down the backside of the berm where it scared up the nesting gulls. It happened exactly as related herein, and needless to say, hundreds of gulls went up like fireworks on the fourth of July!

James froze while the man jolted round to search the bushes with eyes that burned like coals. Then, with a catlike reflex, the man made a mighty leapt from shore to boat where he caught both oars as if natural extensions of his arms. He gave a thrust to separate his boat from shore. The wind caught him and, due to some boulders in the water, his attention momentarily shifted away from James.

Seeing an opportunity to escape without detection, James ran like heck toward his own camp. He ran to beat the wind which carried the wild man toward his camp.

James reached his camp first but not without detection because, as any outdoors man knows, motion makes for detection.

"James!" the wild man shouted, still some distance down the beach, "James!"

Astounded, James went walking with caution toward the man, "How do you know my name?"

"It's Lake," the man replied, "We met in the grocery store at Arlington."

"Lake?" James echoed in disbelief.

"One and the same," Lake replied with a smile.

Drawing close, James saw the fellow who only a few days before seemed a neatly made miner come to town in his best duds with hair and beard well groomed and, a row of pens nicely arranged in his shirt pocket.

The two men met on the beach halfway between what would become their respective camps. Then, with his adrenaline still pumping, Lake explained how he'd been waiting for James in hope of speaking with him. Lake said he'd been living on the river for twenty-five years and, in all that time, he'd never known anyone to do what James had done. Lake didn't seem at all doubtful but, suddenly bewildered, he halted his speech and asked—,

"How did you get behind me?"

James explained what had transpired since last he saw Lake, which had been the day before the west wind began.

Lake spoke in fits and starts like an old radial airplane engine coming to life. In so many words, he told how he'd been living away from what he called "the outside world" for twenty-five years and, until that moment, he hadn't met anyone with whom he could relate.

James wasn't sure what to think except for the obvious, being that Lake was a man on fire.

"Hang on!" said Lake, turning toward his boat, "I'll be right back!" Then returning at once, he continued, "I want you to have this. It's a hat that holds water. It will help you beat the heat. Here! Look! See how it works." Lake went shin deep in the river, dipped the hat in the water, and put it on his head, "See, it's a nice hat. I got it from a kayaker."

"That's mighty kind of you Lake," said James, "but I already have a hat."

"Are you sure?" Lake asked. "This is a really nice hat."

"Thanks again Lake. But I'll stick with the hat I got."

"Oh, well, alright then."

Until then James had been running on schedule to beat the heat exactly as he'd planned. In such a focused way, James also was a man on fire. Therefore James explained that he didn't have his camp made, that he had much work to do before he could turn in, and that he must get his work done if he were to have an early start on the morrow.

Disappointed, Lake nonetheless said he understood. James returned to his boat, built a tent platform of polished gravel, pitched his tent, disassembled the components of his walking machine and loaded his boat so that everything would be ready when he woke.

"I looked forward to a morning in which I wouldn't have to carry loads but instead would only need to stow a few items and shove off."

James had no more than finished his preparations and only needed to eat and hit the sack when he heard a shout—,

"James!" Lake called, approaching.

At once James went forward to meet Lake on the beach halfway between their respective camps. Lake meanwhile came gesturing with a handheld weather radio, "I wanted to warn you, a windstorm is coming."

Knowing that the last wind storm had ended only an hour before, and remembering what Larry had told him back in Arlington regarding the weather in the gorge, that it was nearly impossible to predict; James decided he would continue as he had since day one, taking things as they came.

Lake looked back at the western sky, then returned his eyes to James with concern, "You could reach [the town of] Boardman before the storm hits."

"Thanks for the heads-up Lake, but I'm not going anywhere until I've caught some shuteye."

"Well, if you're not going anywhere," said Lake with a shrug, "why not visit for awhile?"

"I apologize Lake, but I've got to get some food in me and hit the sack."

"I haven't spoken with anyone in twenty-five years!" Lake said, launching his words. Then softening a little, he said, "Yeah, I mean, I've spoke with some people while in town but, I haven't sat down for a real conversation in over two decades."

For once James couldn't say no. So the two men sat down to talk on the beach. The time was 4:00pm. UB showed up directly, stumbling about like a drunk while James made excuses for him, explaining how he'd had a rough morning.

"He's 14 years old," James concluded, petting UB fondly.

"How old do you think I am?" Lake asked.

"I don't know."

"Guess."

"I'm not good at that," James replied.

"Just take a guess."

"Alright, I'd say about 43, give or take a few years."

"I'm 64," Lake proudly stated.

"Really?"

"Yes, really."

James couldn't help being amazed, for other than being leathery, Lake had the physical makeup of a young athlete. He was lean and ripped with muscles from head to toe, completely nimble, entirely fast-footed, and possessed of an intensity fit perhaps only for the wild. Perhaps, if a man were to go into one of those few wild areas yet remaining in the world, he would find a group of animated men squatting around a campfire, sharpening their arrows, speaking of the hunt, laughing and gesturing in fits and starts. Perhaps such men remained young and strong to the end of their days.

"Do you have a base camp somewhere?" James asked.

"No," Lake replied, "can't do that. They'd run me off, the authorities I mean. Have to keep moving. I stay somewhere for awhile, then move on. That's why I know this river like I do, and the Snake River too. I know these two rivers better than any man. Go ahead, ask me anything about these two rivers, I know them both like the back of my hand."

"Well," James began, "I'm pretty well lined-out until the next dam but after that, I'm in the dark."

"Go get your map," Lake ordered, "and we'll have a look."

"I don't have a map," James replied. "I had a good map but it ended at the first dam. I have a hand-drawn map and it's good but, it ends at the next dam."

"I've got a map for you," said Lake, effortlessly springing to his feet.

"I couldn't take your map," James called after Lake.

"It's an extra," Lake said over his shoulder. "A fellow I met on the river gave it to me."

After some fast digging, Lake returned with map in hand. The map wasn't a river chart or even a detailed map but a good overall perspective showing both the Columbia and Snake River from the Pacific Ocean to Lewiston, Idaho. James couldn't know how fortunate he was, but Lake quite likely knew the Columbia and Snake Rivers better than any man who had lived since the building of the dams. Lake poured out a wealth of information that would prove vital in days and weeks to come. The two men continued pouring over the map until James made a fear-based remark about not trusting the Indians whereupon Lake stopped cold and said, "Now you know as well as I, a man's skin color ain't got nothing to do with whether he's good or bad!"

James agreed and Lake was graceful enough to let it go at that, not to mention that Lake had been making fear-based remarks about Mexicans only a few days before (nor were his fears unfounded). To make amends, James told Lake of his request to speak with the chief of the Nez Perce while at the town of Lyle, whereupon Lake said, "I'm half Nez Perce."

James looked on in surprise and, sure enough he could see it, although until that moment he hadn't known that Lake was half Indian.

No more had Lake said he was half Indian than he added he was a shaman and, without missing a beat, began giving instruction on how to live life. Lake had scarcely spoken two sentences however when James interrupted—,

"That sounds like [an ancient Chinese philosophy called] Taoism."

"It is," replied Lake, surprised that the Kansan would know such a thing.

"I didn't know that Indians were Taoists," James said in a perplexed tone.

"They're not," replied Lake. Then with some disappointment, "I try to explain Taoism to them but they don't like it."

Presently remembering what Lake had said about not having a real conversation for twenty years, James looked sideways at Lake. He then said, "I read that book by Lao—, Lao—,"

"Lao-Tzu," said Lake, referring to the man who founded Taoism in China around 600BC.

"Yeah, Lao-Tzu, he's not my cup of tea," said James, adding that he was a Christian. He said no more about it, but in his chest he saw Taoism as a philosophy which, although not without wisdom, was only a dry seed without Jesus. And so it was only natural then, he felt glad to know that Indians didn't want it.

"You must carry a lot of dog food!" said James, petting a large German sheppard, a beagle, and dachshund who had come ashore to vie like puppies for his attention.

"I don't buy any," Lake replied, ordering his dogs to behave. Lake then proceeded to tell how he fed his dogs, which was to club carp over the head with an oar.

"That's a good idea," said James, knowing firsthand how the river, which often stagnated in the desert, teamed with carp. In fact James had been tempted to kill them with his paddle, so easy it would have been. But because James had no good reason outside of thinking them grotesque, he refrained.

Lake once again returned to that which he regarded as highly significant, "No one has ever made it up this river."

"Someone must have," James replied.

"No," said Lake. And turning his natural intensity up a notch, "You don't get it! This is something that has never been done, *and you don't get it!*"

James looked out over the river and thought of what seemed logical, whereupon he replied, "Someone might have paddled by while you weren't looking."

With a frustrated grin, Lake shook his head, "You just don't get it."

James grinned back as if to say, *"I can't help it."*

Lake pitched a pebble into the water and said, "I'd like to know if you make it."

"I could send word," said James. "Is there a way I can contact you?"

Lake went to his boat only to return with a small backpack. Then producing pen and paper, a shiny object slipped out of his pack and into his lap.

"What the heck!" James exclaimed, spotting the cell phone in Lake's lap, "I thought you said you hadn't had any outside contact for twenty-five years!"

"I have a half-brother," Lake said sheepishly. Then picking up the phone and drawing solemn, "This is so I can call him. He helps me out, financially."

James shrugged it off in the knowledge that no man squared one-hundred percent of the time and perhaps men too often gave themselves more credit than indicated on that record of truth being kept in Heaven above.

After trading contact information, Lake asked, "Did you have to get permission from any government agencies to do your trip? You know, like the Corp of Engineers, or the National Parks Service?"

"I didn't ask," James replied, folding a piece of notebook paper and slipping it in his pocket. Then stroking UB, James took in the vastness of his surroundings.

> "Free as a man could be, in the midst of so much beauty, it is easy to understand why Lake used the term 'outside world' when referring to modern society."

"Since starting my journey, I've been having the same dream," James began. "I don't have it so often anymore, but in it, I get called into some government office and they're all very nicely telling me that I should have told them what I was doing. They then tell me, again very nicely, that before I can continue, they have some forms that must be filled out. They then bring out this stack of forms and start asking questions but their questions make less and less sense until finally, they don't make any sense at all."

"Like what kind of questions?" Lake asked.

"Oh you know, nonsense questions. I can't remember them but, questions like, 'How many oranges does it take to build a dog house?'"

Laughing, Lake said, "You're just getting the system out of your system."

And perhaps Lake was right, for James would not have the dream again.

"You'll never be the same," Lake added.

James scoffed.

"You won't be," Lake reiterated.

"I won't change," James rebutted, but of course he would change, even while he remained the same.

Continuing their conversation, Lake explained the way of the warrior and James listened intently.

"Let your mind lay down flat," said Lake. "Let it go flat as the river when it calms. Then let the scenery fill your mind and take the place of all thought—the land, the trees, the bushes, the water, the sky."

The way of the warrior was about focusing in the natural world. The men sat Indian style with their dogs beside the river on the isle of fantastic rocks. They spoke for six hours at which point the sun had turned the sky above the gorge blood red. The two then rose, clasped hands solidly and bid one another farewell.

Back in his camp, James ate an apple, bread, and peanut butter. He then went to bed. The time was 10:20pm and he couldn't sleep after repressing a serious need of it all evening. Not to mention that every time he drifted off, he jolted awake, having seen the burning eyes of the shaman looking in from the ether. James fell asleep at 3:30am. But he would have no regrets. And like so many others who helped him along the way, he hoped to see Lake again someday.

Day 43, Friday, June 25

James woke at 4:00am to find the wind had arrived. The waves were crashing the beach, and his camp would soon be swamped just as Lake had warned. Exhausted in the extreme, James didn't want to get up but had to.

James ate a full but cold breakfast including five raw eggs. He then shoved off only to discover that he couldn't paddle near shore due to vast fields of semi-submerged boulders that stretched like minefields along the south shore. The larger boulders were easy to see but great numbers of smaller boulders appeared and disappeared amid the waves. Thus having no choice but to stay far from shore, James found himself in swells marching in ranks straight up the river. Thankfully the swells were not the biggest he would know, but all the same, they were white-capped, foaming, wild and wooly things that demanded every atom of a man.

"Upon each swell I was lifted up where the wind grabbed hold, and as it did I dug for the heart of the wave and surged forward. Again and again [I surged forward], I was almost flying!"

Of course James wasn't really flying or even going fast in comparison to modern motorized standards, but all the same, he had reached a significant milestone thanks to a skill level that had been gained one paddle stroke at a time. He had finally taken to the swells, and it felt like flying.

At 8:00am, James found a notch in a rocky shoreline where he landed with some difficulty (due to rough water). There he ate a banana, bread and peanut butter. Then shoving off, James continued in leaps and bounds so to speak, and with each swell demanding his attention in the absolute, he scarcely had time to notice how the hills to the south had melted to flat lands.

"Between each swell crest was a trough where, digging and looking over my shoulder, I had only a few seconds to get in sync with the next crest."

"Take in the whole river, but be a part of each wave," the shaman had said, telling James the way of the warrior. It was a good philosophy but, in the foaming swells, the Kansan believed in the way of the knight, *"Go forth and meet the dragon with all the strength that God sees fit to afford you."*

Perhaps the dragon, having seen how the knight had taken to the swells, was not entirely disappointed, even as he continued to stock the knight, ever looking for an opportunity to pounce.

At some point the boulder fields ended and James passed Crow Butte Island which stood across the river near the Washington shore. From there the river took a slight angle to the right which meant the Oregon shore got a reprieve from the wind. James got out his field glasses and sighted the community of Boardman four miles ahead.

Having come within a few miles of Boardman, James landed on

a beach in a small nook. His wristwatch read 11:30am and as always by midday, the desert sun burned hot! James cooked a large steak. While eating, he fell asleep twice but jolted awake just before his face landed in his plate. He then got back on the river and rode the swells.

Like most ports, Boardman had been built by the Army Corp of Engineers and consisted of heavy stone walls around a park of well watered lawns and shade trees. James passed through the gate and into the protected waters within. He carried loads of gear up a gentle bank to a picnic table under a shade tree where he cleaned his canoe inside and out before assembling his walking machine.

At approximately 3:20pm, James began on a short section of road that connected port and town. UB rode on the cart because the blacktop burned like a hotplate under the sun. Not to mention, UB suffered from exhaustion.

James stopped before a campground nestled in a shady grove between port and town.

> "Admittedly, there had been times when I felt glad for the absence of a campground so that I might enjoy the comforts of an inn."

Until then, James had stayed at inns only when no campgrounds were available. Presently, he passed the campground, the idea being that needed supplies were in town, just across the bridge over the railroad tracks.

At the inn, the Kansan entered the lobby and removed his hat. He stepped up to the counter where he apologized for his state, adding that he meant to remedy it directly. He then reached for his debit card but, he couldn't find it.

"Can you pay with cash?" asked the clerk.

"I don't have enough," James replied, checking his wallet.

"Can you call your bank?" asked the clerk.

"I don't know, Ma'am," said James, still searching in vain. Then shaking his head, James dropped his eyes to the floor and, in a rare display of vulnerability, spoke in a tone that matched his state of exhaustion, "I'm a long way from home."

In a manner of speaking, James's tired brain groped in a fogbank until somehow it saw his card in Arlington at the ATM machine in the restaurant. And certainly it must have been helpful that the restaurant in Arlington was the only place James had used his card in his journey to get cash.

The clerk helped James find the phone number to the restaurant in Arlington. And because it was long distance, James used his calling card. The manager at the restaurant had James's card.

Meanwhile, the clerk saw James's relief and understood his card to be safe. She then heard him ask the manager when the restaurant closed, and moreover, heard him vow to get to Arlington even if he had to hitchhike. James then thanked the manager and hung up the phone.

"I can give you a ride," said the clerk without the slightest hesitation. "I get off in ten minutes."

Moved by her kind offer, James spoke just four words, all of which were filled with heartfelt gratitude, "Oh Ma'am, thank you."

Charlotte had a nine-year-old grandson with eyes that could win anyone's heart. Jessie, who appeared to be half White and half Hispanic, had been in the lobby all along, off in a bright corner with a coloring book. Jessie's mother and father were alive but, they were no longer around if James understood correctly. Charlotte didn't say much about it but Jessie's mother was her daughter. Jessie had an exceptionally good relationship with his grandmother. Charlotte appeared to be both Jessie's rock and best friend, very obviously the source of his happiness and good behavior.

For James, who had not ridden in a car since beginning his journey; it seemed a strange sensation to sit back and relax while going seventy miles an hour. He was too tired to make much conversation but that didn't stop him from feeling grateful. He petted UB, gazed out at the passing desert, and recovered his strength mile by mile.

Charlotte would accept no gas money for the round trip of fifty-two miles. James then asked if he might have the honor of taking grandmother and grandson to dinner. And because Charlotte knew the area, James suggested that she choose the venue. Charlotte agreed, then turned off the beaten path and drove to the edge of Boardman where a Mexican restaurant sat beside a potato processing plant with a smoke stack and what sounded like the drone of a processor.

In the restaurant, James ordered the largest dish they had. Then having cleaned his plate, he looked up to see Jessie gazing at him in amazement—,

"*What is it?*" James asked.

"I've never seen anyone finish one of those [platters]," replied Jessie.

The Kansan widened his eyes to match the boy's, "When I was in Celilo Indian Park, I heard that the men in the Lewis and Clark expedition ate sixteen pounds of meat a day!"

The conversation continued, and Charlotte, who was herself a lady without malice, mentioned that the potato processing plant employed a great many Mexican immigrants, one of whom was Jessie's father.

"It was obvious that Charlotte regarded Jessie as a gift from God—no questions asked. Charlotte never said as much nor did she have to, it was very clear she loved him."

Charlotte and Jessie returned James to the inn where they parted with words of thanks and well wishes. James then checked in and got his rig (which he had left in front of a plate glass window under the lobby's carport).

In his room, James took a shower and went to work stringing gear mindlessly about until, overtaken with exhaustion, he hit the sack. The time was 7:00pm. Man and dog slept like the dead.

Day 44, Saturday, June 26

At 6:00am, James went to work on his gear. At 7:30am, he went for breakfast at the restaurant across the way. After breakfast he hunkered down on his journal and caught it up at 3:40pm. He then brought out the rocks he'd collected for Frank and Kathy. Also among items to be sent home were purchase receipts and copies of his journal, copies which he planned to make as soon as he found a copying machine. So it was that, while preparing to go out, James paused to bring out a plastic zip-lock bag. Then, using caution not to tear the paper towel within, he took out Amy's note.

"Master," said James's brain to his heart, "perhaps Amy loved you and you can be grateful that she did. But a woman like her is rarely if ever single. Single for a day perhaps, at the end of which she would have a tail of suitors from New York to San Diego. If only you were rich and Amy was willing, you could pay to fly her in and out for visits along the way. You could have afforded such a thing once upon a time, but that was back when I ruled this roost. Now days, I don't know what we're doing. I only know that we're going to St Louis, and we'll be broke when we get there. So even while Amy might love you, you cannot give her what she needs."

The heart fell silent, sensing the brain to be right. His errand demanded commitment in the complete, and Amy needed more than an old motor home out in the sticks.

For the record, James began his venture with 27,000 dollars and ended with an infinite return on investment plus 2,000 dollars yet remaining in his pocket. Presently understanding there would be a wife for him if it pleased God but in the meantime, his job was to keep putting one foot before the other with faith; James put Amy's note in with other items to be shipped home.

Presently, our lonely traveler went to the grocery store where he met Brenda, a young school teacher who was single and attractive. Upon learning that James was doing the Lewis and Clark trail, Brenda told James about an upcoming section of the trail with which she was familiar, herself having lived beside the Clearwater River. James thanked Brenda and then departed with groceries and ice in hand. Back at the inn, James called home and spoke with Frank. After that, he headed for the laundromat in town.

With his cloths in the wash, James sat on the curb outside the laundromat working on his journal. While he worked, he met a little boy of Mexican heritage named Aaron. Aaron had come to the laundromat with his mother. Aaron was six years old, bright-eyed, happy, and bursting with energy—,

"What are you doing?" he asked James.

"I'm keeping a journal," replied the Kansan, lifting his eyes from the page, looking over the wire rims of his reading glasses.

"I have a journal," said Aaron.

"You do?" asked James, pleasantly surprised, removing his glasses. Aaron then told James about his journal and also about getting an A on his math test. James told Aaron it was good that he had got an A. He then turned and gave a reassuring nod to Aaron's mother who stood folding laundry behind a plate glass window (so that she might know her son was safe). Aaron did not remain long but sped off like a tiny tornado. James returned to his journal and caught it up in short order.

In the laundromat, Aaron and his mother were the only people other than James. After an unrecorded period of time, two Hispanic men entered and proceeded to wait on Aaron's mother like a pair of guards. James didn't speak to the men, nor they to him. Aaron meanwhile continued to run laps around the washing machines. Then skidding to a stop, he turned his attention toward UB but the little dog backed under a chair and growled.

"He's old," said James, "and sometimes a little cranky."

"Will he bite me?" asked Aaron.

"No," James assured the boy, "he won't bite, so long as you pet him nicely!"

Under James's watchful eye, Aaron petted UB softly, then zoomed away. Aaron was obviously a handful for his mother who tried in vain to control him. She completed her work, then called Aaron to her side and prepared to depart with their escorts. As she carried her load past James, a fleeting smile graced her work-weary face as if to tell him she appreciated the kindness he'd shown her boy. The time was 10:00pm.

The Kansan remained alone in the laundromat, looking around himself. The place was a wreck. A front-loading washer with its glass face kicked in sat stuffed with beer cans and trash. Graffiti covered the walls in angry knifelike strokes and appeared to be the work of Mexican gang-bangers. Meanwhile, darkness fell fast on a Saturday night.

James allowed his clothes to dry but didn't bother to fold them until back at the inn where he had much work to do. A need for sleep soon overtook him however so he laid down. The time was 10:40pm.

Man and dog slept well.

Day 45, Sunday, June 27

James rose at 6:30am, a late hour for one who hoped to avoid desert heat but at least it felt good to sleep. At 7:20am, James went across the way for breakfast. He then returned to his room where he considered staying over for an early start on the morrow. Deciding not to wait, he got ice, loaded his cooler, packed his gear, loaded his rig, and departed the inn at approximately 11:00am.

At 11:40am, James arrived at the port where he worked under the same tree as before, transforming land rig to water craft. Meanwhile, five Hispanic males appearing to be seventeen or eighteen years of age came walking into the park which, for whatever reason, was deserted. James continued with the business at hand, ever mindful of his situation. His picnic table sat stacked with high-dollar items like a brightly colored display in a shopping mall while thirty yards away, four Hispanic males seemed without direction except to shuck and jive while keeping their eyes on him. So James kept an eye on them, and sure enough, their leader began to advance. The Kansan picked up the axle of his cart and took a step in their direction before squaring off. The young Hispanic hesitated, then retreated.

With his canoe on the beach, James only had to load his gear and shove off but, as he carried the last load down the gentle bank, he saw the five males approaching. All too aware of his isolation, James continued to prepare his boat for launch. The five males advanced to a distance not greater than twenty-five feet, stopping only where the sand beach rose to meet the green lawn directly above James.

For the record, James's pistol remained packed away, out of reach and unloaded. The teens didn't descend the bank but remained talking among themselves while stealing looks at James. James meanwhile realized that they weren't gang-bangers. Distance had kept him from seeing as much beforehand. Therefore James kept an eye on them as he worked and as soon as one of them stole another look, James waved. Not a happy or tentative wave but an honest wave. The teen waved back and, after some consulting among themselves, their leader came down the bank while his friends remained above.

Daniel had a rare gift with words. And using his gift, Daniel was able to ask, without putting James down, that he not be judged by the color of his skin. Daniel's deft diplomacy wasn't wasted on James who, having seen what he had seen, had reason for concern.

Daniel then asked, "Are you going fishing?"

"I have the licenses and the gear but, I'm yet to get a chance," said James who went on to tell of attempting the Lewis and Clark route.

"I studied those guys in school!" Daniel exclaimed, his dark eyes brightening.

James said he felt fortunate to be doing what he was doing and that so far it had really been something. He then asked, "Who are your friends?"

James and Daniel went up the bank to meet the others where, shaking hands and trading names, James smiled broadly upon learning that one of the youths was named, "Jesus."

"You have the best name possible," James assured the young man.

"The young men were nowhere near gang-bangers but normal teenagers looking for girls on summer vacation as they themselves said."

James told about doing the Lewis and Clark trail. Then bidding them farewell, he descended the bank and shoved off.

Enthusiastically, Daniel called out from shore, "I hope you make it!"

After making it to St Louis, James made the following journal entry:

"If I could compare this work I do with a pen to working metal, then no matter how much I pound, weld, grind, and polish—no matter how much I care about all people, no matter how much I want all people to 'make it,' no matter how many journals I fill trying to figure out this cultural conundrum, no matter how much sleep I lose mulling it over—I always end up with the same four words, 'My people are disappearing.' "

Like a desert that must be crossed before entering the Promised Land, James had to resolve the questions in his heart regarding the cultural issue. It would take years, and all related entries herein are a product of that process.

Presently paddling out the port gate, James looked upon a section of river three miles wide and ten miles long with islands scattered here and there. The scene was so vast, he couldn't distinguish one feature from another. Therefore he went into the middle of it to avoid confusing a peninsula for an island, whereby he might find himself in a dead end. And as always, that Universal Voice that spoke to men in open water said, *"Do not tarry here."*

James paddled hard, working against a light wind. The time was roughly 2:00pm and the sun beat down hot as ever. After making six miles, he landed on a sandy island and immediately laid down in the shade of a shrub. The time was 4:00pm and so hot had it become, James could do little but wait for more shade. He then set up his tent next to a line of shrubs. The line of shrubs didn't parallel the shore but cast their shadow on a stretch of high-water beach running toward the center of the island. As a result, James's camp looked out over sand flats and shallow pools with the river in the background.

The Kansan brought out his stove and put on a 20oz steak. Meanwhile, several deer came out on the sand flats amid the pools and, seeing how the island was very far out in the river, James thought it interesting that deer would be there. Then hearing the voice of a woman, James turned to see a pretty lady in a bikini peaking around a bush at him. She then disappeared.

James got up to investigate and, stepping around a small land point near his camp, he met Michelle, her husband Ernie, and their son Derrick. The family had come in their motorboat to day camp on the island beach. They were very impressed when James told them he was attempting the Lewis and Clark route. Ernie offered James a beer and Michelle offered a glass of wine which James refused even while thanking them kindly for their enthusiasm.

While speaking with Ernie and Michelle, James kneed and pushed two bounding dogs as if in a game, for both had smelt his steak cooking and were trying to get past him. They couldn't get past however because James stood blocking a narrow gap of sand between river and coarse shrub growth. With well wishes, James returned to his camp where he ate his steak, a bagel, and a green bell pepper. James hit the sack after dinner. His wristwatch read 10:00pm. The desert air felt stifling but, within forty minutes, James drifted off and slept well.

Day 46, Monday, June 28

At 6:00am, James packed his camp, ate an abbreviated breakfast and shoved off at 8:00am. The slow repetitive nature of the following entry reflects the wear-and-tear effect that the desert environment had on him:

> "The air was calm and the sun hot. I went slowly under the hot sun. Sometimes there was a breeze but, it was against me. Most often it was calm. Still and hot. Hot. There was no current. The mountains had fallen away. The land held no features. A thin layer of scum covered the water."

As the islands fell behind, the river narrowed to just under a mile in width. Then rounding a bend, James saw a grain elevator beside the south shore with a barge moored alongside. Perhaps it was only the heat and a wish for something besides the languid nature of the place but James suddenly felt an urge to touch the barge. He could hear the augers, so he knew the barge was being filled with grain which he assumed to have come from irrigated fields along the river. The shallows dropped off into the shipping channel, the current suddenly came alive, and James had to fight for every yard.

> "The current coming off the backside of the barge was strong. I paddled hard to get myself in position to pass the back corner [of the barge] at a slight angle so that I wouldn't be swept underneath [it]. Thus passing very close, I reached out my hand and touched the barge. A good solid touch!"

After laboring for days in temperatures exceeding 100 degrees, the desert sun had James feeling a little punchy. And for the record, he had not, until this point, goofed-off since first putting his paddle in the river.

The current died out, the river began a long gentle bend and, for the sake of conserving energy, James began a straight line course through the bend from south shore to north. Once on the north shore, he burrowed into a stand of shrubs to gain their shade where he ate lunch. UB begged and got tidbits. Then they were off again.

Still punchy, James entertained himself by paddling in such a way as to make whirlpools spin off the tip of his paddle. And because the water lay clear beneath a thin layer of scum, he watched as bits of scum descended twelve to fourteen inches inside the tiny tornado-like structures he made. He smiled and even laughed a little. He liked natural dynamics.

Looking up from his whirlpools, James spotted the community of Irrigon on the Oregon shore directly across the river. Then looking through his field glasses, he tried to see if the town had a mini-market where he could purchase ice.

"I don't need ice," James reminded himself, returning to his whirlpools.

"It would be nice to have ice," and he picked up his field glasses for a second look.

"No, I don't need ice," and he returned to making whirlpools. Then remembering his straight course, James decided he couldn't possibly go to Irrigon because doing so would defeat the purpose of his shortcut. So the matter was settled. Then deciding to go to Irrigon, James returned to making whirlpools and thus continued weaving when he should have been on a straight course through the bend. James wasn't in such bad condition but just tired, and happy, in a strange sun-drunk kind of way.

Meanwhile in the Port of Irrigon, James had been spotted and mistaken for a boater in trouble. So a motorboat was dispatched to check on James who was still weaving one way and then another.

James saw the motorboat coming on a beeline and, being unaware of what had transpired at the port, he feared the driver didn't see him. Then growing alarmed, James began waving his paddle in the air to keep from being hit. Needless to mention, waving a paddle is a distress signal. The boat closed the distance rapidly before cutting its engine and coasting to a stop, whereupon its driver asked, "Are you alright?"

"I'm fine," James replied.

"Do you need a tow?" asked the man.

"No Sir," James replied, still at a loss, "but thank you for asking."

"Are you sure?"

"Yes Sir."

"Well alright then," and the man throttled up his engine.

"Wait!" James hollered.

The man throttled down, and James continued, "Sir, if I may ask, is there ice in town?"

"Yes," replied the man, looking somewhat annoyed, perhaps by the ridiculous nature of the question. He then sped back across the river and vanished inside the port.

Even after resolving to do so, James paddled and paddled and almost wondered if he would ever get to port. Never had it seemed to take so long to cross a river but he did at last reach the port gate. Meanwhile on the walls above the gate, a group of boys, some White and some Hispanic watched as the canoeist passed below.

> "The boys didn't appear very friendly at first but that area of the desert was troubled and, from what I could tell, no one escaped its unhappy effect whether they knew it or not. I gave a straight-faced wave and the boys waved back."

Passing through the gate, James continued into sheltered waters surrounded by a park of watered lawns, shade trees, and picnic tables.

Having moored his canoe at the dock, James went up a ramp and into the park where he met Roy (whose real name is withheld for reasons to be told, but not just yet). Roy was a retired trucker and senior citizen. Roy said he had spotted James out on the river and had mistakenly thought him to be a boater with engine problems, whereupon a motorboat was dispatched. James thanked Roy and, promising to return, proceeded toward the park restrooms. On his way back, James met the boys who had been on the wall of the port. The four or five boys were on their way into town but stopped to see what James was about.

> "I told the boys I was doing the Lewis and Clark trail. All the boys said they had places to be and went away directly except for one inspired boy named Christian."

After speaking with Christian, James learned from Roy where he could purchase ice in town. And because it would be a two-mile round trip in the heat, James asked Roy if he could keep an eye on UB. Roy said he would be happy to watch both dog and boat.

In town, an informal Mexican diner served as the only eatery. James ate two burritos and then went to the gas station across the way for ice where, to his surprise, he found a basket of fruit from which he purchased two oranges and a lime.

Back at port, James iced his cooler and, while so occupied, accidentally stepped on one of his oranges which had dropped and rolled behind him. The orange burst and squashed flat under his heavy boot but, not to let it go to waste, James immediately scraped it up off the dock and gobbled it down while a trio of fishermen looked on in surprise.

"If you gentlemen will excuse me," said James, "in the desert, a man can't afford to waste anything."

James returned up the ramp where he asked Roy if he might join him. Roy welcomed James and UB to his picnic table which enjoyed both the shade of a large tree and a breeze that came across the water. Shortly thereafter, a young woman (her real name is withheld) asked if she might join the two men.

Tiffany was a rebel teen stuffed into tight blue jeans and a tube-top that undoubtedly earned her no small amounts of attention. She had done her worst with punk-rock makeup and electric hair dye but, having not graduated to tattoos and piercings, she had no way to mask her natural beauty. Her green eyes were second to none, even as they betrayed what she knew. Her skin was like morning dew, upon which her studded dog collar made for a clue.

Roy meanwhile appeared relaxed as people who have lived a good number of years often are. Probably, Roy's only regret was that his wife had passed on and couldn't be there with him. So it was that three lonely people sat talking and talking. Indeed they talked for four hours. Then James said he had to go and find a place to camp before night set in.

"I know a place where you can camp," said Tiffany, and she told of a nearby spot on the river bank. James said he would check it out. Tiffany then said she was going fishing and, with well wishes, departed.

As soon as Tiffany had gone, Roy said, "Tiffany's only fifteen."

"Fifteen," James echoed in disbelief.

"Yeah, I know," Roy agreed, and with a shake of his head, "they didn't make 'em like that when I was young."

Roy then told James that Tiffany had been raped at knife point repeatedly by a friend of her mother's boyfriend who was staying with them. Roy said the monster had gone to prison. James shook his head with a frown, but at that moment, his eyes were closed to what he'd seen; the Canadian trucker waiting in the wings, Tiffany's mother and her friend who came by to borrow money from Tiffany, the dog collar around Tiffany's neck, and other red flags. Roy spoke of changing times, and little towns without resources to afford police. He ended by saying there wasn't much that one old man on a park bench could do.

James thanked Roy and, with well wishes and a handshake, the two men parted.

Paddling out the port gate, James turned and continued east beside the wall of the port. To his right, a wall of riprap hid him from park and town. To his left, the vast river lay empty. And directly ahead, a lone figure stood on the riprap with fishing pole in hand. She faced upstream so her back was to him, and still he recognized her. Tiffany had changed her blue jeans for a pair of slacks. James would remember her cotton pants were light brown and, soaking wet to the waist.

As though she had eyes in the back of her head, Tiffany turned her shoulders and smiled at James, "Hello."

"Hello," echoed the Kansan, caught in an ambush, filled with lust like hot lead and knowing it. And here comes a place to tell, he hadn't seen it coming.

"What are you doing?" he asked.

"What's it look like?" and she flicked her fishing pole at him playfully.

"Hey!" said James, pointing his finger even as he smiled. Then without knowing what he was saying, "You could get your hook in my eye!"

For a brief moment, each did nothing except to smile at the other. The Kansan then nodded upriver and asked, "Is that the spot?"

"That's it," Tiffany replied, glancing several hundred yards ahead.

Looking ahead, James knew in his heart, he mustn't camp there. Then in a decidedly formal tone, "I'll go have a look," and with a paddle stoke he added, "You take care, Tiffany."

"Goodbye James," Tiffany said earnestly, as though knowing she would not see him again.

James continued to the spot where he found a primitive campsite hidden in the trees with a footpath that lead to the port. He got back in his canoe and shoved off, then waved goodbye to Tiffany who waved back.

"I don't know what Tiffany felt but, I had told her and Roy that I hoped to marry a young woman [of child bearing age] and have a family after I completed my errand. Whatever Tiffany felt, I pray God save her. For while the rebel girl appeared to walk of her own free will on a dark and dangerous path, there was far more to it than that, and probably, it was the only path she knew. And looking back on it all, and perhaps most difficult (and hopeful) of all, I remember the light in Tiffany's eyes. It was a good light in spite of enduring something that no little girl should ever have to endure."

Behind James, Tiffany watched from the port wall until he had disappeared from sight.

James paddled with meaning and made good progress around a long bend in the river. Then having rounded the bend, he spotted the town of Umatilla some five miles ahead.

Still a few miles from Umatilla, James carried loads roughly two-hundred feet across a hard mud flat to a narrow strip of sand beneath a dirt embankment. He hurried to strike camp as darkness fell.

Warning of rising crime in the area, Roy had cautioned James to look out for himself. Lake had done the same, not to mention that James had eyes of his own. He cable locked his canoe to his tent. Then lying in darkness with wind and animals making noises all around, he arrived at a decision which, truth be known, had to be made—,

"I'd rather be dead than paranoid," he said to himself.

Man and dog slept well.

Day 47, Tuesday, June 29

At 6:00am, James had steak and eggs along with the usual trimmings for breakfast. He didn't eat all 20oz of steak but cut a 4oz portion into bite-sized snacks to eat later that day.

While James ate breakfast, UB weighed the consequences of stealing one of the snack-sized steak chunks from a plate on the ground at his master's feet.

Seeing what his dog was up to, James figured it would be alright for UB to have one chunk. So he didn't say anything as UB lowered his nose ever so slowly to the plate. Then, with a sudden thrust, the little dog pushed his nose into the sand and flung a portion of beach onto the plate, covering the bite-sized chunks in a layer of sand and dirt.

"Darn you!" said James, snatching the plate away.

Grumbling, James dropped the steak chunks into a plastic baggy, dirt and all. He didn't dwell on it, not when camp had to be broke. Thus focused, he felt happy to see the water level had risen almost to his camp overnight, for it saved him the work of carrying loads across the mud flats. He shoved off at 9:45am.

James paddled against moderate current until roughly 1:00pm when he arrived at the Port of Umatilla where many summer vacationers were bringing motorboats in and out of the water. The port lay only two miles downstream of McNary Dam, the last dam James would portage on the Columbia River.

In the park of the port, James staged his gear around a picnic table where he looked forward to eating lunch before assembling his walking machine. But when he sat to eat his lunch, he discovered much to his chagrin, the dirt-covered steak chunks which he had placed in a baggy that morning. Alas, UB's scheme came to fruition. UB savored a steak dinner while his master looked on, munching an apple, and shaking his head.

While James assembled his rig, a woman came scavenging in trash cans and what not. She appeared to be sixty or better, slender in build, with a few golden strands remaining in her otherwise gray hair.

"If you don't mind my asking Ma'am, are you as they say, 'Down on your luck?'"

Carolyn replied that she was homeless. The two then spoke while James cleaned his gear. Carolyn never told how she had become homeless, nor did James ask. Carolyn appeared strong in body and intelligent in mind. She never asked or implied that James give her money nor did he. She shed no tear but was deeply distraught. James didn't know what to think but was sincere in his courtesy as always. Then two men approached and Carolyn grew frightened.

The Kansan stood from his work while asking Carolyn who the men were. Carolyn said they were park keepers come to run her off.

James understood the difficult but necessary task before the park keepers. After all, the park was a place for hard working people to get away from life's troubles for a week, often earned through a year of labor. At such times, their need to get away from life's troubles deserved respect. James spared Carolyn from such sentiment however, for he didn't know her story. And because James didn't possess people skills, he could only take a step forward and square off as if to tell the men, *"This woman is my guest."*

The two men stopped short and lingered a moment before retreating. James and Carolyn then spoke for another twenty minutes. James told Carolyn (who believed in God) that the way out of any dilemma was to put one foot before the other with faith in God, step by step. Carolyn agreed, and giving James a hug, she left the park on her own accord.

From the park, James pulled his rig to a campground that sat on a shelf directly above port and river. At the entrance of the campground stood a house with office attached. In the office, while waiting in line, James overheard how things stood with the 4th of July only days away. All campsites were reserved. Subsequently, current policy dictated one-night stays only in any campsite that happened to be open. Thus being forewarned, James stepped up to the counter and made his appeal—,

"Sir, my name is James and I come from Kansas to attempt the Lewis and Clark trail from west to east. I began at the mouth of the Columbia on May 14. Just now, I'm looking at four days between here and Kennewick, and that means I need a day to restock and ready my gear before setting out. So, the long and short of it is, I'm hoping you can make an exception and give me a campsite for two nights."

"No exceptions," replied the man.

Without question, James accepted the man's policy. Then with no one in line behind James, the two men enjoyed a brief but good conversation in which they spoke on a variety of topics including Lewis and Clark. After getting directions to the inn in town, James thanked the man and departed. The time was approximately 7:00pm.

Although James would have enjoyed the shade and breeze of the campground above the port, he harbored no bad feelings for the campground manager. Instead, James respected Pat for running a tight ship. Had Pat not been tough, the campground couldn't have been pleasant, as we shall see.

The Kansan harnessed into his rig and set out pulling but no more had he reached the exit than along came Pat in an ATV—,

"Don't go into town at night," said Pat, pulling alongside with a look of concern. Then glancing at James's walking machine, he added, "especially not with all that."

Like someone with prior experience, James asked, "Are things not good there?"

"Things aren't what they used to be," replied Pat, and albeit no more expressive than the next fellow, Pat's face told of a man who had lived there many years, who had seen the community unravel, who regretted it, and who had decided to move away. It was true, Pat was moving away. And while he could not be blamed, it was a shame.

"You can stay here two nights," said Pat, "I'll work something out."

Pat then showed James to a good tent site with shade, level lawn, picnic table, and water.

"How much do I owe you?" James asked, bringing out his wallet.

"It's on me," said Pat.

James thanked Pat kindly, and Pat departed with well wishes. James then set about making camp. He brought out his stove and cooked a 20oz steak. After dinner, James showered and shaved at the park facility, then hit the sack at 10:30pm and slept like a rock.

Day 48, Wednesday, June 30

When in a campground, James separated his firearm from its bullets in such a way as to eliminate the possibility of disaster should some curious child get into his stuff while he was away. James's extra-measure of precaution involved separating pistol and bullets between tent and cart, plus he put the bullets under padlock.

Having risen to do chores at 5:00am, James headed for town early. UB remained behind because he had blown out a paw on the highway between Arlington and Three Mile Canyon, so he couldn't walk very well.

Exiting the park, James didn't take the main road into town but a shortcut which passed through a neighborhood of low-income housing. James wasn't looking for trouble. Rather, he simply had to have the most direct route to town because he was on foot and would soon have heavy sacks of groceries to carry. So James found a path that made for a shortcut within a shortcut. The path cut through a field directly before a three-story rectangular tenement slum that looked like it had been hit by a storm and never cleaned up. James figured it to be inhabited by Hispanics but whether they were there legally he couldn't know. James harbored no hate for them but simply understood a need to exercise caution because the path was obviously theirs and they might not like him using it.

In town, James got breakfast at a café where a lone cowboy and waitress appeared to be the last of a dying bred.

> "Except to greet me, they spoke few words. But as a natural matter, being that I was one of them, they spoke volumes with their eyes, as if to tell me, sadly, that their realm had fallen."

From the café, James proceeded to the laundromat where he also worked on his journal. Among the mix of races using the laundromat, James was the only white. No one behaved discourteously but all five people kept to themselves so that not a single word was spoken.

James next went to the grocery store and resupplied for the trip to Kennewick. Then, with two large grocery sacks under each arm plus his laundry and journal, James set out for the campground. He took the most direct route, walking through an ally that ran behind the small business district before arriving to the same path he'd taken earlier.

> "That end of the path began between the side of a building and a pile of dirt, broken concrete, and trash. Painted on the side of the building was a Mexican gang marker, like a 'No Trespassing' sign."

James took the path that crossed over a set of train tracks before proceeding toward the tenement slum.

Back at his camp, James met Scott who camped nearby in an RV with his wife and kids. James asked Scott if it would be alright for him to work while they spoke. So the two men got to know one another while James unpackaged and repackaged his groceries, loaded his ice chest and food duffle. Scott departed but returned shortly thereafter to invite James to dinner later that night with his family. James accepted and looked forward to it. Scott then departed and James set out for town by way of the main road which took the long way around.

On his way to town, James stopped at the visitor's center where a kind clerk named Kathy happily went to the trouble of duplicating a map of the Snake River from its confluence with the Columbia River to Little Goose Dam. Kathy worked by lying her large map section by section on a copy machine and making 8 x 11 copies of each section for James who would later cut and paste the pages together. James told Kathy of his hope to go through the locks at McNary Dam (just one mile upstream). Kathy told James he could use the phone (if he had a calling card) to speak with the U.S. Army Corp of Engineers. Thus on the phone with Ann, James told what he was about and then asked if he might go through the lock at McNary Dam. Ann chose her words carefully probably because the Columbia River was classified by law as a navigable waterway and therefore any citizen had the right to travel it. So Ann didn't tell James "No" but did her best to discourage him by emphasizing a "safety concern" regarding "non-motorized boats." To James, any rule requiring a man to have a motor sounded like something made up by engineers. James did not press the issue but, for the record, he believed there would inevitably be incidents of drowning if canoeist and kayakers were allowed to use the locks.

James next called home and left a message for Frank, telling of his itinerary for the next few days. James then thanked Kathy and, wishing not to tie up the phone any longer, walked to a truck stop in town where he called his sister Patricia and left a message. James then returned to his camp and ate a steak, an apple, a large portion of cheese, and bread.

After lunch, James walked to the port where, having picked out a man who looked to know the river, he asked directions for portaging around the dam. The old-timer said it was easy, and proceeded to tell how. After thanking the old-timer, James returned to his camp only to find the old-timer had stopped in his truck with his wife to get a firsthand look at James's walking machine. James was happy to show how his machine worked. Scott soon came and joined the conversation. An assistant park manager also came and joined in.

No sooner had everyone gone than another man came in a car with a canoe on top. Ed had been driving the Lewis and Clark trail and doing a little paddling here and there along the way. Ed had stopped at the visitor's center where Kathy had told him about James. So it was that the two men spoke at length. Ed, who didn't appear to be an assuming fellow, lived on the Chesapeake Bay where he owned a forty foot wood sailboat. Ed commuted to Washington DC where he worked. He had been keeping a photo journal if James remembered correctly but in any case, Ed asked if he could take James's photo. So James stood from the table, walked over to the tip of his canoe where his hat hung and, putting it on with a smile, said, "I want folks to know where I come from."

Unless James's eyes deceived him, Ed was disappointed. So James asked why, at which point, and in no small part because the two men had become comfortable speaking with one another, their conversation turned to the rowel in Kansas between the creationists and evolutionists regarding which curriculum should be taught in public schools. If James understood Ed correctly, Ed wanted to know why anyone would want to teach creation theory with so much scientific evidence on the side of evolution theory.

"Regarding "evolution," I see the slow and methodic mechanism of nature as evidence to that which manifests itself in craftsmanship, being a love of making things, which comes from God who [being The Ultimate Craftsman] is forever about by means that men cannot comprehend beyond the level of their own finite limitations. For example, scientists give the universe a size and age, but in self-evident truth, the universe is infinite (meaning it is unknowable, mysterious, and fantastic).Therefore the origin of man is beyond the reach of science. And yet, the origin of the species is within man's reach, for such are the ways of The Ultimate Craftsman, anyone who cares to reach out will grow in the labor of His love."

James's explanation to Ed wasn't so carefully tailored as the above, and therefore, seeing Ed's pained expression, James feared Ed might be thinking creationists were nuts and perhaps even dangerous. With his heart on his sleeve, James asked Ed not judge him or his people based on a media perception but rather to walk among them (not with an agenda, but with an open heart).

Disappointed though they were, Ed and James parted as two men who both cared deeply about their country, with an earnest handshake.

From 1:30pm to 5:05pm, James sat at his picnic table and caught up his journal. He then organized his gear to be ready to go early in the morning. As he worked, Scott's young son Cole came down the road. Cole was a remarkable little fellow who suffered from a speech impediment due to an ear problem that affected his hearing for the first five years of life. But Cole wasn't about to withdraw because he couldn't speak real well. In fact he was going all out to catch up. So James and Cole got along naturally well, being as both were men on missions. Then at 6:00pm, Cole's sister Kaile came to tell that dinner would be ready in ten minutes. The timing couldn't have been better for James who had just finished his work.

For dinner James joined Scott, his wife LeAnne, their eldest daughter Kaile, Cole, and their toddler daughter Quinn. The food tasted delicious; baked chicken with potatoes, beans, and muffins as good as any James ever had. Best of all for a man far from home was the fact that he was sitting to dinner with a family, like he did back home. Indeed, James was grateful for their hospitality. Later, after good conversation, they moved to James's camp because of its good shade. There they relaxed in lawn chairs, talking until twilight.

James slept well.

Day 49, Thursday, July 1

James got up at 6:00am and took the path to town where he ate breakfast at the café. On his way back to camp, he stopped at the beginning of the path to look at the gang marker before gazing across the field to the tenement slum. He wasn't without feeling for those folks, most of whom weren't gang-bangers but were just poor people barely getting by. It would have been easy to encourage them to pull themselves up, if only it weren't on the ruins of his people and culture.

Back in his camp, James iced his cooler and worked to break camp. Cole came and James employed him. Scott and LeAnne brought sausage and pepperoni, a thoughtful gift for which James thanked them kindly. Then in parting, James shook Cole's hand and said, "I'm proud of you Cole. You're outgoing and that's a sure sign of [your] bravery."

UB's paw had mended and therefore he walked alongside as James pulled a two mile stretch of blacktop that ran straight from campground to dam. To fine-tune the balance of his walking machine, James moved his hands forward or backward on the pull bars a few inches, after which he only needed to leave his hands at rest on the bars while walking. It worked that well but to the eye without mechanical inclination; it probably didn't look like much more than a handle that had been put on a canoe. In fact it was more than that, being a frame, a harness, some hinge points, two wheels, one man, and a few simple principles.

From the foot of the dam, the road turned to climb the shoulder and, in hot morning sun, made for a test. Fortunately, James came to the hill fresh with rest on the heels of fifty days labor, good diet, and human kindness. On the other side of the dam, James entered a tiny park with boat ramp, parking lot, and restroom. He hoped to top-off his water jug before beginning the long stretch of desert ahead but he couldn't find a water spigot. While he looked for a spigot, a hydroelectric company worker pulled up in a service truck—,

"Howdy," said James.

"Good morning," said the man whose name was Dan.

Figuring that Dan would know of a spigot somewhere in the vicinity, James said, "I was just looking for some water."

"I've got water," said Dan, pointing without hesitation to a water cooler on the back of his utility truck.

"I don't want to take your water," James replied.

"I won't drink it all," Dan assured.

James thanked Dan for his hospitality. He then explained his walking machine and also how the idea for attempting the Lewis and Clark trail began one Sunday at his brother's dinner table. After a brief but good conversation, the two men parted with words of thanks and well wishes.

While James worked to convert land rig to water craft, two more dam workers came in a second truck and gave information on the river ahead. Harlan and George then departed with well wishes.

James shoved off at 11:00am and made good progress with a fair breeze at his back. He took a final look back at McNary Dam, then turned to face a giant bend where the river turned north toward Canada. Simultaneously, the flat lands ended and the gorge rose up again.

As James neared the bend, he remembered Lake's warning, *"When you get to that bend, stay on the Washington side. Don't get caught on the east side with a west wind or those swells will have you on the rocks!"*

Until then, Lake's knowledge of the river had been on the money and would continue to prove solid throughout. Not to mention, James had not forgotten the jog at Wind Mountain. So it was, he took action to avoid the upcoming peril:

> "I shot (paddled) a five-mile line [across the river], taking an angle to the Washington shore, along which I planned to remain [until reaching the city of Kennewick]."

Feeling strong and wanting to make hay while the sun shined, James paddled with determination. He didn't stop for lunch but ate sausage and pepperoni while paddling in relatively calm water. He paddled nonstop for seven hours and crossed the 300 mile mark as the crow flew upriver from the Pacific Ocean.

At 6:00pm, James arrived before an island measuring 1/3 mile long and several hundred yards wide. The cigar-shaped island lay along the east shore, roughly one mile downstream from Juniper Canyon. On the downstream end of the island, James found a small cove into which years of pounding swells had packed drifting tumbled weeds together so tightly, as to create something like a scouring pad measuring twenty feet across. James, who needed to cross the giant scouring pad to reach the island shore, tested the surface with great caution. Then realizing it to be safe, he could not help but laugh as he walked across it, for it crunched under his feet like a bowl of cereal.

UB remained in the canoe, watching as his master hiked up a rugged slope to a cliff top overlooking the upstream half of the island. From the cliff, James spotted a patch of level ground on which to camp.

Returning to his boat, James paddled to the upstream end of the island where he moored his craft on a narrow shelf at the base of a cliffy shoreline measuring eight feet in vertical height. From there the Kansan went about the work of carrying loads up the shore which, due to its broken nature, afforded ample footholds and handholds. He brought his canoe up last, then continued to haul loads, including his canoe, up a long desert slope that ended at the base of a great cliff. James didn't camp so near the cliff as to be in danger of falling rocks.

After feeding his dog, James made his own dinner which included a 16oz steak and a quart of water with a lime squeezed in. For comfortable dining, he arranged his cooler and plastic gear locker like table and chair on a vista overlooking river and gorge. The cooler made for a good bench seat. The gear locker made a nice table with a raised rim around its edge like a baby tray. So it was, James dined while evening shadows filled the desert gorge and made for a five-star view at once vast, desolate, and beautiful.

James finished his chores and retired to his tent just as the mosquitoes came out. It had been a productive day. The time was 10:00pm. Man and dog slept well.

Day 50, Friday, July 2

At 6:00am James began his morning routine. Then while eating breakfast, it amazed him that the sun could already be so hot at 7:00am!

The waves had come up with the wind and as a result, James wouldn't be able to put into the river where he had taken out the night before. Scouting revealed an access point in a narrow moat between island and shore. The water lay calm there but not without a catch. James had to haul his boat and gear across the island and then negotiate a near vertical bank measuring twenty feet in height.

> "More often than not, grunt work goes unrecorded because to translate it from reality to ink and paper requires poetry. Otherwise, it comes off as boring when in fact it is a wonderful way of life, out in the great wide open, where a man is free as a bird."

At 10:00am, James shoved off, exited the sheltered moat, and entered the river proper. The south wind blew straight up the river and that made James happy in hope of making good progress. To capitalize on the wind, he moved one-hundred yards out into the river (the depth was 90ft). The rising wind soon turned waves into swells, and shortly thereafter, the swells began to whitecap. James made an occasional joke to lighten the intensity of his work. Then, and for no other reason than because he had developed the skill to do so, James crossed the river, navigating through marching ranks of white-capped swells for a distance of one mile. Then paddling along the far shore at a distance of roughly seventy feet, James glanced at rocks for visual points of reference by which he estimated each swell-surge shoved him forward better than twenty feet. Twenty feet, all at once, swell after swell, he surged forward.

"It was really something. Going in leaps and bounds. Paddling hard. Making tremendous progress!"

James hadn't forgotten Lake's warning regarding the peril of the east shore, particularly dangerous at the Wallula Gap some five miles ahead. At the Wallula Gap, the river narrowed between sheer cliffs to form one of the dramatic spectacles of the gorge. James couldn't miss seeing it, for even at five miles distance, it seemed front-and-center with its towering cliffs and narrowing gap.

Heeding Lake's advice, James headed back toward the west shore where he might pass through the gap in safer conditions. Due to the swells however, James had to cross the river on a long diagonal. And as he crossed in rising wind, the swells grew larger and larger until James found himself navigated on what seemed white-capped walls of thunder. His state was one of total focus, his mental and physical exertion nothing less than absolute.

In such swells, the angle on which James had to cross the river became extremely slight, almost like going straight up the river, and no more had James reached the middle of the river than he spotted a yacht coming straight toward him from the opposite direction. The yacht wasn't a sailing vessel but a cruiser, and James wondered if they understood he couldn't get out of the way. He simply had no choice but to stay in sync with the swells. He had just enough time while changing from right to left to sweep his paddle high in the air like a flag so they might see him. He changed from left to right, right to left, each time sweeping his paddle like a flag, but they did not respond. They simply could not see him amid the crests and troughs.

At last spotting the canoeist, the yacht moved over and passed just two-hundred feet off his port side. Aboard the yacht, a man and woman waved while holding to a rail. The canoeist waved back and then continued in the assumption that any wake from the yacht would be overcome by the awesome power of the swells. Unfortunately, James hadn't understood the strange dynamics of water quite as well as he'd thought. Like ghosts in the flux, a series of wakes were charging toward him. James saw nothing beyond the white-capped swells which acted like walls. In fairness to James, he had no prior experience in such a situation. The first wake broadsided him without warning, nearly flipping him over. In the following instant, before James could recover, a swell hit from behind, then another wake broadsided, then another swell hit from behind. The canoeist was thrown wildly from crest to crest, fighting for all his worth, tossed on a checkerboard pattern of swells and wakes.

Perhaps thinking he had the knight at last, the dragon laughed and shouted, "Checkmate!"

The knight would remember it as one of his more desperate moments. Thankfully, it lasted no longer than a minute, whereupon he continued to the west shore where he enjoyed the full benefit of wind and swells while maintaining the psychological advantage of being reasonably close to shore. And looking to shore, he saw how he was hurled forward thirty feet at a time.

Out in the middle of the river, a lone sail boat undoubtedly from the Wallula Yacht Club looked to be manned by expert sailors, each well focused on task. A beautiful woman in a bikini rode on deck. She wasn't sunbathing however but bracing, not frightened but alert.

Directly ahead rose the Wallula Gap, and passing between its towering cliffs, James couldn't help but be in awe, for even as the river demanded his full attention, his skill level had risen above the immediate area around the bow of his craft, and as a result, he could take in a lot more than before.

"Navigating beneath cliffs that rose up on such a scale as to make the sky look small was truly something. But as impressive as the cliffs were, the swells were the thing. Every time the bow came up (and in such swells it always came up like a cannon), this great wall of energy shot out from under like a shock wave. It was power, pure power, hurling me forward thirty feet adding immediately to sixty, ninety, and so on!"

No sooner had James shot the gap when the gorge suddenly dropped away to flat lands with green hills on the northern horizon. The wind diminished and with it the swells diminished into waves (both wind and waves remained strong). Meanwhile, the opposite shoreline dropped back better than two miles to give the river the appearance of a lake.

James needed a place to rest but landing remained out of the question due to a combination of wind, waves, and rugged shoreline. Therefore when James spotted a rocky cove no larger than a car port, he paddled all out to gain it before the wind blew him past like a leaf on the water. In doing so, James frightened a family of ducks who had taken refuge there. The father and mother duck tried to draw James away from their babies by pretending to have broken wings. Thus portraying themselves as easy prey, they went flapping and flopping from cove to open river while their babies remained swimming about the mouth of the cove like nervous water beetles; little yellow fuzz balls, peeping for mommy and daddy.

Himself in a fix, James simply could not afford to miss his opportunity and, as a result, the ducklings scattered in a panic, fluttering out into the white-capped waves.

"Stupid ducks," said James, "I wasn't going to hurt you," and taking another stroke, "better you drown than I."

The canoeist executed a skillful maneuver directly before the mouth of the cove while peeping ducklings appeared and disappeared amid whitecaps like fishing bobbers. Then, just before the bow of James's craft broke the threshold of the cove, a sudden gust blew his hat off.

"Darn," said James, and he brought his craft about to race toward his sinking hat.

The canoeist snatched his hat from the water and tossed it in his boat but, just before it landed safely, another gust suddenly lifted it out of the boat and sent it another twenty feet upriver. Again, James raced to get his hat. He then paddled with every atom of his worth so that he might still gain the cove but, the wind would not allow him to turn his craft and, he was carried away like a leaf on the water.

"Thanks a lot, God!" James shouted angrily at the sky.

For only the second time in his journey, a large wave broke over the stern and hit James square on the seat of his pants. It happened directly on the heels of his words. Thus the phenomenon brought his head around whereby he saw the ducklings returning safely to the cove.

James shouted the f-word, plus the word, "it." Then as if to tell the Big Man to take His best shot, "Blow all You want!"

A tremendously powerful gust broadsided the canoe.

Frightened, the Kansan cried out, "You could have helped me!" Then, in a pleading tone, "I need to rest!"

The wind subsided, and having escaped his cloud of frustration just long enough to look upriver, James spotted another cove only a short distance ahead. Moreover, the cove had a small tree hanging over it, so unlike the first cove, it offered shade from the sun. And as James would discover, it was unoccupied.

In the cove, James tied off and apologized to God. He then laid back on the stern, put his feet up on the gunwales and snored in shade while the motion of the water rocked him gently. After a half-hour nap, James ate lunch. While eating, he sensed there to be a lesson involving ducks but he couldn't quite grasp it. Only after reaching St Louis would James look back and see that his hat had only been an inexpensive straw hat, easily replaced. Plus he had a cap. Therefore, if he'd needed to get into the cove as badly as he'd thought, he wouldn't have turned and gone after his hat.

Having finished his lunch, James continued paddling north along the west shore. The time was roughly 3:00pm and, perhaps due to the lay of the land, the wind shifted to come hard from the west, so it broadsided and pushed his canoe toward open river. James tried to use the shoreline as a wind block but due to shallow water, he had no choice but to remain out in the crosswind. His difficulty only increased as the shoreline grew irregular, allowing for large coves from which came powerful cross gusts. James understood he mustn't allow the gusting wind to overpower and carry him across the river where, some 2½ miles away along the east shore, things would turn bad, like Wind Mountain kind of bad.

"Do not let the west wind catch and take you over to that east shore!" Lake had warned.

So it was, the mouth of each cove presented a very serious consequence. More than once, high crosswinds nearly overcame James and carried him into open river. In fact, James fought so hard he snapped his paddle in half. The canoeist would crack the blades of several paddles along the length of his journey but only that once did he snap the shank of one clean in two. It happened in a near panic, on the threshold of being overcome by the crosswind. James was fighting hard, trying to bring the bow around toward shore, and he was losing the fight when, as a last resort, he stabbed his paddle down and paddled backward with strokes akin to bench-pressing, "Turn! Turn! Turn!"

"Snap!" went the paddle.

Perhaps the dragon shouted, "This time I have you!"

With catlike reflexes, the knight snatched the broken half of his paddle from the water, threw it in his boat, yanked the tarp open, scrambled forward, grasped hold of his spare paddle and shoveled water like a madman. Thus by the thinnest of margins, he escaped.

Why James retrieved the broken half of his paddle cannot be known except to say he did it on impulse. Presently, the wind abated due to a change in the lay of the land and James continued in much better conditions.

Next came two kayakers headed downstream and meeting them, James asked where they were going.

"We're paddling from Kennewick to Astoria," said the first kayaker, "It's 330 miles, so we should be there in two weeks."

"I began near Astoria," James said, "at Fort Canby."

The first kayaker stared at James in disbelief.

"It can be done," James said with friendly firmness, "I just did it."

"How long did it take you," asked the first kayaker.

"Fifty days," James replied.

"Fifty days!" cried the kayaker, again in disbelief.

The first kayaker, who appeared highly driven, paddled on while the second kayaker, who appeared more relaxed, remained to speak with James. The two men had a brief but good conversation before bidding one another farewell.

The shoreline, which had been clean until that point, became trash strewn and James regarded it an indicator of lawless activity. Also, Lake had warned of gang activity in the area. UB knew nothing of the sort however and therefore had no qualms about letting his master know he needed to go ashore. They landed in a trashy desert cove where what looked to be a teenage Mexican father and mother stood fishing with their toddler playing nearby. No words were spoken although the two men nodded to one another. James let UB do his duty, then continued paddling north along the west shore, approximately six miles from the city of Kennewick.

Collectively called the Tri-Cities Area, the three towns of Kennewick, Richland, and Pasco were located on the confluence of the Columbia and Snake Rivers. At Kennewick, the canoeist planned to resupply before attempting the Snake River leg of his journey. Presently, James knew he couldn't make Kennewick before nightfall. Hoping to find a safe campsite, he paddled through desert lowlands absolutely strewn with trash. A discarded oven lay half submerged along the shore, riddled with bullet holes. Needless to say that after seeing more of the same for several miles, James felt relieved to find a safe place to camp:

> "...and scouting further, I found the shore to be cut off from a network of primitive roads and paths in the desert beyond. It was cut off by a dense thicket behind which lay a bog divided by an elevated railroad track. There wasn't any trash there, not even a cigarette butt. The thicket paralleled the shore with only an animal path running between the two. The shore, itself being a five-foot cut bank, had a collapsed area that gave me access. To make camp, I had to clear dead branches and a fair number of rocks. It took some doing but the site was prime, tucked into the impenetrable thicket, yet open to the river. There I would have shade both evening and morning. Having cleared the site, I brought up my gear and canoe, and then made camp. I didn't cook but ate an apple along with some slices of cheese, two bagels, and an orange. I was in bed by 9:00pm which I considered to be good."

James slept well.

Day 51, Saturday, July 3

At 7:00am, James checked the ice in his cooler and decided to cook his remaining beef supply. He cut a three-pound roast into chunks and cooked it in two batches. Then setting the beef aside to cool, James made and ate breakfast. He then bagged the cooked beef and put it in his cooler. UB came limping and crying with a huge thorn in his paw which James pulled out.

Having shoved off, man and dog proceeded north along the west shore. The morning sky was clear blue, with a light breeze that cooled the skin, and no waves to speak of. They hadn't gone far at all when they arrived at a clean patch of beach where a man sat alone on a log gazing out over the river with his Harley parked alongside. The man, who said his name was Jim, appeared to be enjoying some quiet time. After getting directions on what lay ahead, James thanked Jim and continued toward the city of Kennewick.

Just outside the city, James came to a tiny patch of beach where a single lounge chair had been set up. Behind the chair, through an opening in the trees, James spotted an old k-car parked on a dirt lane. The red car, although faded, appeared without scratch or ding. Likewise, the primitive beach hadn't a speck of trash. Nor was there a soul to be seen except for a single senorita, standing shin deep in the water directly before the Kansan.

That such a woman should be alone astounded James, for she was just that beautiful, with great big Spanish eyes and jet-black hair flowing down her flawless frame to the back of a scant bikini.

In awe, James watched as the senorita flipped her hair over her head so that it landed in the river like a mop before him. Then rising up, she lifted her hair in her hands until, with arms fully extended above her head, she let it fall down her backside. James could scarcely believe what he saw but unless weeks of desert heat had him hallucinating, there she stood, smooth and perfect as a babe, unmarred by tattoos and piercings, and more, far more, indeed almost impossibly if not wholly juxtaposed to her provocative behavior, she stood possessed of a reserved quality which gave her a quiet kind of dignity despite her near nakedness! She was either the devil, or fantastically innocent.

To say the least, our sinner wanted to go ashore, but to invite himself seemed improper. Knowing not what to do, he asked directions to what he already knew. But honest he was and therefore he asked her to verify what he'd been told regarding what lie ahead. The senorita answered his questions warmly and perhaps even a little laughingly, so easily had she put him under her spell. But even while under her spell, James did not forget his errand. Ahead stood an industrial district to be gotten through, and beyond that the city, and the date was July 3rd which meant all the inns might be booked solid, plus there were no campgrounds unless he paddle five miles beyond the five miles that lie ahead, and still there might not be an open campsite. Such were the things that weighed on the canoeist as he paddled ever so slowly, asking directions, and stealing looks.

Having passed the senorita, James couldn't help glancing over his shoulder at her. And in fairness to James, he was lonesome. He'd been on the river for days without anyone to speak with except his dog and such things affected him even though he remained unaware of them. To turn his canoe around might have frightened her however so James kept paddling and glancing back. He fancied her a working-class girl, a hotel maid, getting away on her day off, closing in on age thirty and still dreaming a prince would come and take her away in one of those yachts out in the middle of the river; away to his castle where she could be the princess that she was. That was what James decided. She was an aging girl of great beauty and trapping dreams to match.

The senorita, by then only a dot on the shoreline, vanished from sight as James entered an industrial district where a great many barges sat moored. The canoeist paddled though a narrow water alley between parked barges. Then emerging from the upstream end of the industrial area, he saw the suspension bridge at Kennewick three miles ahead.

No sooner had James seen the suspension bridge than, looking to his right, he saw the mouth of the Snake River and knew he had reached a major milestone. He had successfully canoed up the Columbia River.

James would not enter the Snake River on that day because he first needed to resupply in Kennewick which meant continuing up the Columbia for another three miles beyond the confluence. Presently in need of ice to keep his food from spoiling, James landed at Two Rivers Park, located directly across from where the Snake River emptied into the Columbia.

At the park, James asked a pair of young men where he might find ice for his cooler. Frank immediately launched into directions but when James said he was on foot, Brandon got on his cell phone and called his girlfriend who was in route to the park with Frank's girlfriend. Next thing James knew, he had two bags of ice just like that. James tried to pay Frank and Brandon but neither would accept any money. They said they liked what James was doing. Then wishing him well, they sped away in their ski boat.

From Two Rivers Park, James paddled north toward an inn on a peninsula called Clover Island three miles ahead. The date was July 3rd, so James could only hope the inn had a vacancy. In the meantime, the river buzzed with pleasure crafts on a perfect Fourth of July weekend. Speed boats, ski boats, jet skies, and pleasure cruisers threw off wakes that made James's canoe bob like a cork but, he didn't mind. Then noticing a ski boat that had stopped and raised an orange flag, he feared them to be in some distress. (He didn't know that an orange flag served to warn other boaters away when swimmers were in the water.) Therefore seeing how other boaters avoided them, James suspected there to be some kind of freeway mentality going on and, joining the crowd so to speak, he decided they could call for help on their cell phone. Then worrying they might not have a phone, he turned his craft and began paddling toward them even though they were far out in the river. When the people in the boat realized James might be coming for them, they began to behave nervously. In fact they called their swimmers aboard as the Kansan drew near. Then, when he had all but reached them, they sped away, leaving him baffled.

Directly after paddling under the suspension bridge, James arrived at the manmade peninsula called Clover Island. Clover Island was a kind of luxury port, clean and green, with yachts, first-class restaurant, and an upscale inn. James didn't paddle to the docks located at the back of the peninsula's cove but instead moored his canoe beneath a cliffy bank at the mouth of the cove (for the sake of saving time and energy should there be no vacancy at the inn).

Having tied off to a tree branch that hung out from the mouth of the cove, James grabbed hold of the branch and attempted to swing himself from boat to cliff. Unfortunately, he miscalculated and swung too hard, whereupon he slammed against the cliff, broke a lens out of his sunglasses, bent up the frames, and knocked off his hat. None the worse for wear, James continued twenty feet up to appear suddenly before the inn where he surprised a couple who were just then stepping from a luxury car—,

"Ma'am, Sir, howdy-do," said the Kansan with a tip of his hat. Then brushing off his shirt and straightening his pants, he entered the inn to see if there were any vacancies.

A pair of attractive young lady clerks behind the check-in desk gave James a particularly good room that had become available due to a cancellation. The young clerks also saved James time and work by informing him that he could off-load his gear at a dock directly below the inn's swimming pool which was located just around the corner from where he had moored his craft. James's room wasn't cheap, but it wasn't terribly expensive either, and because he'd just completed a major leg of his journey, he thought it alright to have a room with a prime view of the river.

With his gear in his room, James paddled his empty canoe to the dock at the back of the peninsular cove where he set about the work of assembling his walking machine. The spacious wood-planked dock afforded plenty of room for everybody. Unfortunately, it was covered with goose droppings to such a degree, there wasn't a square foot where a goose hadn't left its calling card. And the droppings were not small but almost the size of something UB would do. James had to be careful as he went about his work and still it was impossible not to get goose stuff on himself and his machine. James didn't get upset but only wondered why with all the high-dollar boats could someone not afford to have the dock cleaned! So he asked and was told that a legal action by animal rights activist was to blame. James wouldn't worry about it while St Louis remained before him but only knew there had to be a better way. James pulled his rig to the inn. The time was approximately 7:00pm.

UB was delighted to have a room. His master meanwhile focused on the next leg of their journey. James's original knowledge of the Snake River had been so sparse; he had envisioned terrible sets of rapids which he would have to portage by hauling his canoe and gear up and down cliffs, using ropes, ascenders, and the harness of his walking machine (which was a modified mountain rescue harness). Lake had assured James that the Snake River wouldn't be a problem with regard to rapids but rather the challenge would come in paddling 150 miles through a desert canyon with no towns, few roads, and scarce opportunity to resupply. Lake had told where the resupply points were but James had been so concerned with the Columbia at the time, he hadn't retained much of what Lake said regarding the Snake.

Even while tired and depleted, James felt happy as he ate dinner from his cooler. He ate a cold steak, one green bell pepper, two bagels, and an orange. After eating, James took a shower and spent another hour planning for the next leg of his journey by which point his wristwatch read 10:00pm. James hit the sack and slept well.

Day 52, Sunday, July 4

At 8:00am, James ate a complimentary breakfast at the inn before walking to town for a full breakfast at a café. Returning to his room, James hunkered down on his journal until 1:00pm but didn't catch it up. He ate lunch in his room then began planning for the next leg of his journey. He needed a new paddle to replace the one he had broken. He needed a good map. He needed a bigger skillet. He needed provisions. He needed to work on his gear. He needed information. He needed to do laundry. He needed to have everything right before entering the mouth of the Snake. He needed to keep moving so as not to fall behind and, as a result, get caught in a blizzard atop the Continental Divide.

The date was July 4 and, calling around on the phone, James found businesses either closed or staffed by kids who didn't know much. This was no bad thing because it forced James to get better organized by way of making a plan for the next day. To do so, James first got a city map from the hotel lobby. He then used map and phone book to locate and mark the places he needed to travel for supplies. Thus he mapped out his route for stops on the morrow and made lists of what he needed at each stop. He also made a list of things for Patricia to bring because they planned on meeting in a State Park ten miles up the Snake River.

After planning, James worked on his journal until 10:00pm when the sound of fireworks brought him to the window. The people of the Tri-Cities were celebrating the 4th, and James enjoyed a first-class view of the fireworks which came from a barge on the river just outside his window.

A little lonesome perhaps, but grateful for his freedom, James slept well.

Day 53, Monday, July 5

At 6:30am, James walked to town for breakfast at the café. UB howled while James ate. Across the dining room, four men sat at a table and James guessed them to be locals who knew the area. When he had finished his breakfast, he walked over to their table—,

"Excuse me gentlemen. My name is James, and I come from Kansas to attempt the Lewis and Clark route going west to east. I put into the Columbia on May 14 at Fort Canby and arrived here day before yesterday. I'll be starting up the Snake River on Wednesday if all goes well but, I don't know much about the Snake, and I need to resupply first. I was hoping you gentlemen might know the area and be able to help me with some information."

A conversation began and the men invited James to pull up a chair. So it was that James met Marty who was Chaplin of the Kennewick Fire Department; Mac a retired policeman; Arnie a retired woodworker; and Roger a construction worker. All four men knew the area well, and by their hospitality, helped James out of that strange inner discomfort called loneliness. In fact all five were soon talking and laughing in good humor.

After awhile, Mac had to go meet his wife. Roger also had to go. Then because the Tri-Cities were spread out over a large area, Marty offered to help James get resupplied for the route ahead. James gratefully accepted.

James hadn't noticed Marty's prosthetic leg until the men got up from the table. Marty walked a little slowly. He was a big man, not big as in overweight but tall and large framed. Marty had been a fireman until he lost his leg. Then as could be expected, he had gone through a time of trial. He became Chaplin for the Fire Department.

Marty had a good-looking 4x4 truck. It was red and white and looked like it belonged beside a fire engine. James had his city map, acquisition list, grocery list, phone numbers, pen and pad inside his empty journal case which presently served as a brief case. UB meanwhile got to ride same as he would back home, looking out the window and wagging his tail. In fact when UB was a young dog, he often rode in the bed of James's truck, his face in the wind, his front paws on the bed side, his back paws on a spare tire.

After purchasing a cast iron skillet at a local hardware store, the two men went to Marty's house where James couldn't help noticing Marty's fishing boat, covered with dust in the car port like it hadn't been used for a long time. Inside the house, the two men sat at a kitchen table pouring over river charts. Marty liked telling about the river. His maps, like his knowledge, were of the highest quality and detail. The Snake River was similar to the Columbia but on a half-scale. Whereas the Columbia had been a mile wide, the Snake was a half mile wide. Whereas the Columbia had been a distance of roughly 300 miles, the Snake would be 150 miles. Also like the Columbia, the Snake passed through a gorge with four hydroelectric dams to portage. James made many notations regarding supply points, miles between supply points, and goods and services available at each point. Then after making some phone calls, the two men drove to Pasco to look at paddles. James didn't find a paddle that suited him but purchased a map and a light blanket to replace his summer sleeping bag. By then it was noontime so James asked Marty if he could buy lunch and they went to a Chinese buffet—,

"I don't know about leaving a small dog tied up outside a Chinese restaurant," said James, fixing UB's leash to a tree.

Marty only laughed and shook his head.

James also laughed even while he made sure they got a table by a window where, as usual, he could keep an eye on UB. James then began telling a recent story about a Chinese restaurant that got busted for serving animals that weren't on the menu—,

"It's true," said James, "it was in the newspaper." Only then did James notice how Marty seemed to be losing his appetite, "Ah heck, what am I saying? [I'm reveling over a rotten apple in spite of all the good Chinese food]. I'm sorry Marty!"

Marty forgave James's poor manners and in fact the two men hit it off as friends. James told Marty of his plan to meet his sister Patricia at Charbonneau State Park on Wednesday. Marty said he might come out to the park (located only ten miles up the Snake River). James thought that would be great but no more had he said so when he silently remembered that he and his sister held different beliefs and therefore had issues, and, there was Marty, looking like a reincarnation of John Wayne with a king-sized Christian cross on his chest. James decided not to worry about it.

After lunch, the men went to an outdoor store in Kennewick where James purchased two boxes of food bars. Then on the way to the grocery store, James realized he'd forgotten his grocery list so they went to the inn where James took the opportunity to show Marty his walking machine. While doing so, an emergency call came in on Marty's radio.

"I've got to go," said Marty. "You're welcome to come if you like. Otherwise, I'll come back."

"Are you sure it's alright for me to come along," asked James.

"Oh yeah."

"Can UB come?"

"Yeah."

Marty turned on his siren and they sped away in his red and white truck.

"What's that code mean?" James asked, listening to the dispatcher.

"It means someone's found a [dead] body," Marty replied.

The men arrived at a corner house in a residential neighborhood where a police officer stood on the front lawn speaking with an emotionally distraught woman. Marty parked at the curbside and James immediately stepped out when in fact he should have waited for Marty but being a little excited, he wasn't thinking. In fact, James had no more then stepped out than the emotionally distraught woman began across the yard for him. At once James realized she had mistaken him for the Chaplin and, it was too late to get back in the truck.

As the distraught woman closed in, James felt a tinge of panic because he had no training in such matters. He removed his hat and glasses, then glanced hopefully at Marty as if to say, "Please hurry!"

Marty had yet to get around the truck when the distraught woman arrived before James, and, while she poured her heart out, James couldn't help thinking that the very last thing he wanted for the poor woman was to end up in a situation like what he had experienced a few times in life when after telephoning some establishment and explaining what he needed in detail, his call got transferred.

"Ma'am," James said earnestly, "I am very sorry for your loss."

Fortunately at that exact moment, Marty came alongside and James was able to introduce him as the Chaplin. So everything worked out smoothly.

Next a policeman came seeking information from the woman. Apparently, a man had died of natural causes related to old age and the distraught woman (a young friend who mowed his lawn) had found the body. The situation was however a little more complicated than that because while questioning the neighbors, the police had learned that another man had visited the house earlier. Therefore a process that James had never witnessed unfolded directly before him. And observing how Marty and the police handled it, James would make the following journal entry:

"They made me feel proud to be an American."

Afterward, Marty took James to the grocery store and then back to the inn. James sincerely thanked Marty, and in turn, Marty assured James that he'd been glad to help. The two men then traded contact information so James could let Marty know how he faired. Then, so Marty would not see his eyes which were welling just a little, James turned to look out the window while saying, "There sure is a lot of good in this world." The two men then parted with a firm handshake.

In his room, James put his groceries in a refrigerator to be transferred (later) to his ice chest. He then drank two cups of coffee, started his laundry, spread out his gear in his room and went to work. He cleaned out his cooler. He cleaned out his water bottles and filled them. He organized all six duffle bags and repacked his plastic storage locker. He worked fast, performing dozens of tasks. He got out the map he had purchased in Pasco. It wasn't a map of the Snake River but a map of the Blue Mountains which included a section of the Snake River, and because it was a large map, it showed the river pretty well. It didn't show the entire section of river that James needed but only half of what he needed, being the length running from the bridge at Lyons Ferry to Lewiston Idaho. Therefore, James pasted the photo-copied map pages from the visitor's center in Umatilla to the backside of the Blue Mountain map. The photo-copied pages showed the first section of the Snake River, being the length from Ice Harbor Dam to the bridge at Lyons Ferry. So his map had a front and back, the first side showing the first section of the Snake River and the second side showing the second section. Finally, James transferred the detailed notations he had made at Marty's house onto his map front and back. The finished product was a custom-made map that would help James make excellent time on the Snake River leg of his journey. Next James mailed letters home along with old maps and receipts.

At 8:00pm, James went for dinner at the inn's restaurant while a pretty young desk clerk named Cathy babysat UB. Returning to his room, James worked on his gear, then brought out his journal and caught it up. He hit the sack at 12:05am. It had been a highly productive day.

James slept well.

Day 54, Tuesday, July 6

At 6:30am, James called a company in the State of Maine and ordered two paddles by overnight air carrier. He then walked to the diner in town where he, Marty, Mac, Arnie, and Roger enjoyed good conversation and breakfast.

"I'll tell you what," said Mac, "at this time of year, and going where you're going [past a few large State Parks], you're bound to meet up with some pretty girls. That is, if you haven't already."

While shaking his head with a smile, James dropped his eyes and said, "I'm trying to be good," and for the record, he would remain completely chaste throughout his journey, not by any strength or wisdom of his own but because he had given his heart to God, and therefore, the Holy Spirit interceded whenever the temptation of the flesh came upon him.

The conversation continued with laughs all around, especially when James told how he'd nearly gotten himself killed by paddling into the path of an ocean freighter. James felt very fortunate for the company he'd found, and that gave him all the more reason to feel troubled over things he'd seen in the desert and in its little towns, and even in Kennewick which was no longer small but still possessed small-town qualities in men like Marty, Mac, Arnie, and Roger. James rarely deviated from the topic of reaching St Louis because it was, after all, an all-consuming task. Presently however, James drew grim and broke with his standard mode of operation—,

"I couldn't help but notice how around town, a lot of windows have bars on them."

Roger was first to break the silence, "It wasn't that long ago, there weren't any bars on any windows."

The five men began on the subject and as their witness, James saw no hate, nor did anyone look down their nose at those who were different, but rather he saw men who were concerned as well they should be.

Mac spoke of a need for local control but the thing James would remember most was the pain in Marty's voice when after telling how he had tried, he said—,

"It's not working."

Roger was younger and understandably frustrated. His people were in decline, their culture collapsing, accelerated by a large influx of illegal aliens. Roger began to say something about how James was about to enter a natural barrier and would come out the other side in a different world, but Roger never got the chance. Mac or Marty cut him off, saying only, "He's [James is] going there, he'll see for himself."

Having completed the Lewis and Clark Trail, James made this entry on the matter:

> "Today, our little towns and farms are dying in a world that is too big to see how a life-sustaining bushel of grain is grown in the land of the free. For a golden bushel of grain sprouts not only from good soil and hard work, but from social stability, itself sprouted from the unity of a people bound by love and loyalty. It is a beautiful thing, a gift from God that feeds the world, and it is dying. I can only hope that we can turn it around before it's too late."

Changing the subject, Arnie asked James if he had a snakebite kit (the men had been discussing it before James arrived that morning and thought he should have one because he was headed into rattlesnake territory). James replied that he didn't have a snakebite kit whereupon Marty offered to take him to get one.

After taking James to get a snakebite kit, Marty dropped James off at the inn with an invitation to grill up some food later that evening. James would have accepted gladly, but because he needed to get some serious sleep before facing the Snake River on the morrow, he declined. As for Marty, he understood.

James went to his room and fell asleep. The time was 11:00am. Soon the phone rang; the local newspaper wanted to do a story. James thanked them for their interest. He said he would be happy to give them an interview but not before he reached St Louis.

Most reporters would understand James's policy of walking before talking. Therefore the following entry belongs here for the sake of James's honor and also for the sake of those reporters who might otherwise end up feeling like they had been treated unfairly:

> "[Somewhere on the trail far ahead,] a woman and man stepped forward with microphone and video camera. I had already explained my policy to another reporter, and perhaps that was why, when I asked if they were with the press, the woman said they were not (perhaps they were only "citizen reporters"). I had just entered a small town and was in extreme exhaustion. People had been stepping forward right and left to help, mostly my people but also some Indians whose territory I had come through, and having been the recipient of such kindness, I simply trusted the woman when she assured me that her partner with the video camera just had a thing for taking video. Unbeknown to me, I would be on TV. The television station was not in the little town but in a nearby big city. "

After speaking with the Kennewick newspaper, James went back to sleep. For the remainder of the day James slept and ate, slept and ate. Outside that, he spoke on the phone with Frank for half an hour. Then when nighttime came, despite sleeping all day, James slept like a log.

Rivers of the North
Chapter VI

Day 55, Wednesday, July 7

At 6:15am, James iced his cooler and began a load of laundry. He went to the diner where he met Marty, Mac, Arnie, and Roger. Good food and conversation followed. Sometimes laughing, sometimes serious, they spoke for an hour or so. Then with words of thanks, well wishes, and handshakes, James departed in the hope of seeing them again someday.

Back in the hotel lobby, James found his paddles had come all the way from Maine. Immediately he took them from their box and inspected them. Both were identical, made of wood, polished to cut through water, with large blades shaped like beaver tails for maximum grab. James lowered his walking machine down a gravel path at the corner of the inn's parking lot situated closest to the suspension bridge and the main river channel. He then brought his gear down from his room, disassembled his walking machine, and loaded his canoe. At 11:30am, with everything ready to go, James left UB in the shade beside the canoe and went for lunch at the inn's restaurant where he ate a hamburger and chips before shoving off at 12:30pm.

Man and dog went in the direction from which they'd come a few days before. So they went downstream, toward the confluence. And because of strong winds that could push and pin them against the east shore, James paddled in the windbreak of a large riprap levy that ran the west bank. Then, after paddling two miles, James set out to cross the Columbia River for the last time. He went on a diagonal, angling his craft to catch the wind like a sail while aiming his bow toward the mouth of the Snake River.

At the land point between the two rivers there was a State Park, and while James didn't need to go ashore, he did so because the park had been named after the Indian maiden who played an important role in the Lewis and Clark expedition. So James paid his respects to Sacahawea.

James hadn't gone far into the mouth of the Snake when he

looked over his shoulder to see the Columbia directly behind. Then paddling a mile further, he took a final look back. Perhaps the dragon watched as the knight paddled away. Perhaps he nodded, and even smiled a little.

Feeling fired up, James paddled hard with a strong wind at his back. Just for fun, he tried to beat a barge to the upstream end of Strawberry Island. The barge traveled in the shipping lane to the south of the island, the canoeist in a small channel to the north. James lost but it didn't matter because, as he came out the upstream end of the channel, he saw Ice Harbor Dam in the distance and therefore knew he was making extraordinary progress.

At approximately 2:00pm, James landed under a shade tree where he ate a banana and energy bar, then shoved off directly. The current came on unexpectedly and rapidly grew to make for some of the toughest sustained upstream paddling of James's journey. Every paddle stroke brought a belabored growl and, this is the place to tell, James wanted to go through the lock at Ice Harbor Dam something fierce!

The dam stood five miles ahead. The official time for opening the lock to public crafts was 6:00pm, and if only he could get there in time, James believed he might have a chance to go through the lock.

> "The current was flat out ripping, nearly impossible to make headway against. I kept paddling for all my worth. Heavy labored controlled breathing; exhale on the power stroke, inhale on the return. Three times while paddling thus, I glanced to shore to gauge my progress only to see I was going backward. There was nothing to do but shift my position in the river, look for better water, and try again. It was a [decision-making] process taking only seconds, for to take longer would be too costly and I could not afford that, as I had but so much energy to spend before I ran out."

Fighting all out in desert heat soon sapped James of strength. And while it may have been frivolous to appeal to the Almighty for help in gaining such a reward, no sooner had James done so than a tiny sliver of cloud came to shield him even while brilliant sunshine illuminated the face of the dam.

"I felt goose bumps. A surge of energy flowed though me."

At 5:00pm, the situation appeared impossible and still James inched forward with two miles to go. He marveled at the dam with its ten waterfalls pouring down into a mist. To the left of the dam, the lock appeared like an attached garage for ships. It had a massive steel door beside which a barrier wall protruded to form a protected channel through which ships might pass without getting wrecked by turbulence from the waterfalls.

The canoeist could not have approached the dam without the experience of the Columbia River behind him and a strong wind at his back. The roar alone was terrific. The energy so destabilized the river, it rose and fell like a great undulating blanket. James aimed for the barrier wall and the protection it provided. Meanwhile on the unprotected side of the wall, tremendous waterfalls gave rise to horrific rapids which in turn gave rise to giant swells like phantoms trapped in an arena beneath the dam. They raced in every direction, crashing into one another, vanishing in explosions of spray and mist. Several charged out at James as he fought to gain the protection of the barrier wall. It was something a man in a canoe would not forget; the sheer walls of the dam, the ten waterfalls, the terrific roar, the rising and falling of the river, the spray and mist.

James finally reached the protected waters behind the barrier wall. At once the roar dampened and the river calmed even as it continued to rise and fall significantly. One-hundred fifty feet ahead where protected channel met dam stood the steel door of the lock. The door was closed but, some distance back from the door, a cord hung beside a large sign that read: "PULL CORD."

James pulled the cord at exactly two minutes before six o'clock.

A mechanical voice crackled to life, "WELCOME TO ICE HARBOR DAM. THE LOCKMASTER HAS BEEN NOTIFIED. PLEASE PROCEED TO THE LIGHT AND WAIT FOR FURTHER INSTRUCTIONS."

Although it was the scheduled time for boats to use the lock, there were no boats in sight. Nor were there any people in sight, no fishermen, no dam workers, no sightseers. There was only the dam itself, the river, the sensation of rising and falling, the muffled thunder of waterfalls, and the great steel door before which the Kansan and his little dog waited.

The light was red but with any hope it would turn green and the door would open.

After waiting five minutes for the light to change, James paddled back and pulled the cord again but no voice crackled to life. So he pulled it again and still nothing happened. James then paddled back to the light where he waited. He was about to give up when from high above, he heard a shout which carried a distinct tone—,

"What [in the hell] are you doing?"

Looking up, James saw the head of a man peering over the top of the massive barrier wall. It was the lockmaster who had come out on a cat walk.

James shouted up the wall, "Sir, I was hoping to use the lock."

"I can't allow that!" shouted the man. "The valves that flood the lock have no adjustment other than full open. When the water rushes in, it creates a lot of turbulence."

"I can't hear you," James shouted.

"I said, I can't let you in there. Once I throw the switch, the river floods the lock chamber [at 50,000 gallons per second] and it's a violent process."

"Yes Sir, I understand," James shouted, at once disappointed but hardly ready to quit. "Sir, can you tell me where I might be able to portage around the dam?"

"Can you get up over there?" shouted the Lockmaster, and he pointed to the secondary wall of the channel behind which the dam butted up against the side of the canyon.

James paddled around the secondary wall and into a corner where he found neither path, staircase, nor ladder, but only a great buttress of basalt boulders. Landing his canoe in said corner presented a challenge due to the rising and falling water. Fortunately, some driftwood floated there and James was able to construct a crude boat ramp in a gap between dam wall and buttress. By employing smaller drift logs as rollers, and using no small physical effort, James pulled his craft out of the water.

"It's okay boy," said the Kansan, comforting his frightened dog. "I'll be back before you know it." He then climbed ten stories up the buttress to a shelf near the top of the dam where he met the Lockmaster.

"Sir, my name is James, and I've come from Kansas to attempt the Lewis and Clark route west to east. I began at the mouth of the

Columbia river on May 14 and . . ." James continued, explaining how he had used his walking machine to get around the dams on the Columbia River. Meanwhile, an armed guard kept watch from a wall directly above.

The lockmaster so liked what James was about, he offered to help James get his canoe up the buttress. James thanked the lockmaster whereupon the two men proceeded to where they might descend the buttress, except that the lockmaster stopped at the edge to look down.

Seeing his expression, James said, "It will be easy with two of us."

"Let me think this over," said the lockmaster who then left to have a word with the guards. On returning, the Lockmaster told James what he had in mind and the two men entered into an agreement the old-fashioned way, with a handshake. As to what they agreed on, nothing can be told, nor was anything written.

Aside from knowing that James made the entire journey under his own power, all that can be known is that James paddled east from Ice Harbor Dam with a tail wind blowing him in the direction of Charbonneau State Park. And so it was, James continued to make excellent progress, paddling roughly 1½ miles on a long diagonal in which he made his first crossing of the Snake River.

At 7:30pm, James landed at a small marina located just outside Charbonneau State Park. The marina sat empty and possessed the quality of a well kept filling station in the middle of nowhere. As James assembled his walking machine, two men came to see what he was about. The men arrived simultaneously although from different directions, each having seen the canoeist paddle in from the river. Frank had come to fish the area. Steve had come to teach young folks how to sail. James was happy to explain his walking machine and all three men had a good conversation. James then inquired about the location of the park pay phone but to his dismay learned there was none. Fortunately, Frank immediately offered his cell phone for which James felt grateful. James then made a call to his sister and asked that she adjust her schedule because he was one-half day ahead of his. Patricia understood; James hoped to cross the Rocky Mountains before the snows began. Therefore she said she could meet him a half-day earlier than planned. James felt fortunate for his sister's flexibility on short notice. James then tried to pay

Frank for the call but Frank kindly refused.

While pulling toward the state park, James passed a sign telling how the park gate closed at dark. And seeing as it was almost dark, James felt all the more fortunate.

On entering the park, James stopped to ask directions from a groundskeeper who was visiting with five or six vacationers sipping drinks in lawn chairs. It was the only time James met with anything less than hospitality from camp people but perhaps they didn't know what to make of a man, punch drunk with exhaustion, claiming to have canoed up the Columbia River. Whatever the case, it wasn't until after James sensed the groundskeeper didn't want him there that UB walked to the end of his leash and defecated directly in front of the groundskeeper. Without being told, the Kansan immediately apologized and felt bad while searching his cart for something to pick up UB's mess. One of the vacationers must have realized that James was down to his last, whereupon he stepped forward and kindly showed James to a dumpster across the road where he happened to know of some plastic grocery bags.

James next asked the groundskeeper where the open campsites were but the man only grumbled and pointed into the twilight. So James continued into the park, himself grumbling. He hadn't gone far however when he decided that they had only gotten off on the wrong foot.

James set up his tent, took a shower, hit the sack at 11:00pm and slept like a rock.

Day 56, Thursday, July 8

Albeit a little slowly, James was up and moving at 6:45am. After breakfast, a groundskeeper came and asked James to move his camp to an unreserved site. Whether it was the same groundskeeper as the night before James couldn't know. He moved his camp with little effort because most of his gear remained in his cart and he didn't have to take down his tent but only carried it a short distance. He worked on his journal until 2:30pm and then went to pay his campground fee at the admissions office which had been closed the night before.

Arriving back at camp, James found Patricia and hugged her

tight. Brother and sister then sat talking for hours during which time James offered Pat a food bar made of chocolate with a granola center—,

"These things taste pretty good," said James taking a bite of his bar and chewing.

"Yeah," said Pat, "these are about the best there are. Did you know these are made for women?"

"Yeah," said James, as if to say, *"so what."* Then shrugging it off, he added, "They taste good, that's all that matters."

Pat then continued, "They put estrogen in them."

James stopped chewing.

"I think they stopped doing that," Pat reiterated, reading the sudden change in her brother's expression.

James brought out his reading glasses to check the packaging but could find nothing indicating estrogen. Again Pat said she thought the manufacturer had stopped the practice of adding the female hormone.

Uncertain, James sat the remaining portion of his bar aside.

"Aren't you going to finish yours?" asked Pat.

"Maybe later," said James but in fact he would never take another bite even though he had an entire box of them packed in his food duffle.

Brother and sister drove to Kennewick where James photocopied his journal, then purchased a few additional groceries and picked up some unneeded gear which he'd left at the hotel office for safe keeping. James gave said gear to Patricia for safe keeping. Next they went for Mexican food and enjoyed a pleasant dinner. Upon returning to the park, James found a note from Marty. Marty had come to the park to visit while James and Pat were out. James was upset with himself for not calling Marty before he and Pat left camp. He then called Marty on Patricia's phone and left a message because Marty wasn't home.

Patricia set up her tent, then brought out a pair of lawn chairs and invited James to sit. The two spoke until late and just as anticipated, they ended up wading through a quagmire together regarding their political differences which wouldn't have pained them so if they hadn't loved one another. Therefore comes a place *not* to tell except to say that brother and sister made it through a quagmire, and it did them good to see one another. James slept well.

Day 57, Friday, July 9

At 7:00am, James cut a roast into chunks and, after cooking them, put them on ice for the journey ahead. He then began breakfast: bacon, eggs, etc. Pat got up at 8:00 and started a pot of coffee. After breakfast, while brother and sister sat and talked, a Park Ranger who had learned of James at the campground office came to offer James his knowledge. James had many questions, especially after learning that Donald had spent a good portion of his career on the remote northern tier of the Missouri River. Donald hadn't been gone long when another Park Ranger stopped to visit. Jeanne had enthusiasm, and lots of knowledge. Then with well wishes, Jeanne departed. James and Patricia continued visiting until alas, James realized that time had passed much too quickly.

James didn't pull his rig to the marina but parked his machine where the green lawn of the park ended at a steep bank with a gentle path leading down to a narrow beach beside the river.

While James went about the work of disassembling his walking machine, a man came and said he had heard what James was about and wanted to help. Al then took forty dollars from his billfold and offered it to James. James refused the money even while sincerely thanking Al for his generous offer. Then seeing how he had pained the man, James did a quick about-face so to speak and gratefully accepted the gift.

Patricia helped carry loads of gear down the bank. Then with words of thanks, well wishes and a big hug, James shoved off and paddled east. Sister stood watching until brother had disappeared from sight.

James paddled with urgency in the knowledge that 140 miles lie between himself and the next town.

"I know I must have found some shade and rested and ate somewhere that day but in the process of catching up my journal, looking back from Monday afternoon to Friday afternoon, my memory evades me, probably because I am very [very] tired."

James would remember paddling past numerous desert marshes with manmade bird nests standing on poles, obviously some kind of wildlife conservation project. He enjoyed the benefit of a light tailwind and made excellent progress. At 8:00pm he began looking for a campsite but found nothing suitable. Still looking at 9:00pm, he knew he had to get off the river if he were to make camp before darkness fell. He retained only a foggy memory of his camp but his journal tells the following:

> "I carried my gear and canoe up a hill to camp atop a bluff overlooking the river from the NW side. There was a green [river or railroad (?)] mile marker near my camp but I don't remember its number. I was roughly sixty feet above the water. I pitched my tent in near darkness. It was a good level sight.

Having paddled a distance of approximately 14 miles, James hit the hay around 10:30pm and slept well.

Day 58, Saturday, July 10

At 7:00am, James carried loads to the river below. He didn't make breakfast because the desert sun burned hot and no shade existed in that place. James shoved off and paddled with a tailwind until 10:45am when he found an excellent pebble beach under a small shade tree. He built a windbreak for his stove and made a large breakfast. Then removing his stove from his U-shaped windbreak, he laid back in it with duffle bags for pads like a lazy chair and drank a cup of coffee, all the while gazing out over the sparkling river.

James shoved off at 1:00pm and paddled hard. The wind came up from the west to raise the swells that marched in white-capped ranks straight up the river. The fishing boats retreated, seeking shelter along the shores. The canoeist meanwhile took advantage by crossing the river on straight line courses through every bend in order to minimize his total distance traveled. He worked hard amid the whitecaps and reaped his reward in leaps and bounds.

> "Until mastered, a canoe is the worst possible craft for rough water travel, but once mastered, it has no equal. Even the kayak, which is fast like the canoe, cannot match its

payload."

Sometime around 4:00pm while cutting a bend in aforesaid fashion, James met with a yacht coming in the opposite direction. Then, and almost exactly as before when on the Columbia River, the canoeist got tossed about on a dangerous checkerboard pattern of wakes and swells. At least he was not taken off guard, thanks to prior experience. The first wake broke over the side and drenched UB but, in that heat, it was almost a blessing. Afterward, James decided to stay near shore for the remainder of the day. So it was, he continued in sheltered water, paddling, singing, and gazing up cliffs that rose to meet the blue sky.

At 6:00pm, James crossed the river in high wind and swells to gain Wind Dust State Park. The park seemed old and almost worn out compared to Charbonneau Park, but the latter was big and brand new whereas the former had perhaps only been broken in like a comfortable pair of shoes. Upon landing at the boat ramp, James met a man named Wayne.

"I met you at Umatilla," said Wayne.

"I am sorry Sir, but, I cannot remember," James replied.

"You had just reached the top of the hill at the dam," said Wayne, and breaking into a smile, he added, "You were really huffing and puffing."

"Oh yeah," said James, himself breaking into a smile, "I remember now."

James felt surprised to learn that ice wasn't available at Wind Dust Park. On his custom made map, James had written the word "ice" beside Wind Dust Park. On closer inspection however, James saw that he'd written "ice" with an arrow at the end of which he'd written "28 miles ahead". Realizing as much, James thought he should push on while his ice supply lasted. Wayne told James of a place upstream where he could take out to portage around Lower Monumental Dam (the dam stood three miles ahead). James thanked Wayne for the info, then filled his water bottles and shoved off.

No more had James reached the portage spot than he saw Wayne fishing along the shore. Perhaps Wayne, who couldn't go out in his motorboat until the wind died down, had decided to fish there so he could help James carry his canoe up the slope to the road above. Whatever the case, James felt fortunate for the help, for by then, he was plumb worn out.

Having carried the canoe up to the road, James and Wayne shared winded words of thanks and well wishes before parting with a handshake.

After bringing up his gear and assembling his rig, James ate a large portion of summer sausage, a large portion of cheese, two bagels, one apple, and a grapefruit. James then set out pulling the road toward Lower Monumental Dam which stood only one mile ahead. The dam wasn't releasing water but, such was the power of the wind, it drove swells to the dam like a stampede into a box canyon. And truly, it made for a treacherous sight to behold.

Laboring in exhaustion, James pulled his cart up the mile-long grade without knowing what lay beyond the dam (he hadn't thought to ask Wayne). Meanwhile, time had gotten away from him. So he worried for finding a campsite before dark. Fortunately, when he came over the shoulder of the dam at 8:30pm, he found a simple camping area on a gravel shelf above the river. Needless to say, he felt relieved.

The Kansan set up his tent and ate bread, peanut butter, and a grapefruit. By then his wristwatch read 10:00pm. He hit the sack and slept well.

Day 59, Sunday, July 11

James broke camp at 7:00am. He didn't make breakfast because the sun burned hot and no shade existed.

While transforming his land rig to water craft at the boat ramp below the camping area, James met Tom and his wife Lisa. Tom said their dog of many years had died. Then, with an understandable measure of reluctance, he gave James a can of dog food that he'd been keeping around.

James said nothing about it but, when the two men parted with a handshake, he was surprised at the weakness in his own grip. Then, climbing to seat himself in his canoe, he felt slow and unstable whereas he'd always been sure and swift. Such was the price of his remarkable progress. And still there was no time to rest. For such was his situation, he had to make hay, especially while the wind blew favorably. So he paddled upriver with the wind at his back. And as he went, he kept an eye out for a patch of shade in which to make breakfast.

At 10:30am, James made a windbreak for his stove by arranging rocks, driftwood, and gear under a small tree that overhung a sliver of rocky beach.

> "Breakfast was awesome [in that beautiful place]. Then same as before, I removed the stove and lounged in the windbreak. It was a comfortable [2½ hour] brunch."

The canoeist continued paddling upriver. The wind wasn't as strong as the day before and James considered it a blessing in lieu of his exhaustion. He caught a second wind from within and although it didn't pack a serious punch, it allowed him to paddle with consistent strength. Thus feeling twice blessed, he continued in favorable conditions both inside and out. At 3:00pm he ate lunch in a shady nook. He then slept one-half hour, snoring and dreaming before shoving off.

Probably because Lower Monumental Dam wasn't releasing water, the river seemed more like a lake winding through a desert canyon. And because it was the height of the vacation season, and because the wind had become light perhaps due to the lay of the land, James entered a popular area where many pleasure boats motored about. The approximate time was 5:00pm and, almost at once, James noticed a ski boat in the middle of the river flying the orange flag, and because he hadn't yet learned what the orange flag meant, he felt concerned that no one had stopped to help them. So he set out to see if he could be of some assistance, but just as he drew near, the people started their engine and sped away:

> "I was in a desolate area, so the people couldn't have been local folks but vacationers. Most were pleasure boaters: ski boats, speed boats, jet skies, and cruisers. I saw a father and mother in a ski boat pulling their three little ones on a raft behind, all squealing for joy. I also saw a father on a jet ski with his three children holding tight, hugging together and having the time of their lives. I wish they were not afraid of me. I was sorely battered about by their wakes but I was not upset even though exhausted. For their part,

they sure did seem afraid. Fishermen were outgoing almost to a man but the pleasure boaters seemed disinterested if not downright paranoid. Perhaps they were suburbanites, insular, fed on a steady diet of bad news. I realized that my thoughts were only theories and therefore I decided to put them to a test. I aimed my canoe toward a pleasure boat that sat in the water. I paddled directly toward it and sure enough, the boat started up and sped off. Again I aimed my boat at a pleasure boat and it also sped off, then another. I paddled toward a boat that pulled a skier round and round in a tight circle, and it also sped away (having first picked up its skier). I couldn't help but laugh, for I had cleared off an entire section of river. The air fell quiet, the water settled, and the canyon filled with peace. Immediately thereafter, a fox came from the shrubs to get a drink. Very slowly I paddled toward it while speaking softly. And while the pretty little thing appeared full of apprehension, it let its curiosity [or thirst] get the better of it. I coasted to within a canoe length! Then floating in place, I told the little fellow how pretty he was. He or she was small, lean, healthy, gray, with big ears, and some black on its tail. UB started barking while wagging his tail. The fox turned and vanished into the shrubs."

At approximately 7:00pm, James spotted the bridge at Lyon's Ferry State Park and knew he had made very serious progress. He paddled another mile and had nearly made the bridge when seeing how his map might be outdated in comparison to what lie ahead, he looked for a source of information only to see pleasure boats floating here and there.

Feigning disinterest, James paddled as though he were crossing the river and nothing more when in truth his objective was a family in a pleasure boat. The family flew no orange flag but had a swimmer some distance from their boat and therefore wouldn't be able to escape if all went according to plan. James waited until the right moment, then turned his canoe toward the boat and waved in friendly fashion like a man who sought some assistance. The man at the wheel very plainly saw James wave but didn't wave back. Therefore, James went to plan B and veered to separate the man from his wife who was in the water.

James took off his hat, "Excuse me Ma'am, but may I ask if there is ice and food at the State Park?"

The lady in the water smiled and seemed perfectly at ease with the courteous Kansan. She was more than a little attractive, about forty years of age, blond and by all appearances in excellent form. She was also a mother if James remembered correctly. Meanwhile her husband, who was just out of earshot, looked on with concern. The good lady told James that ice and food were not available in the State Park located on the north shore but rather at the private marina and campground on the south shore (at the other end of the bridge). The Kansan thanked the good lady for saving him a lot of work, which was no small thing.

No more had James reentered the middle of the river than along came a yacht with a couple at the rail, smiling and waving like mannequins, or movie stars. James meanwhile scrambled mightily in anticipation of their wake, seeing that they would pass within fifty feet! Afterwards, having only just avoided being overturned, James couldn't help being astonished by their obvious detachment.

James continued to the marina where he landed at 8:00pm. Straight away, two fishermen came forward and James enjoyed explaining his walking machine for them. Then learning that the marina store had closed for the evening, James feared his food would spoil without ice. One of the fishermen then set out to find the owner of the store and shortly thereafter returned with a bag of ice in each hand. James thanked Gene and tried to pay him for the ice but Gene refused, saying that he liked what James was doing. Leo then invited James aboard his boat for a beer. James thanked Leo kindly but declined, saying he had to finish assembling his rig and make camp before darkness fell.

Harnessed into his rig, James followed Gene who showed him to the tent area, a shady shelf high above and behind the rest of the campground. Jean then departed with a handshake, well wishes, and words of thanks from James.

Having spent too much time on things for which only exhaustion can account, like taking too long to select a campsite among dozens of campsites, James lost his race against the onset of night. He fumbled about while trying to erect his tent in the dark. Fortunately, a fisherman came and offered his white fuel lantern.

James accepted gratefully, then slung a rope over a tree limb to which Will tied his lantern. With plenty of light, James set up his tent and ate bread and peanut butter before returning Will's lantern with words of thanks.

Directly after returning Will's lantern, James hit the sack. His wristwatch read 11:00pm. As the crow flew, he had paddled nineteen miles. Overall in three days, he'd come fifty six miles including the portage of Lower Monumental Dam.

Man and dog slept well.

Day 60, Monday, July 12

At 8:00am, James went to the marina store for breakfast. The marina had no laundromat or telephone but the food and friendly hometown atmosphere were good. Back in his camp, James worked on his journal, breaking periodically for conversations with other campers and also to have a hamburger at the marina for lunch before catching up his journal at 5:15pm. James then went for fish and chips at the marina and, while there, prepaid for three bags of ice which he meant to get in the morning before shoving off. He then returned to his camp where he knew he should go to sleep but chose instead to go next door where he talked with Will and Greg until dark (the three men had their camps in a row on the high shelf that overlooked campground and river). Then at 10:30pm or thereabouts, after much good conversation, James retired to his tent and slept well.

Day 61, Tuesday, July 13

At 7:00am, James took out a large roast he'd purchased back in Kennewick. He cut the roast into chunks, each chunk being about three or four bites in size. He then cooked the chunks in batches, bagged them, and put them on ice in his cooler. The idea was to let the chunks cool, then drain out the ice melt and put in more ice. James meant to eat the chunks while paddling upriver.

Having put the cooked beef on ice, James cooked and ate breakfast, then went to Greg's and Marlene's who had invited him for coffee. Greg appeared to be in his fifties, a tall tree trunk of a man, part Native American with an outgoing nature and, if James guessed correctly, an old alpha dog who could still take most comers. Greg's wife Marlene was petite and pretty with red hair. After coffee, Greg and Marlene offered James a ride to the tiny town of Starbuck. James had planned on putting into the river that morning but accepted their offer readily in the knowledge that Starbuck had a small grocery store. So it was, Greg's and Marlene's hospitality came at a perfect time, what with James being near the halfway point in a 150 mile run.

Riding in the car on the way to Starbuck, James got to see what the desert looked like above the gorge. Not one tree grew in that realm; just sand and shrubs, hills and sky, which somehow made for that beauty unique to deserts.

In Starbuck, James, Greg, and Marlene went to the town diner where Greg kindly insisted on picking up the tab for James. They then went across the street to a grocer where James's good fortune continued. The lady who owned the place had gone for fresh produce that morning. So the produce section, which was a large cardboard box, contained a good many green bell peppers and James, who quite possibly ate more green bell peppers than any other man on earth, bought them all.

On the way back to the campground, Greg detoured twelve miles upriver to show James Little Goose Dam. At the dam, Greg handed James a pair of binoculars and, looking across the river, James saw a place to portage around the dam. Also across the river, James saw a campground over-grown with weeds. He asked Greg about it and learned that since the terrorist attacks of 9/11, the road across the dam had closed to public traffic, effectively cutting off the campground. On the way back to Lyon's Ferry, Greg brought up the debate surrounding the dams. Some folks were for the dams, others wanted to see the river returned to its natural state. Greg didn't say what side of the debate he was on. James only said he seen no positive results from all the equipment and manpower he'd seen going into saving the Salmon. This did not mean James was for or against the damns, and no more was said on the subject. James loved nature for what it was, a gift from God. He liked getting out in nature, and in his blessed life, he had enjoyed no small amount of fishing. He considered the largemouth bass to be king of fish. However, he'd never seen a steelhead salmon. Then one day while visiting his sister in the Cascade Mountains, James was walking on a gravel lane when this tremendous fish leapt into the air above the meadow. It fought its way up into the air, all power and muscle, thrashing and flashing in the sun. Then, it soared. Indeed, it seemed to hang suspended like a rainbow, like the best of the best, and in fact that was what it was, an eagle of the sea, come to spawn in the mountains. In the next instant, it vanished in a culvert pipe flowing like a faucet from the side of a grade. It had been something to see and James would not forget it. The run of the salmon represented a quality that James valued greatly in his own heritage. The migration of the pioneers, like the run of the salmon, came from a God-given will that set their hearts and feet in motion. It called them to leave their world like the salmon that left the ocean never to return. It called them to make flesh and blood sacrifices of their own lives. And although James was yet to figure it out, he was in midstream.

"If God made the world for a reason, and if God is the source of all wisdom, then in the big picture, how am I to find answers to the problems that face my people while I myself depend on an infrastructure which, being destructive to God's Creation, must also be destructive to His intention? In this way, I am a salmon come before a 'dam.' Of course, some people would take this and run with it. They would say it means that people who drive big SUV's are part of the 'dam' problem. But such rhetoric is itself a dam because the SUV people are in fact some of the kindest people on earth, and for their efforts this earth is a better reflection of Heaven. Yes, the modern industrial infrastructure is destructive, but it is also creative. And because I haven't the wisdom to get myself beyond the 'dam' [conundrum of knowing which choices are more of one than the other]; I pray to follow the One who can."

Back at the campground, James spent the afternoon and evening visiting with Greg, Marlene, and Will who, with their tents in a row, made up the population of the tent area. First they visited at Will's table, then at James's table, and finally at Greg's and Marlene's table where they sat for hours sampling homemade foods and telling stories. Will was a retired sheriff and told one heck of a tale. Greg also had good tales to tell, being a retired logger. Both men seemed to have a lot to them and James, who was younger, mostly listened. They visited until midnight, then all said goodnight.

James slept well.

Day 62, Wednesday, July 14

James broke camp at 6:00am, pulled his rig down the hill, and transformed it into a water craft. Then with canoe moored and ready to go, he went for breakfast at the marina which opened at 8:00am. James would regret not remembering the names of the good lady and gentleman who owned the marina. He would however remember the name of his waitress. Crystal would have been hard not to notice, such was her excellent work ethic, not to mention she was a beautiful young woman. Crystal said she had a canoe that her father had given her. She said her father had taught her how to canoe and she liked paddling on the river.

From the marina James returned to his canoe where Greg and Will just happened to be returning from an early morning fishing trip. James thanked them for their hospitality and asked Greg to thank Marlene for him. Then with firm hand shakes, James bid them well and shoved off.

"From Lyon's Ferry I paddled toward Little Goose Dam twelve miles upstream. The day promised to be hot. Hot, as in desert hot which requires reminding, lest it be forgotten. The time was approx 9:30am. From the east, a slight breeze came against me but I felt rested from my stay at Lyon's Ferry, so I paddled hard and made good progress even as the breeze continued to mount. The bridge at Lyon's Ferry disappeared three miles behind as I rounded a bend. Then, [I paddled] three more miles to the next bend. The hills rose steeply from the river to form the walls of the gorge. Not hills to a flatlander but mountains worn by time, each a barren blanket of desert rising up to meet the blue."

The breeze grew into a headwind that the canoeist matched with determination, strength, and strategy. Then, having paddled seven miles total, James saw what he believed to be an opportunity to escape the headwind which, having grown steadily, would soon overpower him. His opportunity began at an abandoned campground which logically must have been connected by road to the other abandoned campground at the dam five miles upstream. In fact there was a road between the campgrounds, used occasionally by dam workers in service vehicles. So James figured on beating the wind by pulling the road to the dam. He hoped to then portage around the north shoulder of the dam and make camp. That was his plan.

While assembling his rig at the first abandoned campground, James and UB cooled off by taking dips in the river. Then while eating lunch in a patch of shade, James discovered his pre-cooked beef was going rancid. He ate half of it and planned to eat the other half that night because he felt certain it would not keep until morning.

On the day prior, when James had seen the abandoned camp ground at the dam, he had also seen a paved road running through the campground. Therefore, on seeing the second abandoned campground, James assumed the two campgrounds to be connected by a paved road. As it turned out, the road between the campgrounds was a mixture of pea-gravel and sand in which the narrow wheels of his cart sank repeatedly. The wind died completely. No cloud blocked the sun. No shade existed. Half a mile had somehow come between river and road on the hottest part of the day in the middle of July and, there was our novice, pulling his cart into the desert.

Soaked in sweat, James pulled while UB sat atop the cart, wrapped in a white towel, his face a picture of agony. In fact such was UB's desperation; he tried to jump ship but his master barked orders for him to stay. The official temperature for the day may have been 105 in the shade but that didn't tell the tale on baking hot gravel. Still, James figured he'd be alright because he could see what he believed to be the dam. In reality he did not see the dam but the top of a remote power relay station which sat just beyond the next rise, shimming like a mirage.

James pulled for all his worth, believing that the cool river was just over the rise. Even as his strength was drained out, he laughed in anticipation of how good it would feel to reach the end and stumble into the water. Over and over again, the wheels of his cart sunk in sand and pea-gravel but he kept driving with his legs—,

"Lord," James said, glancing up with pleading eyes.

UB also spoke with his eyes, looking out from within his blanket, *"James, you're killing me!"*

"I'm sorry boy," said James, hoarse with heat and exhaustion, "sorry for getting us into this mess, but, we only have to make it over this rise."

Slow as a tortoise, James ground out the yards.

"A railroad track came to parallel the road at a distance of about 40 feet on grade cut into the side of the canyon, which put it about 15 feet above the plane of the road. As I understood it, the track had been decommissioned. Therefore it surprised me to hear a train coming. The train measured only several cars in length. The engineer slowed the train way down and, as he went by, he hung out the window to his waist while looking at me with utmost concern."

For his part, James walked extra tall, nodded, and gave a sure wave as if to say, *"Don't worry about me, I know exactly what I'm doing."*

The train throttled up and passed on. Then using up the last of his strength, James crested the rise in anticipation of finding the dam.

Standing before the power relay station, James's hopes went up in smoke. Far away, the dam shimmered like a distant hope, greatly distorted by heat waves that seemed to have become one with the shrill screams of cicadas.

Two miles lay between man and dam but it may as well have been twenty. James looked to the river with hope but, it lie across a half mile wide carpet of thorns buzzing with yellow jackets (and most likely crawling with rattle snakes, not to mention tarantulas and scorpions). A man could get into trouble fast in the desert and perhaps no man had ever done so faster than James. He glanced about for shade but there was none. His head ached and felt swollen. He wasn't thinking clearly or he would have poured water from his cooler over his head. He did at least think to douse himself with regular drinking water but he didn't because he found his drinking water had gotten downright hot and taking a hot shower to cool off made no sense, not to mention he feared running out of drinking water. He tried to crawl under his cart but scorching hot gravel forbade it. Likewise, most of his rig had gotten too hot to touch. It seemed James was trapped in an oven and, if a way out existed, his normally fluid mind could not find it.

"Lord," James said in the pleading voice of a child, glancing about in a sea of heat waves. Only then did James see a corrugated drainage pipe coming out the side of the railroad grade.

James placed UB on the ground, "Come boy."

UB whimpered, unable to negotiate the thorny animal path that led to the pipe.

"Sorry boy," said James, returning to fetch up his dog before proceeding to the pipe.

In the pipe, James sat with his back against cool corrugated steel. Cooling him further, a breeze came through the pipe from a mountain ravine. Meanwhile, his raspy breaths echoed like an animal come to die. Powdery dirt clung to him like flour but he took no notice. Half laughing and half crying, James figured he'd found God's rescue chamber for idiots. He thanked the Lord for his good fortune, then closed his eyes and drifted off.

Waking a short time later, James fetched his cooler and dry food duffle into the pipe to preserve his food stores. He then napped restlessly for several hours. At 7:00pm, he emerged from the pipe and continued pulling toward the dam. Soon the hills cast their cooling shadows over the road for which James felt more than a little grateful.

At 8:00pm, the Kansan reached the dam only to find his way blocked by a tall fence and gate. Beside the gate was an opening large enough for pedestrians to pass and, looking beyond it, James could see that the road continued up and over the shoulder of the dam. However, a sign on the fence beside the opening warned people not to pass without first calling for assistance using a telephone mounted beside the gate.

On the telephone, a recorded voice told James to leave a message because it was after hours. James gave his name, where he was from, and what he was doing. He requested a security escort and said he would wait for a guard to come as per the instructions on the sign by the telephone. James then pitched his tent amid the weeds of the abandoned campground. He ate the remaining semi-rancid meat.

By then the time was 10:00pm, so he hit the sack.
Man and dog slept well.

Day 63, Thursday, July 15

James broke camp at 4:00am, having awakened by wristwatch alarm. He planned to cross the river and gain the south road which passed the dam unhindered. James knew there wasn't a fence or gate to bar the south road and therefore it had to be legal. In the meantime, he couldn't afford to wait for security to come and tell him what he already knew, especially not when they probably wouldn't arrive until after 8:00am, by which point the west wind might be driving swells to the dam like a stampede into a box canyon (the west wind had already begun).

James needed to cross the river and fast. Once across the river, he would have to haul his boat up an imposing buttress but he would deal with that once he got there. In fact his original decision to portage the north shoulder had been based on avoiding the south buttress, but that no longer mattered, he couldn't afford to stay where he was.

The Kansan figured the worst place to cross any river had to be below a hydroelectric dam in a canyon. The exception of course being those times when the floodgates were closed and no wind raised the waves. Fortunately, the floodgates were closed. Unfortunately, the wind had begun to raise the waves. Therefore with urgency, trepidation, and exhaustion weighing on him, James disassembled his rig and carried loads as fast as he could down a gentle riprap bank located directly below the campground. It was an intense way to start a day. Then, just as he readied to shove off, the wind died. It was one of those moments—and there were more than a few—when James looked to the sky with a large measure of gratitude.

James paddled for all his worth, "Please God, don't let them open those floodgates."

Had the floodgates opened, James wasn't so close as to suffer immediate death but figured he'd first hear a loud buzzer to warn of the impending event. In such a situation, James meant to turn and paddle downstream like no tomorrow. However, if the wind were to return at such an inopportune moment, he would be trapped. James took no pleasure in risking his life, none whatsoever. Needless to say, he paddled as hard as his strength allowed.

The canoeist made it across without event, and because the lock stood on the south side of the dam, he gained piece of mind by gaining the protection of the barrier wall, should the floodgates open.

The buttress came next, a nearly vertical pitch of basalt boulders where dam met canyon. At least it wasn't a tall buttress, rising no more than forty feet to a shelf and a service road. James tied off with some difficulty and then set about the much more difficult business of hauling loads up the buttress. He began with his plastic storage locker because it weighed among the heaviest of his items. Thus he went up the buttress, moving the locker from ledge to ledge. About halfway up, a sharp volcanic edge pierced the bottom of the locker—,

"Ah shucks!"

Up and down the buttress James climbed until only his boat remained. Then, having no other choice, James dragged his canoe up the buttress. He climbed like a monkey and pulled like a donkey, holding the boat with one limb and climbing with his other three. The steep angle helped to keep the weight of the craft off the rocks somewhat and that at least was good. Three-quarters of the way up however, a single slip put a gouge in his boat that would forever serve up memories of the place. In fact it was the largest scar his boat would receive on that side of the Continental Divide. Fortunately, the quality of the boat skin, being thick and flexible plastic, prevented it from being pierced.

Up top, the Kansan had his gear scattered about and had only begun to assemble his rig when a sheriff showed up in response to the call James had made the evening before. The amiable sheriff, who looked to be of retirement age, took the edge off what had been a trying morning. Having learned that James was from Kansas, the sheriff said he had graduated from Kansas University. If James heard the sheriff correctly, he hadn't been back there for many years. The sheriff smiled as if remembering a bygone era.

James made no mention of it but the sheriff would have been a student back in the day when, as Frank had told James, no doors were locked on campus. And something else good from that bygone era, hanging above the fireplace in the Student Union, was a Hawkins Frontier Rifle! The rifle had hung above the hearth for untold decades. Then one day, it was gone. Whether it had been stolen or just taken down cannot be known.

After breaking the ice, the good sheriff asked, "Do you have any bombs or explosives?"

"No Sir," replied James, taken aback.

"Do you mind if I search your gear?"

"No Sir," James replied.

While the Sheriff searched, James hid his exhaustion and hoped the sheriff would not scatter his stuff too much about the place. The sheriff did not. Then about halfway though his search the sheriff rose up, looked at James, and called it good. And to tell the truth, the dam was safer with James there than without.

The sheriff told James he was free to continue and the two men parted with a handshake. As the sheriff drove away, an official from the Army Corp of Engineers came in a pickup truck—,

"You should have portaged on the other side of the dam," said the engineer, stepping from his truck with a pained expression. "If you had portaged on the other side, you wouldn't have had to climb up that buttress."

By that point James felt happy just to be getting the job done. He knew the engineer had only just arrived at the dam for work a short time earlier and therefore couldn't know the full story.

"I'd be happy to give you a lift to the boat ramp [on the other side of the dam]," added the engineer. "We can put your boat in my truck."

"Thank you for you kind offer, Sir," James replied, "but I have to walk and paddle every step and stroke of the way." James then explained how he used his walking machine to get around the dams.

Ron then asked, "Is there anything I can help you with?"

"You wouldn't happen to have ice in there would you?" asked James, gesturing to the dam.

"No, I'm afraid not," replied Ron.

"How about fresh water?" James asked.

"Now that I can help you with," and Ron took James's empty water jugs. Ron was missing one arm but it didn't seem to slow him down. He drove away only to return directly with jugs full of fresh water. James thanked Ron and the two men spoke briefly. Ron then departed with well wishes and a handshake.

James pulled his rig up a grade to a switchback, then pulled over the south shoulder of Little Goose Dam. From there a small gravel lane paralleled the river on a manmade shelf at the base of a cliff. James hadn't gone fifty yards however when he heard a shout, "James!"

The Kansan turned to see a guard in a watchtower. The guard waved and shouted, "Good luck!"

"Thanks!" James shouted. Then turning to the remote setting ahead, the boy in James found it easy to fancy himself leaving a distant desert outpost on the edge of an unexplored wilderness. The time was 8:30am.

After two miles, the road ended in a tiny access park consisting of a boat ramp, vaulted toilet, and two campsites side by side, each with fire ring and picnic table under a small grove of trees beside a gentle shoreline. The campsites were primitive, having no electricity or running water but shade, breeze, and solitude abounding.

James converted his land rig to water craft and made breakfast. UB begged and got the bacon grease. Ron came with his dog in his truck and the two men sat talking about dogs and the river. Ron didn't stay long but departed with well wishes. James fell asleep on a picnic table where he dreamed heavily for one hour. Then a lone fisherman named Dave came in an old pickup truck. James and Dave greeted one another but had no conversation because James was fixing to go and Dave was occupied making his camp in the other site.

At about 11:00am, James shoved off and made good time, paddling with a breeze at his back. To manage the heat, he capitalized on almost every shade patch he found. Such places of refuge were rare, cast on the water by shrub or overhanging rock. Once in a patch of shade, James would tie off and fall asleep, snoring for thirty minutes. He would then eat a small meal and continue paddling.

> "The river, which had widened, appeared like vast fields of water, calm water, not mirror calm but gently glimmering under blue sky. Vaster still was the desert, that all-surrounding realm of sand and shrubs which, although beautiful, seemed a place where nature itself became

languid. To say the least, the going could have been monotonous had there not been something more, just there, in the absence of life's clutter. A man could miss it if he were distracted but the desert had a way of melting everything else away until a man found himself looking into infinity. Then, with his soul awakened to the sense of it, he would find but a thin veil between himself and the face of his Creator."

While paddling alongside a large island, James spotted a small fishing boat motoring toward him. The boat came on until having drawn near; it cut its engine and coasted to a stop.
"Hello," said Dave, smiling from under the brim of his hat.
"Howdy," said James, recognizing who it was.
"Catch," Dave said, suddenly tossing a bottle of water.
James caught the bottle and at once knew it was ice cold, "Oh, thank you Sir!"
"You're welcome."
The two men talked about fishing while each man enjoyed a bottle of ice water. Then with words of thanks and well wishes, James continued paddling.
After paddling a distance of twelve miles, James reached the bridge at Central Ferry State Park. His wristwatch read 6:00pm. At the park office, James asked permission to camp along the shore in order to avoid converting his water craft to land rig but the park managers informed him that such a thing wasn't possible. Having no problem with the rules, James filled his water jug and continued paddling upriver another mile before finding a primitive beach of smooth fist-sized stones. The natural strip of beach was peppered with chest-high shrubs below a 12-foot cliff of sandy hard-packed earth mixed with stones. James leveled a section of beach to make a tent platform. Then having pitched his tent, he unloaded his canoe and, as usual, reloaded it alongside his tent. But when he reloaded it, he set it up on driftwood rollers.
The driftwood rollers were fairly straight round logs the size of small fence posts which were abundant there. James laid the rollers atop slightly larger drift logs. In such a way, he made a ramp on which his canoe could roll downhill for a distance of thirty feet from campsite to water's edge. Of course James meant to use the

roller-ramp in the morning, thereby avoiding the work of unloading and reloading.

For dinner James ate beef franks wrapped in sandwich bread with a side of cold cucumber slices and an orange for desert. By then his wristwatch read 10:00pm, so he hit the sack. And because he didn't use his rain fly, he looked up at a star-filled sky.

Man and dog slept well.

Day 64, Friday, July 16

At 5:30am, James woke with hands tingling as if he'd slept on them. He didn't think much about it but only rubbed his hands together to restore circulation, then opened and closed them several times before breaking camp.

James crossed the river to make breakfast on the shaded side of the gorge. He and UB then shoved off. The time was 9:00am.

> "The breeze was against me but I was determined to make progress and, I knew how to beat the heat. I had learned to spot the shady nook under overhanging rock or shrub. Such places were rare and had to be taken advantage of in the heat of the day. Every two hours or so, I found such a place. Then tying off, I laid back on the stern with my feet up on the gunwales. I fell asleep at once, dreaming for 30 minutes. Then waking, I would eat a mini-meal of apples, cheese, and bread, or beef franks and cucumbers, along with fruit. Then I was off paddling again. And if I got hot, I would lean over the side of the boat and submerge my head plus hands and wrists in the water. Then I would go on. And if I got hotter yet, I would jump in the water. It was quick and efficient travel, straight through the heat of the day."

James sang songs as he paddled, often times making them up. Usually he had the river to himself. In fact the river was his by statute of law. He owned it as an American, or at least that was how the law read but in truth it was a gift from God. There were all kinds of birds, as well as raccoons, badgers, fox, deer, and beaver. Several times, James saw entire families. A mother raccoon restrained one of her babies who'd gotten overly curious about James. A mother badger did the same with one of her young.

At some point in the late afternoon, James heard what sounded like the approach of hot rod with throttle and exhaust pipes full open. Using his field glasses, he saw a bright yellow speed boat, sleek and fast looking. It cut its engine and stopped under a cliff a mile ahead. All went silent and then, the gorge, which was tremendously deep in that area, filled with music.

Except for his own singing, James had forgotten about music, having heard none for two months. Therefore in a state of delight, James sang along—,

"*Carefree highway, got to see you my old friend. Carefree highway, got the morning after blues, from my head down to my shoes.*"

The boat kept playing songs by Gordon Lightfoot and James sang along to each one. But as James neared the boat, it fired up its engine and sped away. James felt bad because they had fled when he had only wanted to say "howdy."

At 6:00pm, James landed and made camp in a place similar to the night before. He ate the same dinner as the night before and then went to bed. His wristwatch read 9:30pm.

Man and dog slept well.

Day 65, Saturday, July 17

At 6:00am, James again woke with hands tingling as if he had slept on them. He rubbed them same as the morning before, then shaved and trimmed his hair. He brought out his last clean t-shirt. He meant to look presentable when he reached Boyart State Park, a resupply point which according to his map lay six miles upstream. He cooked his last four eggs and last three pieces of bacon which he ate along with a green bell pepper and orange. He had completely run out of cold storage supplies and there yet remained one-half inch of ice in the bottom of the inner cooler (the cooler within a cooler). So James felt pleased because his system had worked well. He broke camp and shoved off. His wristwatch read 9:45am.

Six miles passed without event except that a grain barge passed close by and James made fun of riding its wake, "Yee Ha!"

At 12:00pm, the canoeist made port at Boyart State Park where he had a good conversation with a fisherman named Jake who told about a fishing contest that sounded like a lot of fun. If James remembered correctly, the contest was to see who could catch the most of a species of fish which, being an alien invader, was destructive to the river's natural ecosystem.

James next pulled his rig to the marina which consisted of a store, restaurant, and inn where, as fortune would have it, James had no more than stepped inside and told what he was about when the folks who owned the place said they had just sent a man to the grocer in Clarkson and, if James needed to resupply, they could call him on his cell phone. The owners had supplies there at their marina but of course they did not have a butcher counter or produce section. James, who could scarcely have been more delighted by their kind offer, made a shopping list that may have appeared to be a "give me an inch and I'll take a mile" kind of deal. The owners of the marina were gracious, and James thanked them kindly.

The Kansan spent the rest of the day working on his journal, gear, laundry, and food supplies. Plus he made a few phone calls back home. He worked until 9:00pm then hit the sack on the floor as always when at an inn.

James slept well.

Day 66, Sunday, July 18

At 6:00am, James woke with hands tingling and weaker than before. In fact, his hands had gotten progressively worse over the past three mornings. Worriedly, James rubbed and opened and closed his hands before going about his business. He worked on his journal from 7:00am to 4:00pm, breaking only for lunch. From 4:00pm to 5:00pm he organized his gear and iced his cooler. Then stepping out, James went down the hall and into a commons area where he spied a large T-bone steak with baked potato steaming on a plate. Also on the counter alongside the steak sat a fresh salad. James paused to gaze longingly at what just happened to be his favorite meal. Then as fortune would have it, the chef came forward and informed James that there had been a banquet in the restaurant and one person hadn't shown up. The chef then offered the meal at a discount price. James hit the jackpot once again.

After an excellent steak dinner, James returned to his room and caught up his journal at 8:30pm. He then did some final work to his gear and hit the sack at 10:00pm.

Man and dog slept well.

Day 67, Monday, July 19

At 5:30am, James woke to find his hands tingling, sore, and terribly weak. The problem came from a combination of two factors; the first being that of fatigue brought about by gripping a paddle tight while shoveling water. The second factor being that James's hands had been severely damaged when he was nineteen. Besides being crushed, part of James's right hand including his thumb had been completely severed except for the flap of skin that made up the palm. James also lost a portion of bone from his left forearm (his arm wasn't shortened because the bone grew back around a pin). Fortunately, due to some savvy ambulance personnel, James had been delivered into the skilled hands of a top notch surgeon who pinned, wired, and stitched him back together. James had a very tiny disability rating. The surgeon had told him about it in private and James never passed the information on to anyone.

Presently, James called his sister who as we already know was a registered nurse. Patricia put James at ease, telling him he only needed rest and ibuprofen. Rest was the main thing. Patricia was adamant about it and James promised he'd stay put for a few days. No more had James gotten off the phone however than he remembered he had to get over the mountains before the snows began. So he decided against his sister's caring advice. He also decided against taking ibuprofen or any medication. He wasn't against medications but would avoid them in everything except emergencies. He rolled up his bedroll, then moved food supplies from refrigerator to ice chest. He ate breakfast and then loaded and pulled his cart to the boat ramp.

At the ramp, James met Joe and Terry who were taking an old sailboat down the Snake River with plans to continue down the Columbia to the Pacific Ocean and then up to Alaska. Joe was sixty-one and looked to be a good old boy of modest means. His girlfriend Terry was twenty-five, pretty, and finely made.

"What a dream!" James exclaimed in a moment of unrestraint.

Next to join the conversation came a fisherman named Cliff. Then moving on with well wishes and handshakes, James had no choice but to apologize for his lame grip. He claimed it only a temporary thing. He then began his routine of unloading, disassembling, and reloading. While he worked, rain began to fall. Then a rumble came through the gorge and, seeing a dark storm rolling down river, James figured it might rain for an hour or a week but he wasn't going to wait to find out which.

From the marina, James needed to travel only two miles before reaching Lower Granite Dam. But in those two miles, he would have to cross the river in order to gain a service road on the far shore by which he could pull his rig over the south shoulder of the dam. James paddled as hard as his strength allowed while crossing the river on a long diagonal. By the time he reached the halfway point, the storm had advanced to loom like a dark wall above the dam. In fact, it threw lightning bolts over the dam! UB hunkered down beneath the tarp while his master labored against rising wind and rain. Then in a driving storm, they gained the safety of the far shore.

James beached his craft on a natural gravel bar that rose gently to the service road above. A few giant drift logs lay about that beach and because no trees grew in that realm, James figured them to be from the Rocky Mountains.

The storm passed as James carried loads to the road where he assembled his rig. Then in bright sunshine he set out pulling toward the dam. He stopped in a rare patch of shade along the way to eat three pieces of bread with peanut butter and an orange for desert. He then began up a long sun-baked grade that went over the south shoulder of Lower Granite Dam:

"'We've seen bigger hills,' I told UB [who walked alongside]."

Slowly but surely the Kansan pulled his cart up and over the shoulder, then proceeded another two miles to a remote boat launch at the end of the road.

At the boat launch, James sought a patch of shade in which to put his ice chest and dry food duffel so the ice and food within might last as long as possible. He set said items under the eve of a bush near the boat launch. And because the bush was of modest size, James decided to put all his duffle bags in its shade to keep them from heating up and then transferring their heat to the ice chest once loaded in the boat with the tarp snapped down tight. So the bush ended up looking somewhat like a Christmas tree with red, green, yellow, and blue duffle bags under its eves. Meanwhile as James worked to transform his land rig to water craft, a nest of yellow jackets that lived in the ground under the bush came out to see what the problem was.

"Once upon a time while climbing up a slope, I accidentally put my hand through a rotten log and into a hornet's nest. I went running through the woods like a man on fire with my sister running behind, screaming for me to lie down and play dead. I refused to play dead, at least until I reached a point of desperation, whereupon I dropped and lay motionless, at which point it hardly mattered that the hornets abandoned me because they'd already stung me from head to toe."

Presently remembering the aforesaid misadventure and wishing not to repeat it, James rushed to get his gear away from the bush. The hornets kept coming out and, needless to say, James worked with great urgency, stuffing his belongings into his boat whichever way he could.

By the time James had loaded his boat, the hornets had worked themselves up into a cloud around the bush.

"UB," James called. "Here boy! Hurry!"

A hornet tried to sting James but he swatted it down and stomped it.

"Sorry," James said to the dying hornet, "but I couldn't allow you to go back and tell the others."

With hornets zooming this way and that, the canoeist paddled away as quickly as he could, his poorly loaded craft listing badly to one side. He may have set a personal best for speed in going from land to water but of course he had to land again and properly load his craft. While doing so, he ate cold cuts with cucumber and a bagel. He then set out paddling east. His wristwatch read 11:00am.

The storm had passed, the wind had died, and because the dam allowed no access from the State Park behind, James had the river to himself.

Then, as if it were meant to be, James entered what appeared to be the deepest section of gorge anywhere in his journey. Again and again, he marveled at the heights to which the gorge walls rose. The cliffs went straight up from the water hundreds of feet and the canoeist wouldn't have been able to see what lay higher above except for a series of little side canyons that fed into the gorge every 1/2 mile or so. The little side canyons allowed James to see how the cliffs of the gorge rose up to meet a near-vertical desert slope which continued up dramatically to another system of cliffs which looked like mesas in the sky. From bottom to top, the distance must have measured at least 3,000 feet!

> "I was in awe. I couldn't stop gazing up at the endless heights and their awesome beauty. I felt as if I were in God's own dwelling. I paddled but scarcely looked to see where I was going, and, I didn't regret having no camera, for no camera could have done justice to what I saw. Somehow, a mule deer appeared from that high realm, negotiating the cliffy bank. She came down a spree slope for a drink. She didn't see me. I paddled toward her and passed silently by. The river had become like glass. A ferret came next, also wanting a drink. It saw me and darted into a hole but came back out, its curiosity having got the better of it. I glided past and, in that moment, we were eye to eye. The east wind came up but I didn't mind. Sometimes the wind was with me, sometimes against me. That's how it was."

Against the wind, James disregarded the pain in his hands and made good time.

> "The day was perfect. Not nearly as hot as usual, with cloud puffs often shading me—and all in a realm of awe. It passed too fast but shall last long in my memory. A special day, a gift."

At 6:00pm, James began to keep an eye out for a place to camp but could find none due to sheer gorge walls. Meanwhile, a storm had begun to brew. James kept looking but there were no places to camp. He stopped to scout a rocky outcrop, then another and another but found nothing. Then the storm hit with a vengeance. High wind and heavy rain came first from one direction, then from another. Fortunately there were no swells which may have been due to the orientation of the river in that area. James had no choice but to keep paddling in an all-out squall. And there was something new which was in fact a clue to what lie ahead, it had become cool. The time was approximately 7:00pm.

> "The wind swept the rain in tremendous sheets across the surface and, the river boiled."

Reaching another outcrop, James hoped to find a campsite but came up empty. So he paddled toward the next outcrop a half mile ahead and, as he did, the erratic wind organized into a steady gale traveling powerfully upriver. As a result, James went swiftly from one prospect to another until at last he found a campsite. And an excellent campsite it was. Not only that but, in the moment he found it, the wind subsided and the downpour turned into light rain. So it was, the Kansan stood on a beach of polished rocks, dripping wet, and feeling blessed.

James went to work at once, building a tent platform of rocks, sand, and dirt about twenty feet from shore and five feet above water level. He toweled his tent dry before covering it with the rain fly. While he worked, he asked UB to go and do his dog duty so he wouldn't wake his master in the middle of the night. UB wanted in the tent so badly however, he refused to go anywhere but only sat shivering and whining. James maintained his patience, encouraging UB while he worked until UB did as asked. James then toweled UB off and put him on his dog bed in the tent where he would be cozy.

Having changed into a pair of gray gym shorts, James took his jeans to the river and worked (without soap) to scrub them clean because they had gotten very dirty and he didn't wish to use his only other pair of jeans so soon. Force of habitat had him washing his clothes with scarcely a stitch on but in fact, after months of desert heat, the air had turned cold, the river had turned cold, and although light, the rain and breeze made it all the colder! So it was that James first felt the effects of the Rocky Mountains which stood directly ahead even as they remained out of sight due to the depth of the gorge.

James didn't think about why it had turned cold but only knew it had been a long day and he was no spring chicken, yet there he was knee deep in the river, exposed to the elements, feeling healthy as a horse. He laughed happily. Then lifting his eyes with gratitude, he was dumbstruck by what he saw.

Above James, a very brilliant and perfectly formed rainbow spanned the gorge with a leg atop either side. And being framed by cliffs, the rainbow divided the sky same as a dam would a river. But that wasn't the half of it, for on either side of the rainbow, the sky was dramatically different. On one side the sky appeared dark blue, and on the other side light blue. There wasn't any fade but only the rainbow starkly dividing the sky like day and night. The light blue lay ahead of James and the dark blue behind. Obviously, James saw some kind of refractory phenomenon but he wasn't thinking along any such lines—,

Laughing and crying all at once, James knew the Lord had come before him.

"Lord," James said, his voice breaking like that of a child.

God then spoke, and while James heard no audible voice, in his heart, he knew exactly what his Creator was saying—,

"I'm right here James. You need only keep putting one foot before the other with faith, and I promise you, good will come of it."

Day 68, Tuesday, July 20

Having slept heavily until 6:45am, James woke and immediately realized his hands were improved, vastly improved!

"I was following the Maker of miracles but I did not expect anything other than what He told me. I understood I was not to define what 'good' meant but simply to trust Him. I did not need a reason to trust Him, but I had one all the same. My father died of a heart attack when I was one and, in a manner of speaking, my mother, brother, sister, and I suddenly found ourselves in a PT-109 situation. Mom never remarried but, besides loving me and taking care of me and making sure I went to church every Sunday, the greatest thing she ever did for me was to get down on her knees before me when I was six years old and tell me that a woman could not show a man how to be a man. She then turned me around so that I was facing a group of men whereupon she told me to go and watch, listen, and learn. I took my mother's charge to heart. And with a fatherless void in my chest, I had all the incentive I needed. As a result, I have studied a great many men, not with conscious intent, not as part of an academic study, not with anything but a void to fill in my chest, a void which felt as big as space itself. Into that void, I shoveled everything from John Wayne to Woody Allen. I shoveled until I was plumb full. And when I had filled myself up, I was as confused as ever. That's right, I didn't know who I was, and all the knowledge in the world couldn't help me. Then I heard my long-forgotten friend Jesus calling, and somehow, almost like groping in the dark, I found my way back to Him. He took what I had put inside and brought it to life. And when He did, it was like nothing I can describe except to say my void filled with light, my eyes could see at last, my stars and planets were put in order and I was filled with joy."

The walls of the gorge were set back from the shore in that place and although poor in quality, grass covered the ground as opposed to desert sand and shrubs. It was a sign that the desert had begun to give way. Also telling were the large amounts of drift wood along the shores.

James hung his tent fly on a large branch of driftwood to dry. He spread his wet jeans, shirt, and socks out on smaller branches. He turned his tent inside out and shook it out. There wasn't any shortage of work to do, little chores and not-so-little chores. James made a shade canopy using driftwood poles, rope, and tarp. Then in the shade of the canopy, he precooked a large batch of meat. Afterward, James mixed the leftover meat juice with UB's dog food in a bowl and said—,

"Yummy, this smells so good, I could eat it."

UB, who seemed to have lost his appetite of late, showed no interest.

James bagged the cooked beef and then cooked a breakfast of steak and eggs with all the trimmings. UB meanwhile snuck off to eat a dead salmon that lie rotting on the shore. Fortunately, James saw and dashed across the beach to grab UB by the nap of his neck, lifting him away from the poisonous flesh just as he was opening his mouth to take a bite.

UB began yelping.

"You're not hurt!" James barked, both fearful and frustrated because UB hadn't been eating like he should.

After breakfast, James went about the business of breaking camp while UB lie like a dead fish on the shore. Then, when his master called him to the canoe, UB could hardly negotiate the rocks. Days of desert heat had worn him out. He was gaunt and weak. James had also lost weight but not like UB. James carried UB to the boat and, it worried him not only to feel how little UB weighed, but because UB seemed to have given up. James didn't complain but only worried.

Without making light of UB's difficulty, here comes a place to tell, James penned UB as a literary fall guy when in truth UB lived a dog's dream seventy percent of the time. But in the other thirty percent, UB experienced some rough patches, among which the Snake River run would be his worst. So the worst was almost over for UB and in fact he would shine in the mountains ahead while James got his turn at becoming thin.

James shoved off at 11:00am, laboring hard to make progress against a headwind. And as he went, he worried for UB who lay limp at his feet.

"Please don't die on me, UB," James asked.

The Kansan prayed for his dog. He confessed it to be a stupid request, what with all the human suffering in the world. He then opened UB's food bowl and UB slowly took a bite, then another and another until he had eaten all his food. It was the beginning of UB's recovery.

As mentioned, James saw no horizon down in the gorge but somewhere not so far ahead rose the Rocky Mountains. As evidence, blackberry patches began to show up along the shores. James gorged himself on the delicious fruit while keeping an eye out for bears. He then continued paddling with purple stains down the front of his white t-shirt.

At 4:00pm the canoeist landed in a patch of reeds, then walked onto a beach where three men were camped—,

"Howdy Sirs. My name is James and I come from Kansas. I'm attempting the Lewis and Clark route from west to east. I started at the Pacific Ocean on May 14, and I hope to reach Three Forks Montana by the end of September." The Kansan then held out his map and asked, "I was hoping you might be able to tell me where I am exactly? I think I know but, it's hard to be sure."

One of the men smiled and said something to the others about James being the man he'd met. James then recognized Cliff whom he'd met at Boyart State Park. Cliff, Dave, and Rulen were all near retirement age or better. A good conversation followed in which Rulen told James that a few men were still using the Oregon Trail back when he was a kid. Rulen said there were no prairie schooners with families by that late date but an occasional bachelor still made his way to Oregon with a donkey and cart. Amazed, James asked Rulen when he had seen such a thing. Rulen said it was before the war (WWII). Rulen then lifted his arms like Atlas, flexing powerful muscles while asking James to guess his age. Rulen as it turned out was seventy-three years old but with the physique of a much younger man. James then told a brief pioneer tale about a young husband and wife who arrived by "prairie schooner" to the newly opened Kansas Territory in the 1850s. Their dream was to own a well-stocked farm of 160 acres. At that time a fever was sweeping the frontier and the young couple fell so ill they could hardly help themselves. Life became misery inside their tiny dirt floor cabin. First their infant child died, then the mother who was dying, asked her husband to take her home to New York where she died. The young pioneer did not give up, but remarried and returned to Kansas where he helped build the town that James grew up in. The pioneer and his second wife raised a family there. Then when his second wife of many years died, the old pioneer married a young school teacher and raised a second family there in the same small town. He lived to see all his many children to adulthood, one of whom would be James's father's father. James always smiled when telling the part about the old man marrying the young woman. After all, it gave him hope to know he existed because his great grandmother had found it in her heart to love an old man.

A sudden gust struck and would have blown away the campers

shade canopy except that James grabbed it. The three men then invited James to stay for dinner. They had a fine-looking stew in a big cast iron kettle with beef, potatoes, and onions. James wanted to stay but the gust had signaled a change in wind direction which meant he would no longer have to fight a headwind but could take advantage of a strong tailwind. So James thanked the men even as he declined, saying he had to go in order to catch the wind while it lasted. Cliff thought James might make it to Lewiston Idaho that evening. James said it was too far but he hoped to make it to Chief Timothy State Park. Thus with words of thanks and well wishes, James departed.

A strong tailwind saw James making excellent time, paddling hard, riding swells, cutting all bends on a straight line course. At one point, while looking to shore, James laughed and told UB—,

"We may as well have a motor on the back!"

Chief Timothy State Park lay concealed from the northern approach and therefore the canoeist overshot it. He realized his mistake at once but, due to high wind, he had no choice but to continue upriver. And that wasn't so bad because simply to access an overnight campsite in a State Park meant a lot of work, what with his walking machine to assemble and disassemble. A primitive campsite would better suit James's needs for a single night.

While yet in the vicinity of the park, James saw three young men on jet skis having a good time. They were jumping swells and wiping out. To protect themselves from the cold water, they wore wet suits, another indication that a new realm waited just around the bend so to speak. James watched as they raced out to catch the wake of a passing barge and because James happened to be in a good position to do so, he also decided to jump the wake but from the opposite side. He didn't think it would be a big wake but in fact the barge was empty and (as James learned in the beginning of his journey) a tugboat traveling at speed, under no load, in close proximity, could throw off a very large wake.

The canoeist cut it close and attacked the wake only to realize his mistake too late—,

"Diamond Wave!"

Up the face of the wave and into the air went the canoe. Then, as the bow turned down, James knew he'd found trouble. Like a spear the canoe penetrated the secondary wake to a quarter of its length! The craft rebounded nicely thanks to the tarp but as it did, it clipped the top off the secondary wake which then cascaded down the tarp to drench James. UB meanwhile was half drowned as the wake collapsed on him. The canoe did not swamp thanks in part to its large size. Afterward, James continued across the river where he bailed water and decided to stay near shore for the remainder of the day. While bailing water along the shore, he spoke briefly with a young couple.

James needed a campsite, but the river had come up against a great cliff—at the bottom of which—Highway 12 ran like a straight piece of string atop a riprap buttress that extended east for as far as the eye could see. So James had no option except to paddle hard and ride swells swiftly along the buttress while hoping for a change in the lay of the land which might in turn provide a campsite. James couldn't know it, but the cliff and buttress continued unbroken to Lewiston Idaho four miles ahead.

Arriving at the outskirts of town, James saw a cliff painted with graffiti. He hadn't seen any graffiti since leaving the Columbia Basin but now the graffiti read entirely different. Instead of angry gang markers there were only hearts inside which were written things like—,

"Jim + Sue."

There were no knifelike strokes, no cryptic words, nor broken bottles or trash, but only hearts pierced by arrows and love-based scripts—,

"Rick Loves Beth Forever."

Some of the graffiti was old and faded, some of it new, but none of it bad. James had found what Roger had tried to tell him about. And finding it, he knew it wasn't the kind of thing people would discover by watching network news.

"I have concluded, upon completing the trail, that the so called mainstream media gives the goodness of small town and rural America as much attention as would a Roman soldier give a Christian who lie dying beside the road."

Up ahead, the riprap buttress took a hard jog and James found himself in a situation similar to Wind Mountain but on a miniature scale. Drawing on experience, he used a zigzag strategy. In other words, he dug hard for open river in the troughs between the crests, then turned to ride each crest as it came upon him before going down in the next trough where he could once again dig for open river. Skilled as James had become, he respected the jog and save for the most demanding moments, sang to relieve tension.

Once safely around the jog, the canoeist spotted the mast of sailboats in a marina and therefore knew he had completed the Snake River leg of his journey.

"We've made it, UB," James said, paddling just 200 yards from the marina, unaware of a low profile barrier floating on the marina perimeter.

By the time James saw the floating barrier which had been masked by waves and fading light, it was too late. He dug hard to make the mouth of the marina but the wind blew too strong. He found himself in a bad way and would have been swept against the barrier had it not been for God's grace. For just there, on the same riprap shoulder that had run unbroken for miles, a tiny strip of beach lay no wider than ten feet. Still, at a distance of thirty yards it was no free gift, which is to say, James had to fight for it.

Having landed safely, James discovered the tiny beach (known locally as "Rooster's Landing") was not only a beach but a short gravel driveway leading through a veil of dense green vegetation to Highway 12 which went straight into town. And himself coming to stand before the highway after assuming it and the river had separated, James felt doubly blessed.

While James assembled his rig, the water calmed and a bright red speedboat came from the marina to race up and down the river a few times before retiring. Darkness fell and with it came the mosquitoes but the Kansan foiled them, pulling away toward town. Actually there were two towns, one on either side of the river, connected by a single bridge. On the Washington side, the town of Clarkston had been named for Captain Clark of the Lewis and Clark expedition. On the Idaho side, the town of Lewiston was named after Captain Lewis.

It had become pitch dark, and although traffic flowed light, James felt glad for his slow-moving vehicle sign. He had no other worries in that place, for although dark, there had been no bad graffiti, trash, or other warning signs. So it was that James felt safe and therefore could enjoy the blessings of success which, when coupled with deep exhaustion, made for a natural high closer to freedom than words could describe. In fact, it made for a lesson that would not be taken for granted.

On the edge of town, James spoke briefly with man who came alongside in a car, looking for his teenage daughter. Just inside town, James stopped at the first inn he found where, as fortune would have it, the inn keeper had just finished baking a batch of huckleberry muffins (having picked the berries herself earlier that day). Dora gave James two of the freshly baked muffins.

"Oh Ma'am," James said with a tone of appreciation which only a man come from the river could know. "Thank you."

UB was happy to have a room. The time wasn't recorded but it was near midnight by the time James unloaded his rig, took a shower, and hit the hay.

Man and dog slept well.

Day 69, Wednesday, July 21

James rose at 6:30am and told UB, "Scouting begins with breakfast at the local diner."

James left his rig at the inn and proceeded to get breakfast at the diner. He then proceeded to the Clarkston Chamber of Commerce where UB enjoyed the attention of an attractive young lady clerk. Girls always liked UB. From the Chamber of Commerce, man and dog continued to the bridge where Highway 12 crossed the Snake River into Lewiston. James measured the sidewalk on the bridge to determine if it was wide enough to accommodate his rig (without blocking pedestrian traffic). No more had James measured the bridge than he happened to see Rulen on the river below. The seventy-three year old was at the oars of a large wooden fishing boat, powering with shoulders and arms to drive the bow upon a grassy bank in a shaded park.

Inspired, James shouted, "Rulen!"

Rulen looked about.

"Up here!" James shouted.

James proceeded down to the park where he told Rulen that Cliff had been right with regard to making Lewiston by nightfall. The two men spoke briefly and as often would be the case, James wished he had more time. Rulen had come to town for supplies and, because he had his truck in the parking lot, he gave James and UB a ride to the Army Corp of Engineers Office which was only a hop-skip-and-a-jump across the park.

In the office of the Corp of Engineers, James stepped up to a counter and told what he was about.

"You're in luck," said a friendly clerk, gathering up some brochures, "We just happened to have a man here who knows all about Lewis and Clark."

"Thank you Sir," said James, "but what I need is to see a chart of the Clearwater River."

As the clerk combed cabinets, he seemed befuddled, "I'm sure we have some charts or maps here somewhere."

In fairness to the clerk, he was almost certainly a volunteer, and a good one at that, both courteous and genuinely eager to help. Nor can any bad reflection be made here on the Corp of Engineers.

> "Having met a good number of Corp members on the trail (and omitting what I heard at the Lewis and Clark [Re]Interpretation Center on Cape Disappointment), I hold them in very high regard."

While the clerk searched the cabinets, James found a map of town on a display rack and took it to the counter. Then opening the map, he asked the clerk if he knew where one might find someone with experience navigating the Clearwater River. The clerk gave directions to a river outfitter.

James and UB proceeded over the bridge into Lewiston and then several blocks further to the outfitter. It had been a good suggestion on the clerk's part, but James came up empty handed even as he met with courtesy.

Out of leads, James followed his nose to a boat repair shop on a back street where he met a man in greasy coveralls—,

"Excuse me, Dave," said James, reading the man's name tag while extending his hand for a shake.

"Name's Bill," replied the man, shaking hands.

James told Bill about his journey and at once the two men were on good standing. Bill invited James inside where, having spread a large map of the Clearwater River out on a work bench, he poured out a wealth of information. Then with words of thanks and well wishes, James departed for the inn.

The time was 11:00am or thereabouts. Man and dog had crossed the bridge and were headed east along the north side of Highway 12 when, looking across the highway, James saw a man and girl at a phone booth. James didn't think about it at the time but the man bore a noteworthy resemblance to a TV cartoon character known as "Beavus" except older. So James saw a white man in his mid-thirties which he believed, rightly or wrongly, to be hardened by a life of drugs and smalltime crime. The girl appeared to be from Guatemala or perhaps Equador, age fourteen, uncommonly pretty but dressed exactly like a prostitute. Her expression was one of confusion wrapped around a core of anger. She obviously didn't want to be there but the man had hold of her slender upper arm.

While clutching her, the man glanced about as if anxiously waiting for someone on the other end of the phone line to answer. Meanwhile in James's heart, an alarm bell rang.

Noticing James, the girl gazed as if to ask for help. But then again, she may only have wanted to get away from her stepfather. Or perhaps she knew no better than to ask for a better pimp. James however wasn't operating on that kind of intellectual level. Rather, he only sensed her to be in peril, whereupon his fluid mind formulated a plan to get in close and, if necessary, take the man down.

In the next second, the man followed the girl's eyes to James whereupon his tension visibly doubled. But what if he was not a criminal? What if he was only a frustrated stepfather who mistook James for a john? Whatever the case, a tiny atom of uncertainty made James question what he saw.

In the next second, the girl broke free. She didn't run or cry for help but strode quickly away from the man although in confusion as if she knew not where to go or to whom to turn. She didn't come in James's direction perhaps because she had come to sense that he would see her returned to where she came from (which wasn't entirely true, for had James the resources, he would have seen her returned home, but not into the hands of bad people). The girl hadn't taken six steps when the man caught and forcibly ushered her away, retreating quickly from the street, vanishing into a door on the side of a small pizza place that sat back from the road.

James immediately veered into a café just there on his side of the street—,

"Ma'am," said James, striding quick for the counter, "I need to call the police."

"Yes Sir," said the waitress, asking no questions but only reading the look in his eyes and the inflection of his voice.

James called 911 and then headed for the door.

"Where are you going?" asked the waitress who had overheard the call.

"I'm going to make sure he doesn't get away," replied James.

"Don't do that!" cried the waitress. "He could be armed and innocent people in there might get hurt."

Almost immediately, a police cruiser pulled in across the street and James went to meet the officer. They then walked through the little pizza place but the man and girl were gone. The officer didn't question the people there but went to cruise the neighborhood. James didn't know what to think. Perhaps he had jumped to conclusions but then again, he knew what he'd seen. Still, there was that one atom of doubt. But if only for the sake of the little girl, he hadn't let it stop him. Perhaps at the worst, he would only have embarrassed himself.

Having told the officer he would be across the street and to please let him know whatever the outcome, James sat brooding in the café. The waitress came and offered James anything he wanted on the house. James thanked her for her kind offer but accepted only a glass of water.

"I should have acted on my gut instinct," James told her, shaking his head.

"You did the right thing," replied the waitress.

James only shook his head in frustration.

"The man may have been the girl's father," said the waitress.

"No," James replied, "he was *not* her father."

James was upset because he hadn't taken action as his heart commanded.

The police couldn't find the man and girl. James thanked the waitress for her kindness and then returned to his room at the inn where he remained unhappy regarding what he'd seen.

"Whatever I saw, it wasn't good."

Day 70, Thursday, July 22

At 6:30am, James rose and went to the local diner but found it closed so he continued to a mini-market where he purchased a roadmap showing the Clearwater River. Then returning to the diner at 8:00am, James ate breakfast. Back at the inn, James worked on his journal. On the night before, with permission from the inn keeper, he had cooked in his room, making batches of beef to eat on the trail ahead. He had also done his laundry in the bathtub and hung it to dry. Presently, James went out for lunch, then to the Chamber of Commerce where he copied his journal. From there he made an unplanned stop at a barber shop where he had a good conversation with Larry and the men. After getting his hair cut, James went to the hardware store and purchased a plastic storage locker to replace the one he had damaged on the buttress of Little Goose Dam. He went to the post office and mailed his journal copies home. And because James was yet on the edge of the desert, he was drenched by the time he got back to his room at 4:00pm. So he washed his shirt in the sink and hung it to dry before working on his gear.

Putting his shirt back on, James walked to a drive-in diner for dinner where he had the fish platter and a nice conversation with a waitress. Then returning to his room, James worked on his journal but did not catch it up. He packed his gear, which he had spread about the room. All preparations were finished at 10:30pm, after which he slept well.

Day 71, Friday, July 23

At 5:30am, James rose and said his morning prayer as always. He packed his bedroll and loaded his rig. He stopped in the front office and bid Dona the innkeeper goodbye, then set out pulling under a blue sky. The time was 7:00am.

At the local diner, a waitress took a picture of James's walking machine. After breakfast, James went to the grocery store where he stocked up on supplies. From the grocer he pulled to the park where he'd seen Rulen a few days before. In fact he went to the same gentle shore where Rulen had landed his boat, in the shade of a tree growing between the river and bike path. From that spot, James could see straight across the Snake River, directly into the mouth of the Clearwater River.

While James went about the amphibious business of transforming land rig to water craft, a man came riding a bicycle and stopped to talk. The man was missing one arm and looked like he might be semi-homeless. James greeted the man with the same genuine respect and courtesy which he showed every man and woman. Straight away, the man seemed intent that James should not put into the river there but should pull the bike path instead. James declined even as he thanked the man for his advice. The man then began to complain about how people were always treating him badly. James offered practical suggestions on how the man might deal with customers who, as the man put it, were slow to pay for work he'd done on their bicycles. To no avail, the man grew progressively negative until alas, he had become downright mean.

James gave the man a look as he rose from his work and slipped his wrench in his back pocket, whereupon he started toward the man.

Falling silent, the man dropped his eyes.

"I'm not going to hurt you," said James, "I only want to tell you something."

"What's that?" asked the man.

"Look at me," said James, whereupon the man lifted his eyes.

"Any experience can affect a man for better or worse," said James, "It's up to the man to decide which it shall be, and his decision will affect others."

"Oh I know that," the man quipped, and he tried to launch back into negativity.

"I ain't buying it," James interrupted. And after a pause, "Just think about what I told you."

The man seemed anxious to get away but James had unconsciously taken hold of his handle bars. Once released, the man quickly peddled away and, having traveled what he thought to be a safe distance, tried to make the last word negative but James drowned him out with a shout—,

"Think about what I said!"

Shoving off, James immediately crossed the Snake River and entered the mouth of the Clearwater River. In doing so the canoeist entered the State of Idaho. Then paddling one-hundred yards further, a sudden and dramatic change took James by surprise. Just like that, the murky desert water turned crystal clear.

Having come 500 miles as the crow flew, James expected that within several days he would begin his walk over the mountains. But until then, it appeared that he was in for some delightful paddling. Indeed, the mountain water was so clear and pure and natural, it filled James with joyful anticipation.

Because James's approach to the Rocky Mountains had been by means of a trench in the earth, he never saw them until he was in them. He could not know then, that the river literally came out of the mountains right there! He had reached the Rockies!

Encountering the first signs of current, which was not anything unusual, the canoeist decided to cross the 1/8-mile-wide river in hope of finding easier water.

Upon arriving to the north shore however, he found more of the same swift current—,

"We've seen worse," James told UB, as if it were all in a day's work.

Even while laboring against current, James continued to marvel at the crystal clear water. In particular, he noticed how the stony bottom passed underneath like a cobblestone road, seemingly close enough to touch although in truth it lay ten feet below. And that was not the half of it, what with the sky being bright blue, and the landscape growing greener by the paddle stroke, the day seemed full of promise.

Next James noticed a family of geese swimming along the shore in an attempt to escape him. And because the little ones couldn't swim as fast as their mother, it wasn't very long before James had gotten parallel with them. Both parties were moving upstream with the geese about 15 feet offshore and the canoeist 30 feet offshore. The geese were only a small family, being a mother and three juveniles.

"I'm not going to hurt you," James said, hoping to pass and leave them unbothered.

The nervous mother goose only increased her speed, all the while glancing back and forth between her young and the intruder. Then one of her young broke ranks, not to run, but to protect his mother's exposed flank. The little fellow proved not only brave but strong, for so hard was he swimming that he had soon passed his mother even as he caused her great distress.

Such was the little fellow's focus on James, he didn't bother to look where he was going, and, he went in front of his mother like a driver who veers into the lane of another. She nailed him on his bottom with a sharp peck, whereupon he jumped with a squawk before scurrying to get back in line with his siblings.

James chuckled.

Meanwhile, the current kept mounting until the canoeist found himself fighting for every yard.

"One yard at a time," said the Kansan, digging for all his worth, "One yard at a time!"

A battle of yards became a battle of feet, then a battle of inches, and then a battle for nothing. Exhausted but not defeated, James unfolded his pulling frame and began towing his craft through shallows along the shore.

Although big and wide, the river had suddenly changed to take on the character of a mountain stream with gravel bars of polished stones around which swept small sets of rapids. Knee deep in the rapids, James struggled for every yard. Even in the smooth patches of water between the rapids, such was the force of the river, it sprayed up and forward from his thighs to form umbrella-like sheets though which he could not see the bottom. Thus he went blindly with regard to placing his feet among the slick stones. Several times he slipped, fell, and went completely under.

"Oh well," James said to himself in jest after falling and going under, "now I don't have to worry about getting wet."

James continued in hope that he had only entered a difficult stretch of river and things would soon improve. He was yet to find easier water when he saw an official-looking truck parked on a gravel lane above the north shore.

James beached his boat and went up to ask why the current was so strong.

"Excuse me, Sir. My name is James and I come from Kansas to attempt the Lewis and Clark route west to east." James then nodded toward the river, "Just now, I'm hoping to canoe to the town of Orofino but the current has come up against me and, I'm wondering what's going on because I was led to believe that the river was navigable. Perhaps this is only a rough stretch. Could you tell me Sir, does the water smooth out in a mile or two?"

The man in the truck replied, "You were told correctly about the river being navigable except for one thing, the floodgates have been opened at Dworshak Dam."

Rob, who was employed by the City of Lewiston, went on to tell James that the floodgates would remain open for the remainder of the summer.

James nodded with a sense of relief simply for knowing even though it seemed like bad news. James and Rob then spoke for fifteen or twenty minutes on a variety of subjects including the topic of finding a good woman and settling down on a homestead. Then with words of thanks and well wishes, James returned to his boat, disappointed over the seemingly bad news about the river even as he remained determined.

Although not recorded, the time was roughly 1:00pm. The air temperature had risen quickly and was probably on its way to the century mark. Meanwhile the water coming down from the mountains was so cold, James laughed as he towed his boat, fancying his head to be in the Sahara while his feet were in the Arctic. In reality it wasn't so bad. The hard part was pulling his boat against rapids and swift the current. For hours he labored like a beast of burden.

By 4:00pm James had managed only five miles from where he began at the confluence. Thus deciding it was time to switch from water craft to land rig, the Kansan scouted a fishing path through the trees up to the shoulder of Highway 12. Then on the way back to the boat, James let UB in on his plan, "We'll wait till the cool of evening boy, then we'll pull the road to Orofino."

The town of Orofino was the point at which James planned to begin his walk over the mountains. And that being the case, James paused to ask himself an obvious question, *"Why pull the canoe to Orofino if I'm not going to use it anymore?"*

James would use his canoe again but not until spring when he began the second year of his journey. Presently, he didn't know how fortunate he was, for although Orofino would prove a beautiful little mountain town, Lewiston was the place from which to resupply if he were to successfully complete the first year of his journey.

Unaware of the above, James sat on the stern of his craft with his feet in the shallows, gazing out over the river—,

"Master," began the brain with a measure of trepidation, "if I may suggest a retreat?"

"Do not speak of such things in my presence," replied the heart.

The Kansan had scarcely been wrestling with himself for ten minutes when he heard voices coming round the bend. He couldn't see to whom the voices belonged or even make out their words but one thing was for certain, they sounded bright and cheerful as songbirds.

Songbirds, in the form of four beautiful maidens, came floating together in a clutch, down the middle of the river. The girls were sunk down low in their inner tubes, so they didn't see the Kansan who had stood up to get a better look at them. Then noticing him, one of the maidens called out—,

"What are you fishing for?"

"I'm not fishing," James shouted across the water.

"Then what are you doing?"

"I'm trying to get up this river!" came the reply with a hint of boyish frustration.

After a moments silence, one of the maidens called out to James, "Sir, I'm not going to lie to you, you're looking mighty good from here."

The brazen maiden probably mistook James at distance for a younger man but whatever the case, James only smiled and, while shaking his head said, "Thank you," although not loud enough for them to hear.

After consulting among themselves, one of the girls called out, "May we come over there?"

"Yes, you may," replied James with a friendly shout.

The girls began paddling with arms and feet but could make little progress against the current. So they were swept past, but at least they remained together, and that was good because the river was wide and swift.

"Shall I come to you?" the Kansan shouted, his paddle in hand.

"Yes," came the reply, "please do."

All too happy to leave his present impasse behind, James called UB to the boat and paddled after the maidens. Meanwhile, the four young ladies managed to gain an eddy beside a gravel bar where they floated like a group of damsel flies.

As James neared the maidens, he overheard one of them utter, "Oh my God," which was almost certainly not a commentary on

James's good health, at least not as much as it was a reaction to the rash decision that she and her girlfriends had made. For there they were, isolated between wooded slope and river without a soul in sight, and as we shall see, that wasn't the half of it.

Having got close enough to see the girls faces, James realized his good fortune. For same as birds of a feather flock together, they were young women of extraordinary beauty.

"Ladies," spoke the Kansan, "am I glad to see you." Then taking another paddle stroke, James began to tell what he was about when, seeing them more fully, he fell dumbstruck even as the momentum of his craft carried him in among them—,

"I had no idea," he said, in shock and awe.

Looking uncertain, one of the maidens asked, "Would you like us to cover up?"

"Um," replied James as his jungle mechanic, who had jumped to his feet, shouted commands while trying mightily to pick the lock on his cage.

Now comes a place to remove the young ladies from the picture for a moment. Indeed, here comes a place to forgive their indecency and put everything on James's shoulders for the purpose of addressing his responsibility, or irresponsibility. And while the young ladies mustn't be let off the hook entirely, here it must be told that however perfect their natures were; their natures were never fully revealed to James. James did however see into their eyes and therefore knew they were good souls. They were wholesome country girls without a course word between them, much less a tattoo or strange body piercing. They were in their early twenties, having just graduated from university that spring. They had come together on that summer day for a goodbye celebration before going their separate ways into the wide world. Thus in the knowledge that their group was dissolving and therefore wishing to celebrate the close friendship they had shared, the former campus queens had obviously shared some beverage by which means they had become more exuberant than normal. They were not drunk but under the influence. In addition to that, they had chosen to do their celebrating in nature, and nature seemed to have had its own special effect on them. So there they were, the only four souls on the river with James, and probably, such an event couldn't have happened again even if James could have continued paddling around the world ten times.

The maidens had just asked James if he would like them to cover up, and his reply will be known soon enough, but this is a place to ask their question in another way. Would it have been brave of our knight to make the young ladies feel at home about their behavior, or would it have been brave of him to encourage them to the modest path their pioneer foremothers took to build the home of the brave? Would it have been right of him to go along in a self-serving society where people exposed their bodies as a way of making statements about their freedom, or would it have been right of him to follow the path of his forefathers who risked and often gave their lives so that others could be free? And in the event that such sacrifices have been forgotten, would it have been better to stand in the buffet line while the Titanic took on water so to speak, or would it have been better to remember, and get on with the business of deploying the lifeboats? The young ladies were awaiting his reply. They were sunk down low in their inner tubes like little girls. They were looking up at him with uncertainty.

It would have been easy for James to do the right thing if only other Christians had been there to shake their fingers. But James wasn't even thinking clearly enough to consider how he would later explain himself to them. And of course God was watching, but James had forgotten about that. So there he was, floating in an eddy, pleasing his eyes upon the four maidens, assuring them that they were fine as they were. And so it was, they smiled and were happy even as he failed them.

What happened next will be known soon enough but first comes a place to tell that the young lady's names have been withheld. The young ladies must have some names however for the telling of this true story and therefore they shall be given names and numbers. Their assigned names will change but their numbers will remain the same. In other words, each young lady shall begin with one name and end with another even as her number remains unchanged. Therefore to begin, the ladies shall be known as: Siren No. 1, Siren No. 2, Siren No. 3, and Siren No. 4. In fairness, James shall be known as Lizard.

Finally, with regard to the sirens, their assigned numbers represent nothing other than the order in which they introduced themselves to James:

"My name's _____," said Siren No. 1, bravely putting out her hand.

"Pleased to meet you Siren No. 1," said the canoeist, taking her hand in his. "I'm Lizard."

"I'm ____," said Siren No. 2, exuberantly extending her hand.

"I'm ____," said Siren No. 3, putting out her hand with down home sophistication (meaning thoughtfulness in the consideration of others).

"I'm ____," said Siren No. 4, quietly extending her hand.

UB, who was the only innocent one in the group, enjoyed no small attention from the sirens who had gathered round the gunwales.

"Are you okay?" asked Siren No. 3, petting UB while looking up at Lizard.

"Oh, yes Miss," replied Lizard, smiling with embarrassment even as he remained formal, "It's just that, well, it's not every day a man finds himself surrounded by, well, by so much beauty."

The sirens thanked the lizard for complimenting them on their beauty, and they returned his compliment in kind. Meanwhile it was only natural that the sirens held to the gunwales while reaching in to pet UB and therefore, with two sirens on either side, gathered close around a craft with serious space limitations; Lizard could not help being aware of their hands which, incidentally or not, were making contact with his thighs!

Siren No. 1 then asked, "So, what were you going to tell us?"

"Oh yeah," said the lizard, having completely forgotten, "I'm attempting the Lewis and Clark route. And, I was glad to see you because I couldn't go any further upstream, being as the current had come against me. But, I couldn't bring myself to give up. So, I was stuck there."

"What will you do now?" asked Siren No. 3.

"I'll return to Lewiston," Lizard replied.

"We're going to Lewiston!" cried Siren No. 2.

After what appeared to be a quick consensus among themselves, the sirens invited Lizard to join them. Therefore the lizard put his paddle away because he couldn't use it anyway, not with the sirens gathered close and smiling up from the slow swirling eddy.

"Would you like a [alcoholic] beverage?" asked one of the sirens, offering up a cold one.

"No thank you," replied Lizard, blindly feeling a measure of pride for showing restraint!

The sirens then began paddling with their feet to bring the canoe out of the eddy and into the river where the current took hold and carried them away.

Floating, Lizard told the sirens how a great many people had stepped forward to help him and their kindness was the real story. Too bad Lizard could not see how upright he held himself while speaking of lofty things, or he would have known what a pious hypocrite he had become!

In turn, the sirens told Lizard of how they had gotten their inner tubes earlier that day. The old boy at the tire shop hadn't had any used inner tubes to give them but then out of the blue, he up and gave them brand new tubes for free! The young sirens were far more sweet than coy and Lizard couldn't help laughing, for in his mind's eye he saw them entering a tire shop and gathering around some good old boy who never stood a chance, at least not against sirens who looked so wholesome and beautiful, they could have played *Elli May* from the *Beverly Hillbillies*, or *Mary Ann* from *Gilligan's Island*.

"Are you sure you wouldn't like a beverage?" asked one of the sirens, offering up a cold beer.

"No thank you," replied the lizard.

"You look just like _____ _____," said Siren No. 3 to Lizard.

"Who's _____ _____?" asked Lizard, having never heard of the man.

"You don't know who _____ _____ is?" Siren No. 1 asked as if everyone in the world knew who the man in question was."

"No," replied Lizard, "I do not."

"He's a country western singer," said Siren No. 4.

"Yeah," replied Siren No. 2, "and all the girls love him!"

Lizard didn't tell the sirens he'd been living in a cave but confessed he didn't know the man. Then on unanimous suggestion from the sirens, Lizard promised to try modern country music once he got back to Kansas. When he got back, he discovered a new kind of music, Christian Country Music. As for Modern Country Music, James was glad to know about it.

> "Some of it, in all truth, is the best country western music ever, perhaps because those who make it are answering a call to remember that which is of immeasurable

value. In this way, I believe that modern country music can help my people hold on to what they love, just so long as its singers and songwriters do not follow my bad example on this particular day, which wasn't at all like a Christian knight but more like something on the order of a Babylonian in cowboy boots."

"You really do look just like _____ _____," affirmed one of the sirens, to which the other three agreed. All then proceeded to advise Lizard, telling how he only needed to keep his hat and sunglasses on, whereupon he could go around telling girls he was _____ _____, and they would believe him.

Lizard only smiled, charmed by the way in which the sirens had let him know he was getting on in his years. In fact, they were giving tips on how he might get around it.

"Are you sure you wouldn't like a beverage?"

Lizard accepted the beer.

"Aren't you going to drink it?" asked one of the sirens who watched as Lizard put it in his boat without opening it.

"I'll drink it later," said Lizard, unable to keep a smile from those who dabbled their feet in the water without a care for anything other than the thrill of living.

Still floating backward as if under a spell with the sirens gathered close around, Lizard wasn't looking where he was going or even aware that he was going backward. Therefore, he couldn't see the rocks which protruded into the river ahead. Nor could he see the rapids they created.

As the rapids took them by surprise, Siren No. 2 was abruptly swept away!

"Siren No. 2!" cried Young Lady No. 1 as she jumped into the rapids after her friend.

James stabbed his paddle into the river and strained for all his worth to keep his canoe from getting sideways and sweeping over the girls. Meanwhile, young lady No. 4 went to the stern to grab hold of young lady No. 1 who had grabbed hold of young lady No. 2. Straining while looking over his shoulder to keep an eye on the girls, James checked the river and brought his boat into the calm eddy beside the rapid where he jumped in and went behind the stern where young lady No. 1 and young lady No. 4 had pulled young lady

No. 2 into the shallows. All three maidens were okay. Young lady No. 3 was also okay.

All together, everyone seemed to have gotten sober. James got back in the boat and the episode ended up to be no big deal but it could have been tragic because, although only a small rapid, the power of the river was deceptive, very deceptive, and what with alcohol added to the mix, what seemed nothing could have crossed a line into something that had people weeping in disbelief and asking why. In other words, it would have seemed a freak thing had young lady No. 2 drowned but such things happened and James would have forever had it on his chest like a stack of bricks, not to mention, his errand would have been destroyed.

Back on the float, James kept an eye on the river ahead while suggesting that the young ladies take precautions to avoid a trip to the poky courtesy of the local sheriff. The maidens obliged except for young lady No. 2 who had suffered some loss of personal property in the rapids. Fortunately, James happened to have one t-shirt made of a material thicker than average.

After digging out the shirt, James returned to the subject of how amazing his journey had been with regard to all the kind people who had stepped forward. And in fact it would be the case from one end of the trail to the other. People gave James their time, their enthusiasm, their money, they cooked him meals, took him out to eat, brought him food and water, washed his cloths, gave him places to sleep, they helped him to repair his equipment, they drew him maps, they gave him gifts, they stopped and offered him rides and whatever else was needed. They were forever stepping forward, from one end of the trail to the other, and in all the worthy wonders James would record in 4,000 miles of canoeing and walking through America, he would not find any so worthy as they.

Presently, and even though James was hardly a good orator, the young women were courteous and in fact showed no small interest in what he said.

> "God's grace did not end at the gate of St Louis. For years after I was dirt poor [even as I worked my tail off writing this account] and people kept coming forward, giving me cloths, food, and the like in such abundance as to be astounding."

The group soon arrived at a small green park on the outskirts of Lewiston. James bid the young ladies farewell although in doing so he confused young lady No. 1 with young lady No. 4 but only in name. James had never been very good at names but had a knack at remembering other things. Beautiful young lady No. 1 was the brave one. Beautiful young lady No. 2 was the passionate one. Beautiful young lady No. 3 was the considerate one. And Beautiful young lady No. 4 was the quiet one. Presently, the girls didn't have a cell phone between them but went away across the park to the highway where they put their thumbs out to catch a ride without a fear in the world.

Having turned to his gear, James heard one of the girls call out across the green, "God bless you!"

It was beautiful young lady No. 3. She was waving, getting ready to hop into a pickup truck that had pulled over.

"And may God bless you!" James shouted joyfully.

Having assembled his rig, the Kansan pulled to an inn located beside the park. It was 8:30pm by the time he got established in his room and began planning for the next day. He needed to trade his canoe for a pack animal. A pack horse spirited enough to make the 500 mile journey over the Great Divide and at the same time, steady enough to share mountain passes with eighteen wheelers. James also needed to find a babysitter for UB, whom he thought too old to survive the mountains. But as we already know, UB would so recover from the desert, as to be given a chance. And further improving UB's odds, James didn't have money for a good horse and therefore would carry his backpack instead. In fact James spent $3/4^{ths}$ of his budget in the first $1/4^{th}$ of his journey. Therefore, the last $3/4^{ths}$ of his journey would be camping and cook fires with almost no stays in inns. By such means, James would have maximum people contact because he camped in many town parks and other places where the people could see and easily approach him. He and UB would walk over the Rocky Mountains, canoe the mighty Missouri, and arrive at Fort Dubois in Saint Louis on October 18, 2005. And not only would UB make the entire journey, he came out of it as fit as a pup!

Sparing all other detail, it is enough to know that bears, bandits, blizzards, and beautiful women waited on the trail ahead. But as James would say, that wasn't the half of it.

Below is James's final entry from his 4,000 mile journey on the Lewis and Clark Trail:

"Stepping ashore, I was not so very excited, but just plain happy, not tearful, but just plain grateful. For such a gift had I been given, God had fitted it to me like a tailor, working patiently, day in and out, over the past two years, and now, I wore it like a comfortable coat for whatever was to come. With UB under my arm, I went up the riprap shore, walked across the green, and read the plaque that marked the end of my journey. It read:

THE JOURNEY BEGINS HERE."

Note to Fellow Christian Canoeist and Kayakers:

You may have noticed the canoeist on the back cover of this book is holding his paddle totally wrong. His incorrect pose was decided on intentionally because I thought he looked like a bold knight in that pose, which only goes to show that, without God, I was a fool going to his death, but with God, all things are possible.

All glory be to God.

www.ingramcontent.com/pod-product-compliance
Lightning Source LLC
Chambersburg PA
CBHW050614300426
44112CB00012B/1501